INSTINCTIVE BEHAVIOR

INSTINCTIVE BEHAVIOR

THE DEVELOPMENT OF A MODERN CONCEPT

Translated and edited by

CLAIRE H. SCHILLER

Introduction by

KARL S. LASHLEY

Contributors:

D. J. KUENEN · KONRAD LORENZ

NICHOLAS TINBERGEN · PAUL H. SCHILLER

JAKOB VON UEXKÜLL

International Universities Press, Inc.

NEW YORK

Contents

INTRODUCTION, by Karl S. Lashley ix

NOTE BY THE TRANSLATOR xiii

PREFACE, by Nicholas Tinbergen xv

PART I

A STROLL THROUGH THE WORLD OF
ANIMALS AND MEN

A Picture Book of Invisible Worlds 5

Jakob von Uexküll

Introduction 5
Space in the *Umwelt* 13
Operational Space 14
Tactile Space 19
Visual Space 19
The Farthest Plane 21
Receptor Time 29
The Simple *Umwelten* 31
Form and Motion as Perceptual Cues 36
Goal and Plan 42
Receptor Image and Effector Image 46
The Familiar Path 50
Home and Territory—*Heim und Heimat* 54
The Companion 57
Search Image and Search Tone 62
The Magic *Umwelten* 64
The Same Subject as an Object in Different *Umwelten* . . . 73
Conclusion 76

PART II

1. COMPANIONSHIP IN BIRD LIFE

Fellow Members of the Species as Releasers of Social Behavior .   83

Konrad Lorenz

1. Introduction: Uexküll's Concept of "Companion"   83
2. Methods and Principles   90
3. "Imprinting" the Object of Instinctive Social Reactions . . 102
4. The Innate Releasing Mechanism of the Companion . . . 110
   Summary and Discussion 116

2. THE NATURE OF INSTINCT

The Conception of Instinctive Behavior 129

Konrad Lorenz

1. The Spencer-Lloyd Morgan Theory 131
2. McDougall's Instinct Theory 156
3. The Reflex Theory of Instinctive Behavior 163
   Summary 173

3. TAXIS AND INSTINCT

Taxis and Instinctive Action in the Egg-Retrieving
    Behavior of the Greylag Goose 176

Konrad Lorenz and Nicholas Tinbergen

1. Theoretical Aspects of Taxis and Instinctive Action . . . 176
2. The Problem 185
3. Observations on the Egg-Rolling Movements 187
4. Experiments 192
   Summary and Conclusions 206

4. FEEDING BEHAVIOR IN YOUNG THRUSHES

Releasing and Directing Stimulus Situations in *Turdus m.
    merula L.* and *T. e. ericetorum Turton* 209

Nicholas Tinbergen and D. J. Kuenen

1. Introduction and Statement of the Problem 209
2. Materials and Methods 211
3. The Release 213
4. Orientation 221
5. Control Experiments in the Field 232
6. Evaluation and Summary 233

5. COMPARATIVE STUDY OF BEHAVIOR 239

    Konrad Lorenz

    1. The Evolution of Instinctive Behavior 239
    2. The Physiology of Instinctive Behavior 245
    3. Automatism and Reflex 249

6. INNATE MOTOR ACTION AS A BASIS OF LEARNING

    Manipulative Patterns in the Chimpanzee 264

    Paul H. Schiller

    1. Development of Problem-Solving 265
    2. Free Play 269
    3. Play with Boxes, String, etc. 278
        Conclusions 284

7. THE PAST TWELVE YEARS IN THE COMPARATIVE
    STUDY OF BEHAVIOR 288

    Konrad Lorenz

    BIBLIOGRAPHY 311

    INDEX 321

Introduction

KARL S. LASHLEY

The study of animal behavior during the present century has developed along two distinct lines, the products of professional psychologists in America and of zoologists in Europe. In America the prevailing interest has been in the phenomena of learning. The early studies of Lloyd Morgan and of Thorndike directed interest to animals as material for experiments on the modifiability of behavior and set a pattern for later work. The great mass of literature has dealt with general problems of learning for which the animals, as well as the maze or problem-box, serve merely as experimental apparatus. The choice of animals for study has been determined largely by their ready availability and the ease with which they can be reared and handled under the restricted conditions of the laboratory. Animals with highly specialized and elaborate instincts do not adapt readily to captivity and the selection of forms suited to cage life has militated against observation of inherited types of behavior. Partly as a consequence of this selection, the "anti-instinct" movement, typified by the writings of Watson, Dunlap, and Kuo, came to dominate psychological theory. The few recent studies of instinctive behavior produced by American psychologists have been inspired by interest in hormone control and have dealt more with physiological mechanisms than wth details of behavior.

In Europe the comparative study of behavior has been chiefly in the hands of zoologists, whose interests were in taxonomy, evolution and ecology rather than in learning theory. Experienced in field work and familiar wjth a wide variety of animals, they have followed the lead of the Peckhams, Whitman, Wheeler, and von Uexküll. They have traced patterns of instinctive activity among related species and have shown that behavior may be as clear an index of phylogenetic relationship as are physical structures. They have observed the great variety and complexity of instincts exhibited by animals under natural conditions and have made important progress in analyzing the situations which elicit such behavior. They have also succeeded in breaking down many complex activities into their component elements and in tracing adaptive interaction of behavior and environment. On the basis of these observations a general theory of the nature of instincts has been built. Physiological interpretations of the mechanism of instincts are as yet tentative and play little part in the system. The general approach to the study of behavior has been termed *ethology,* the science of racial characteristics.

Until recently these studies, published in German and in journals with limited circulation, were almost unknown in America. To make them available to English readers the translation of the papers included in the present volume was planned and begun by the distinguished Hungarian psychologist, Paul Harkai Schiller, shortly before his tragic death in 1949. He wished not only to present important papers but to illustrate by their selection the development of behavioral studies from the rather naïve and anthropomorphic speculations of the early decades to the modern methods of experimental analysis.

The papers in the collection are classics in the development of the science of ethology. They illustrate the maturation of the concepts of behavior during the period which they cover and are historically important. Since they were published at different times and addressed to different audiences, there is naturally some repetition in the reports and discussions of experiments and observations, but omission or condensation of these was not permissible, since it would have destroyed the continuity and perhaps distorted the meaning of the individual papers.

For pioneer investigators like Romanes in England, Washburn in America, and von Uexküll in Germany, the central problem of comparative psychology was, "What is the nature of the animal's experience; how does the world appear to it?" The monograph by von Uexküll, Part I of this book, is an example of this approach to the problems of behavior. The author is chiefly concerned with the sensory capacities of various animals and seeks to give a picture, in terms of human experience, of the world as it appears to them. The interpretations are sometimes farfetched, as in the speculations concerning the time-sense of the tick, and although the descriptions of the animals' worlds give the reader a feeling for their experiences, this empathy is illusory and sometimes misleading. Gradually the view has gained acceptance that questions concerning the animal's mind are meaningful and can be answered only in terms of the interaction of the animal with its environment.

The later papers included in Part II of this book are among the most original and important contributions to analysis of instinctive behavior. They still show some influence of the earlier point of view, in that they deal chiefly with sensory components of behavior and are oriented toward life histories and ecology rather than toward the physiology of reaction. The American reader is likely to feel in them a lack of rigorous controls such as have been developed in narrower laboratory studies. This defect is still apparent in more recent publications by ethologists and is, in fact, inherent in all attempts to unravel the intricate network of environmental influences which activate and modify innate behavior mechanisms. Only continued and painstaking dissection of behavior, bit by bit, can define the many variables, but the work of the ethologists is an impressive start toward the solution of genetic contributions to behavior. It demands the attention of all serious students.

Many of the observations described here have been summarized by Dr. Tinbergen in his book, *The Study of Instinct,* published since the translations were begun. However, the more recent theoretical discussions of ethologists can be more clearly understood and evaluated with the historical background provided by these papers. They reveal a continuity of approach and methods, although the theoretical interpretations have been considerably modified as additional facts have appeared.

In his Preface, Dr. Tinbergen points out that ethologists have paid little attention to problems of learning. Dr. Schiller had planned a program for studies of learning which had much in common with the views of ethologists. In his *Handeln und Erleben* (Berlin, 1944) he stressed the continuous interplay of environment and behavior, and the predominant importance of innate organization in determining the character of action and the course of learning. The size, shape, weight, and other properties of objects immediately elicit appropriate handling. This in turn changes the properties and relations of the objects and elicits new manipulations. The animal has a repertoire of innate manipulative responses to the elements of every situation. Dr. Schiller emphasized that a knowledge of these responses is the only safe starting point for psychological investigations of learning. The innate action patterns form the basis of psychological development. As they change the total situation, they alter its perceptual characters. The range and complexity of perceptual capacities increases as the elemental reactions are combined into more elaborate acts. The combination and condensation of action patterns is the basis of learning, providing both the material and the motivation for higher forms of learning.

The sixth paper in this volume reports Dr. Schiller's study, not previously published, of the innate reactions of the chimpanzee in first contacts with various objects. It shows that much of the behavior which has been thought to be learned and which has been adduced as evidence of insight is, in reality, an expression of innate manipulative tendencies. Playful manipulation is the instinctive response to objects. The acts are performed with no prescience of usefulness and in the problem situation the very acts which might solve the problem may be performed in such a way as to prevent success. The appropriateness of the act for such a task as getting food is discovered only by chance. The putting together of jointed sticks is not "to make a longer stick." The use of the joined sticks in reaching food is discovered only after interest in the act of joining them has waned. The insight is the immediate, one-trial learning to use the innate manipulative acts in the manner discovered by chance, and the generalization of the acts to other, similar situations. Dr. Schiller's study is limited to motor manipulations but an extension of the same concepts to the manipulation of ideas may well lead to the conclusion that man has failed to identify his own instincts because he calls them intelligence.

The translation has presented some unusual difficulties because many of the concepts of ethology are novel and are expressed in a technical language for which no English equivalents have been developed. Dr. Claire H. Schiller has met this difficulty competently in rendering a fair and adequate interpretation of the texts, but she has had to devise English expressions which may not always convey to the reader the exact meaning of the German terminology. She therefore has added a word of explanation of some of the terms which are most likely to be confusing.

Note by the Translator

The most puzzling terms are those by which von Uexküll seeks to represent the relations between the objective world and the world as it appears to the animal. To deal with the latter he has coined a number of words which are almost untranslatable and much of his introduction is devoted to explaining their meaning. The term *Umwelt* (self-world or phenomenal world) has been retained. It is the world around an animal as the animal sees it, the subjective world as contrasted with the environment. The effects of stimulation appear in this *Umwelt* as elementary sensations, *Merkzeichen*, which, organized and projected into the object, become meaningful perceptions, conceived by the animal as the properties of that object, *Merkmal*. The perceptions are transformed in the nervous system into *Wirkzeichen*, the impulses to action. Action upon external objects modifies them to produce *Wirkmal*, changes in the object which produce additional stimulation, translated as functional or effector cues.

Übersprungbewegung is translated as displacement activity, a term used technically by Tinbergen himself in his English publications. Displacement activities are innate behavior patterns which occur as substitutions for the motor pattern proper to an instinct, when a surplus of motivation is somehow prevented from discharging through its own, normal paths. They are found most frequently in one of two situations: strong activation of two conflicting drives, or strong motivation of one drive with lack of adequate external stimulation.

Some of the material quoted by the various authors from American and English sources was not available in its original form and may not, in its present retranslated form, conform exactly to the original text.

C. H. S.

Preface

NICHOLAS TINBERGEN

Whenever I meet American behaviorists I am struck by the very great difference in approach between them and us. It seems to me well worth while to try and compare the ways of behaviorism with those of ethology. To do this thoroughly would require a much more intimate knowledge of behaviorism than I can boast; also, it would require much more space than I can in fairness claim.

It is, I think, of great importance to recognize that the two types of approach are fundamentally the same in that they both have, as their object, an observable phenomenon, and in that they are both "objective." Both schools study behavior, and not a mysterious "psyche," nor unobservable subjective phenomena. Both aim at descriptions, and at formulations of problems, concepts and conclusions that are as objective as in any other natural science. It is true that both often use words borrowed from everyday language, words which, stemming from a period in which subjective and objective thinking were not yet separated, are charged naturally with blended subjective and objective meaning. But both try to overcome the dangers of this by giving new, purely objective definitions. This fundamental identity of approach justifies the expectation that both fields will ultimately merge into one.

However, in spite of this general similarity, many differences in actual procedure exist between the two schools. In the following I shall not enter into the problem of how these differences originated, nor is it my intention to discuss all the differences I can see. I shall merely point, very briefly, to some of the more obvious ones, in the hope that this may promote mutual understanding and appreciation.

1. Ethologists are zoologists, and as such interested in the three major problems of biology: that of the function or survival value of observed life processes; that of their causation; and that of their evolution. Behaviorists concentrate on the second of these problems, that of underlying causes, and practically ignore the others. Many psychologists are not even

interested in them. Anyone who is aware of the paramount importance of insight into adaptedness, selection, and evolution to general biology will agree that this is a serious gap in a science concerned with life processes.

This lack of balance in the behaviorist's interest has made him neglect true comparative study. The zoological training of ethologists has made them aware of the great value of comparison as an aid to evolutionary study. It is, of course, impossible to discuss the matter fully here, but briefly the difference between comparison as applied occasionally in the *Journal of Comparative and Physiological Psychology* and by comparative ethology amounts to this: in ethology (and in zoology in general), comparison aims at more than merely stating that one animal is different from another, or that they are similar. It aims at establishing homologies and analogies. This leads to the distinction of true affinity on the one hand and convergence on the other, and through this to a description of the course evolution must have taken. This, as will be clear to anyone who has followed, however superficially, the development of the science of evolution, is the indispensable prerequisite to studies on the causation of evolution.

Some aspects of this approach have been discussed by Lorenz in the paper on comparative behavior study presented in this volume. Since this paper originally appeared, progress has been made, although much more work is of course needed.

2. Behaviorists concentrate on other types of behavior than do ethologists. Behaviorism is concerned more with learned than with nonlearned behavior. Ethologists consider that learning is a change in something, and that it must pay to study this something before the change occurs. This difference in interest coincides with a different selection of animal types: behaviorists concentrate on mammals, ethologists on lower vertebrates and invertebrates. On the whole, the interest of ethologists is wider as regards the variety of animal types studied. In 1942 I gave some facts demonstrating this, comparing the contents of a representative behaviorist journal with those of the only European ethological journal then in existence. Beach has recently shown that this difference still exists, and has emphasized it once more. It must be admitted that this comparison is not wholly in favor of ethology: the neglect of mammals and of problems of learning is a serious gap in ethology. There are some notable exceptions, it is true, and there is also a growing tendency to fill this gap, but as yet most of the ethological work has been mainly on innate behavior found in birds, fish, and insects.

3. Ethologists tend to spend much time in preparing full and accurate descriptions of the whole behavior pattern of selected species, as

preliminaries to further study, whereas behaviorism has for the time being abandoned this task, and concentrated on detailed analysis of the causation of selected simple units of behavior. It is true that some behaviorists have done a considerable amount of this descriptive work—the admirable achievements of the Yerkes group may be mentioned as an example—and also that no ethologist has yet given a really "complete" description of the behavior pattern of any one species. Yet it cannot be denied that ethology has at present a stronger trend to broad description, and to discovery of phenomena to be explained, than behaviorism.

As a consequence of this state of affairs, behaviorists can teach ethologists much about analytical and experimental procedure, but ethologists see more of the more highly integrated levels of behavior, of phenomena of interaction between units and systems, and have hit upon a wide range of problems untouched by behaviorists.

It seems to me that the differences in interest, together with the fact that ethology is a comparatively young and small (though rapidly growing) school, are in the main responsible for the different development of the two schools. Ethology is in a stage of renewed reconnaissance; most of the work is still in a qualitative stage, although a beginning has been made with quantitative studies of special problems; behaviorism has penetrated deeply in some problems, notably problems of learning as seen in some species. While I feel that ethology can learn much from behaviorism concerning the experimental study of learning, behaviorism might profit by studying the work of ethologists as far as broadness and balance of approach are concerned.

Thus it seems to me obvious that both schools have their merits and their shortcomings. Although the fundamental identity of object and of approach justifies the hope that one day the two fields will fuse, we are at present very far from attaining this ideal. It is worth considering what has so far prevented this fusion.

The difference in interest is without doubt the primary cause. But another equally important factor has been sheer ignorance of each other's work. This ignorance is partly due to the fact that most of the ethological work has been published in the German language, and most of the behaviorists' work in English. Apart from this, there is an even more serious language barrier: the technical vocabularies of the two schools differ widely. Behaviorism being the senior and more sophisticated school, its load of technical concepts and terms is much the larger. It is almost impossible for us ethologists to read and understand behaviorists' papers; usually we are drowned in the first page. While I am aware of the fact that we too are rapidly developing a technical jargon of our own, ours is undoubtedly still the more simple of the two.

It is, of course, highly desirable that this lack of mutual understanding be remedied. This can only be done by considerable efforts on both sides. Close contact is of primary importance. This can be promoted by personal discussions, and by the presentation of work in a language that the other school can understand. Paul Schiller's initiative, which he was unfortunately prevented from carrying out because of his untimely death, may prove an important step, and we owe a great deal to Mrs. Schiller for having taken the trouble of completing the tedious task of translating this series of papers.

Since the war, ethological research, which used to have its headquarters on the European Continent, has been taken up in Britain, and the postwar literature has been partly written in English. Also, on the Continent the development of ethology has accelerated. Hence, the papers written before the war cannot be considered a fair sample of the present state of ethology. It may be helpful, therefore, if I add some references to more recent work, which, I think, will show that ethology is developing in a direction which will appeal to behaviorists.

A number of papers appeared in the proceedings of a symposium held in Cambridge by the Society for Experimental Biology (1950). Shortly afterwards, the first attempt at a coherent introduction to the whole field appeared in book form (Tinbergen, 1951). Since this book was completed in 1948, nine years have passed in which a series of new reports have been published.

"Ethograms," or broad and detailed descriptions of the normal behavior of a species, are appearing in increasing numbers. Baerends produced two monographs, one on a digger wasp (1941), another on several species of cichlid fish (1950). Kortlandt (1940a), O. Koenig (1951) and L. Koenig (1951) published ethograms of the European cormorant, the bearded tit, and the bee-eater, all in German. A representative sample of similar work published in English is Hinde's monograph on the great tit (1952). In several of these papers description is followed up by analytical work on special problems. The paper on wolves by Schenkel (1947), and those on various other mammals by Eibl-Eibesfeldt (1950a, 1950b, 1951), reveal the increasing interest in mammals.

An analysis of the stimuli responsible for the release of a simple response before learning sets in has been made by Tinbergen and Perdeck (1950) who used the begging response of the newly born herring gull chick. This work is being continued with greater precision by Weidmann, who uses the black-headed gull. Similar work has been done by Drees (1952) on saltid spiders. This work was a preliminary to systematic exhaustion experiments which are now applied by various workers as a means of investigating the nature of the internal factors determining the readiness to show specific behavior patterns (Prechtl, 1953; Hinde, 1954). Another systematic attempt in this direction is Van Iersel's recently published study (1953) of the external and internal factors which determine the shift from sexual to parental behavior in the male three-spined stickleback.

Since the discovery of "displacement activities" by Kortlandt (1940b) and Tinbergen (1940), new work has been done on this phenomenon. Tinbergen gave a new review (1952), and since then a new example has been carefully studied by Moynihan (1953). The recognition of the nature of displacement activities, and of other results of the simultaneous activation of two or more drives, has been a great help in understanding the causation of various types of "display," such as courtship, threat and anti-predator behavior. A summary of the present state can be found in Tinbergen (1953); examples of the type of study and of the kind of conclusions it leads to are Hinde's study of the reproductive behavior of the chaffinch (1953) and Moynihan's forthcoming monograph on the black-headed gull (1954).

An understanding of the functions and the causation of these types of display, combined with comparative study of closely related species, begins to lead to evolutionary conclusions. This work is only in its beginning, as anybody will understand who is aware of the amount of work involved. Some promising results have been obtained by Crane (1941) for fiddler crabs, by Lorenz (1941) for dabbling ducks, by Hinde (1952) for tits, by Baerends (1950) for cichlid fish, and by Moynihan (1954) for gulls. It is now at least possible to say something about the origin of display movements, about their causation, and about the special type of adaptive evolution they have undergone. This type of work clearly demonstrates the necessity of studying function, causation, and evolution together, without neglecting any one of these three aspects.

These recent studies are all logical continuations of the work sampled in the present volume. They concern problems which are obvious to anyone who observes the normal behavior of animals in their natural habitat, but which have been neglected almost entirely by behaviorism. A true science of behavior, however, cannot afford to neglect them. Whatever the shortcomings of ethology are, I am convinced that it will prove to be of positive value to the future development of the science of behavior, animal and human.

INSTINCTIVE BEHAVIOR

Part I

Part

A Stroll Through the Worlds of Animals and Men

A Picture Book of Invisible Worlds[1]

JAKOB von UEXKÜLL (1934)

Introduction

This little monograph does not claim to point the way to a new science. Perhaps it should be called a stroll into unfamiliar worlds; worlds strange to us but known to other creatures, manifold and varied as the animals themselves. The best time to set out on such an adventure is on a sunny day. The place, a flower-strewn meadow, humming with insects, fluttering with butterflies. Here we may glimpse the worlds of the lowly dwellers of the meadow. To do so, we must first blow, in fancy, a soap bubble around each creature to represent its own world, filled with the perceptions which it alone knows. When we ourselves then step into one of these bubbles, the familiar meadow is transformed. Many of its colorful features disappear, others no longer belong together but appear in new relationships. A new world comes into being. Through the bubble we see the world of the burrowing worm, of the butterfly, or of the field mouse; the world as it appears to the animals themselves, not as it appears to us. This we may call the *phenomenal world* or the *self-world* of the animal.

To some, these worlds are invisible. Many a zoologist and physiologist, clinging to the doctrine that all living beings are mere machines, denies their existence and thus boards up the gates to other worlds so that no single ray of light shines forth from all the radiance that is shed over them. But let us who are not committed to the machine theory

----

1 Illustrated by G. Kriszat.

consider the nature of machines. All our useful devices, our machines, only implement our acts. There are tools that help our senses, spectacles, telescopes, microphones, which we may call *perceptual tools*. There are also tools used to effect our purposes, the machines of our factories and of transportation, lathes and motor cars. These we may call *effector tools*.

Now we might assume that an animal is nothing but a collection of perceptual and effector tools, connected by an integrating apparatus which, though still a mechanism, is yet fit to carry on the life functions. This is indeed the position of all mechanistic theorists, whether their analogies are in terms of rigid mechanics or more plastic dynamics. They brand animals as mere objects. The proponents of such theories forget that, from the first, they have overlooked the most important thing, the *subject* which uses the tools, perceives and functions with their aid.

The mechanists have pieced together the sensory and motor organs of animals, like so many parts of a machine, ignoring their real functions of perceiving and acting, and have even gone on to mechanize man himself. According to the behaviorists, man's own sensations and will are mere appearance, to be considered, if at all, only as disturbing static. But we who still hold that our sense organs serve our perceptions, and our motor organs our actions, see in animals as well not only the mechanical structure, but also the operator, who is built into their organs, as we are into our bodies. We no longer regard animals as mere machines, but as subjects whose essential activity consists of perceiving and acting. We thus unlock the gates that lead to other realms, for all that a subject perceives becomes his perceptual world and all that he does, his effector world. Perceptual and effector worlds together form a closed unit, the *Umwelt*. These different worlds, which are as manifold as the animals themselves, present to all nature lovers new lands of such wealth and beauty that a walk through them is well worth while, even though they unfold not to the physical but only to the spiritual eye. So, reader, join us as we ramble through these worlds of wonder.

Anyone who lives in the country and roams through woods and brush with his dog has surely made the acquaintance of a tiny insect which, hanging from the branches of bushes, lurks for its prey, be it man or animal, ready to hurl itself at its victim and gorge itself with his blood until it swells to the size of a pea (Fig. 1). The tick, though not dangerous, is still an unpleasant guest of mammals, including men. Recent publications have clarified many details of its life story so that we are able to trace an almost complete picture of it.

From the egg there issues forth a small animal, not yet fully developed, for it lacks a pair of legs and sex organs. In this state it is already capable of attacking cold-blooded animals, such as lizards, whom it waylays as it sits on the tip of a blade of grass. After shedding its skin several times, it acquires the missing organs, mates, and starts its hunt for warm-blooded animals.

After mating, the female climbs to the tip of a twig on some bush. There she clings at such a height that she can drop upon small mammals that may run under her, or be brushed off by larger animals.

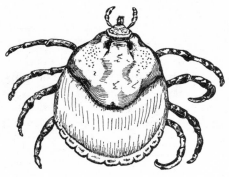

Fig. 1
Tick

The eyeless tick is directed to this watchtower by a general photo-sensitivity of her skin. The approaching prey is revealed to the blind and deaf highway woman by her sense of smell. The odor of butyric acid, that emanates from the skin glands of all mammals, acts on the tick as a signal to leave her watchtower and hurl herself downwards. If, in so doing, she lands on something warm—a fine sense of temperature betrays this to her—she has reached her prey, the warm-blooded creature. It only remains for her to find a hairless spot. There she burrows deep into the skin of her prey, and slowly pumps herself full of warm blood.

Experiments with artificial membranes and fluids other than blood have proved that the tick lacks all sense of taste. Once the membrane is perforated, she will drink any fluid of the right temperature.

If after the stimulus of butyric acid has functioned, the tick falls upon something cold, she has missed her prey and must again climb to her watchtower.

The tick's abundant blood repast is also her last meal. Now there is nothing left for her to do but drop to earth, lay her eggs and die.

The tick's life history provides support for the validity of the bio-logical versus the heretofore customary physiological approach. To the physiologist, every living creature is an object that exists in his human world. He investigates the organs of living things and the way they work together, as a technician would examine a strange machine. The biologist, on the other hand, takes into account each individual as a subject, living in a world of its own, of which it is the center. It cannot, therefore, be compared to a machine, but only to the engineer who operates the machine. If we ask whether the tick is a machine or an operator, a mere object or a subject, the physiologist will reply that he finds receptors, that is, sense organs, and effectors, that is, organs of action, connected by an integrating device in the central nervous system. He finds no trace of an operator.

To this the biologist will reply, "You mistake the character of the organism completely. No single part of the tick's body has the nature of a machine; everywhere operators are at work." The physiologist will continue, undeterred, "We can show that all the actions of the tick are reflex[2] in character and the reflex arc is the foundation of all animal machines (Fig. 2). It begins with a receptor, which admits only certain

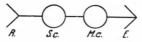

FIG. 2
Reflex arc
R. Receptor; S.c. Sensory cell;
M.c. Motor cell; E. Effector

influences such as butyric acid and warmth, and screens out all others. It ends with a muscle which moves an effector, a leg or proboscis. The sensory cells that initiate the nervous excitation and the motor cells that elicit the motor impulse serve only as connecting links to transmit the entirely physical waves of excitation (produced in the nerves by the receptor upon external stimulation) to the muscles of the effectors. The entire reflex arc works by transfer of motion, as does any machine. No subjective factor, no engineer or engineers appear anywhere in this process."

"On the contrary," the biologist will counter, "we meet the operator everywhere, not merely machine parts. For all the cells of the reflex arc are concerned, not with the transfer of motion, but with the transfer of the *stimulus*. And the stimulus must be 'perceived' by a subject; it does not occur in objects." Any machine part, such as the clapper of a bell,

[2] Reflex originally means the intercepting and reflecting of a light ray by a mirror. Transferred to living creatures, the reflex is conceived as the reception of an external stimulus by a receptor and the stimulus-elicited response by the effectors. In the process the stimulus is converted into nervous excitation, which has to pass through several stations on its way from the receptor to the effector. The course thus described is referred to as a reflex arc.

produces its effect only if it is swung back and forth in a certain manner. To all other agents, such as cold, heat, acids, alkalies, electric currents, it responds as would any other piece of metal. The action of living organs is fundamentally different from this. Since the time of Johannes Müller we know that a muscle responds to all external agents in one and the same way—by contraction. It transforms all external interference into the same effective stimulus, and responds to it with the same impulse, resulting in contraction. Johannes Müller showed also that all external influences affecting the optic nerve, whether ether waves, pressure, or electric currents, elicit a sensation of light. Our visual sensory cells produce the same perception whatever the source of stimulation. From this we may conclude that each living cell is an engineer who perceives and acts, and has *perceptual* or *receptor* signs (*Merkzeichen*) and impulses or *effector signs* (*Wirkzeichen*) which are specific to it. The manifold perceiving and acting of the whole animal may thus be reduced to the cooperation of all the tiny cells, each of which commands only one receptor sign and one effector sign.

In order to achieve an orderly collaboration, the organism uses the brain cells (these, too, are elementary mechanics) and groups half of them as "receptor cells" in the stimulus-receiving part of the brain, or "perceptive organ," into smaller or larger clusters. These clusters correspond to groups of external stimuli, which approach the animal in the form of questions. The other half of the brain cells is used by the organism as "effector cells" or impulse cells, and is grouped into clusters with which it controls the movements of the effectors. These impart the subject's answers to the outer world. The clusters of receptor cells fill the "receptor organs" (*Merkorgan*) of the brain, and the clusters of effector cells make up the contents of its "effector organs" (*Wirkorgan*).

The individual cells of the perceptor organ, whatever their activity, remain as spatially separate units. The units of information which they separately convey would also remain isolated, if it were not possible for them to be fused into new units which are independent of the spatial characters of the receptor organ. This possibility does, in fact, exist. The receptor signs of a group of receptor cells are combined outside the receptor organ, indeed outside the animal, into units that become the properties of external objects. This projection of sensory impressions is a self-evident fact. All our human sensations, which represent our specific receptor signs, unite into perceptual cues (*Merkmal*) which constitute the attributes of external objects and serve as the real basis of our actions. The sensation "blue" becomes the "blueness" of the sky; the sensation "green," the "greenness" of the lawn. These are the cues by which we recognize the objects: blue, the sky; green, the lawn.

A similar process takes place in the effector organ. The isolated effector cells are organized into well-articulated groups according to their effector signs or impulses. The isolated impulses are coordinated into units, and these self-contained motor impulses or rhythmical impulse melodies act upon the muscles subordinated to them. And the limbs or other organs activated by the separate muscles imprint upon the external objects their effector cue or functional significance (*Wirkmal*).

Figuratively speaking, every animal grasps its object with two arms of a forceps, receptor, and effector. With the one it invests the object with a receptor cue or perceptual meaning, with the other, an effector cue or operational meaning. But since all of the traits of an object are structurally interconnected, the traits given operational meaning must affect those bearing perceptual meaning through the object, and so change the object itself. This is best expressed briefly as: *The effector cue or meaning extinguishes the receptor cue or meaning.*

Beside the selection of stimuli which the receptors let through, and the arrangement of muscles which enables the effectors to function in certain ways, the most decisive factor for the course of any action is the number and arrangement of receptor cells which, with the aid of their receptor signs, furnish the objects of the *Umwelt* with receptor cues, and the number and arrangement of effector cells which, by means of their effector signs, supply the same objects with effector cues.

The object participates in the action only to the extent that it must possess certain qualities that can serve as perceptual cue-bearers on the one hand and as functional cue-bearers on the other; and these must be linked by a connecting counterstructure.

The relations between subject and object are best shown by the diagram of the functional cycle (Fig. 3). This illustrates how the subject and

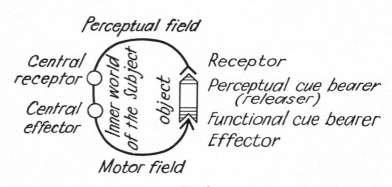

FIG. 3

Functional cycle

the object are dovetailed into one another, to constitute a systematic whole. If we further consider that a subject is related to the same or to different objects by several functional cycles, we shall gain insight into the first principle of *Umwelt* theory: all animals, from the simplest to the most complex, are fitted into their unique worlds with equal completeness. A simple world corresponds to a simple animal, a well-articulated world to a complex one.

And now let us set into the schema of the functional cycle, the tick as subject, and the mammal as her object. It shows at a glance that three functional cycles follow each other in well-planned succession. The skin glands of the mammal are the bearers of perceptual meaning in the first cycle, since the stimulus of butyric acid releases specific receptor signs in the tick's receptor organ, and these receptor signs are projected outside as an olfactory cue. By induction (the nature of which we do not know) the processes that take place in the receptor organ initiate corresponding impulses in the effector organ, and these impulses induce the tick to let go with her legs and drop. The tick, falling on the hairs of the mammal, projects the effector cue of shock onto them. This in turn releases a tactile cue, which extinguishes the olfactory stimulus of the butyric acid. The new receptor cue elicits running about, until it in turn is replaced by the sensation of heat, which starts the boring response.

We are admittedly confronted here with three successive reflexes. Each is elicited by objectively demonstrable physical or chemical stimuli. But anyone who is content with this statement and assumes that it solves the problem proves only that he has not grasped the basic question. We are not concerned with the chemical stimulus of butyric acid, any more than with the mechanical stimulus (released by the hairs), or the temperature stimulus of the skin. We are concerned solely with the fact that, out of the hundreds of stimuli radiating from the qualities of the mammal's body, only three become the bearers of receptor cues for the tick. Why just these three and no others?

What we are dealing with is not an exchange of forces between two objects, but the relations between a living subject and its object. These occur on an altogether different plane, namely, between the receptor sign of the subject and the stimulus from the object.

The tick hangs motionless on the tip of a branch in a forest clearing. Her position gives her the chance to drop on a passing mammal. Out of the whole environment, no stimulus affects her until a mammal approaches, whose blood she needs before she can bear her young.

And now something quite wonderful happens. Of all the influences that emanate from the mammal's body, only three become stimuli, and those in a definite sequence. Out of the vast world which surrounds the tick, three stimuli shine forth from the dark like beacons, and serve as guides to lead her unerringly to her goal. To accomplish this, the tick, besides her body with its receptors and effectors, has been given three receptor signs, which she can use as sign stimuli. And these perceptual cues prescribe the course of her actions so rigidly that she is only able to produce corresponding specific effector cues.

The whole rich world around the tick shrinks and changes into a scanty framework consisting, in essence, of three receptor cues and three effector cues—her *Umwelt*. But the very poverty of this world guarantees the unfailing certainty of her actions, and security is more important than wealth.

From the example of the tick we can deduce the basic structural traits of the *Umwelt*, which are valid for all animals. However, the tick possesses another most remarkable faculty, which affords a further insight into these worlds.

The lucky coincidence which brings a mammal under the twig on which the tick sits obviously occurs very rarely. Nor does the large number of ticks ambushed in the bushes balance this drawback sufficiently to ensure survival of the species. To heighten the probability of a prey coming her way, the tick's ability to live long without food must be added. And this faculty she possesses to an unusual degree. At the Zoological Institute in Rostock, ticks who had been starving for eighteen years have been kept alive.[3] A tick can wait eighteen years. That is something which we humans cannot do. Our time is made up of a series of moments, or briefest time units, within which the world shows no change. For the duration of a moment, the world stands still. Man's moment lasts 1/18 of a second.[4] We shall see later that the length of a moment varies in different animals. But whatever number we wish to adopt for the tick, the ability to endure a never-changing world for eighteen years

[3] The tick is built for a long period of starvation. The sperm cells harbored by the female during her waiting period remain bundled in sperm capsules until mammalian blood reaches the tick's stomach—they are then freed and fertilize the eggs, which have been reposing in the ovary. The perfect fitting of the tick to her prey-object, which she finally seizes, contrasts strikingly with the extremely low probability that this will actually ensue. Bodenheimer is quite right in speaking of a *pessimal* world in which most animals live, that is, the most unfavorable one conceivable. But this world is not their *Umwelt;* it is their environment. An *optimal Umwelt,* that is, one as favorable as possible, and a *pessimal environment* may be considered the general rule. The point is always survival of the species, no matter how many individuals perish. Because of the optimal *Umwelt,* the environment of a species must be *pessimal* or the species would gain the ascendancy over all others.

[4] This is corroborated by motion picture technique. When a film strip is projected, the single pictures must jerk forward successively, and then stand still. To show them distinctly, the jerky motion must be concealed by interposing a screen. The human eye does not perceive the blackout involved if the eclipse of the picture occurs within 1/18 of a second. If the time is lengthened, insufferable flickering ensues.

is beyond the realm of possibility. We shall therefore assume that during her period of waiting the tick is in a sleeplike state, of the sort that interrupts time for hours in our case, too. Only in the tick's world, time, instead of standing still for mere hours, stops for many years at a time, and does not begin to function again until the signal of butyric acid arouses her to renewed activity.

What have we gained by realizing this? Something extremely significant. Time, which frames all happening, seems to us to be the only objectively stable thing in contrast to the colorful change of its contents, and now we see that the subject sways the time of his own world. Instead of saying, as heretofore, that without time, there can be no living subject, we shall now have to say that without a living subject, there can be no time.

In the next chapter we shall see that the same is true of space: without a living subject, there can be neither space nor time. With this, biology has ultimately established its connection with the doctrine of Kant, which it intends to exploit in the *Umwelt* theory by stressing the decisive role of the subject.

Space in the Umwelt

Like a gourmet who picks the raisins out of a cake, the tick has selected butyric acid alone from among the things in her environment. We are not interested in knowing what taste sensations the raisins give the gourmet. We are interested solely in the fact that the raisins become sign stimuli in his world, because they have special biological meaning for him. Nor do we ask how butyric acid smells or tastes to the tick; we merely register the fact that butyric acid, because it is biologically meaningful to the tick, becomes a receptor cue for her.

Suffice it to say that in the tick's receptor organ there must be receptor cells which send out their signs, as we assume that the gourmet's receptor cells send out theirs. The tick's receptor signs give the stimulus of butyric acid a meaning in her own world, by transforming it into a perceptual cue, as the gourmet's receptor signs give the raisin stimulus a meaning in his world.

The *Umwelt* of any animal that we wish to investigate is only a section carved out of the environment which we see spread around it—and this environment is nothing but our own human world. The first task of *Umwelt* research is to identify each animal's perceptual cues among all the stimuli in its environment and to build up the animal's specific world with them. The raisin stimulus leaves the tick quite cold, whereas the indication of butyric acid is of eminent importance to her. In the gourmet's world, on the other hand, the stimulus of raisins, not of butyric acid, is accented.

As the spider spins its threads, every subject spins his relations to certain characters of the things around him, and weaves them into a firm web which carries his existence.

Whatever the relations between a subject and the objects in his environment, they always take effect outside the subject, and that is where we must look for the perceptual cues. In some way, therefore, these are spatially fixed and, since they follow each other in a certain sequence, they are time-bound as well.

We are easily deluded into assuming that the relationship between a foreign subject and the objects in his world exists on the same spatial and temporal plane as our own relations with the objects in our human world. This fallacy is fed by a belief in the existence of a single world, into which all living creatures are pigeonholed. This gives rise to the widespread conviction that there is only one space and one time for all living things. Only recently have physicists begun to doubt the existence of a universe with a space that is valid for all beings. That such a space cannot exist is evident from the fact that all men live in three distinct spaces, which interpenetrate and complement, but in part also contradict one another.

Operational Space

When we move our limbs freely with our eyes shut, we know the exact direction and extent of these motions. Our hands trace paths in a space called our *motor sphere,* or our *effector space*. We measure all these paths by infinitesimal units, which we shall call *directional steps,* since we know the direction of each step perfectly, through kinesthetic sensations or *direction signs*. We distinguish six directions, or three pairs of opposites: right and left, up and down, forward and backward.

Comprehensive experiments have shown that the shortest steps which we can measure with the index finger of an outstretched arm are of about 2 cm. These steps evidently do not provide a very precise measurement for the space in which they are taken. Anyone may easily find out how inaccurate they are by trying to bring together the forefingers of both hands with his eyes closed. He will find that the attempt usually fails, and they miss one another by anything up to 2 cm.

It is of the utmost importance to us that paths once traced are retained very easily. This is what makes writing in the dark possible. This faculty is called *kinesthesia,* a word that explains nothing.

However, effector space is not merely a motor space built up of a thousand intersecting directional steps. It contains and is ruled by a sys-

tem of planes placed perpendicularly to one another, the familiar coordinate system, which is the basis of all spatial definitions.

It is imperative for anyone who deals with the problem of space to
become aware of this fact. Nothing could be simpler. By holding one's
hand vertically, at right angles to the forehead, and moving it right and
left with eyes closed, the boundary between the two becomes obvious. It
coincides approximately with the median plane of the body. By holding
one's hand horizontally and moving it up and down in front of the face,
the boundary between above and below can easily be ascertained. For
most people, this boundary is at eye level, though many people locate it
at the height of the upper lip. The boundary between in front and behind shows the greatest variation. It is found by holding up one's hand
palm forward and moving it back and forth at the side of the head. Many
people indicate this plane near the ear opening, others indicate the
zygomatic arch as the border plane, and by some it is even placed in front
of the tip of the nose. Every normal person carries around with him a
coordinate system composed of these three planes and firmly connected
with his head (Fig. 4), thus providing his operational space with a solid
framework for his directional steps.

Into the changing throng of directional steps which, as motor elements, cannot give the effector space any solidity, the static planes introduce a firm scaffolding that ensures order in functional space.

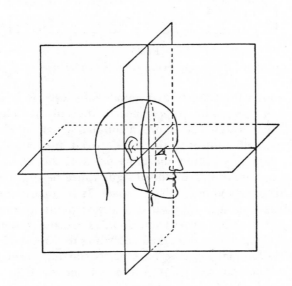

FIG. 4
The coordinate system of man

Cyon's great contribution is that he traced the three-dimensional character of our space to a sense organ situated in the middle ear, the so-called semicircular canals (Fig. 5), whose position roughly corresponds to the three planes of operational space. This relationship is so clearly proven by numerous experiments that we can make the assertion: all animals possessing the three canals also have a three-dimensional operational space.

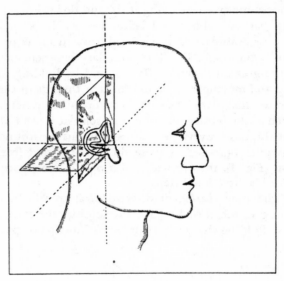

FIG. 5

The semicircular canals of man

Figure 6 shows the semicircular canals of a fish. It is obvious that they must be of paramount importance to the animal. This is further evidenced by their internal structure, a tubular system in which a liquid moves under nervous control in the three spatial directions. The motion of the liquid faithfully reflects the movements of the whole body. This indicates that the organ has an added significance beyond projecting the three planes into the animal's effector space. It is apparently destined to act as a compass—not as a compass that always points to the North, but as a compass for the fish's own "front door." If all the movements of the whole body are analyzed and marked according to three directions in the canals, then the animal must be back at its starting point whenever it has reduced the nervous markings to zero as it moves about.

There is no doubt that a compass for the front door is a necessary implement for all animals with a fixed home, be it a nesting place or a spawning ground. Determination of the front door by visual cues in visual space is insufficient in most cases, since the entrance must be found even if its aspect has changed.

The ability to find their front door in a purely operational space can also be demonstrated in insects and molluscs, although these animals have no semicircular canals.

The following is a very convincing experiment. A beehive is shifted to a location of 2 meters from its original site while most of the bees have flown out. It will then be found that the bees gather in the air, at the spot where the flight hole—their front door—was previously located. Not until five minutes later do the bees turn and fly toward the hive.

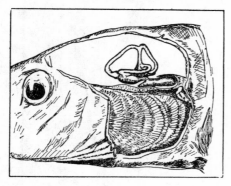

FIG. 6
The semicircular canals of a fish

In a later stage of these experiments, it was found that bees whose antennae were cut off immediately flew toward the hive in its new position. This means that their orientation is mainly operational only while they possess antennae. Without these, they orient themselves by optical impressions in visual space. In normal life, therefore, bees' antennae must somehow assume the role of a compass for the front door, which shows them the way home with greater certainty than do visual impressions.

Even more striking is the "homing" of the snail, *Patella* (Fig. 7). *Patella* lives on the rocky ground between the zones of ebb and flood tides. The big specimens use their hard shells to scoop a bed out of the rock. Here they spend the time of ebb, pressed hard onto the rock. At high tide they begin to wander and graze over the rocks around them. As soon as the tide recedes, they return to their beds. In so doing, they do not always use the same route. The eyes of *Patella* are so primitive that with their aid alone the snail could never find its way home. It is equally unlikely that it could be guided by a scent cue. The only alternative left

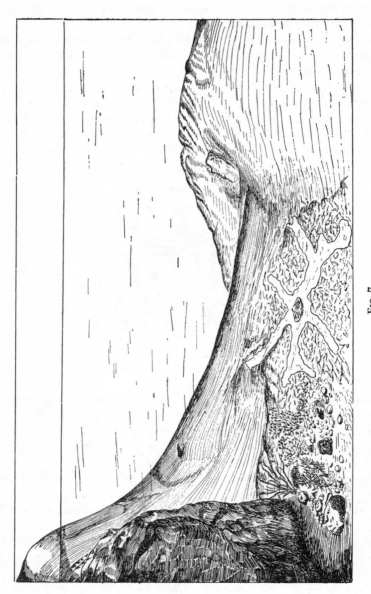

FIG. 7

Homing of the snail *Patella*

is to assume the existence of a compass in the animal's operational space, although we do not know its nature.

Tactile Space

In tactile space, the elementary structural unit is a stationary one: the *locus*, not a motor magnitude as is direction. Locus also owes its existence to a subjective receptor sign; it is not a configuration inherent in surrounding substances. This has been proved by Weber. If the points of a compass are placed on the nape of a subject's neck at a distance of more than 1 cm., the two are clearly distinguished. Each of them is in a different place. If they are now moved down the subject's back without changing the distance between them, they come closer and closer together in his tactile space, until they finally coincide.

It follows that, in addition to the receptor sign of tactile sensation, we also have receptor signs for location. These are called *local signs.* Each local sign, projected into the outside world, furnishes a place or site in tactile space. The skin surfaces that release the same local sign in us when touched, vary exceedingly in size, according to their importance in touch. Next to the tip of the tongue, which explores the oral cavity, the fingertips contain the smallest units and are therefore able to differentiate the largest number of places. When we finger an object, our exploring fingers cover its surface with a delicate mosaic of sensory units. The place-mosaic of objects in an animal's world, both in tactile and visual space, is given by the subject to the things in his *Umwelt,* and does not exist in his environment.

When fingering an object, the places or *loci* are combined with the directional units, and both serve to give it form.

In many animals, tactile space is of prime importance. Rats and cats remain quite unhampered in their motions even if they have lost their vision, so long as they have their tactile hairs. All nocturnal animals and all cave dwellers live primarily in tactile space, which represents a blending of places with orientational units.

Visual Space

Eyeless animals who, like the tick, have a photosensitive skin probably have identical skin regions to produce local signs for both light stimuli and tactile stimuli. Visual and tactile *loci* coincide in their world.

Only in animals with eyes are visual and tactile space distinctly segregated. In the retina of the eye, very small elementary sections, the visual elements, lie close together. Each element of vision has a corresponding place in the *Umwelt,* since there is a local sign for each visual element.

Figure 8 illustrates the visual space of a flying insect. It is clear that, owing to the global structure of the eye, the section of the environment that reaches one visual element grows with increasing distance, and that ever more comprehensive parts of the environment are covered by one place. In consequence, objects receding from the eye become smaller and smaller, until they shrink to a single locus, at which point they vanish. For the place or locus represents the smallest spatial vessel within which there are no differences.

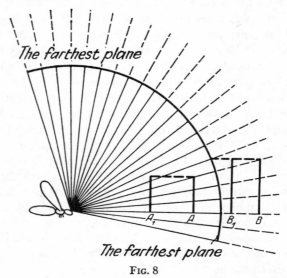

FIG. 8

The visual space of an insect in flight

In tactile space, objects do not grow smaller. And this is where visual and tactile space enter into conflict. A cup grasped with the outstretched arm and guided to the lips grows in visual space, but does not change its size in tactile space. In this case tactile space predominates, because an impartial observer does not see the cup grow.

The roving eye, like the feeling hand, spreads a subtle mosaic of places or sites over all the things in the subject's world. The delicacy of this mosaic depends on the number of visual elements which grasp the same sector of the environment.

Since the number of visual elements varies greatly in the eyes of different animals, the place-mosaics in their environments must differ correspondingly. The coarser the place-mosaic, the more details will be lost, and the world as seen through the eyes of a fly must appear considerably cruder than it does to the human eye.

Since any image can be transformed into a place-mosaic by superimposing a fine mesh or lattice on it, this method makes it possible to render the differences between the place-mosaics of various animal eyes.

By diminishing a picture more and more, photographing it again with the same lattice, and then re-enlarging it, we shall obtain a progressively coarser mosaic. Since the lattice photographed with the picture is disturbing, the coarser mosaic-images have been reproduced as water colors, without the lattice. Figures 9a to 9d were made by the lattice method. They enable us to gain insight into the world of an animal if we know the number of visual elements in its eye. Figure 9c corresponds roughly to the image furnished by the eye of a housefly. It is easy to see that in a world which contains so few details, the threads of a cobweb must vanish completely, and we may say: the spider spins a web that remains totally invisible to its prey. Figure 9d corresponds approximately to the image registered by a mollusc eye. It shows that the visual space of snails and clams contains nothing beyond a number of light and dark areas.

In visual as in tactile space, connections between places are established by directional steps. When preparing an object under a reducing glass, which acts by condensing a large number of places onto a small area, we find that not only the eye, but also the hand which guides the dissecting needle, takes much smaller direction steps corresponding to the points that have been drawn close together.

The Farthest Plane

Unlike operational and tactile space, visual space is surrounded by an impenetrable wall, which we call the horizon or the farthest plane.

Sun, moon and stars wander without any difference in depth on the same most distant plane, which surrounds all visible things. The location of the farthest plane is not rigidly fixed. When I took my first walk out of doors after a serious case of typhoid, the farthest plane hung down before me at a distance of about twenty meters, like a colorful tapestry on which all visible things were depicted. Beyond the twenty meters, there were no nearer and farther objects, only larger and smaller ones. Even the cars that drove past me did not become more remote, only smaller as soon as they reached the farthest plane.

The lens of the human eye has the same function as the lens of a photographic camera—namely, to focus the objects before it sharply onto the retina, which is the counterpart of the photosensitive plate. The lens of the human eye is elastic and can be bent by special ciliary muscles. This curving has the same effect as focusing the lens in a camera.

When the lens muscles are contracted, "forward" directional signs appear. When the elastic lens distends the relaxing muscles, directional

FIG. 9a

A village street, photograph

Fig. 9b

The same village street, photographed through a screen

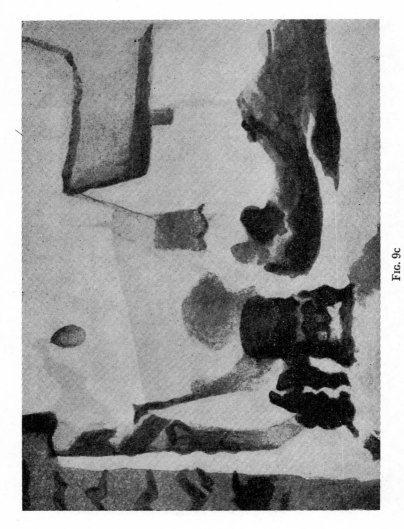

Fig. 9c

The same village street as seen by a fly

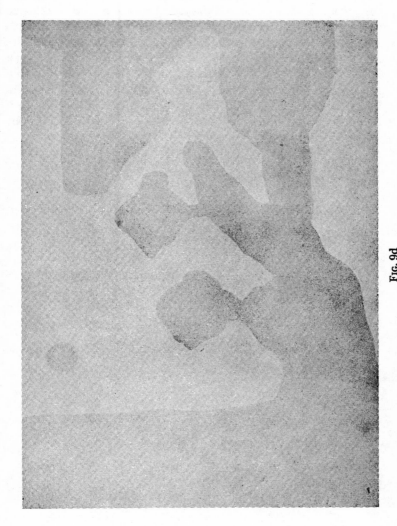

FIG. 9d
The same village street, seen by a mollusc

signs appear which signal "backwards." When the muscles are totally relaxed, the eye is set for a range of from ten meters to infinity.

Through the muscular movements, we recognize the things in our environment as being near or far within a radius of ten meters. Outside this orbit, objects at first become only larger or smaller. The infant's visual space ends here with a farthest plane that encompasses his entire world. Only gradually, step by step, do we learn to push back the most distant plane with the aid of distance signs, until, at a distance of 6 to 8 km., it sets a limit to the adult's visual space, too, and the horizon begins.

The difference between the visual spaces of a child and a grownup is portrayed in Figure 10, which reproduces an experience described by

Fig. 10
The farthest plane of a child and of an adult

Helmholtz. He reports that as a little boy he was passing the Potsdam garrison church, and noticed some workmen on the gallery. Thereupon he asked his mother to reach down some of the little dolls for him. Church and workmen were already on his farthest plane, and so were not distant, but small. Thus he had every reason to believe that his mother could fetch the puppets down from the gallery with her long arm. He did not know that in his mother's world the church had altogether different dimensions and that the people on the gallery were not small, but far away. It is hard to decide where the farthest plane begins in the *Umwelt* of an animal, for it is difficult to determine experimentally at what point an object approaching the subject in his environment becomes nearer as well as larger in his specific world. Attempts at catching flies show that the approaching human hand makes them fly away only when it is about half a meter from them. Accordingly, it would seem justifiable to suppose that their farthest plane is at this distance.

But other observations suggest that the most remote plane also appears in other ways in the housefly's world. We know that flies do not simply circle around a hanging lamp or chandelier, but interrupt their flight abruptly whenever they have flown half a meter or so away, and then fly close by or under it again. This behavior is like that of a yachtsman who is anxious to stay within sight of an island.

Now the eye of a fly (Fig. 11) is built in such a way that its visual elements (rhabdoms) are long nerve configurations, which must intercept

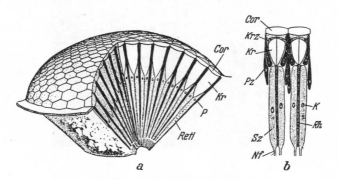

FIG. 11

Structure of the compound eye of a fly (schematic)
a: Whole eye, from which a section is dissected on the right
(according to Hesse)
b: Two ommatidia
cor: Chitincornea; *K:* nucleus; *Kr:* crystalline lens; *Krz:* lens cell; *Nf:* nerve fiber; *P:* pigment; *Retl:* retinula; *Rh:* rhabdom; *Sz:* visual cell

the image projected by their lenses at varying depths, depending on the distance of the object seen. Exner has surmised that we might here be dealing with a substitute for the muscular lens apparatus of the human eye. Assuming that the optic apparatus made up of the fly's visual elements functions as a portrait lens, the chandelier would vanish at a certain distance, and thus cause the fly to return. As an illustration of this phenomenon, compare Figures 12 and 13, which represent a chandelier photographed without and with a portrait lens.

FIG. 12
Chandelier as seen by man

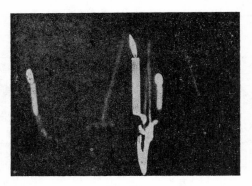

FIG. 13
Chandelier as seen by fly

Whether the farthest plane encloses visual space in this or another manner—it is always there. We may therefore picture all the animals around us, be they beetles, butterflies, flies, mosquitoes or dragonflies that people a meadow, enclosed within soap bubbles, which confine their visual space and contain all that is visible to them. Each soap bubble harbors different *loci,* and in each there exist the directional planes of operational space, which give its space a solid framework. The fluttering birds, the squirrels leaping from branch to branch, or the cows that browse in the meadows—all remain permanently surrounded by their soap bubbles, which define their own space.

Only when this fact is clearly grasped shall we recognize the soap bubble which encloses each of us as well. Then we shall also see all our fellow men in their individual soap bubbles, which intersect each other smoothly, because they are built up of subjective perceptual signs. There is no space independent of subjects. If we still cling to the fiction of an all-encompassing universal space, we do so only because this conventional fable facilitates mutual communication.

Receptor Time

Karl Ernst von Baer has made it clear that time is the product of a subject. Time as a succession of moments varies from one *Umwelt* to another, according to the number of moments experienced by different subjects within the same span of time. A moment is the smallest indivisible time vessel, for it is the expression of an indivisible elementary sensation, the so-called *moment sign*. As already stated, the duration of a human moment amounts to $\frac{1}{18}$ of a second. Furthermore, the moment is identical for all sense modalities, since all sensations are accompanied by the same moment sign.

The human ear does not discriminate eighteen air vibrations in one second, but hears them as one sound.

It has been found that eighteen taps applied to the skin within one second are felt as even pressure.

Kinematography projects environmental motions onto a screen at their accustomed tempo. The single pictures then follow each other in tiny jerks of $\frac{1}{18}$ second.

If we wish to observe motions too swift for the human eye, we resort to slow-motion photography. This is a technique by which more than eighteen pictures are taken per second, and then projected at a normal tempo. Motor processes are thus extended over a longer span of time, and processes too swift for our human time-tempo (of 18 per second), such as the wing-beat of birds and insects, can be made visible. As slow-motion photography slows motor processes down, the time contractor speeds them up. If a process is photographed once an hour and then presented at the rate of $\frac{1}{18}$ second, it is condensed into a short space of time. In this way, processes too slow for our human tempo, such as the blossoming of a flower, can be brought within the range of our perception.

The question arises whether there are animals whose perceptual time consists of shorter or longer moments than ours, and in whose *Umwelt* motor processes are consequently enacted more slowly or more quickly than in ours.

The first experiments of this kind were made by a young German scientist. Later, with the collaboration of another, he studied especially the reaction of the fighting fish to its own mirror image. The fighting fish does not recognize its own reflection if it is shown him eighteen times per second. It must be presented to the fighting fish at least thirty times per second. A third student trained the fighting fish to snap toward their food if a gray disc was rotated behind it. On the other hand, if a disc with black and white sectors was turned slowly, it acted as a "warning sign," for in this case the fish received a light shock when they approached their food. After this training, if the rotation speed of the black and white disc was gradually increased, the avoiding reactions became more uncertain at a certain speed, and soon thereafter they shifted to the opposite. This did not happen until the black sectors followed each other within 1/60 second. At this speed the black-and-white signal had become gray. This proves conclusively that in the world of these fish, who feed on fast-moving prey, all motor processes—as in the case of slow-motion photography—appear at reduced speed.

An instance of time contraction is given in Figure 14, borrowed from the above-mentioned work. A vineyard snail is placed on a rubber ball which, carried by water, slides under it without friction. The snail's shell is held in place by a bracket. Thus the snail, unhampered in its crawling movements, remains in the same place. If a small stick is then

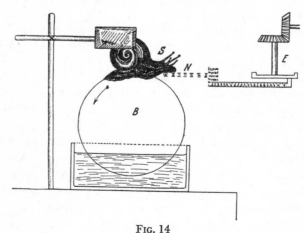

FIG. 14

The snail's movement

B: ball; *E:* eccentric wheel; *N:* rod; *S:* snail

moved up to its foot, the snail will climb up on it. If the snail is given one to three taps with the stick each second, it will turn away, but if four or more taps are administered per second, it will begin to climb onto the stick. In the snail's world a rod that oscillates four times per second has become stationary. We may infer from this that the snail's receptor time moves at a tempo of three to four moments per second. As a result, all motor processes in the snail's world occur much faster than in ours. Nor do its own motions seem slower to the snail than ours do to us.

The Simple Umwelten

Space and time are of no immediate use to the subject. They become significant only when numerous receptor cues, which would vanish without the temporal and spatial framework of the *Umwelt*, must be discriminated. In very simple *Umwelten,* however, which harbor but a single perceptual cue, there is no need for a framework of this kind.

In Figure 15, the environment and the *Umwelt* of the *Paramecium* are shown side by side. *Paramecium* is covered with dense rows of cilia,

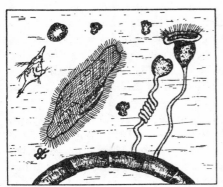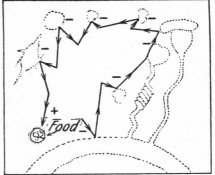

Fig. 15
Environment and *Umwelt* of the *Paramecium*

whose lashing drives it swiftly through the water, while it revolves continually on its longitudinal axis. Of all the different things in its environment, its *Umwelt* takes in only the ever-identical receptor cue which, whenever, wherever, and however the *Paramecium* is stimulated, impels it to the motion of escape. The same obstacle cue always elicits the same fleeing reaction. This consists of a backward motion, followed by a lateral deflection, whereupon the animal again begins to swim forward. By this, the obstacle is removed. We may say that in this case the same receptor cue is always extinguished by the same effector cue. The small animal comes to rest only when it reaches its food, the bacteria of putrefaction, which alone of all the things in its world do not emit stimuli. These facts show how nature is able to fashion life according to her plan, with a single functional cycle.

A few multicellular animals, such as the marine medusa *Rhizostoma*, are also able to get along with a single functional cycle. Here the entire organism consists of a swimming pump mechanism, which draws the plankton-filled sea water into itself unfiltered, and ejects it again, filtered. The sole manifestation of life consists in the rhythmic up-and-down swinging of the elastic umbrella. The ever-constant pulsation keeps the animal floating on the surface of the ocean. At the same time the stomach distends and contracts alternately, driving the sea water in and out through fine pores. The liquid content of the stomach is propelled through labyrinthine digestive canals, whose walls absorb the nourishment and the accompanying oxygen. Swimming, feeding, and breathing are carried out by the same rhythmic contraction of the muscles on the edge of the umbrella. To ensure continuity of this motion, eight bell-shaped organs are located on the periphery of the umbrella (represented symbolically in Fig. 16), whose clappers strike a nerve end at each beat. The stimulus thus produced elicits the next umbrella-beat. In this way the medusa gives herself her own effector cue, and this releases the same receptor cue, which again elicits the same effector cue *ad infinitum*. In the medusa's world, the same bell signal rings all the time, and dominates the rhythm of life. All other stimuli are cut off.

In the case of a single functional cycle, as in *Rhizostoma*, we can speak of a reflex animal, for the same reflex runs all the time from each bell to the muscular band at the umbrella's edge. Moreover, the term may even be extended to animals with several reflex arcs, such as other medusae, so long as these reflex arcs remain mutually independent. Thus there are medusae which have tentacles with self-contained reflex arcs. Moreover, many medusae have a mobile mouth *(manubrium)* with a muscular system of its own, which is connected to the receptors on the umbrella's edge. All these reflex arcs operate quite independently and are not directed by a central organ.

An external organ that contains a complete reflex arc is aptly termed a *reflex person*. Sea urchins possess a large number of such reflex persons, each of which performs its own reflex function by itself, without central control. To illustrate the contrast between animals built in this way and higher animals, I have coined the phrase: when a dog runs, the animal moves its legs; when a sea urchin runs, the legs move the animal.

Sea urchins, like porcupines, carry a large number of spines which,

FIG. 16
A marine medusa with peripheral organs

however, are developed as independent reflex persons. Besides the hard, pointed spines, which are attached to the lime shell by means of a ball bearing and are able to turn a forest of spears against any stimulus-emitting object that approaches the skin, there are delicate, long, muscular tube-feet for climbing. Furthermore, certain sea urchins have four kinds of claws (cleansing claws, clapping claws, snapping claws, and poison claws or *pedicellariae*) scattered over their surface.

Although some of these reflex persons act in unison, they work quite independently of each other. Thus in response to one and the same chemical stimulus emitted by the sea urchin's enemy, the starfish, the spines part, the poison fangs spring forth in their stead and bury themselves in the enemy's suction feet.

We may therefore refer to a *reflex republic* in which, despite the utter independence of each reflex person, absolute domestic peace reigns. For the tender tube-feet are never attacked by the sharp snapping fangs, which normally seize every approaching object. This peace is not dictated by a central organization, as in our case, where our sharp teeth are a constant danger to the tongue, avoided only by the appearance of the receptor signal of pain in the central organ. For pain inhibits the pain-eliciting action. In a sea urchin's reflex republic, which has no superior center, domestic peace must be secured differently. It is achieved by the presence of autodermin, a substance secreted by the skin. Undiluted, autodermin lames the receptors of the reflex persons. It is diffused throughout the skin in such great dilution that, upon contact of the skin with a foreign body, it remains ineffective. As soon as two skin surfaces meet, however, it becomes effectual and prevents release of the normal reflex of snapping by the *pedicellariae*.

A reflex republic such as a sea urchin may well have numerous receptor cues in its *Umwelt,* if it consists of numerous reflex persons. But these receptor cues must remain completely cut off from each other, since each functional cycle operates in utter seclusion.

The tick's life manifestations, as we have seen, consist substantially of three reflexes. Even this represents a superior type of organism, since the functional cycles, instead of using these isolated reflex arcs, have a common receptor organ. In the tick's world the prey may therefore possibly exist as an entity, even though consisting only of butyric acid stimulus, tactile stimulus and heat stimulus.

For the sea urchin, this possibility does not exist. Its receptor cues, which are composed of graduated pressure stimuli and chemical stimuli, constitute totally isolated magnitudes.

Some sea urchins respond to any darkening of the horizon by a movement of spines which, as shown in Figures 17a and b, is displayed equally toward a cloud, a ship, and the real enemy, namely, a fish. Even so, our representation of its *Umwelt* is not sufficiently simplified. We cannot think in terms of the sea urchin projecting the receptor cue of darkness outward into space, since it has no visual space. What actually happens

Fig. 17a

The sea urchin's environment

Fig. 17b

The sea urchin's *Umwelt*

is better conveyed by the analogy of a wad of cotton passing lightly over its photosensitive skin.

Form and Motion as Perceptual Cues

Even supposing that each receptor cue of the various reflex persons is provided with a local sign and that thus each is in a separate place in the sea urchin's world, it would still be impossible to join these *loci*. Consequently this *Umwelt* must of necessity lack the receptor cues of form and motion, which presuppose a combination of several places.

Form and motion appear only in higher perceptual worlds. Now, thanks to experiences in our own world, we generally assume that the shape of an object is the receptor cue originally given, and that motion is added only as an attendant phenomenon, a secondary receptor cue. However, for many animal worlds this is not true. Not only are static form and moving form two mutually quite independent receptor cues, but motion may even appear as an independent receptor cue, without form.

Figure 18 shows the jackdaw on the hunt for grasshoppers. It simply cannot see a sitting grasshopper. The jackdaw does not snap after it unless it hops. One is at first inclined to suppose that the jackdaw is familiar with the form of the grasshopper in repose, but that owing to the intersecting blades of grass it cannot recognize the grasshopper as an entity, as we have difficulty in finding a familiar form in a puzzle picture. According to this hypothesis, the form only separates from the interfering subsidiary images at the time of the jump.

In the light of further observation, however, we may assume that the jackdaw does not know the form of the stationary grasshopper at all, but is adapted to the moving form only. This would explain the "death-feigning" reaction of many insects. If their static form does not exist in the perceptual world of the pursuing enemy, then by "pretending to be

FIG. 18
Jackdaw and grasshopper

dead" they disappear entirely from their enemy's sensory world and cannot even be found if sought.

I have built a "fly rod" consisting of a small stick from which a pea is suspended on a thin thread. The pea is covered with a sticky gum. If by a slight motion of the stick the pea is swung back and forth in front of a sunny window sill on which a number of flies are sitting, many of them will invariably throw themselves on the pea, and some will remain stuck to it. These are always males. The whole process represents a misdirected nuptial flight. The flies circling around a chandelier, too, are males lunging at females flitting by. The swinging pea deceptively imitates the perceptual cue of the female in flight. In repose it is never taken for a female. We may well conclude from this that static female and female in flight are two different receptor cues.

Figure 19 proves that motion without form can feature as a perceptual cue. It presents the scallop in its environment and in its *Umwelt*. In its environment, within range of its hundred eyes, is the scallop's most dreaded enemy, the starfish, *Asterias*. So long as the starfish is at rest, it affects the scallop not at all. The starfish's characteristic form is no sensory cue for the scallop. As soon as the starfish moves, however, the scallop responds by pushing out its long tentacles, which act as olfactory organs. They approach the starfish and receive the new stimulus. Thereupon the scallop rises and swims away.

Experiments have shown that shape and color of a moving object are wholly indifferent. The object appears as a perceptual cue in the scallop's world only if its motion is as slow as that of the starfish. The scallop's eyes are not set for either form or color but solely for a certain motor tempo, which corresponds exactly to that of its enemy. However, even this does not characterize the enemy precisely enough. First, a scent cue must intervene, to elicit the second functional cycle, which removes the scallop by flight from the vicinity of its enemy, and by this effector cue conclusively extinguishes the enemy's receptor cues.

The existence of a receptor cue for form was long surmised in the *Umwelt* of the earthworm. Darwin early pointed out that earthworms handle both leaves and pine needles according to their shapes (Fig. 20). The earthworm drags leaves and pine needles into its narrow cave. They serve it both for protection and for food. Most leaves spread out if one tries to pull them into a narrow tube petiole foremost. On the other hand, they roll up easily and offer no resistance if seized at the tip. Pine needles, on the other hand, which always fall in pairs, must be grasped at their base, not their tip, if they are to be dragged into a narrow hole with ease.

It was inferred from the earthworm's spontaneously correct handling

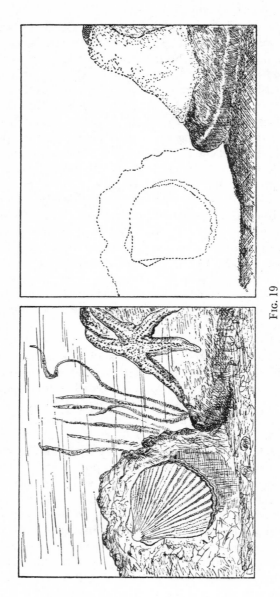

FIG. 19

Environment and *Umwelt* of the scallop

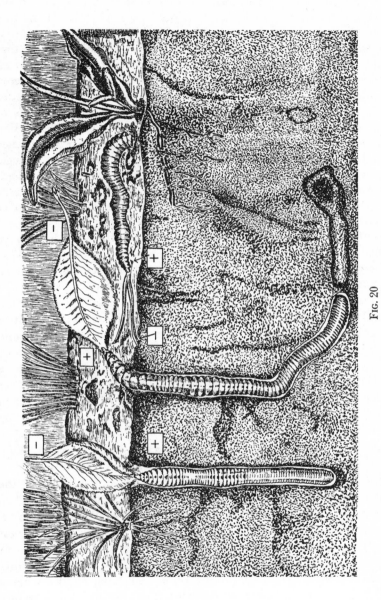

Fig. 20

Taste discrimination in earthworms

of leaves and needles that the form of these objects, which plays a decisive part in its effector world, must exist as a receptor cue in its perceptual world.

This assumption has been proven false. It was possible to show that identical small sticks dipped in gelatine were pulled into the earthworms' holes indiscriminately by either end. But as soon as one end was covered with powder from the tip of a dried cherry leaf, the other with powder from its base, the earthworms differentiated between the two ends of the stick exactly as they do between the tip and base of the leaf itself. Although earthworms handle leaves in keeping with their form, they are guided not by the shape but by the taste of the leaves. This arrangement has evidently been adopted for the reason that the receptor organs of earthworms are built too simply to fashion sensory cues of shape. This example shows how nature is able to overcome difficulties which to us seem utterly insurmountable.

Thus the hypothesis of form perception in earthworms had to be abandoned. It became even more urgent to answer the question: what are the lowest animals in whose *Umwelt* we may expect to find form as a perceptual cue?

This question has since been solved. It has been possible to show that bees alight by preference on figures that exhibit broken forms, such as stars and crosses, whereas they avoid compact forms, such as circles and squares. Figure 21, which was designed on this basis, contrasts a bee's environment with its *Umwelt*. The bee is seen in its environment, a blooming field, in which blossoming flowers alternate with buds. If we put ourselves in the bee's place and look at the field from the point of view of its *Umwelt,* the blossoms are changed to stars or crosses according to their form, and the buds assume the unbroken shape of circles. The biological significance of this newly discovered quality in bees is evident. Only blossoming flowers have a meaning for them; buds do not.

Now, as we saw in the case of the tick, relations of meaning are the only true signposts in our exploration of *Umwelten*. Whether the broken forms are physiologically more effective, does not matter from this aspect.

These studies have reduced the problem of form to the simplest formula. It is enough to assume that the receptor cells for local signs in the receptor organ are segregated into two groups, those in one according to the schema "broken," those in the other according to the schema "compact." There are no further differentiations. If the schemata are projected outward, "receptor images" of a very general nature result. Excellent new investigations reveal that in the case of bees these are filled with colors and scents.

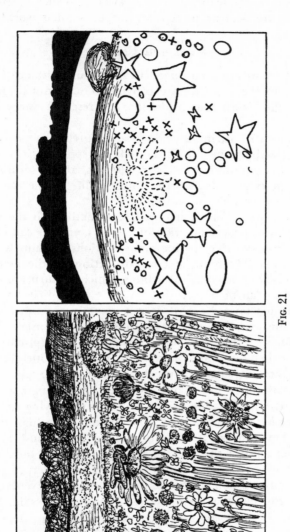

FIG. 21

Environment and *Umwelt* of the honey bee

The earthworm, the scallop, or the tick have no such schemata. Consequently there are no true perceptual images in their worlds.

Goal and Plan

Since we humans are accustomed to carry our existence laboriously from one goal to the next, we are convinced that animals live in the same fashion. This is a fallacy which has led research astray again and again.

True, no one will attribute goals to a sea urchin or an earthworm. But even in describing the life of the tick, we spoke of it as waylaying its prey. By this expression we have already, albeit unintentionally, smuggled our petty everyday worries into the life of the tick, which is dominated by a pure plan of nature.

It must therefore be our first objective to extinguish the will-o'-the-wisp of a goal in our contemplation of *Umwelten*. This can only be accomplished by coordinating the life manifestations of animals under the viewpoint of a plan. Perhaps later certain actions of the highest mammals may prove to be teleological actions, which in turn are dovetailed into the over-all plan of nature.

Actions directed toward a goal do not occur in any other animals at all. To prove this assertion, the reader must be given insight into a few *Umwelten,* which preclude all doubt. According to information I have received concerning the sound perception of night moths, it makes no difference whether the sound to which the animals are adjusted be the sound manifestation of a bat or one produced by rubbing a glass stopper —the effect is always the same. Night moths which, owing to their light coloring, are easily visible, fly away upon perceiving a high tone, while species which have protective coloration alight in response to the same tone. The same sensory cue has the opposite effect in their case. It is striking how the two opposite kinds of action are governed by a plan. There can be no question of discrimination or purposiveness, since no moth or butterfly has ever seen the color of its own skin. The plan revealed in this instance appears even more admirable when we learn that the artful microscopic structure of the night moth's hearing organ exists solely for this one high tone of the bat. To all else, these moths are totally deaf.

A fine observation by Fabre revealed the contrast between goal and plan long ago. He placed an eyed hawk moth female on a sheet of white paper, where she moved her abdomen about for some time. He then put her under a glass bell next to the sheet of paper. During the night, swarms of males of this very rare species came flying in through the window and crowded together on the white paper. Not a single male heeded the female who sat next to it under the glass bell. Fabre was unable to ascertain what kind of physical or chemical stimulus emanated from the paper.

Experiments made with grasshoppers and crickets have been more instructive in this respect. Figure 22 is an illustration of these experiments. A specimen, fiddling in lively fashion, is sitting in a room before a microphone. In a neighboring room the sex partners gather in front of a loudspeaker and pay not the slightest attention to a specimen sitting under a glass bell, who fiddles in vain, since the sounds she makes cannot be heard. Thus the partners make no advances whatever. The optical image is ineffectual.

Both experiments show the same thing. No goal is pursued in either case. But the seemingly strange behavior of the males is easily explained if examined under the aspect of a governing plan. In both cases a specific receptor cue initiates a functional cycle, but, since the normal object is eliminated, the proper effector cue, which would be necessary to extinguish the first perceptual cue, is not produced. Normally, another receptor cue should intervene at this point and activate the next functional cycle. The nature of this second receptor cue must be investigated more closely in both cases. In any event, it is a necessary link in the chain of functional cycles which lead to mating.

All right, the reader will say, we must give up purposive action for insects. They are ruled directly by the plan of nature, which determines their perceptual cues, as we have seen in the case of the tick. But no one who has ever observed a mother hen hastening to the aid of the chicks in a poultry yard can doubt the existence of true goal actions. Very fine experiments have fully clarified this particular case.

Figure 23 illustrates the results obtained in these experiments. If a chick is tied to a peg by one leg, it peeps loudly. This distress call makes the mother hen run immediately in the direction of the sound with ruffled plumage, even if the chick is invisible. As soon as she catches sight of the chick, she begins to peck furiously at an imaginary antagonist. But if the fettered chick is set before the mother hen's eyes under a glass bell, so that she can see it but not hear its distress call, she is not in the least disturbed by the sight of him.

Here again, we have an interrupted chain of functional cycles, not a goal action. The perceptual cue of peeping normally comes indirectly from an enemy who is attacking the chick. According to plan, this sensory cue is extinguished by the effector cue of beak thrusts, which chase the foe away. The struggling, but not-peeping chick is not a sensory cue that would release a specific activity. It would be quite incon-

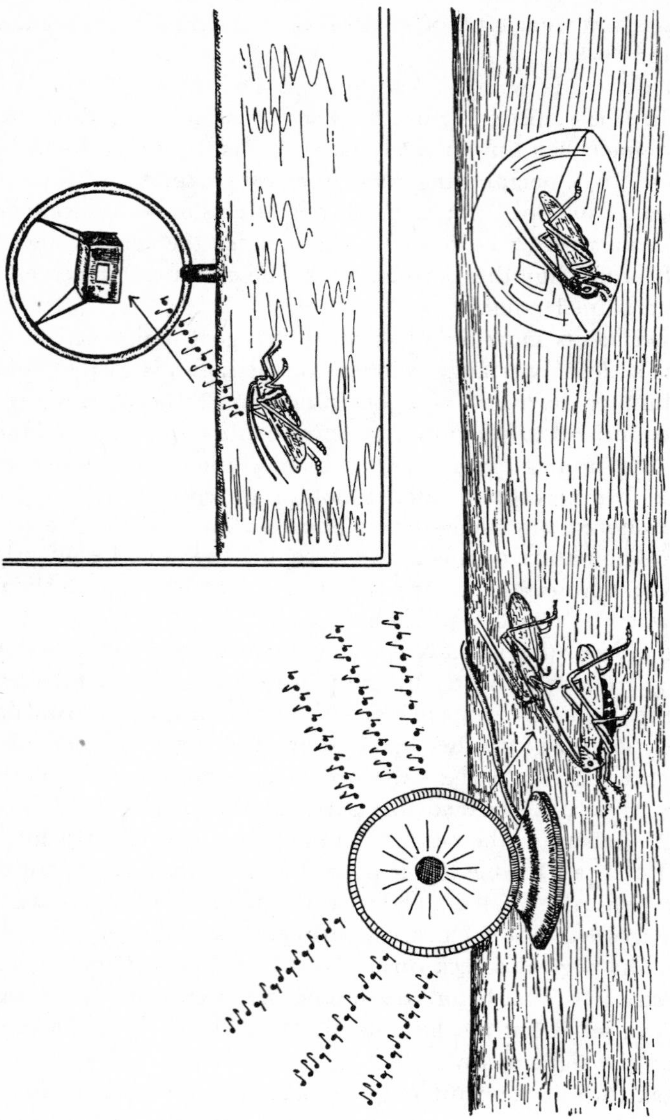

Fig. 22

Grasshoppers before a microphone

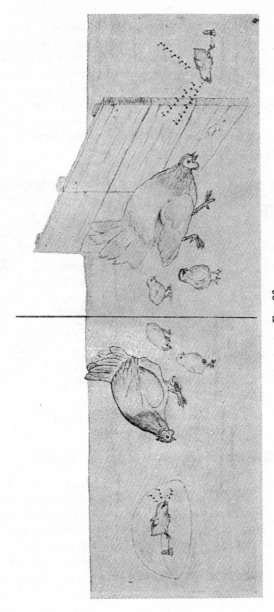

FIG. 23
Hen and chicks

gruous if it were, too, as the mother hen is in no position to loosen a noose.

The hen shown in Figure 24 behaved even more oddly and aimlessly. Together with a clutch of eggs of a white stock, she had also hatched one egg of her own black breed. Toward this chick, which was her own flesh and blood, she behaved quite inconsistently. She hurried in the direction of the black chick's peeping, but when she perceived it among the white ones, she pecked away at it. The auditory and the visual cues of the same object elicited two contradictory functional cycles in her. Evidently the chick's two sensory cues had not been fused into an entity in the hen's world.

Fig. 24
Hen and black chick

Receptor Image and Effector Image

If we contrast nature's plan with the subject's goal, we will not have to discuss the question of instinct, which does not really get anyone anywhere. Does the acorn need an instinct to grow into an oak tree, or does a host of bone-forming cells work instinctively to form a bone? If we deny this and substitute a plan of nature as a regulating factor, then nature's designs will also be recognized as swaying the spinning of a cobweb or the building of a bird's nest, since no subjective goal is involved in either case.

Instinct is merely a product of perplexity, a concept which must answer if we gainsay the superindividual plans of nature. These plans are disputed because it is hard to conceive the nature of a plan, since it assuredly is neither matter nor force. Yet it is not so difficult to gain an idea of the plan, if one bears a concrete example in mind.

The most beautiful plan will not drive a nail into the wall, if you have no hammer. But the finest hammer is not enough either, if you have no plan and rely on chance. Then you hit your fingers.

Without plans, that is, without the sovereign ordinances of nature, there would be no order in nature, only chaos. Every crystal is the product of a plan of nature, and when physicists present Bohr's beautiful atom models, they exemplify the plans of inanimate nature which they seek.

The sovereignty of nature's living plans is expressed most clearly in the study of *Umwelten*. To trace them is one of the most enthralling pursuits. We shall therefore not let ourselves be turned aside, but will calmly continue on our stroll through the *Umwelten*.

The processes illustrated in Figure 25 (facing p. 60) give a series of findings gleaned from studies of the hermit crab. It has been found that the hermit crab requires an extremely simple spatial schema as a receptor image. Any object of a certain order of magnitude with a cylindrical to conical outline can assume meaning for it.

As the figures show, one and the same cylindrical object—in this case, a sea anemone—changes its meaning in the crab's world according to the crab's prevailing mood.

The same crab and the same sea anemone are before us all the time. But in the first case the crab had been robbed of the actinians which it had carried on its shell. In the second case even its shell had been taken from it, and in the third case a crab that wore both shell and actinians had been left to starve for some time. This is enough to put the crab into three different moods. According to these moods, the sea anemone changes its meaning for the crab. In the first case, where the crab's shell lacks the protective mantle of actinians, which repel its enemy, the cuttle-fish, the receptor image of the sea anemone assumes a "defense tone." This is expressed in the action of the crab, which plants the sea anemone on its shell. If the same crab is robbed of its shell, the sea anemone's receptor image gains a "dwelling tone," which is expressed in the crab's attempt, albeit a futile one, to crawl into it. In the third case, that of the starving crab, the receptor image of the sea anemone assumes a "feeding tone," and the crab begins to devour it.

These observations are of especial value because they show that, even at the level of arthropod worlds, the perceptual image furnished by the sense organs can be supplemented and changed by a "functional image" (effector image) dependent on the action which it elicits.

To clarify this remarkable state of affairs, experiments were carried out on dogs. The problems was stated very simply and the answers of the dogs were unequivocal. A dog had been trained to jump up on a chair before it at the command, "chair." Then the chair was removed and the command repeated. It was found that the dog now treated as chairs all the objects on which it could sit, and jumped up on them. Let us put it this way: a series of other objects, such as crates, shelves, overturned stools, assumed a "sitting tone." Moreover, this was a "dog sitting tone" and not a human sitting tone. For many of these "dog chairs" were not at all suitable as human seating accommodations. It could also be shown that "table" and "basket" assumed a special tone for the dog, a tone that depended entirely on the actions which it performed with them.

But the real problem, in all its implications, can only be analyzed in man. How do we manage to see *sitting* in a chair, *drinking* in a cup, *climbing* in a ladder, none of which are given perceptually? In all the objects that we have learned to use, we see the function which we perform with them as surely as we see their shape or color.

I had taken a young, very intelligent and agile Negro with me from the heart of Africa to Dar-es-Salaam. The only thing which he lacked was a knowledge of European tools. When I bid him climb a short ladder, he asked me: "How am I to do that, I see nothing but rods and holes?" As soon as another Negro had shown him how to climb the ladder, he could do it easily. From then on, the perceptually given "rods and holes" held a climbing tone for him, and he recognized them everywhere as a ladder. The *receptor image* of rods and holes had been supplemented by the effector image of his own action; through this it had acquired a new meaning. The new meaning manifested itself as a new attribute, as a *functional* or *effector tone*.

This experience with the Negro indicates that we have developed an effector image for each of the functions which we perform with the objects in our specific *Umwelt*. This effector image we inevitably fuse so closely with the receptor image furnished by our sense organs, that in the process the objects acquire a new quality, which conveys their meaning to us. and which we shall briefly term the *functional tone*.

If an object is used in different ways, it may possess several effector images, which then lend different tones to the same perceptual image. A chair may occasionally be used as a weapon. It then assumes another functional image, which manifests itself as a "thrashing tone." In this strictly human case, as in that of the hermit crab, the subject's mood determines which functional image will lend its tone to the perceptual image. Effector images can be surmised only in animals whose actions are controlled by central effector organs. All animals that operate on a purely reflex plan, such as the sea urchin, must be excluded. Elsewhere, however, the influence of effector images reaches far down into the animal kingdom, as shown by the hermit crab.

If we wish to use the functional images to paint the *Umwelten* of animals further removed from us, we must constantly bear in mind that they are the performances of animals, projected into their *Umwelt*, and that they lend meaning to perceptual images only by their effector tone. The vital things in an animal's world furnish a perceptual image. To reproduce these vital things, and to grasp the full significance of their perceptual images, we shall supply these images with a functional tone. Even at a level where there are as yet no spatially articulated receptor images, as in the tick, we may say that the meaning of the only three effective stimuli that reach her from her prey stems from the functional tones (connected with the stimuli) of dropping down, of running around and of boring in. To be sure, the selective activity of the receptors, these entrance gates of the stimuli, plays the lead; but what lends this activity unerring certainty is the functional tone connected with the stimuli.

Since functional images can be deduced from the easily recognizable performances of animals, the objects in the *Umwelt* of a foreign subject become more tangible and gain new meaning.

If a dragonfly flits toward a branch to perch on it, the branch not only exists as a receptor image in its world, but is also distinguished by a sitting tone, which marks it above all other branches.

The *Umwelt* only acquires its admirable surety for animals if we include the functional tones in our contemplation of it. We may say that the number of objects which an animal can distinguish in its own world equals the number of functions it can carry out. If, along with few functions, it possesses few functional images, its world, too, will consist of few objects. As a result its world is indeed poorer, but all the more secure. For orientation is much easier among few objects than among many. If the *Paramecium* had a functional image of its performance, its entire world would consist of homogeneous objects, all of them bearing the same obstacle tone. To be sure, such an *Umwelt* would leave nothing to be desired as far as certitude is concerned.

As the number of an animal's performances grows, the number of objects that populate its *Umwelt* increases. It grows within the individual life span of every animal that is able to gather experiences. For each new experience entails a readjustment to new impressions. Thus new perceptual images with new functional tones are created.

This may be observed especially in dogs, who learn to handle certain human implements by turning them into canine implements. Nevertheless, the number of dog objects remains considerably smaller than that of our objects. To illustrate this fact, let us imagine a room in terms of the functional tones connected with the objects in it, first by man (Fig. 26), secondly by a dog (Fig. 27), and thirdly by a housefly (Fig. 28) *(see* between pp. 60-61).

In the world of man, the functional tones of the objects in a room can be represented by a sitting tone for a chair, a meal tone for the table, and by further adequate effector tones for plates and glasses (eating and drinking tone). The floor has a walking tone while the bookcase displays a reading tone and the desk a writing tone. The wall has an obstacle tone and the lamp a light tone.

If we represent the recurrent similar functional tones by identical colors in the dog's world, only feeding, sitting, running, and light tones are left. Everything else displays an obstacle tone. Owing to its smoothness, even a revolving piano stool does not have a sitting tone for a dog.

Finally, for the fly, everything assumes a single running tone, except for the lamp whose significance has already been pointed out, and the crockery on the table.

Flies orient themselves with great ease in the environment of our room. As soon as a pot of hot coffee is set down on the table, they gather around it, because its heat acts as a stimulus to them. They wander over the surface of the table, which for them has a running tone. And since flies' feet are equipped with taste organs, whose stimulation releases a protruding of the proboscis, they are held fast by their food, while all other objects induce continued wandering. Here it is particularly easy to lift the fly's *Umwelt* out of its environment.

The Familiar Path

The best way to find out that no two human *Umwelten* are the same is to have yourself led through unknown territory by someone familiar with it. Your guide unerringly follows a path that you cannot see. Among all the rocks and trees in the environment there are some which, strung together in sequence, stand out as landmarks from all the others, although they are not apparent to a stranger.

The familiar path is entirely dependent on the individual subject. It is therefore a typical *Umwelt* problem. The familiar pathway is a spatial problem, and draws both on the subject's visual and functional space. This is evident from the way in which a familiar path is described —something like this: turn right behind the red house, then straight ahead for a hundred paces, and on to the left. Three kinds of sensory cues are used to describe a route: (1) visual cues, (2) the direction planes of the coordinate system, (3) directional steps. In this case we do not use the elementary directional pace, i.e., the smallest possible motor unit, but the customary summation of elementary impulses required to take one walking step.

The walking pace, that is, the regular motion of a leg forward and backward, is fixed so definitely and is of the same approximate length in so many people, that until quite recently it served as a common length measure. If I tell someone to walk a hundred paces, I mean that he is to give his leg the same motor impulse a hundred times. The result will always be the same approximate distance traversed. If we travel over a certain stretch repeatedly, the impulses given while walking remain in our memory as directional signs, so that we automatically stop at the same place, even if we have paid no attention to visual cues. Thus the orientational signs are of great importance for the familiar path.

It would be highly interesting to determine how the problem of the familiar path is worked out in the *Umwelten* of animals. Scent cues and tactile cues are surely decisive factors in building up the familiar path in many of their *Umwelten*. Thousands of experimental series have been made in the past decades by numerous American scientists who tried to determine how soon an animal was able to learn a certain pathway, through requiring widely varied animals to orient themselves in a maze. They have not seen the point: the problem of the familiar path. They have neither investigated the visual, tactile or scent cues, nor given thought to the application of the coordinate system by the animal— that right and left is a problem in itself, has never struck them. Nor have they ever debated the question of the number of paces, because they did not see that in animals, too, the pace may serve as the measure of distance.

In short, the problem of the familiar path must be attacked all over again, despite the prodigious amount of observations available. Beside its theoretical interest, the way a dog retraces the familiar path in his *Umwelt*, for example, also has eminent practical value in view of the tasks which face the seeing-eye dogs of the blind.

Figure 29 shows a blind man led by his dog. The blind man's world is a very limited one: it extends only as far as he can feel his way with his feet and cane. As far as he is concerned, the street through which he passes is plunged in darkness. His dog, however, must guide him home over a certain path. The difficulty of training the dog lies in introducing into the dog's *Umwelt* specific perceptual cues which serve the blind man's interests, not the dog's. Thus the route along which the dog leads the blind man must be plotted along a curve around obstacles against which the man might stumble. It is especially hard to teach a dog the meaning of a mailbox or an open window—to give it perceptual cues for things which it would normally pass by unheeded. The edge of the curb,

FIG. 29
Blind man and his dog

over which the blind man might stumble, is equally hard to introduce
into the dog's world, since under ordinary circumstances a freely running
dog scarcely notices it.

Figure 30 portrays an observation made with young jackdaws. As may
be seen, the jackdaw flies around the whole house, but then wheels and
retraces its former, familiar course for the return flight to its starting
point, which the jackdaw did not know again when it approached it
from the other side.

It has recently been found that rats long continue to use an accustomed detour, even when the direct path is open to them.

Now the problem of the familiar path has been taken up anew in
fighting fish, and the following results were obtained: in the first place,
it was found that the unfamiliar has a repellent influence on these fish.
A glass plate with two round holes, through which the fish could glide
with ease, was placed in the aquarium. If the food was presented behind
the hole, the fish took quite a while to glide hesitantly through the hole

FIG. 30
The jackdaw's familiar path

and snatch the food. Next the bait was shown laterally from the window —the fish soon followed after. Finally, the lure was presented behind the second window. Nevertheless, the fish invariably swam through the familiar hole and avoided using the unfamiliar.

Then, as shown in Figure 31, a partition was built into the food side of the tank at right angles to the glass plate, and the fish lured around the

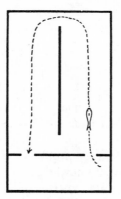

FIG. 31
The familiar path of the fighting fish

partition by means of the food. If the food was now shown on the other side of the partition, the fish swam straightway around it, still following the long familiar path, even if it could have reached the bait by swimming toward it in front of the partition. The familiar route here involved visual and orientational cues, and possibly directional steps as well.

On the whole, we may say that the familiar path works as a stretch of lightly fluid medium within a refractory mass.

Home and Territory—Heim und Heimat

The problem of home and territory is closely related to the familiar pathway.

As a starting point, it will be best to choose the experiments with sticklebacks. The male stickleback builds himself a nest, whose entrance he likes to mark by a colored thread—a visual path cue for the young? The young grow up in the nest under the father's care. This nest is his home. But his territory reaches beyond the nest. Figure 32 shows an aquarium, in opposite corners of which two sticklebacks have built their nests. An invisible borderline crosses the acquarium and divides it into two regions, each of which belongs to one nest. This area, which belongs with the nest, is the stickleback's territory, which he defends vigorously and successfully even against bigger sticklebacks. In his own territory the stickleback always wins.

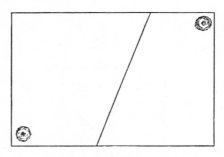

FIG. 32
Nest and territory of the stickleback

Territory is a pure *Umwelt* problem. It is an entirely subjective product, for even the closest knowledge of the environment does not give the slightest clue as to its existence.

The question now is, which animals possess a territory and which ones do not? A housefly, which, in flying back and forth, covers a certain section of space around the chandelier, does not, by virtue of this fact, necessarily have a domicile.

A spider, on the other hand, which builds a cobweb in which it is constantly active, possesses a home that is at the same time its territory.

The same is true of the mole. It, too, has built itself a home and a territory. An orderly system of caves is spread out underground like a cobweb. But, in addition to the single tunnels themselves, its domain also comprises the whole section of earth encompassed by them. In captivity, it plots its tunnels so that they resemble a cobweb. We were able to demonstrate that the mole, thanks to its highly developed scent organ, not only finds its food easily within the tunnel, but that it can also smell food in the solid earth beyond the tunnel, up to a distance of some 5 to 6 cm. In a close-knit system of passages, such as the mole builds in captivity, the entire area of soil extending between the passages would be controlled by its senses. In nature, where the mole draws its tunnels farther apart, it can control the earth within a certain radius around each tunnel by scent cues. Like the spider, the mole travels repeatedly through this network of passages and gathers up everything in the way of prey that has strayed there. In the midst of this network of tunnels, the mole builds itself a cave padded with dry leaves—its home proper, where it spends its leisure hours. The underground passages are all familiar pathways to the mole; it runs forward and backward along them with equal speed and skill. Its field of prey extends as far as its passages reach. This whole field is at the same time the mole's territory, which it defends unto death against all neighboring moles.

The faculty with which the mole, a blind animal, finds its way unerringly in a medium which to us seems completely homogeneous, is astonishing. If trained to a certain place where the mole gets its food, it will find this place again, even after the passages leading to it are totally destroyed. The mole cannot possibly be guided by olfactory cues in so doing. Its space is a purely operational space. One must assume that, by reproducing its orientational steps, a mole is able to retrace a pathway that it has once traveled. As in all blind animals, tactile cues connected with the directional steps must here play an important part. It may be assumed that orientational cues and directional steps unite to form the basis of a spatial schema. If the mole's network of passages, or part thereof, is destroyed, it is able, with the aid of a projected schema, to re-create a new network resembling the old.

Bees also build themselves a home, but the area all around the hive, where they seek their food, while being their field of prey, is not a territory which they would defend against intruders. In magpies, on the other hand, we may speak of home and territory, for their nest is built within a region inside of which they tolerate no other magpies.

Eventually, we shall probably find that countless animals defend their field of prey against members of their own species, thereby making it their territory. Any tract of land, if the territories were drawn into it, would resemble a political map for each species, their borderlines determined by attack and defense. It would also appear that there is no free land left, but that everywhere territory touches territory.

It is most interesting to observe that between the nests of many birds of prey and their hunting grounds, a neutral zone is inserted, where they strike no prey at all. Ornithologists are probably right in supposing that this arrangement was made by nature to prevent birds of prey from striking their own brood. When, so to speak, the nestling has become a branchling and spends its days around the parental nest, hopping from limb to limb, it might easily incure the danger of being struck by its own parents by mistake. As it is, the nestling spends its days unmenaced in the neutral zone of the protected territory. This protected territory is sought out by many songbirds as a nesting and brooding site, where they can bring up their young in safety under the great robber's protection.

Special consideration should be given to the ways and means by which dogs mark their territory for members of their own species. In a park were certain spots where two large hounds urinated in their daily outings. The places which they marked with their scent cues were always spots particularly conspicuous to the human eye also. Whenever both dogs were walked at the same time, a urinating competition ensued.

As soon as a high-spirited dog meets a strange dog, the former invariably shows a tendency to furnish the nearest conspicuous object with "his visiting card." Moreover, if a dog penetrates into the territory of another dog, which is earmarked by that dog's scent signals, he will successively seek these out and paint them over carefully. A spiritless dog, on the other hand, will pass shyly by a strange dog's scent marks in the latter's territory, and not betray his presence by any scent signals.

As shown in Figure 33, the great bears of North America also have a habit of marking their territory. Standing erect to its full height, the bear rubs off the bark of a lone, far-visible pine with its back and snout. This acts as a signal to other bears to give the pine a wide berth, and avoid the whole district where a bear of such dimensions defends its territory.

Fig. 33
A bear marking his territory

The Companion

I recall vividly the picture of a rumpled duckling that had been hatched together with turkey chicks and had attached itself so closely to the turkey family that it never went into the water, and painstakingly avoided other small ducks that came from it, fresh and clean.

Soon thereafter, someone brought me a very young wild duck, which followed me about at every step and turn. When I sat down, it leaned its head on my foot. I had the impression that my black boots were the attraction, for sometimes it also ran after the black dachshund. I concluded from this that a black moving object was enough to replace the image of the mother for it, and had the young duck put out near its maternal nest, that it might find its family again.

Today I have come to question whether this ever happened, for I have been informed that goslings of the greylag goose, when just taken from the incubator, must be pocketed and taken to a grey goose family at once if they are to attach themselves willingly to members of their own species. If they remain a little longer in human company, they will reject all companionship with their own kin.

The phenomenon we are dealing with in all these cases is a confusion of perceptual images. This occurs frequently, especially in the world of birds. What we know about the receptor images of birds is as yet insufficient to draw positive conclusions.

In Figure 18 we watched the jackdaw on the hunt for grasshoppers. We got the impression that the jackdaw possesses no receptor image whatsoever for the grasshopper in repose, and that therefore the grasshopper does not exist in the jackdaw's *Umwelt*.

Figures 34a and b illustrate another observation concerning the receptor images of jackdaws. Here a jackdaw is seen in a posture of attack against a cat carrying another jackdaw in its mouth. Jackdaws never attack a cat when it is not carrying any prey. Only when the cat's dangerous teeth are put out of action by holding the prey between them does the cat become an object of attack to the birds. This seems to be a highly

FIG. 34a
Jackdaw in posture of attack against cat

FIG. 34b
Jackdaw in posture of attack against bathing trunks

judicious action by the jackdaw. As a matter of fact, however, it only conforms to a plan of nature, and runs its course independently of insight.
For the bird assumed the same posture of attack when a pair of black
bathing trunks was carried by. Nor was the cat attacked when it carried
a white jackdaw. The receptor image of a black object being moved past
the jackdaw promptly releases a posture of attack.

A receptor image held in such general terms can always give rise to
mistakes. This has already been shown in the sea urchin, in whose world
cloud and ship are constantly confused with the enemy fish, because the
sea urchin responds in the same way to any darkening of the horizon.

In birds, however, we cannot get away with such a simple explanation. As regards social birds, we have a wealth of contradictory observations involving a confusion of receptor images. Only recently have we
succeeded in analyzing out the main principles in the typical case of a
tame jackdaw, "Jock."

Jackdaws living in a colony have a lifelong "companion" with whom
they carry out the most widely varied activities. If a jackdaw is raised in
isolation, it by no means relinquishes the companion. If the jackdaw
finds none of its own species, it will adopt "substitute companions."
Moreover, a new substitute companion may take over for each new
activity. Lorenz was kind enough to send me Figure 35, wherein the
different companion relationships may be seen at a glance. In her youth,
the jackdaw Jock had Lorenz himself for a mother companion. She
followed him everywhere; she called him when she wanted to be fed.
After Jock had learned to get her own food, she chose the maid for her

love companion and performed the characteristic courting dances in front of her. Later on Jock found a young jackdaw who became her adoptive companion and whom she fed in person. When Jock prepared for long flights, she tried, in the manner of jackdaws, to make Lorenz fly with her, by taking off close behind his back. When this attempt failed, Jock attached herself to flying crows, which now became her flight companions. Clearly, there is no uniform perceptual image for the companion in the jackdaw's world. Nor could there be one, since the role of the companion changes all the time.

Fig. 35
The jackdaw "Jock" and her four companions

In most cases, the receptor image of the mother companion is not determined at birth as to form and color. On the other hand, the mother's voice frequently is.

"One should," Lorenz writes, "determine, in a specific case of a mother companion, which mother signs are innate and which ones are individually acquired. The uncanny thing is that, if the fledgling is only taken from its mother a few days, or even hours after hatching (grey goose, Heinroth), the acquired mother signs are engraved so deeply that one would swear they were innate."

Fig. 25

Changes in significance of *Actinia* in the *Umwelt* of the hermit crab

Fig. 26

The room in terms of the functional tones connected with its object by man

Fig. 27

The room in terms of the functional tones connected with its objects by a dog

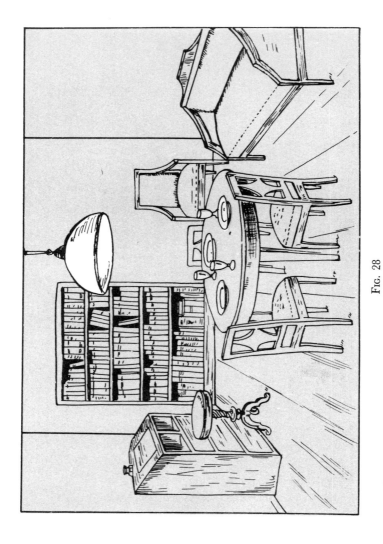

Fɪɢ. 28

The room in terms of the functional tones connected with its objects by a horsefly

The same thing happens in choosing the love companion. Here, too, the acquired signs of the substitute companion are so definitely engraved that an inconvertible perceptual image of the substitute companion is created—once the first exchange has occurred. In consequence, even animals of the same species are rejected as love companions.

This is shown very clearly by a delightful experience. In the Amsterdam Zoo there was a pair of bitterns, whose male had "fallen in love" with the director of the Zoo. So as not to hinder their mating, the latter did not appear for a considerable length of time. The result was that the male became accustomed to the female. A happy union ensued, and when the female was sitting on her eggs, the director risked showing himself again. But what happened? No sooner had the male caught sight of his former love companion, than he chased the female away from the nest and seemed to hint with repeated bows that the director was to occupy the place due him and continue the business of brooding.

The receptor image of the child companion seems in general to be outlined more firmly. Here the gaping bills of the young are probably the most important factor. But here again, one may find that hens of pure strain, such as orpingtons, will mother young kittens and baby bunnies.

Again, as Jock shows, there is more leeway in the case of the substitute companion for free flights.

If we consider that the jackdaw treats bathing trunks in motion as an enemy, that is, they obtain the functional tone "enemy," we may say that they are a substitute foe. Since there are many enemies in the jackdaw's world, the appearance of a substitute enemy, especially if it only happens occasionally, does not affect the perceptual images of the jackdaw's real enemies. Not so with the companion. The latter exists only singly in the *Umwelt,* and once a functional tone is lent to a substitute companion, it is impossible for a true companion to make a later appearance. Once the perceptual image of the maid had acquired the sole "love tone" in Jock's world, all other perceptual images had become ineffectual.

If we consider (a phenomenon not without analogy in primitive people) that in the world of jackdaws all living creatures, that is, moving things, are divided into jackdaws and non-jackdaws, and furthermore, that the borderline between them is drawn differently according to personal experience, it will perhaps be possible to understand that such grotesque mistakes as the ones just described should occur. It is not the perceptual image alone that decides whether one is faced with a jackdaw or non-jackdaw, but the functional image of the subject's own attitude.

This alone determines what perceptual image will acquire the prevailing companion tone.

Search Image and Search Tone

Again I begin with two personal experiences, which will best illustrate what is meant by the search image, a factor of great importance in the *Umwelt*. When I spent some time at the house of a friend, an earthenware water pitcher used to be placed before my seat at luncheon. One day the butler had broken the clay pitcher and put a glass water bottle in its place. When I looked for the pitcher during the meal, I failed to see the glass carafe. Only when my friend assured me that the water was standing in its usual place, did various bright lights that had lain scattered on knives and plates flock together through the air and form the water bottle. Figure 36 conveys this experience. The search image annihilates the perceptual image.

The second experience is this: One day I stepped into a store where I had a large bill to pay, and drew out a 100 Mark bill. It was quite new and slightly bent, so that it did not lie flat on the counter, but stood on

Fig. 36
The object sought obscures the perception

its edge. I asked the cashier to give me my change. She declared I had not yet paid. I tried in vain to point out to her that the money was right under her nose. She became irritated and insisted on immediate payment. At this point I touched the bill with my forefinger, so that it fell over and came to lie the right way. The lady uttered a small cry, then took the bill and felt it, full of apprehension that it might dissolve into thin air again. In this case, too, the search image had obviously extinguished the perceptual image.

All my readers have probably had similar experiences of seeming magic.

Figure 37 was published in my "Biology." It symbolizes the different processes that interlock in human perception. If a bell is set up before

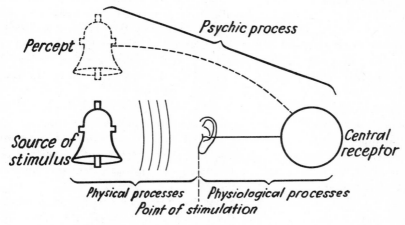

FIG. 37

The processes in noting

someone and sounded, it appears in his environment as a source of stimulation, from which air waves penetrate to his ear (physical processes). In the ear, the air waves are transformed into nervous excitation, which is conveyed to the receptor organ of the brain (physiological processes). Now the receptor cells intervene with their receptor signs and project a perceptual cue or meaning into the *Umwelt* (psychological process).

If besides the air waves coming to the ear, ether waves also reach the eye, which in its turn sends excitation to the receptor organ, then their receptor signs of sounds and colors are combined to form an entity which, projected into the phenomenal world, becomes a perceptual image.

The same graphic illustration can be used to explain the search image. In this case we will assume that the bell lies outside the visual field. The receptor signs of the sounds are projected directly into the *Umwelt*. But connected with it is an invisible optical receptor image, which serves as a search image. If after searching, the bell enters the visual field, then the perceptual image now resulting is fused with the search image. If they differ too widely, it may happen that the search image eliminates the perceptual image, as in the aforesaid instance.

Search images undoubtedly exist in the *Umwelt* of dogs. When the master orders his dog to retrieve a stick, the dog, as shown in Figure 38, has a quite specific search image of the stick. Here we may also examine how closely the search image corresponds to the perceptual image.

It is reported that, if a toad has consumed an earthworm after a prolonged period of starvation, the toad will immediately throw itself on a match that bears a certain resemblance in shape to the earthworm. This leads us to believe that the recently consumed earthworm acts as a search image—as indicated in Figure 39. On the other hand, if the toad has allayed its first hunger with a spider, it has a different search image, for now the toad will snap after a bit of moss or an ant, which, however, does not agree with it very well.

Now we do not always look for a definite object with a single receptor image, but far more often for one that corresponds to a specific functional image. Instead of a specific chair, we look around for something to sit on, that is, for a thing that may be connected with a certain performance tone. In this case we cannot speak of a search image, but only of a search tone.

The earlier example of the hermit crab and sea anemone demonstrates how important a part the search tone plays in the *Umwelt* of animals. What we referred to as the hermit crab's different moods there, can now be much more accurately termed the varying *search tone* with which the crab approached the same perceptual image, giving it at one time a protective tone, at another time a dwelling tone, and again an eating tone.

The hungry toad at first sets out to seek food with just a general feeding tone. Only after it has consumed an earthworm or a spider does it acquire a more specific search image.

The Magic Umwelten

There can be no doubt that a fundamental contrast prevails everywhere between the environment which we see spread around animals, and the *Umwelten* that are built up by the animals themselves and filled with the objects of their own perception. In our study so far, these

Fig. 38

The dog and his search image

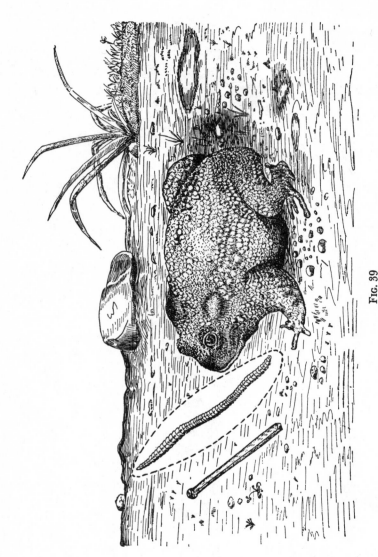

FIG. 39

The toad's search image

Umwelten have as a rule been the product of receptor signs roused to activity by external stimuli. We have already seen exceptions to this rule: the search image, the tracing of the familiar pathway, and the demarcation of the territory, which could not be attributed to external stimuli, but were free subjective products. They evolved as a result of repeated personal experiences by the subject.

If we now continue on our way, we shall enter worlds that feature very effective phenomena which, however, are visible to the subject alone and are bound to no experiences, or at most are related to one single experience. We shall call *Umwelten* of this kind *magic* worlds.

An example may illustrate how deeply many children live in magic worlds. In his *Paideuma*, Frobenius tells of a little girl who was quietly acting out for herself the fairy tale of Hansel and Gretel, the wicked witch and the gingerbread house, with a matchbox and three matches. Suddenly she cried out: "Take away the witch, I can't bear to look at her horrid face any more." This typically magical experience is indicated in Figure 40. Undoubtedly, the wicked witch appeared bodily in the little girl's *Umwelt*.

FIG. 40
The magical appearance of the witch

Explorers have often come upon experiences of this kind among primitive peoples. It is maintained that they live in a magic world, where fantastic phenomena mingle with the perceptually given things around them. If we look more closely, we shall meet the same magic formations in the *Umwelt* of many a highly cultured European.

The question now arises: do animals also live in magic *Umwelten?* Magical experiences are frequently reported in dogs. But these reports have not hitherto been sifted critically enough. On the whole, however, it will probably have to be conceded that dogs relate their experiences in a manner that is magical rather than logical. The role which the master plays in the dog's world is surely conceived magically, not broken down into cause and effect.

A zoologist friend of mine tells about an undoubtedly magic phenomenon in the *Umwelt* of a bird: He had brought up a young starling in a room. The bird never had a chance to see a fly, let alone to catch one. One day he saw the starling suddenly rush toward an invisible object, catch it in mid-air, return with the object to its perch, peck away at it with its bill as any starling will do with a captured fly, and finally swallow the invisible thing (Fig. 41). There was no doubt that the starling had had the apparition of an imaginary fly in its *Umwelt*. Evidently the starling's whole world had been so charged with the "feeding tone," that even without the appearance of a sensory stimulus, the functional image of fly-catching, which was in readiness, forced the perceptual image to appear, and this released the entire action chain. This experience indicates that otherwise utterly puzzling actions by various animals should be interpreted magically.

FIG. 41
Starling and imaginary fly

Figure 42 portrays the behavior of the pea-weevil larva, which was studied by Fabre. In good season, the larva bores a channel into the still soft flesh of a young pea, all the way to the surface. This tunnel is not used until, after the larva's metamorphosis, the grown beetle crawls out of the pea, which has hardened in the meantime. It is quite sure that we are here dealing with an activity which, though conforming to a plan, is yet utterly senseless from the weevil larva's point of view, for no sensory stimulus of the future beetle can possibly reach its larva. No

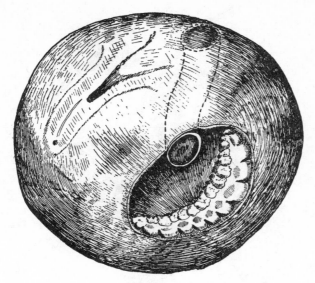

FIG. 42

The magical path of the pea-weevil larva

receptor sign shows the larva the path which it has never trodden and that it must nevertheless take, unless it is to perish miserably after its transformation into a beetle. The way lies before it, clearly written, as in magic characters. The familiar path, acquired through experience, is here replaced by the innate pathway.

Figures 43 and 44 show two further instances of the innate pathway. The female of the funnel-roller begins to cut an intricately curving line of prescribed form along a birch leaf at a specific point (which she may possibly recognize by its taste). This enables her afterwards to roll the leaf into a funnel, into which she will lay her eggs. Although the beetle has never followed the path and the birch leaf shows no indication of it, the path must yet lie before her perfectly clearly, as a magic phenomenon.

The same applies to the flight routes of migratory birds. The continents bear the innate route, which only birds can see. This is certainly true of young birds, who set out unaccompanied by their parents, whereas for the others the acquisition of a familiar path is not beyond the realm of possibility.

Like the familiar pathway, with which we have dealt extensively, the innate way also leads through both visual and functional space. The sole difference between the two is that in the case of the familiar path a series of receptor and effector signs, which have been established by pre-

FIG. 43

The magical path of the funnel-twister

vious experience, succeed one another, while in the case of the innate path the same series of signs is given directly, as a magic phenomenon. To the uninitiated observer a familiar path in a foreign *Umwelt* is just as invisible as is the innate path. And if we assume that the familiar pathway becomes manifest to the foreign subject in his own *Umwelt*— of which there is no doubt—then there is no reason to deny the phenomenon of the innate pathway; since it is composed of identical elements, the projected perceptual and functional signs. In the one case they are elicited by sensory stimuli, in the other they chime in harmonious succession, like an inborn melody.

If a certain route were innate in a man, it could be described in the same terms as a familiar path: a hundred paces to the red house, then round to the right, and so forth.

If we choose to call significant only what is given to the subject by the evidence of his senses, then, of course, only the familiar path will be called meaningful, not the innate. Even so, it remains planful to the highest degree.

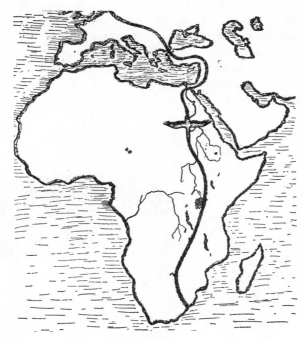

FIG. 44

The magical path of the migratory bird

A strange experience reported by a contemporary scientist indicates that magical phenomena play a far greater part in the animal world than we suspect. He had fed a hen in a certain stall, and let a guinea pig into the stall while the hen was picking up the grains. The hen was beside herself and fluttered about frantically. From then on, she could never again be persuaded to consume food in this stall. She would rather have starved amid plenty of the finest grain. Evidently the apparition of the first experience hovered above the stall like a magical shadow, as Figure 45 attempts to convey it. This occurrence corroborates the surmise that when a mother hen rushes toward the peeping chick and chases away an imaginary enemy by violent bill-pecks, a magic apparition has similarly arisen in her *Umwelt*.

As we have progressed farther in our study of the *Umwelten*, the conviction has grown on us that effective factors occur in them, to which no objective reality can be ascribed. We met the first of these in the place-mosaic, which the eye imprints on the things in its *Umwelt*, and which is no more present in the environment than are the directional planes that support space in an *Umwelt*. It has been equally impossible to find an environmental factor to correspond to the subject's familiar pathway. The distinction between territory and hunting ground does not exist in the environment. No trace of the *Umwelt's* vital search image can be found in the environment. Now we have finally come upon the magical phenomenon of the innate path, which mocks all objectivity and yet gears designfully into the *Umwelt*.

FIG. 45
The magical shadow

There are, then, purely subjective realities in the *Umwelten;* and even the things that exist objectively in the environment never appear there as their objective selves. They are always transformed into perceptual cues or perceptual images and invested with a functional tone. This alone makes them into real objects, although no element of the functional tone is actually present in the stimuli.

And finally, the simple functional cycle teaches us that both receptor and effector cues are the subject's manifestations, and that the qualities of objects included in the functional cycle can be regarded as their bearers only. Thus we ultimately reach the conclusion that each subject lives in a world composed of subjective realities alone, and that even the *Umwelten* themselves represent only subjective realities.

Whoever denies the existence of subjective realities, has failed to recognize the foundations of his own *Umwelt*.

The Same Subject as an Object in Different Umwelten

The foregoing chapters described single strolls into various regions in the unexplored territory of the *Umwelt*. They were arranged according to problems, to obtain a uniform view in each case. Even though we have dealt with some fundamental problems, no completeness has been achieved or aimed at. Many problems await conceptual formulation, while others have not yet developed beyond the stage of formulating questions. Thus we know nothing so far of the extent to which the subject's own body enters into his *Umwelt*. Even the question of the significance of one's own shadow in visual space has not been experimentally attacked.

The pursuit of single problems is indeed important for *Umwelt* research; but it is not enough if we wish to gain a comprehensive view of the relationships between different *Umwelten*. In a limited field, such an over-all picture can be obtained by answering the question: How does the same subject show up as an object in different *Umwelten,* in which it plays an important part? As an example, I choose an oak tree, which harbors many animal subjects, and is destined to play a different role in the *Umwelt* of each. Since the oak also appears in various human *Umwelten,* I shall begin with them.

Figures 46 and 47 are reproductions of two drawings, which we owe to the artist Franz Huth. In the thoroughly rational world of the old forester, who must decide which trees of his forest are ready to be felled, the oak doomed to the ax is nothing more than a few cords of wood, which he seeks to measure accurately (Fig. 46). The knobby bark, which happens to resemble a human face, goes unheeded by him. Figure 47 shows the same oak in the magical world of a little girl, whose forest is still inhabited by gnomes and hobgoblins. The little girl is terribly frightened when the oak tree looks at her with its evil face. The whole oak has become a threatening demon.

In the grounds of my cousin's castle in Estonia there stood an old apple tree. A huge lichen had grown on it, which vaguely resembled the face of a clown, but no one had ever noticed this resemblance. One day my cousin had a dozen Russian seasonal laborers brought in, who discovered the apple tree and thereafter gathered before it daily for worship, murmuring prayers and crossing themselves. They declared that the fungus must be a wonder-working image, because it was not made by hand of man. To them, magic processes in nature appeared quite natural.

FIG. 46
Forester and oak tree

But let us return to the oak tree and its inmates. To the fox (Fig. 48), which has built its lair between the roots, the oak tree has come to mean a solid roof, which protects the fox and its family from the hazards of the weather. It has neither the utility tone of the forester's world, nor the danger tone of the little girl's, but solely a protective tone. How it is shaped beyond that, does not matter in the fox's world.

In the owl's world (Fig. 49) the oak tree also has a protective tone. Only this time it is not the roots, which lie wholly outside the owl's realm, but the mighty limbs that serve it as a protecting wall.

To the squirrel, the oak tree, with its many ramifications, providing a wealth of comfortable jumping boards, gains a climbing tone, and to the songsters which build their nests in its farthest crotches and branches, it offers the supporting tone which they need.

Corresponding to the different functional tones, the perceptual images of the oak tree's numerous inmates, too, are differently shaped. Each *Umwelt* carves a specific section out of the oak, whose qualities are suit-

FIG. 47
Little girl and oak tree

able bearers for both the receptor and effector cues of their respective functional cycles. In the ant's world (Fig. 50) all the rest of the oak vanishes behind its gnarled bark, whose furrows and heights become the ant's hunting ground.

‾The bark-boring beetle seeks its nourishment underneath the bark which it blasts off (Fig. 51). Here it lays its eggs. Its larvae bore their passages underneath the bark. Here, safe from the perils of the outside world, they gnaw themselves farther into their food. But they are not entirely protected. For not only are they persecuted by the woodpecker, which splits off the bark with powerful thrusts of its beak; an ichneumon fly, whose fine ovipositor penetrates through the oakwood (hard in all other *Umwelten*) as if it were butter, destroys them by injecting its eggs into the larva (Fig. 52). Larvae slip out of the ichneumon eggs and feed on the flesh of their victims.

In all the hundred different *Umwelten* of its inmates, the oak tree as an object plays a highly varied role, at one time with some of its parts, at another time with others. Sometimes the same parts are large, at

FIG. 48
Fox and oak tree

others they are small. At times its wood is hard, at others soft. One time the tree serves for protection, then again for attack.

Should we attempt to epitomize all the contradictory properties which the oak tree as an object displays, only chaos would result. And yet they are all but parts of a subject firmly structured in itself, which bears and harbors all these *Umwelten*—not comprehended and never discernible to all the builders of these *Umwelten*.

Conclusion

What we have found on a small scale in the oak tree is enacted on the life tree of nature in vast dimensions.

Out of the millions of *Umwelten*, whose abundance would result in confusion, we shall pick out only those dedicated to the investigation of nature—the *Umwelten* of different scientists.

Figure 53 shows the *Umwelt* of an astronomer, which is the easiest to portray. High on his tower, as far as possible from the earth, sits a human being. He has so transformed his eyes, with the aid of gigantic optical instruments, that they have become fit to penetrate the universe up to its most distant stars. In his *Umwelt*, suns and planets circle in festive

FIG. 49
Owl and oak tree

procession. Fleet-footed light takes millions of years to travel through his *Umwelt* space.

And yet this whole *Umwelt* is only a tiny sector of nature, tailored to the faculties of a human subject.

With slight alterations, the astronomer's image can be used to gain a conception of the deep-sea researcher's *Umwelt*. Only here, instead of constellations, the fantastic shapes of deep-sea fish wheel around his sphere with their uncanny mouths, long tentacles and radial light organs. Here again, we glance into a real world, which constitutes a small sector of nature.

The *Umwelt* of a chemist, who tries to read and write the enigmatic context of nature's substance-words with the aid of the elements, as with 92 letters, is hard to render distinctly.

We shall succeed better in representing the *Umwelt* of a nuclear physicist, for the electrons circle around him in much the same way as the constellations wheel around the astronomer. Only here no cosmic calm reigns, but a mad rush of infinitesimal particles, from which the

FIG. 50
Ant and oak tree

physicist blasts off even tinier ones by bombarding them with diminutive projectiles.

If another physicist investigates the ether waves in his own *Umwelt*, he again resorts to entirely different means, which furnish him a picture of the waves. Now he can ascertain that the light waves, which stimulate the human eye, combine with all other waves, without displaying any differences. They are just waves, nothing more.

Light waves feature altogether differently in the *Umwelt* of a physiologist who studies the senses. Here they become colors, with laws of their own. Red and green fuse into white, and shadows, thrown onto a yellow surface, become blue. Processes unheard-of in waves, and yet the colors are just as real as are the ether waves.

The same contrast exists between the *Umwelten* of a student of air

FIG. 51

Bark-boring beetle
and oak tree

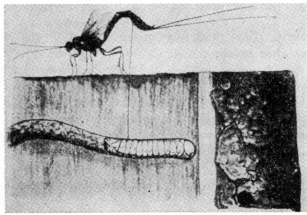

FIG. 52

Ichneumon fly
and oak tree

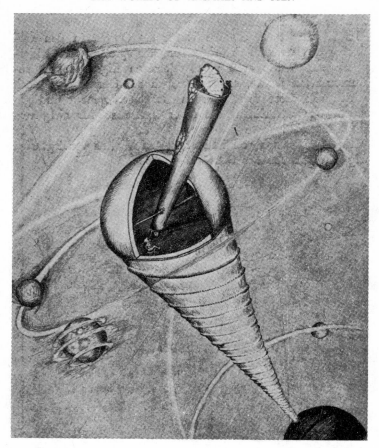

FIG. 53
The astronomer's *Umwelt*

waves and of a musician. In the one there are only waves, in the other only sounds. Yet both are equally real.

So it goes on. In the behaviorist's *Umwelt* the body produces the mind, and in the psychologist's world the mind builds the body.

The role which nature plays as the object of different scientists' worlds is highly contradictory. Should one attempt to combine her objective qualities, chaos would ensue. And yet all these diverse *Umwelten* are harbored and borne by the One that remains forever barred to all *Umwelten.*

Behind all the worlds created by Him, there lies concealed, eternally beyond the reach of knowledge, the subject—Nature.

Part II

1

Companionship in Bird Life

Fellow Members of the Species as Releasers of Social Behavior[1]

KONRAD LORENZ (1935)

I. Introduction: Uexküll's Concept of the "Companion"

What we ordinarily call an object is created in our environment in somewhat the following way: we gather the stimuli that come to us from some one thing, and refer them collectively to that thing as a common source of stimulation. Then we project them outwards, into the space around us, and localize them there. For instance, the lenses in our eyes register a picture of the sun on the retina; but we do not experience it there, as "light," in the same way as we feel the "heat" of a picture of the sun, projected upon some part of our skin by a glass lens. On the contrary, we see the sun as far away from ourselves, high up in the sky, where it is immediately localized by perception, and not by any process of our conscious mind.

In our grasp of the objects in our world we are thus dependent on the senses, whose communications we are able to localize in space. This, after all, is the only way in which we can grasp the inherent, spatial coherence of single stimuli, which gives a "thing" its objective unity and which is the basis for Uexküll's simple definition of the object: "An object is that which moves in unison."

Man's chief localizing senses are touch and vision. We therefore speak of tactile space and of visual space. When it comes to the sense of hearing, our localization is far less accurate, so that the term "auditory space," as applied to humans, is extremely rare. But it remains to be seen

1 Dedicated to Jakob von Uexküll on his 70th birthday.

83

whether the same conditions prevail among all animals. Owls are able to localize acoustic stimuli at least as well as optical ones, and bats far more so. It may be that these animals have an auditory space in the same sense that we possess a visual space.

The gathering of the stimuli which belong to various sense modalities and are emitted by one object into one coherent "thing," is no doubt closely linked with a localization of these stimuli at a common source in space. The development of an object by summation of its stimuli can be observed within ourselves, especially if, for some reason or another, the process is slowed up. For instance, when we awaken from narcosis or even from unusually deep sleep, familiar objects frequently do not appear as themselves. We see lights and hear sounds, but it takes a certain length of time—the time required to bring deliberate observation into play—before we are able to localize the source of these impressions, whereupon they converge into solidity, into a tangible object.

It is a remarkable achievement of the central nervous system that an object, regardless of its position, distance or illumination, and despite the varying impressions which our sense organs receive, appears to have the same size, shape and color within a wide range of these differences. At a greater distance a person appears no smaller than when he is nearby, although, in the picture upon our retina, his dimensions are greatly reduced. We see that a picture hanging on the wall is a rectangle, even though the image imprinted on our retina when we look at it upwards, from an angle, is that of a nonrectangular parallelogram. A piece of white paper looks white even under poor lighting conditions, although it reflects less light than black paper radiates in bright sunshine. How this constancy is secured is a question for the psychology of perception to answer in detail. For our purposes it is enough to state that, even in higher animals, the constancy of objective qualities can as a rule withstand only minor variations in the stimuli that reach the animal's receptors, as compared to man.

The different living conditions of various animal forms entail varying ranges in perceptual conditions, wherefore it is comprehensible that the resistance of things to these changes in the worlds of animals also varies greatly from one species to another. Often the biological significance of such variations is evident. Experiments by Bingham and Coburn showed that chickens did not recognize certain signals to which they had been trained, if these were shown in a reversed position. To crows, on the other hand, the spatial position in which the training objects were presented made no difference whatsoever. A bird like the crow usually flies in circles while on the lookout for his prey, and it is, of course, vitally important that he should recognize the objects which he sees on the ground beneath him, regardless of the direction of his flight, and regardless of the position of their images on his retina.

Man endeavors to master his world and its phenomena through insight into their causal relationships. For him, it is essential to unite the single stimuli into objects of his world. In fact, it constitutes the basis of all his knowledge.

The animal, on the other hand, and the lower animal in particular, is essentially fitted into his world by innate behavior. Intelligence plays no part in the way he reacts to environmental stimulation; therefore a material or objective comprehension of his world is not a biological necessity. It is enough if an instinctive reaction which must respond to a specific object in order to maintain the species is set off by *one* of the stimuli which that object sends out, provided this stimulus characterizes the object so unmistakably that erroneous responses to similar stimuli from other objects do not occur so frequently as to impair its survival value. To prevent this from happening, several stimuli are usually merged in a very simple stimulus combination, to which an "innate releasing mechanism" (IRM) responds. The form of such a releasing mechanism must have a certain minimum of general improbability, for the same reasons that the bit of a key is given a generally unusual form.

There is an essential difference between these *innate* mechanisms and the *acquired* mechanisms which release conditioned reflexes and learned reactions. While the former seem to be extremely simple, all animals appear to make the latter as complex as possible.

If an animal, in the course of its training, is not forced to select certain characters from a given multitude (which can be accomplished by constantly changing the rest), he will as a rule be trained to the totality, the "complex quality" of all the stimuli presented. "Take a dog," writes von Uexküll, "who is trained to react to a certain chair upon the command, 'on the chair.' It is possible that he will not recognize as chairs all the objects that answer the purpose of sitting, but only one particular chair, in one particular place." What "may occur" involuntarily over and over again, in the deliberate training of the highest mammals by man, is the rule in the self-training of mentally lower-ranking animals. If an animal has trained himself to a stimulus situation which has led to success one or more times, he cannot, of course, know —without an "insight into causal relationships"—which of its characters are unessential, and which are basically responsible for the result achieved. Biologically speaking, it is therefore perfectly sensible for the animal to combine all the stimuli into one complex quality, and to adopt this for the releasing factor of his acquired reaction. Blindly, and without distinguishing between what is essential and what is not, he repeats the behavior that has once been successful, but only in a wholly identical situation. An animal can, of course, also be trained to only one cue, for instance, the "triangular." This can be accomplished by keeping one character constant and varying all the others. But wherever a selection of key stimuli is achieved *without* applying such pressure, *there,* in my opinion, we are dealing with the rudiments of an "insight into relevant relations."

In contrast to these individually acquired releasing mechanisms, the innate ones are, from the very first, built into an over-all system of instincts; this system is specific to the species, and its essential characteristics are determined in advance. Therefore, it is only consistent with the principle of economy if as few cues as possible are included in a releasing mechanism. The sea urchin *Sphaerechinus* has a very highly specialized escape-and-defense reaction to his chief enemy, the starfish, *Asterias.* A single, specific chemical stimulus emitted by the starfish suffices to set off this reaction. This type of release of a highly complicated motor pattern, adapted to a specific biological process, by one single stimulus, or at any rate by a relatively simple set of stimuli, is typical for the majority of innate reactions.

Judging from their general behavior, we must credit higher animals with an objective grasp of their world. One might expect that they also had an objective picture of the objects of all their instinctive activities. This should be particularly true where the object of a reaction is a fellow member of the species. Strangely enough, however, this does not seem to be the case. I venture to offer an explanation why it is even less of a biological necessity for fellow members of the species to retain their subjective identity as releasers in various functional cycles than it is for the objects of other instincts.

Even in the highest vertebrates, an object-directed innate behavior sequence is often activated by only a very few of the stimuli which that object emits. If several functional cycles have the same "thing" as their common object, each of these cycles may respond to entirely different stimuli emanating from it. Out of all the stimuli which the object emits, the IRM of an instinctive act chooses a small number, as it were, and reacts to them selectively, thus initiating the action. Owing to their simplicity, the IRM's of two innate reactions sometimes do not share even one of the stimulating factors which activate them, even though they have a common object. The releaser of an innate motor pattern normally emits all the stimuli correlated to both mechanisms simultaneously. In an experiment, however, because the releasing mechanisms are so simple, the set adequate for each can be presented artificially, and one mechanism may be activated by two different objects. In this way, we can separate two functional cycles tuned to one common object. Inversely, and for the same reason, one object may release two antagonistic reactions, each of which should, biologically, have a separate object. This occurs most often in the case of instinctive acts whose object is a fellow member of the species. For example, in various species of ducks the mother's defense reaction can also be elicited by the alarm call of young birds of different species. Other fostering reactions, however, are highly specific to the species and are strictly determined by definite colors and markings on the head and back of the children. Therefore it is quite logical that a mallard duck leading her young should come valiantly to the rescue of a musk duckling crying for help and then, the next instant, subject it to "unspecific treatment": she may attack and kill it as an "alien animal near her own young," solely because it does not have the mallard head and back markings which elicit further care.

Consistent treatment of another member of the species, therefore, as it occurs in natural conditions where instinctive activities function normally, is not necessarily the result of an inherent connection of reactions in the acting subject. Rather, it is often achieved by the purely extraneous circumstance that the releaser, the fellow member of the species, emits all the stimuli correlated to the various releasing mechanisms collectively. The functional design of innate behavior patterns localizes the biologically necessary element of unity in the stimulus-emitting object, rather than in the acting subject.

Let us suppose that two or more instinctive actions must be performed with the same object to secure their survival value. This unity in dealing with the object can be safeguarded in two ways. First, the releaser may be conceived objectively and appear identical in all of the subject's functional cycles. Secondly, the relatedness of different instinctive activities may be centered in the object, in which case this object has no subjective unity in the subject's world. This second type of coherence obviously depends to a great extent on the qualities of the object, and it is the one with which we are concerned at this point.

If the object of a drive is some foreign body in the environment, such as natural prey or nest-building material, the releasing mechanisms which respond to it can only be governed by characters inherent in the suitable object. These cues are often few in number and kind. There is a definite upper limit to the improbability of the IRM's which they can compose. They may, within limits, be released accidentally, in the "wrong" place. This reduces the value of what an innate reaction and its IRM can achieve, and materially enhances the survival value of objects whose identity is subjective.

The situation is quite different if the common object of two or more instinctive acts is an individual of the same species as the acting subject. The structural designs of organs and of innate reactions within a species are parts of one, indivisible functional plan. The releasing mechanisms, parallel with the corresponding properties of the object, may attain an almost unlimited degree of general improbability, which practically excludes the possibility that the action will erupt in the "wrong" place. Elsewhere, I have used the term *releasers*[2] for individual devices that activate ready-made IRM's and set off specific innate action chains in fellow members of the species. These devices may be organs or conspicuous behavior patterns. Most often they are a combination of both. All social releasers represent a compromise between two biological needs: utmost simplicity and utmost general improbability. At sight of a peacock's tail, the splendid plumage of a golden pheasant, or the throat markings of a young grosbeak, people often exclaim: "How strange!" This naive astonishment is really most fitting. The throat of a nestling grosbeak, for instance, is so "strangely colorful" simply because, together with the instinctive act of gaping, it is the key to the parents' innate feeding reaction. Its colorful design has the biological value of preventing "mistaken" responses to other, accidentally similar stimuli. Sometimes a social releaser is not improbable enough. Certain African waxbills *(Estrilda astrilda)* in the nestling stage have a throat design that is almost as highly specialized as the young grosbeak's. Yet they have a breeding parasite who "copies" the key; his young have almost exactly the same coloration and markings on head and throat as the young waxbills.

There are practically no bounds to the specialization of releasers and their perceptual correlates. It can assure consistent behavior toward a member of the species who is the object of various instinctive activities as efficiently as can his subjective unity in the world of the animal who performs these acts. In mentally low-ranking animals, such as birds, this type of extreme joint differentiation of releaser and released reaction can be achieved more easily than a subjective identity running through all the functional cycles.

We may say in conclusion that an inanimate object, or a member of another species, is treated as a material entity more often than a member of the same species. To restate, quite roughly, my position: a number of improbable releasing mechanisms are needed to initiate the various actions that go into the construction of a nest. A stick used for this function does not have enough striking properties to build up these mechanisms. Therefore the bird learns to know it in an instinct-training interlocking,

2 Releasers in this sense are not just anything that elicits a response. To set them apart, both Lorenz and Tinbergen later called them *social releasers,* and this is the term we shall use henceforth. [Translator's note.]

with considerable constancy in all the functional cycles that stand in relation to it. A nestling can be the bearer of infinitely complex characters, for which an endless number of response patterns are in readiness, to wit, a specifically marked gaping throat for the feeding reaction; a strikingly colored ring of feathers around the anus, for the reaction of excrement removal; a cry which means that the young bird is cold, and calls forth the hovering reaction.

In the natural life of a species, releasers and innate responses together secure consistent treatment of its members, even though the latter are not conceived as entities. A constancy of the latter type may perhaps prevail in the acquired, or "insightful" (intelligent), noninstinctive behavior of the highest animals. But the identity is lost with the slightest change in the subject's physiological condition and consequent instinctive attitude toward what he perceives. Humans, with their reasoning power, are able to estimate the effects of their own instinctive-emotional attitude and prevent it from being projected outward and changing the character of the things around them. Even so, an instinctive motor response to a purely subjective change in the environment sometimes breaks through. For instance, one may bump into a door in the dark and kick it, even though he "knows better" all the time. Thus, even in man, the same thing may at one and the same time appear stable in its subjective, and unstable in its objective (behavioral) aspect. In an animal, be it the highest, such a reasoned distinction between sensory and motor processes surely need not be given a thought.

We may safely say that in the world of most birds a fellow member of the species has a different character in each of the functional cycles (according to von Uexküll) where he acts as a partner. The distinctive role which other members of the species play in the life of a bird has aptly been called that of the "companion" *(Kumpan)* by Jakob von Uexküll. After all, the word "companion"—for instance, drinking or hunting companion—stands for a fellow human related to another in one functional cycle only, and the higher stirrings of the mind or soul have little or nothing to do with a companionship of this sort.

The "companion" in bird life has a twofold interest. He is intriguing from the viewpoint of *Umwelt* research, which I shall adopt in this paper. And sociologically he is so important as to warrant even closer scrutiny.

Jakob von Uexküll's personal urging has given me the courage to attempt a presentation of the very complex issues at stake.

II. Methods and Principles

1. OBSERVATION

This study is based on facts gleaned for the most part from random observations. For purposes of biological and in particular behavior research, various species of birds were kept in living conditions closely resembling their natural environment, many of them in complete freedom. I was particularly interested in colony breeders, such as jackdaws, night herons and little egrets, whose sociology I meant to explore to the best of my ability. My main efforts centered on the system of instinctive actions in these species, which accounts almost entirely for the structure of these bird societies.

If one attempts to make a given species unfold its full life cycle in captivity, with all its innate action chains, one gains some insight into the functioning of its instincts. The miscarrying actions and pathological disintegration occurring in captivity are particularly revealing, and much of the blind juggling with environmental factors is removed from the subsequent experiments. I have reported earlier on the methods used in studying systems of instincts (Lorenz, 1932). Moreover, when animals are kept with this purpose in mind over the years, many unintended, incidental results are obtained. If several species are kept simultaneously, new situations always arise. I often noticed reactions to a stimulus which I had not deliberately set. But since it was the only change in the accustomed, natural environment, it must have caused that reaction. The value of such chance experiments is that they are registered by a truly unbiased observer. Because there are such fine variations in the behavior of many animals, especially in their expressive motions and sounds, it is most important for the observer to be free from any hypothesis.

Most of the facts which are utilized in this paper to throw light on the problem of companionship were gathered in this way, as incidental results of the planned ethological research. They were not collected with a purpose in mind, but accumulated by themselves over the years. This accounts for their incompleteness, which the subsequent experiments could mend only slightly. However, all this need not, to my mind, stop us from making use of the data. By presenting my opinions, right or wrong, at this early stage, I hope also to learn of similar observations by other animal lovers and zoologists.

2. EXPERIMENTS

Claparède favors experimental work rather than observation because the latter depends on chance and is too time-consuming. I maintain, on the other hand, that, unless we know the natural behavior of a species, experiments are largely worthless. In my opinion, comparative psychology must be regarded and pursued as a biological science, even though this may involve ignoring a number of widely acknowledged studies in animal psychology for the time being. We must have at least a rough idea of the over-all system of instinctive actions in a species, and know how it functions in the natural conditions where it was evolved. Without it, even experiments with a purely intellectual approach can tell us nothing about the learning ability or the intelligence of an animal. His behavior does not indicate how much of it is genetically determined and how much the result of learning and intelligence. Without knowing an animal's system of instincts thoroughly, it is impossible to tell how hard a problem appears to him. The species studied may have an innate reaction that happens to fit into the experimental situation and is released in it. In this case, a behavior pattern that has nothing to do with intelligence may be classed as an intelligent performance.

Hempelmann describes in his *Tierpsychologie* how titmice in an experimental setup hold down their food with a foot. Bierens de Haan (1933) reports the same pattern in goldfinches. Both compare this behavior with that of other birds who do not use their feet for the same purpose, as though the behavior of titmice and goldfinches indicated a higher mental rating. Neither mentions that this motor pattern is instinctively innate, reflex-like in these two species. It has no more to do with intelligence than the human habit of incessantly twitching our eyelids to keep the cornea from drying out. It is a learning achievement that titmice and goldfinches are able to apply their innate reaction in a new, nonnatural situation. Like an unchanging tool, a rigid instinctive action can at times be turned to new uses. But there is a difference between building a new tool intelligently and being trained to use an old one.

Before starting on experimental work, we must know more than the natural, innate behavior of a species. In order to study one specific pattern, we must be familiar with all of them, including the individually variable ones. One source of error that is overlooked in many maze and puzzle-box experiments is that any panic, particularly in the highest animals, reduces the mental faculties to a minimum. If a mentally high-ranking and therefore easily excitable bird is even slightly frightened in the course of a detour experiment, his mental performance immediately falls far below that of a much duller animal, which does not react with fear to the same environmental change. Tame and shy specimens of the same species thus give a very different performance. These results are irrelevant. They are as wrong as it would be to judge the intelligence of *homo sapiens* by the behavior of the audience when Vienna's Ring Theater burned in 1881. The doors of the theater opened inward instead of outward, and it was beyond the panicky crowd to solve this detour problem. Extensive general observation must precede experimental work, if such fine psychological distinctions, individual as well as typical, are to be appraised correctly and experimental errors avoided. Such observation should at first have no definite aim. Anyone who does not think he has the time for it had better leave animal psychology strictly alone.

Perception is probably the only field where psychology can do without a thorough knowledge of the innate behavior of its experimental subjects. Here the reaction to a stimulus presented is in itself incidental, and important only inasmuch as it represents an objectively measurable, characteristic response to a specific perception.

3.　OBSERVATIONS BY OTHERS

I will readily admit that observation has one great drawback: it is hard to convey to others. Experimental conditions can be reproduced, pure observation unfortunately cannot. Therefore it does not have the same objective character. The observer who studies and records behavior patterns of higher animals is up against a great difficulty. He is himself a subject, so like the object he is observing that he cannot be truly objective. The most "objective" observer cannot escape drawing analogies with his own psychological processes. Language itself forces us to use terms borrowed from our own experience. We speak of postures of "fright," expressions of "rage" and the like. It is easier to avoid such analogies in lower animals who are farther from us in the system. Surely no objective observer has ever associated the attacking reaction of a termite warrior with fury, or the defense pattern of a sea urchin with fright.

But it would be idle quibbling to throw out the whole terminology of human psychology when describing animal behavior. However, these terms should always be used in the same sense. Biology has had to coin words to describe the psychological behavior of lower animals, since there were none in the vocabulary. These words are used consistently in the same strictly limited sense which their initial user gave them. On the other hand, terms that have been used all along to describe the inner life of humans have carried their ambiguity with them into scientific literature. The reverse has happened, too. The word "instinct" has nearly lost its scientific usefulness since it has become a colloquial term.

In using observations which others have made, we meet with another difficulty. Some people use terms of human psychology only where they see true homologies, others apply them even where the analogy is only an apparent one. When a shrimp's antennae touch the tentacles of a sea anemone, we may describe its escape reaction by saying, "Now it is scared." Or, when a young male bird cannot quite utter his courting call yet, we may say, "Now he wants to say something and can't yet." But these remarks are made in quotes, whereas many observers (even psychologically trained ones) often put such statements on paper without making it clear whether they are meant with or without quotes.

But the greatest source of errors in using observations made by others is that no two people who look at the same thing see the same thing. Everyone lives in a world of his own. If a person has not noticed something in a certain animal, he is not entitled to make a negative statement about it. If I use only my own observations and those of scientists with a kindred point of view, I am not prompted by narrow-mindedness or by a wish to conceal facts that contradict my hypotheses. I do so because this is the only way to read between the lines and to exercise a criticism akin to self-criticism, the only way really to understand what I have written down. It is a great help to be personally acquainted with an author. If I read an observation made by my friend Horst Siewert, for instance, I know fairly well what the animal he observed was actually doing at the time. When I read Lloyd Morgan's observations, on the other hand, I have only a vague notion of what he is describing. This is not meant to disparage the value of observations made by various authors. But to rate them equally would be most misleading.

For these reasons, the present paper will include observations by very few scientists beside myself. First and foremost among them is my paternal friend Heinroth. Long before I met him, my views on animal psychology tallied so completely with his that it is hard to decide how much of his intellectual property I have appropriated. Luckily, this point need not be settled. At any rate, I hope that I may be pardoned if I should at times present his ideas without particular mention of his name.

4. The Population Observed

My observations, planned and chance experiments, were made on the following birds, which I kept over a number of years but allowed freedom of flight: 15 small white egrets, 32 night herons, 3 tufted herons, 6 white and 3 black storks, many mallard ducks, call ducks (*Hochbrutenten*), and domesticated musk dusks, 2 summer ducks, 2 greylag geese, 2 common buzzards and 1 honey buzzard, 1 royal eagle, 7 cormorants, 9 kestrels, about a dozen golden pheasants, 1 sea mew, 2 terns, 2 big sulphur-crested cockatoos, 1 Amazon parrot, 7 monks, 20 common ravens,

4 hooded crows and 1 carrion crow, 7 magpies, well over 100 jackdaws, 2 common jays, 2 Cornish crows, 2 grey cardinals, and 3 bullfinches. I give the number of specimens because I believe that the largest possible number should be kept within each species, to guard against undue generalizations. All individuals were not, of course, kept at one time, especially in the species whose numbers are high. As a matter of fact, the "keeping" experiments stretched over many years.

It will be seen that domestic forms account for a very small part of the population. Findings about them will be used with the utmost caution. In my opinion, the chief concern of animal psychology should at present be the study of innate behavior patterns, rather than variable, learned and intelligent ones. As I have said before, if we do not know the innate behavior of an animal, we can never tell what it can achieve by learning and intelligence. A close study of instinctive actions in domesticated animals, especially among birds, and a comparison with the corresponding wild forms, shows that domestication causes mutational losses of behavior elements similar to those it creates in organs. Trying to study instinctive actions in domestic species always strikes me a little like wanting to study the structural colors of bird feathers in a white Peking drake. Even such a course would be preferable: one could at least see the losses in the drake, whereas in behavior patterns one cannot. Moreover, we must bear in mind that the behavior of birds is almost wholly instinctive. The coloration of wild forms can be inferred from the markings of differently spotted domestic ducks which display white spots on various parts of their bodies. In the same way one might, with some skill and biological flair, reconstruct the instinctive behavior of wild birds from that of their domesticated forms. Brückner's study (1933) of domestic fowl is very revealing in this respect. He does say, in his introduction: "Even if the primary social instincts of these animals should be deflected, there is nothing to prevent us from studying conditions as they are now." But he tries, most successfully, not to evaluate abnormal reactions. I should like to cite one error from his otherwise excellent paper, an error due to neglecting the appearance of divergences in chains of innate actions and the way they "meander around." The passage is as follows: "Not all clucking hens lead equally well. Some are noted for the magnificence of their leading, and are borrowed for this purpose. Others perform this important task poorly. Whether they are good or bad leaders is a question of temperament and personality." When an innate behavior pattern "fades out" to a greater or lesser extent, this may perhaps be referred to as a difference in "personality," but certainly not one in temperament. At any rate, every healthy wild hen, whether Bankiva or golden pheasant, is by nature an ideal hen. Within the normal spread of a wild species no parent bird performs her task poorly. At most, it may happen as a mutation in a single individual, who is doomed to remain without offspring.

The adaptiveness of domesticated forms has its own laws. These are undoubtedly quite different from those of the normal wild strain. What are the factors in the heritage of a species such as the mallard duck, that have preserved the feather markings in all their beauty and wealth of detail over thousands of years? These markings drop out in domestication, where they are replaced by haphazard variations within a comparatively short time. We do not know the reasons. The laws that govern the behavior of domestic species are superseded and, to a great extent, neutralized by others of an entirely different nature. This competition of two totally diverse principles, one of which borders on pathology, results, if not in chaos, at any rate in a state of great confusion, which more than offsets the slight advantages to be gained from using domestic animals. These advantages can be expressed in terms of the ease with which the animals can be procured and kept. Before studying variations, we must know the basic theme. I admire the studies on domestic chickens by Katz, Schjelderup-Ebbe, and more recently by Brückner. Yet I venture the opinion that their findings would have had a far more general bearing, had they worked with an undomesticated species such as the greylag goose. This applies particularly to Brückner's study on the disintegration of the family in domestic fowl. The dissolution which he describes occurs only in the domesticated form. Only the domestic hen drives her chicks from her by "hacking" at them, because only the domestic hen begins to lay new eggs before her chicks have left her. The chicks have kept the normal reactions of the wild form, which no longer harmonize with those of the hen; because she is bred to incessant laying, her instinctive activities have been changed, or rather foreshortened. I have read in the literature about wild mother birds driving away their young; but in each case I was able to prove that the breaking up of the family was initiated by the young. The innate activities of parents and offspring begin at the same time; they are correlated within the system of actions of a species; and they cease together, unless man, by systematic breeding, turns the parent bird into an egg-laying machine. When friction appears in the interlocking instinctive processes of parents and young, a pathological factor seems indicated.

5. MY THEORETICAL POSITION IN REGARD TO THE PROBLEM OF INSTINCT

The ideas and hypotheses presented in this paper are based on a very definite theoretical stand regarding the problem of instinct. It seems necessary, therefore, to outline that position briefly.

Many biologists believe that instinctive behavior is a phyletic fore-runner, as it were, of the more variable behavior patterns which we call "acquired" or "insightful" (Wolfgang Köhler). Lloyd Morgan, in *Instinct and Experience,* describes how learning can grow out of instinctive behavior in a flowing transition: experience gradually modifies the existing instinctive foundations and achieves a better adaptation to specific goals. Many German animal psychologists share this view. It is a thankless task to oppose current opinions, but I consider it my duty not to let authority sway me.

It is my belief that instinctive reactions are basically different from all other types of behavior, whether simple, automatic acts, complex actions acquired through training, or the highest, insightful achievements of the mind. I fail to see a dividing line between pure instinctive actions and chains of unconditioned reflexes, though I emphatically reject a strictly mechanistic explanation even for the pure reflex. I believe that there is no homology between instinctive actions and all acquired or insightful behavior, even though there may be a far-reaching functional analogy in some cases. Nor do I believe that genetic transitions exist between the two types of behavior.

These views were first developed quite naively. It seemed to me that they must be self-evident to anyone who knew anything about animals. Not being very well read at the time, I simply based my earliest studies on them.

I am quite aware that in the present state of our knowledge the points which I make, and which, for the time being, I offer as mere working hypotheses, cannot be proved. I shall present the facts which tally with my position and lend it probability. But before doing so, I wish to prove that the prevailing view, which holds that innate reactions can be influenced by experience, is purely dogmatic, and that it can claim even less factual material for its basis than my own.

Morgan uses the flight-learning of young swallows as a classical example to show how a basic innate pattern is adapted and modified by the addition of experience. I cannot agree that the gradual progress in a young bird's flying skill is final proof of any such thing.

Before we speak of learning, we should first make quite sure that a simple process of maturation is not at work. Like a growing organ, the developing instinctive action of a young animal may go off before it has completely matured. The maturation of an innate reaction and of the organs needed to discharge it need not necessarily coincide in time. If the action develops before the organ, the situation is simple. Ducklings of all species have very small and quite useless wings. Yet in their fighting reaction, which can be released in the first days of life, they show exactly the same coordination of wing movements as adult birds: they thresh away at the enemy with bent wrists. After assuming the genetically determined fighting posture, which is adapted to the adult bird's proportions, the short wings of the ducklings cannot touch the opponent. Inversely, the development of the organ may precede that of the instinct which directs its use. In this case, the relationships are not so clear. In many birds, such as swallows, but far more distinctly in large birds such as storks, eagles and the like, the flying equipment is ready to function before their flight movements are coordinated. When the maturation of these coordinations is about to "catch up" with the advanced development of the organ, it looks exactly as if the young bird were learning. Actually, an internal process of maturation is proceeding along strictly determined lines. We shall return later to some few learning processes that take place in addition to these processes of growth.

Carmichael (1926) kept amphibian embryos under constant narcosis in a weak chloretone solution. Strange to say, this did not check their organic development; but it did suppress all movement completely. When he let them "waken" in late stages of development, their swimming motions were the same as those of the normal controls which had been "practicing" these motions for days. The experiment cannot, of course, be repeated with young birds, but several facts seem to indicate that the same conditions prevail. Young ring doves (*Columba palumbus*) leave their nest very early, when their pinions are still very short and their quills soft. The young of the cave-breeding rock pigeon are evidently safer in their nest, as they do not leave it until their primaries and tail feathers are fully grown and horny. Rock pigeons at this stage in their development have had no flying experience at all, while ring doves of the same age have been flying for days. Yet there is not the slightest difference in the flying ability of the young.

Secondly, neither Morgan nor any one of his followers give consideration to the existence of a phenomenon which I have called "instinct-training interlocking" in an earlier paper (Lorenz, 1932). This is the singular fact that, in numerous behavior patterns of birds and other animals, innate and acquired links alternate directly in a functional unit of behavior. If the inserted acquired components are overlooked, a variability wholly foreign to its nature is attributed to the purely instinctive behavior pattern.

An instinct-training interlocking should be conceived as a chain of unconditioned reflexes, with a conditioned reflex wedged in between. A more complex pattern may even contain several. Very often such a reaction chain is set off by the conditioned reflex. In complicated interlockings, as in the simplest conditioned reflexes, the acquired component is often the releasing factor. It consists of a set of characters which the reacting subject composes into a pattern. This acquired releasing mechanism, when activated, initiates the reaction chain which, from then on, is purely reflexive. O. Koehler calls Pavlov's nomenclature a "watering down of the reflex concept." I fully agree with this, and would like to substitute the term "reflex-training interlocking" for the expression "conditioned reflex" to point out that two dissimilar factors are involved.

The movement with which the red-backed shrike (*Lanius collurio L.*) impales its prey is a case in point. The impaling pattern is not entirely innate in the young bird. It does not at first react instinctively to the thorn on which the insect will be impaled.[3] The motor component, on the other hand, is innate, and the bird knows from the start that the insect must be impaled on a solid object. A young bird reared in isolation soon begins to perform the motions of impaling with a morsel of food in its beak. At first, it makes these movements at random, anywhere in its cage. Even if there are suitable thorns or nails, the bird pays no attention to them. Holding the morsel in its beak, the bird flits back and forth between the bars and rungs in its cage. From time to time, it makes the queer little pulling, jerking motions provided in the structure of the action chain for the purpose of impaling. These little jerks occur especially when the bird meets with resistance in its gliding. As a result, the jerky pull ensues as soon as the morsel once happens to catch on a nail or thorn. Within a very short time the bird learns to recognize thorns as the objects of its otherwise innate behavior pattern. Such processes definitely have the character of learning. They often, as it were, fill gaps in chains of innate actions. At these points, a "faculty to acquire" takes the place of a missing link between the adjoining, purely innate actions in the chain.

If we compare instinct-training interlockings with similar functions in various species of birds, we often find that a certain element is innate in one species, while in another the functionally analogous link is individually acquired. This substitution of a faculty to acquire a behavior pattern which is innate in another species is particularly clear when young birds "learn" to fly. Very often one species is able to judge distances correctly and find landing sites properly as soon as it leaves the nest, without previous experience; another has to acquire it over a long period by trial and error. Sometimes there is evidence of a biological need: young reed warblers, water starlings, and several rockbirds, for whom it would be disastrous to miss their landmarks, have a highly developed

---

[3] Lorenz later revised his stand on this particular case, when G. Kramer found that some shrikes, which he reared on silkworms, had an innate mechanism directing their reaction to a sharp point or thorn. See Lorenz (1950). [Translator's note.]

innate faculty to localize their goals in space. Common ravens, on the other hand, who leave their nests gradually, have both the ability and the time to acquire the corresponding skills individually. What we call play, in Groos's sense, is a factor of great importance in many of these acquiring processes. Whenever there is playful activity in the developing behavior of a young animal, we may safely assume that it contains variable, acquired elements.

The vicarious appearance of acquired behavior on the one hand, and of innate activities on the other, indicates that the two are analogous functions, in Werner's interpretation, and it is highly unlikely that there should be transitions between them.

In general, the reaction chains of mentally low-ranking animals include far fewer acquired links than those of higher organisms. If we ask how the two types of reaction behave in evolution, I would advance the following hypothesis: innate behavior on the one side, and acquired and insightful behavior on the other, are not successive stages, either ontogenetically or phylogenetically, but represent two divergent lines of development. Wherever one of the two is very highly differentiated, it displaces the other to a considerable extent. Where instinctive behavior has been gradually curtailed, and learning ability and insight have progressed, I see no evidence for a gradual change from the former to the latter. I do not think such a change is possible. I do not believe that the rigid instinctive links of a reaction chain become more plastic, more susceptible to the influence of experience with the progress of learning ability and intelligence. What happens is rather that they drop out entirely, one by one, and are replaced by conditioned or intelligent behavior patterns. Moreover, the innate links may be retained, and new, variable elements inserted between them. Like all hypotheses of evolution, this one, too, can only be substantiated by making a survey of homologous behavior patterns in allied species. Considering how little we know today about the instinctive actions of higher animals, it is something to be able even to attempt such a survey. No such facts can be advanced to support the opinion that experience has a gradually growing influence on innate activities. As an attempt at such a survey, let us compare the hiding reactions of two *Corvidae*. A jackdaw wishing to hide food which it carries in its beak reacts blindly to environmental stimulation, and usually hides the food in the deepest and darkest nook or cranny available. The jackdaw is incapable of learning, through experience, that hiding becomes meaningless if other jackdaws observe it in the process. Nor does it ever find out that certain spots are inaccessible to its human friends, and that valuable stolen objects are safe from them there. The closely related common raven is far superior in learning ability and intelligence. It learns at an early age that there is sense in hiding only if no one sees it in the act, and that humans, being unable to fly, cannot reach certain places. When and where the common raven hides, contrary to the jackdaw, is not innately determined. In every other respect, the raven's hiding reaction is as rigid as is the jackdaw's. The motor co-ordinations themselves never change, and they are identical in both birds. Experimental changes in the natural conditions for hiding show that the raven does not visualize a goal any more than does the jackdaw —a typical phenomenon for genetically determined actions.

It is essential to study the total behavior of as many and as closely related species as possible. I predict that such a study will bring to light far better and clearer typological sequences.

In an earlier paper to which I have referred before, I adopted Ziegler's definition of instinct. I realize that this definition, which is based on reflex theory, does not account for certain important phenomena of regulative "wholeness." Bethe has shown that the innate coordinations of locomotion are highly regulative in various animals. If I stressed the rigidity of instinctive actions at the time, I meant their absolute rigidity in the face of experience and intelligence. The same experiments by Bethe show clearly that the regulative faculty of instincts is a form of plasticity that has nothing to do with learning or experience. Wherever the coordination of walking movements could be regulated in Bethe's experiments, the adaptation was an immediate *fait accompli* after inter-ference! Bethe's findings strengthen rather than weaken the contention that instinctive actions are impervious to experience. They fit very well into the brief definition of instinct by Driesch: "Instinct is a reaction that is complete from the outset."

It is hard to prove the negative statement that instinctive actions cannot be influenced by learning. Nor is it a definition. Yet I know of nothing better to do than to add a second negative statement to the first one. In this way my conception of instinctive behavior will at least be somewhat narrowed.

In his excellent *Purposive Behaviour in Animals and Men,* Edward C. Tolman (1932) says: "Wherever there is learning ability in reference to a specific goal (and where, except in the very simplest tropisms and reflexes, would this not be the case?) we have the objective appearance and the definition of what is properly called a purpose."

This objective definition of a purpose in the terminology of behavior-ism is most valuable. In my opinion, all types of noninstinctive behavior, whether they are accomplished by training or insight, can be summarized as "purposive behavior." However, instinctive acts are so obviously lack-ing in purposive variability ("pliability relative to some end") that this "behavioristic" definition of the purpose can be used for a negative state-ment about them. I must take serious exception to the view that "learn-ing ability in relation to a specific goal" is only lacking in the simplest tropisms and reflexes. A complex chain of instinctive actions is generally more rigid than a simpler one. The starfish's or the paramecium's simple reaction of turning right side up is more likely to show some plasticity than the comb-building behavior of a bee. Von Uexküll once said: "The amoeba is less of a machine than the horse." We may say similarly that the highly specialized activities of a bitch caring for her puppies reveal their reflex nature far more clearly than the simple but conditioned saliva "reflex" of Pavlov's dogs. Although highly specialized instinctive acts include conditioned as well as unconditioned reflexes, we may safely say that the latter predominate in the most highly differentiated reaction chains, such as are found, for instance, among state-forming insects.

The simpler innate behavior patterns of higher vertebrates are hardly ever long chains of purely instinctive acts. Most of them are intricate integrations of innate and acquired elements. With our scanty research methods, they are often hard to analyze, and will scarcely ever be completely solved. This, however, is no reason why their acquired and reflex factors should not be strictly separated.

Yet another characteristic of purposive behavior, defined by Tolman, can be used to restrict our concept of instinctive behavior. He writes: "Releasing stimuli are not sufficient in themselves. Animal behavior can-not go off *in vacuo*. It needs an additional 'support', something to sustain it. A rat cannot 'run along a passage' without a real floor against which to brace its feet, or real walls along which to steer."

It is hardly possible to point out a more impressive feature of instinc-tive actions than their property to "go off *in vacuo*" when the specific releasing stimuli are lacking. If an innate behavior pattern, for want of adequate stimulation, is never released in captivity, the threshold for this stimulation, strange to say, is lowered. This can go so far that the activity in question finally breaks through and "goes off" without any detectable releasing stimulus. It is as though the latent behavior pattern it-self finally became an internal stimulus. Let me recall the instance of the starling who performed the full motor sequence of a fly-hunt without a fly, as described in the above-mentioned paper. One would think that the presence of flies was the most important and indispensable "behavior support," as Tolman words it, for the discharge of fly-hunting behavior. And so it would be, if the bird were aware of a purpose when it hunts. As it is, this observation proves clearly that the bird is not. The animal follows no purpose, however obscure, but the "blind plan" (von Uexküll) of its instincts. The degree of differentiation and the survival value of this plan has as little to do with the animal's mental faculties as has the biologically meaningful structure of its organism.

In my concept of instinctive action, built up as it is for the most part on negative premises, I make no claim to an explicit definition. The ideas which I have set forth have proved their worth up to a point as working hypotheses in analyzing animal behavior. In the light of our knowledge to date they certainly stand up better under criticism than the current opinions that instinct can be adaptively modified by experience. It remains to be seen to what extent future findings will corroborate them.

III.   "Imprinting" the Object of Instinctive Social Reactions

In complex behavior patterns, consisting of innate and acquired elements, the object of an instinctive act is often the acquired component. I have tried to illustrate this in several instances (Lorenz, 1932). As a rule, the object is acquired by something very much like training. However, in a certain group of instinctive acts—those relative to fellow members of the species—where the motor response is innate while the releaser is not, the acquiring process is basically different and cannot, to my mind, be identified with learning.

To the casual observer it is usually surprising, or even incredible, that a bird should not invariably recognize other members of its species innately and quite "instinctively," and react to them accordingly. However, very few birds do so. Contrary to all mammals that have been studied in this connection, young birds of most species, if reared in isolation, do not recognize other birds of their species when they are brought together. In other words, another individual of the same species does not release the behavior that normally responds to it. On the other hand, young birds of most species, if isolated from their peers and raised by humans, will respond to them with instinctive acts that relate to birds of their species.

This behavior seems so odd, so "crazy," that it strikes anyone who first meets it when he rears birds as a pathological symptom, which he interprets as a "prison psychosis" or some such phenomenon. When it appears again and again, in perfectly healthy specimens of the most varied species, and even in animals who have grown up in full freedom, one gradually comes to realize that it is a standard reaction, and that in most birds the adequate object of an instinctive social reaction is not innately determined. This object is acquired in the course of individual life, through a process which is so singular that it calls for detailed discussion.

If we hatch the egg of a curlew (*Numenius*) or of a great godwit

(*Limosa*) in an incubator, and adopt the young bird as soon as it is hatched, it will have nothing to do with us as foster parents. The fledgling flees at sight of a human, and displays none of the instinctive actions modeled on its parents, except possibly in delicately tuned dummy experiments of a sort that, unfortunately, no one has yet made. In these two species, and in several other autophagous birds, that hatch in advanced stages of development, these instinctive acts can only be released by grown birds of their own species. In the idiom of *Umwelt* research, one might say: the young bird has an innate mechanism or "schema" of the parent. The nestling's innate image of the parent bird consists of enough characters so that its parent-specific motor patterns will be sure to respond only to an adult bird of its own species. The number of these key stimuli can be determined in cases where, by imitating them, we can successfully release the reactions dependent on the parents.

We have the same experience if, instead of a curlew, we adopt a greylag gosling that was hatched by its own parents and has lived with them for a few days. None of the gosling's reactions to its parents can be elicited by a human being. However, if a greylag gosling is taken into human care immediately after hatching, all the behavior patterns which are slanted to the parents respond at once to the human being. In fact, only very careful treatment can induce incubator-hatched greylag goslings to follow a grey goose mother. They must not be allowed to see a human being from the moment they break their shell to the time they are placed under the mother goose. If they do, they follow the human being at once. Heinroth (1910) has described this process very accurately: "I have often had to try and place an incubator gosling with a pair that was leading very young birds. In so doing, one meets all sorts of difficulties, which are typical for the whole psychological and instinctive behavior of our birds. When you open the lid of an incubator where young ducklings have just broken their shells and dried off, they will at first duck and sit quite motionless. Then, when you try to pick them up, they scoot away with lightning speed. Quite often they jump to the floor and hide beneath various objects, and one has a hard time getting hold of the tiny creatures. Not so young goslings. They look at you without betraying any sign of fear; and, if you handle them even briefly, you can hardly shake them off. They peep pitifully if you walk away, and soon follow you about religiously. I have known such a little creature to be content if it could just squat under the chair on which I sat, a few hours after I had taken it from the incubator! If you then take such a gosling to a goose family with young of the same age, the situation usually develops as follows. Goose and gander look suspiciously at the approaching person, and both try to get themselves and their young into the water as quickly as they can. If you walk toward them very rapidly, so that the young have no chance to escape, the parents, of course, put up a spirited defense. This is the time to place the small orphan among the brood and leave in a hurry. In the excitement, the parents at first regard the newcomer as their own, and show an inclination to defend it as soon as they see and hear it in human hands. But the worst is yet to come. It doesn't even occur to the young gosling to treat the two old birds as geese. It runs away, peeping loudly, and, if a human being happens to pass by, it follows him: it simply looks upon humans as its parents." Heinroth goes on to say that a gosling can be placed under a mother goose successfully if put in a sack as soon as it is taken from the incubator, so that it never even gets to see a human being. He maintains, and rightly so, that newborn greylag goslings really look at the first creature they see upon entering the world "with the intention of stamping its picture accurately on their minds; for, as I have said before, these pretty, fluffy creatures do not seem to recognize their parents instinctively as members of their own species."

I have given this behavior of greylag goslings so much time and space because it is a classic example of the process under discussion. The young bird has no inherent knowledge of the object of its childhood reactions. This knowledge is gained through a single impression, to which it is only receptive at a critical period in its life. Moreover, the grey goose obviously "awaits" this impression at its susceptible period, that is, it has an innate urge to fill out this "gap" in its instinctive equipment. It should also be stressed that the genus *Anser* is an extreme in that very few characters of the parent companion are innate in the newborn bird. Except for their instinctive response to the specific alarm call of the species, they really seem to have no innate reaction to parent stimuli. They do not even seem to respond instinctively to the call note of the parents, as do so many small autophagous birds.

The process of imprinting differs radically from the acquisition of the objects of other instinctive acts whose releasing mechanism is not innate. Whereas in the latter case the object seems always to be acquired by self-training, or learning, imprinting has a number of features which distinguish it fundamentally from a learning process. It has no equal in the psychology of any other animal, least of all a mammal. However, I would point out certain analogies in human psychology, which appear in the form of pathological fixations on the object of an instinct.

First among the points that distinguish imprinting from ordinary learning is that the object acquisition in question can only take place within a brief critical period in the life of an individual. In other words, a very specific physiological state in the young animal's development is required to accomplish it.

Secondly, once the physiologically critical period is over, the animal knows the imprinted object of its innate reactions to a fellow member of the species exactly as though this knowledge were innate. It cannot be forgotten! Yet, as C. Bühler (1927) in particular points out, it is essential to anything learned that it can be forgotten! Of course, since our knowledge of this field is in its infancy, it is too early to claim definitely that the imprinting process is irreversible. I infer that it is so from a fact frequently observed in hand-raised birds. Once their instinctive social reactions are transposed to a human being, their behavior does not change in the least even if they are later kept for years with other members of their own species and without human company. Such treatment cannot make them adopt other birds of their species as their equals, any more than a bird which is captured when fully grown can be induced to regard a human being as a member of its species. (Their behavior toward substitute objects, which seems to be an exception to the foregoing, will be discussed later.)

These two facts—first, that later behavior is determined at a critical period through external influence, exerted by a fellow member of the species; and secondly, that this process of determination is irreversible—establish a striking analogy between the origin of the system of instinctive behavior patterns and processes familiar from developmental morphology.

If, at a certain point in the development of a frog embryo, cellular tissue from the ectoderm in the ventral region-to-be, which would normally develop into a piece of abdominal skin, is transplanted to the region of the future medullary tube, it develops into a section of spinal cord, in accordance with its location. The cells are influenced by the principle of organization of their environment. Spemann calls this phenomenon "induction." Induction by the environment compels us to distinguish between "prospective potency" and "prospective meaning" of a cell. The ectoderm cells transplanted in this experiment had the prospective meaning of a piece of ventral skin. Without experimental interference they could not have turned into anything else. But at the same time they had another faculty, which normally remains latent: that of developing into a piece of spinal cord. Thus their prospective potency outweighed their prospective meaning. However, if the same experiment is repeated in a later stage of development, or the ventral ectoderm cells are transplanted back to their place of origin after they have turned into spinal cord, we find that their prospective potency is identical with their prospective meaning. After this second transplantation the replanted ventral ectoderm cells still turn into spinal cord at their new location, as they would have done after the first transplantation, and the second experiment produces a monster. Their prospective meaning is "determined" by the influence of the environment, by induction. The cellular tissue does not "know" instinctively what it will turn into. Its final organic character is imprinted by its environment. This determination occurs at a certain phase in its development. Once it is completed, the tissue cannot "forget" its destination again. The presumptive spinal cord which has been retransplanted into the ventral skin can no longer be "re-determined" so as to be ventral skin! But there are other animals, such as the tunicates, where, as early as the two-cell stage of the embryo, each of the cells is already fully determined as to its later function, where there is hardly any induction, where one cell of the artificially divided two-cell stage literally produces half an organism, where single cell complexes in later ontogenetic stages, if isolated, always develop into the same organs or parts of organs as they would have done with their sister cells. These cells, therefore, are not affected by their environment. Each cell in an embryo of this kind instinctively "knows" exactly what it has to do. The mosaic of delicately interadjusted functions of independent parts constitutes a whole organism, whose parts do not mutually influence each other. Such embryos are called "mosaic embryos" as distinguished from the "regulative embryos" first described.

Similarly, we might well distinguish between mosaic and regulative systems of instincts, and apply the idea of inductive determination to instinctive reactions whose object is not innately known to an animal, but is molded by the environment, especially by a fellow member of the species. There are a great many analogies between the functional plan of an animal's instincts and the functional plan of its organic structure.

When a fourteen-day-old jackdaw directs its reactions toward its real parents, they have the prospective meaning of parents to the young bird. But at this time the instinctive actions dependent on fellow members of the species still have a far wider prospective potentiality of object selection. The parents, who already function as such, can still be displaced by another object. When the young jackdaw is first taken from the nest, it shies away from humans, because it already knows its parents by sight. Nevertheless, the parent companion, the releaser of the jackdaw's childhood reactions, can still be re-determined in another sense. A few hours later it will beg from its human foster parent; after about twenty days it is fledged; it begins to follow him in its flight, and its parent-centered drives can then no longer be re-determined "to jackdaws." Nor can a jackdaw who has remained with its parents be transposed to humans at the same age. Prospective meaning and prospective potency are now one.

Two phases must be distinguished in the development of motor responses that are innate, but whose objects are not. There is an initial, usually very short phase, when the bird searches for the object that fits his innate movement; and a second, longer phase, when it has found the object to which its instincts respond, but during which "re-determination" is still possible. In some birds, as in the aforesaid autophagi, where a single impression is decisive, the second phase is extremely short. In their case, the entire mental development which insessorial birds undergo during their long nesting period is crowded into the few hours which they, too, spend in the nest.

As I have said before, the critical period for imprinting is the shortest and follows soonest after hatching in diverse groups of autophagous birds. I can say from my own experience that young mallards, pheasants and partridges, once they have followed their mother for only a few hours, will not trail a human being. Consequently these species can only be kept successfully if they are hatched artificially. Otherwise, humans elicit such violent escape reactions in the young birds that they may forget to eat, and perish. I believe it is quite possible that a single release of the trailing reaction may imprint the picture of the mother. I think this applies particularly to partridges. I have tried to rear partridge chicks brought to me by peasants who had caught them while mowing. The chicks were so young that they could not even stand all the time, but had to squat on their heels after every few steps. I know this stage well; it lasts only a few hours after the chicks have dried, and while it lasts, the mother leads them only a few yards at a time. Yet these baby partridges died, because they huddled and fled as soon as they were brought into the light to be fed. They would not eat until they were too feeble to live. On the other hand, if partridges are hatched artificially, they are immediately tame with their foster parents, and easy to bring up.

The critical period for inductive determination, for imprinting the object of an instinctive act coined on a fellow member of the species, is not always so easy to ascertain as it is in the case of a greylag goose's or a partridge's behavior toward its parents. For this, there are two reasons.

· One difficulty is that a number of characters may facilitate imprinting to the adequate object, while they make imprinting to a different object harder. The young bird has an innate disposition to react positively to such stimuli. As a result, if the bird has first responded to an inadequate object, it can still be transposed to a fellow member of the species at a time when the reverse process is no longer possible. For instance, a young golden pheasant responds instinctively to the pheasant hen's call note by running toward the source of the sound (a thing which the greylag gosling does not do!). As a result, a pheasant that has been accustomed to humans can be readapted to the hen at a stage in its development when a "transplantation" from pheasant hen to human being is no longer feasible. Experiments by people who can really imitate bird calls successfully would be most revealing; unfortunately, I am not one of them.

A second difficulty is that the critical imprinting periods for the objects of two different innate reactions often overlap. This state of affairs seems to be quite common among birds with long nesting periods. I have noticed especially in sparrows that specimens who were isolated at a relatively late date would respond to humans with their reactions to parents; but their sexual instincts, which are likewise innate but whose releasers are not, would respond to a fellow member of the species. I witnessed a particularly striking instance of this when I once kept nine jackdaws of the same age. Three of them were unfledged when they came to me, the rest almost fully fledged. While they all begged from me, they were all tame. But when their childhood reactions were extinguished, the birds that had been captured later in life suddenly became shy, whereas the other three began to court me. Accordingly, it seems as if in the jackdaw the object of sex behavior was imprinted before the stimulus dependence of the young bird's innate reactions to its parents is finally determined. The process of imprinting does not appear to have been entirely completed, because at this time I was still able to record an occasional readaptation "to jackdaw," a thing that never happened in later phases.

Different functional cycles relating to a fellow member of the species are conditioned to the adequate object at different stages of individual development. This is of vital importance. It is one of the reasons why in captivity, in planned or accidental experiments, the various functional cycles can be "set" for different objects. I once had a young jackdaw reared in complete isolation, who was conditioned to me in all its jackdaw behavior, except for two functional cycles: the activities of flying with the flock, and those of feeding and caring for other young jackdaws. The first of these had been conditioned to hooded crows when its group instinct matured. They were the first flying *Corvidae* the jackdaw ever saw. Later, when it shared its attic with a whole flock of other jackdaws, it still kept flying with the free hooded crows. It did not regard the other jackdaws as flight companions. Every morning, when I had let the birds out, this one rose high into the sky and started to search for its flight companions, the hooded crows, whom it always succeeded in locating unerringly. But when its parental reactions matured it suddenly adopted a recently fledged young jackdaw, whom it led and fed in a manner perfectly typical of the species. It is really a matter of course that the object of nursing behavior (activities involved in care of the offspring) must be innate. It cannot be acquired through earlier imprinting, since the bird's own young are the first it sees. In the life of this particular jackdaw a human being featured as the parent companion, hooded crows as flight companions, and a young jackdaw as the child companion!

Imprinting is often effected through the influence of parents and siblings, and yet it must determine the young bird's behavior toward all members of its species. For this reason, in the imprinted as in the innate mechanism of another individual of the species, only supra-individual properties typical of the species are selected from the picture of parent, brother or sister, to be imprinted permanently. It is remarkable enough that this can be accomplished in normal conditions; but it is even more amazing that the stimulus dependence of innate social reactions in a man-raised bird should be shifted, not to one human being, but to the species *homo sapiens*. A jackdaw who has adopted a human being for a parent and has become a completely "human bird" will not address its awakening sex impulses to its former parent companion. It will "fall in love," suddenly and unpredictably, with a comparative stranger, of either sex, but always with a human being. It even looks as if the former parent companion were not eligible as a "mate." But what are the signs by which this bird can tell that humans are "humans"? A great many questions of this sort are still unanswered.

One more problem must be discussed at this point. Who are the fellow members of the species that determine the releaser of an instinctive action chain?

In cases where imprinting comes long before the instinctive act itself, it must obviously be induced by a member of the species which is connected with the bird in another functional cycle. In all probability, the jackdaw's sexual instincts are modeled on its parent companion. At any rate, provided its human keeper gives a young jackdaw so much time and care that he functions as a full-fledged parent, the bird's sex behavior will be slanted to human beings even if it is raised with several brother and sister companions. In Heinroth's experience, many other birds such as owls, common ravens, partridges and the like, who had grown up with their own siblings, were sexually dependent on humans.

In other species the siblings determine future sex behavior. The mallard ducks mentioned earlier (p. 87), whom I mothered consistently, were sexually normal, while a musk drake reared with them was imprinted "to mallards." Since this brother and sister community of mixed species stayed together into the following spring, I am unable to state when imprinting takes place.

Birds raised in complete isolation often slant all their instinctive actions to humans, even in species where imprinting normally stems from the sibling companion. Since a human being never functions as a brother or sister to a bird, it appears that the process of imprinting is not necessarily dependent on one specific companion.

IV. The Innate Releasing Mechanism of the Companion

The innate releasing mechanisms of several object-directed instinctive activities are not interdependent. Each of them responds to different characters in the object and is independent of the response of the others. We were able to show that this independence is particularly complete in the case of innate reactions whose object is a fellow member of the species.

Through imprinting, the bird acquires a mechanism of a different nature for an individual of the same species. Like a learned mechanism, it is distinguished from the IRM's of instinctive reactions by its great wealth of characters.

In natural conditions, innate releasing mechanism and acquired schema for another member of the species form a functional unity. Only in experimental conditions can the social reactions be distributed among various objects. In the natural life of a species the behavior patterns released by innate mechanisms, which are unconditioned reflexes, are integrated into a uniform functional system by the imprinted mechanism of the companion. The complex character of the acquired companion mechanism fits in between the single, mutually independent releasing mechanisms of various reactions, as a "follow-the-dots" pattern for children fits in between the perforations which have no intrinsic relation to one another, but require a functional design to connect them. The "wholeness" of this design is determined by other factors. An innate mechanism of the companion exists only under the assumption that a specific imprinting process assembles the independent, innate characters of the companion into one schema. Inversely, however, the imprinted mechanism of the companion depends in its origin on the innate mechanism. Imprinting is always directed to a certain object by the response of one or more instinctive reactions with correlated innate releasing mechanisms. The trailing reaction of young partridges is released by the mother's instinctively recognized leading call. A single occurrence of this reaction determines its dependence on the complex quality of the mother companion. One might say that the innate part mechanisms provide a framework of independent points in empty space. The pattern which is to be imprinted is somehow "pressed in between," as von Uexküll puts it.

Innate and acquired mechanisms, like innate and acquired action, form a functional entity. The components are pieced together directly and without subjective connections, and they may vary from species to species to such an extent that either the imprinted or the innate releasing mechanism for a member of the species is ousted to the vanishing point from the repertoire of a species.

In the first case, the innate responses constitute a "mosaic," and only the social releasers in the object insure that it will function uniformly. The fellow member of the species is a different environmental object, a different companion in the functional cycle of each instinctive activity that has a correlated releasing mechanism. Consequently we cannot really speak of "a parent companion" in the world of such birds, since the parent keeps turning up as something new: once as "feeding companion," then again as "warmth companion," "leader companion," and so forth. The young curlew described above is an extreme mosaic type of behavior patterns dependent on a fellow member of the species.

But other birds do not react so blindly to innate social releasers. In their world the imprinted or, generally speaking, the acquired releasing mechanism for another member of the species prevails, and the latter is undoubtedly much more uniform here. This applies particularly when selective recognition of an individual companion is involved. Greylag goose siblings remain compatible for years, although they practically never mate. In other species of ducks, the young continue to be on friendly terms with their parents for years and will resume the old family relationship even after they have raised their own offspring. Here again, the specific pattern of a fellow member of the species does not conform strictly to the concept of "companion," but this time for opposite reasons.

It is astounding that, within one class of vertebrates, we should meet behavior closely related to the rigid instinctive patterns of lower invertebrates on the one hand, and, on the other hand, reactions comparable to corresponding human behavior. This is precisely what makes the observation of birds so rewarding.

The extreme "mosaic type" of the curlew and the extreme "regulative type" of the greylag goose are rare. Between them, there exists every conceivable intermediate stage of alternating innate and acquired mechanisms for fellow members of the species. If imprinting is not typical of the species, the resulting "miscarriages" in an animal's behavior toward its companion are most instructive. Even where the acquired mechanism of the companion is of great importance, IRM's may still respond. This causes ambivalent behavior which, in its utter lack of consistency, clearly shows how abnormal imprinting has disturbed the specific functional plan of innate and acquired companion mechanisms. A jackdaw whose entire behavior is dependent on man, who is friendly to its human guardian and hostile to other jackdaws, may yet display an instinctive defense reaction if its human foster parent grabs one of the other jackdaws. Conversely, the absence of a specific social releaser in an acquired, nonadequate companion may cause similarly inconsistent behavior. In the Zoo at Schönbrunn (Vienna), a white female stork was married to a black male stork, with whom she used to build a nest every year. The two species have slightly different greeting ceremonies when they enter the nest. The white stork accompanies her entrance with the familiar clappering, while the black stork utters curious hissing sounds. As a result, the two storks, who had been married for years, always eyed each other suspiciously and anxiously throughout the greeting ceremony. The white female in particular often seemed about to attack her mate when he absolutely refused to clapper. Heinroth describes similar inconsistencies in a mixed pair of rock pigeon and ring dove.

Species like the greylag goose know only a few properties of the parent companion innately. Yet it would be wrong to say that they have no IRM's at all. Owing to the small number of effective key stimuli, their mechanisms are incredibly broad, although they do have certain limits. Even when a newborn grey gosling has as yet no specific object to follow, it is not possible for just any random "thing" to become its leader companion. In order to activate its trailing reaction, the object must have certain properties. Above all, it must move. But it need not necessarily be alive: we know of cases where very young grey geese tried to attach themselves to boats. Size is evidently not one of the innately effective key stimuli.

A budgerigar (*Melopsittacus*) with whom I worked in the spring of 1933 was very interesting and yet very different in its behavior from the greylag goslings just described. When this bird was one week old, it was taken from the nest and reared in complete isolation. Until it became fledged, the bird was kept in an opaque container, so that it could hardly see the people who took care of it. Then it was moved to a cage, where a blue-and-white celluloid ball was fastened to a resilient stem so that even ordinary climbing or flight movements would set it in motion. This setup was not entirely my own invention; I had met a talking budgerigar reared in isolation by Grasl in Vienna, who raised them professionally. This bird courted a budgerigar dummy attached to the ceiling of its cage. Since I was sure that the bird's innate companion mechanism was so scanty in cues that it would not necessitate such a close copy of another budgerigar, I chose the celluloid ball as the simplest possible dummy for the first experiment. I succeeded fully in shifting my budgerigar's social reactions to the ball. Very soon, the bird stayed near the swinging ball all the time; it was the only place where it would sit down to rest; and the bird performed upon the ball the innate motor patterns of "social skin care," as found in the mutual preening of all parrots. With great accuracy, it went through the motions of preening small feathers, although, of course, the ball did not have any. After the bird had groomed the ball in this fashion for some time, the bird offered its own neck to the ball with the typical motion of a parrot asking to be scratched, and sometimes actually succeeded in getting its neck stroked by the still swinging ball.

The budgerigar's innate mechanism for another member of its species seems to be more detailed spatially than the greylag goose's. The bird treated the ball in every respect as if it were the head of another parakeet. All the attentions which the bird showered upon the ball were of the kind that *Melopsittacus* usually lavishes on the head of another parakeet in the normal course of instinctive behavior. Whenever the ball was fastened close to the bars of the cage, so that the bird could cling to it at any height, the bird always managed to keep the ball exactly on a level with its head. If the ball was fastened above the horizontal bar on which the bird was accustomed to sit, so that it was in front of the bird below head level, the bird seemed at a loss; it did not quite know what to do with the ball, and displayed distinct signs of "embarrassment." If the ball was unfastened and simply thrown on the floor of the cage, the bird became silent and cowered in a corner, just as a budgerigar would react to the death of the only fellow parakeet who has shared its nest.

I could observe only one behavior pattern in this bird that was directed toward the body, not the head of its partner. Courting males of this species have a habit of reaching toward the female's body with one foot, mostly in the region of the rump, while chattering excitedly and strutting up and down in front of her. When my parakeet grew older and began to court his ball, he displayed this behavior pattern especially when I fixed the spring so that the ball swung at its upper end. When the parakeet courted the ball in this position, he often reached out with his foot toward the spring that held it. I believe this was the same motion as the one I have just described in normal males. If the ball was attached differently, the bird occasionally trod into empty space under the ball! Unfortunately, he died before attaining full sexual maturity.

The budgerigar's innate mechanism for other members of its species, then, seems to be articulated spatially into a head and a body. The innate mechanism of the mother companion in greylag goslings is not so articulated.[4] This is probably because the adult parakeet has instinctive actions which are released by diverse parts of the companion's body, whereas there is no such differentiation in the greylag goose.

The innate mechanism of the jackdaw's "flight companion" is more specific than that of the greylag goose's parent companion or the parakeet's social companion. The jackdaw's flight behavior is dependent on the following properties: the ability to fly, blackness, perhaps the general form of a *Corvida* and other characters. Into this schema, whose function it is to isolate jackdaws and safeguard survival, additional sign stimuli may be imprinted, with the result that a hooded crow is sometimes "superimposed on it," as von Uexküll words it. A human being cannot fill this pattern, because he lacks too many of its characteristics. The absence of single properties given in the innate mechanism, as we shall see, does not necessarily mean that the schema cannot be filled by an imprinted object that does not fit into it exactly. The interplay of innate mechanism and imprinting is especially clear in cases in which so few, and yet specific, key stimuli of the companion are innate, that the corresponding stimuli can be provided artificially in the experiment.

Raising mallard ducklings from the time they hatch, and trying to elicit as many of their instinctive reactions to their parents as possible, the experimenter gets the impression that the result is not quite satisfactory. Speaking of artificially hatched mallard ducklings, Heinroth says: "If there are several birds, their need for society and companionship is amply satisfied; they hardly miss the leading mother bird, nor do they attach themselves to human beings. They are not really shy; they eat out of your hand, but dislike being touched, for they always preserve a certain measure of independence. In their behavior toward man, mallard ducklings and greylag goslings accordingly represent two distinctly opposite poles, as far apart as conceivable within one group." At first, my experiences checked fully with Heinroth's. I, too, had found that mallard ducks, and even the near-wild forms of domestic ducks, such as the so-called call ducks *(Hochbrutenten)*, which carry over 50 per cent wild blood in their veins, would not accept a nurse of another species, be it a human being or a foster mother bird. On the other hand, the young of heavy, domestic ducks easily transfer their childhood instincts, especially their urge to follow, to humans or to a domestic hen who mothers them. But this loss of specificity in responding to a stimulus situation results

---

4 Portielje (1926) has shown by ingenious dummy experiments that the defense reaction of the great bittern *(Botaurus stellaris)* which is always aimed against the face of the enemy, gets this orientation simply from the situation "smaller circle above bigger body." The bird has an innate mechanism of the predator segregated into "head" and "body"!

from domestication and is found in the most diverse domestic birds. It
it regrettable that, from these entirely atypical and obscure instincts of
domestic animals, sweeping generalizations are made and irresponsibly
applied to "instinct." Mallard ducklings in possession of all their instincts will not even respond to mother ducks of another species. For
instance, if they are hatched by a musk duck *(Cairina moschata)*, they
lose this foster mother while she is still setting on the nest: they simply
run away from her. And yet *Cairina* and *Anas* can easily be crossbred!
Now mallard ducklings, to all appearances, will immediately adopt a
domestic duck as a foster mother, regardless of her markings, although
her visual image differs from a mallard mother at least as much as a
Cairina. But she has one thing in common with the wild duck: her habits
of social intercourse, especially the call notes, which have hardly changed
in the course of domestication. A *Cairina* mother, at best, quacks hoarsely
and softly, but as a rule she is silent, while the mallard or domestic duck
sounds her call almost constantly when leading her young. In the light
of my findings, where the mallard duck's mother companion was replaced by a human being, a musk duck or domestic duck, it seemed to
me that the innate mother call was the critical cue which the mallard
ducklings missed in all the substitute mothers, except in the domestic
duck. Since the leading call of the mallard mother is fairly simple to
imitate, I resolved to put this idea to the test. In the early summer of
1933, I adopted three wild ducklings hatched by a call duck, and six
crossbred ducklings, mallard and call duck, that had been hatched by
their own mother, a wild duck of pure strain. The animals were all of
the same age, and I took them out as soon as they were hatched. Even
while they were drying, I busied myself with them and kept quacking
my imitation of the call note to them. In the days following, which,
luckily, were the Pentecost holidays, I devoted myself exclusively to
quacking. The fruits of this activity, which certainly was self-denial in
the purest sense of the word, were soon forthcoming. The very first time
I put the ducklings out in a meadow and walked away from them, quacking constantly, they began at once to "peep their abandonment," a behavior which, in one form or another, is typical of all autophagous birds.
Precisely as the real mother duck would do, I responded to the peeping
and returned to the ducklings. Then once more I walked away, quacking
again, whereupon the entire flock promptly began to move, and followed me in close formation. From then on, the ducklings trailed me
almost as eagerly and surely as they would have followed their real
mother. The further course of the experiment indicates that the mother's
call is probably the essential characteristic of the mother companion to
the wild duckling, and that the visual stimuli are imprinted individually

upon the young bird. At first, I had to quack continually; if I stopped, the children would begin to "peep their abandonment." Not until they were older did they treat me as their mother companion even when I was silent.

In single cases, therefore, it is possible to determine which quality the mother companion must possess, and which of her properties the young bird acquires during his early life.

[Since publication in book form made necessary some condensation of the original papers, Sections V-IX of this monograph have been omitted here. They contain reports of interesting and valuable observations, as reviewed in the following Summary, and lend support to interpretation of the behavior described above, but do not introduce additional theoretical concepts.]

X. Summary and Discussion

This paper does not claim to be a study centered on a strictly defined research topic. It is rather an attempt to introduce order and method into a great number of phenomena which have hitherto been more or less disjointed. Such a study must, of course, have the nature of a program or outline. Owing to our type of approach, the few answers which we have obtained cannot be condensed into a few words. I shall endeavor to offset this handicap by giving the summary by sections, discussing each of the few actual results as they appear. Often we shall meet new questions, and I consider it a merit of my work that it points to a broad field for research which, up to the present, has hardly been touched.

A. Recapitulation by Sections

I. The Concepts of Companion (Kumpan) and Social Releaser

Animals emit many stimuli which affect the sense organs of other members of their species. Of these, we tried to identify the ones that release social reactions in their widest sense within the species. We have found that the stimuli and sets of stimuli to which an animal responds instinctively with specific reactions are of a very different type from those whose releasing value is acquired.

I have adopted von Uexküll's term, "releasing mechanism," for the receptor correlate to a releasing stimulus combination, for the readiness to respond specifically to a certain key combination, and thus to activate a certain behavior pattern.

Innate releasing mechanisms are particularly important in birds. If the releasing mechanism of a reaction is innate, it always corresponds to a relatively simple set of single characters, which together represent the key to a specific instinctive act. Out of the abundance of stimuli, the IRM chooses a small number, to which it responds selectively, and releases the action.

This key combination must have a minimum of general improbability, so that the reaction will not be released accidentally in the biologically "wrong" place.

The releasing mechanism of an action chain may have to be acquired even though the motor response itself is innately determined. We have called such behavior patterns "instinct-training interlockings." In contrast to innate releasing mechanisms, the individually acquired mechanisms which activate them correspond to very complex sets of stimuli. As a rule, they respond to "complex-qualities," none of whose innumerable properties can be changed without at the same time changing the quality of the whole, and jeopardizing the release of the reaction. I regard this difference between innate and acquired releasing mechanisms as an essential difference between instinctive behavior and learning.

IRM's are especially important in reactions to members of the same species. If an action is set off by something in the environment, its innate mechanism can only be adapted to stimuli which are inherently a part of that thing. To go back to the simile of the key, we might say that the form of the key bit is predetermined. The necessary general improbability of the mechanism has an upper limit, which is reached when the ready-made negative of the lock corresponds as far as possible to the positive of the key bit. On the other hand, for social reactions which are released by a fellow member of the species the development of both IRM and its pertinent stimulus key lies within the species' phyletic evolution. Organs and instinctive actions which serve solely to emit key stimuli attain a high degree of differentiation, always parallel to the development of corresponding releasing mechanisms which are available to them. We have called such organs and instinctive movements social releasers.

Social releasers are unusually common among birds. It is hardly an exaggeration to say that all particularly conspicuous colors and forms of plumage have a releasing function of some sort. The type of reaction released cannot be inferred from the form of the releaser. It is quite inadmissible, for instance, to refer all releasers to one specific reaction, such as the female's selection of a mate.

To regard these structures and motions as releasers is, to my mind, the only hypothesis that accounts for the combination of simplicity and improbability which is their most general and most outstanding quality.

II. *Specialization*

The high specialization of IRM and releaser causes very curious behavior on the part of many birds toward other members of their species.

If two or more instinctive acts have a common object, there are two ways to ensure that it will be treated consistently, as one object. First, the subject may have an objective conception of the object. Secondly, all the instinctive acts referring to one object may be united in that object. The releasers and correlated IRM's of innate reactions to fellow members of the species may be highly specialized. This differentiation may go so far that, as a result, the object of instinctive behavior is treated as consistently in natural living conditions as it would be if its identity were conceived subjectively. Many birds have actually chosen this path, and avoided the need to comprehend the material identity of conspecific fellows subjectively. The system of their instincts focuses the uniting factor in the object that emits the stimuli rather than in the subject that receives them. In the subject's world, the object is not an entity. Jakob von Uexküll coined the term *Kumpan* (companion) for a fellow member of the species who is only treated identically in one functional cycle, and I have adopted this term for the present paper.

III. *Imprinting*

To my mind, the most important result gained from our study of innate reactions to fellow members of the species is this: in the realm of animal behavior, we cannot identify all that is acquired with experience, nor all acquiring with learning. In many cases, for instance, the adequate object of an innate reaction is not recognized instinctively as such. The animal comes to know it through a unique process, which has nothing to do with learning.

In a number of instinctive reactions to fellow members of the species, the motor response is innate, but recognition of its object is not. The same applies to many other innate behavior patterns, which come to be interlocked with conditioning in the course of individual growth. The difference lies in the way the releasing factor is acquired.

Innate social behavior whose releaser must be acquired becomes dependent on an object in the young bird's world at a very definite stage in its development. This selection may go hand in hand with the motor awakening of the instinctive act, but it may also precede it by months, or even years. In normal, free life, conditions are such as to make sure that the object selection of instinctive activities whose biologically adequate object is a fellow member of the species will be directed toward such a one. If, in the psychological phase of object selection, the young bird is not surrounded by members of its own species, the bird will aim its reactions at some other object in its environment, usually at a living creature if one is available, but failing that, even at a lifeless object.

Two facts distinguish this process of object acquisition from true learning, and make it comparable to another acquiring process, which we know by the name of inductive determination from the field of embryology. In the first place, it is irreversible, whereas it is essential to the concept of learning that whatever has been learned can be either forgotten or extensively modified. Secondly, it is restricted to very specific and brief stages in individual development, often lasting only a few hours.

Imprinting is the name we have given the process by which the releaser of an innate reaction to a fellow member of the species is acquired. This type of conditioning makes a unique and enigmatic selection from the properties of the object: it only centers on supraindividual characters. If the imprinting processes of a young bird are guided experimentally toward an animal of another species, we find that once imprinting is completed, the respective functional cycles are adjusted to that species. It is a complete mystery how the bird can zoologically "identify" the species to which he wrongly "feels he belongs."

Finally, I should like to point out that irreversible fixations on the objects of certain instinctive activities have been known to occur in human psychopathology. Purely symptomatologically, the picture is the same as that of birds whose process of object selection was not typical for their species.

IV. *The Innate Releasing Mechanism of the Companion*

Imprinting never determines all the characteristics of another member of the species that acts as companion to a bird in one functional cycle. A framework of innate releasing mechanisms always exists for the ones that have to be acquired. Out of their entirety, a complete innate schema of the companion, of broader or narrower scope according to the kind and number of IRM's, is built up. Even in cases in which this comprehensive schema is very broad, in which it contains only very few IRM's, it directs imprinting toward the adequate object in the young bird's natural life. In an experimental setup, the key stimuli of single innate mechanisms can at times be identified by deliberately trying to effect imprinting upon inadequate objects in young birds. From the qualities of these objects it is often quite easy to infer what properties are indispensable in "filling out" the innate mechanism of the companion.

The interrelationship between innate mechanism of the companion and imprinting of the object differs widely in various species. There is every transition from species like the greylag goose, whose innate companion mechanism consists of very few characters, to others whose releasing mechanisms are almost all innate, so that very little leeway is left for imprinting. We may safely say that, among birds, the latter extreme is the more primitive one.

V-IX. *Parent, Offspring, Sex Companion, Social Companion, Sibling Companion*

Five different cases were discussed. In each, a specific fellow member of the species plays an outstanding part in the bird's life. I have borrowed von Uexküll's terms of the parent companion, child companion, etc., for these companions in higher functional cycles; although, to be quite consistent, we should have carried our analysis further, into the single functional subcycles, and followed up the environmental picture of another member of the species in each of these.

The IRM's of these companions in higher "cycles of functional cycles" were investigated as far as possible. On the basis of numerous observations, we discussed to what extent the IRM can be filled out by an inadequate object.

Next, the individual characterization of the companion was studied in each of the five main functional cycles.

In each of the five cases we then discussed the releasing behavior patterns of the various companions, which the animal needs in order to discharge his single part functions. In other words, we studied the companion as the releaser of reactions which make up a single functional cycle.

Finally, we discussed the connections between subcycles within each of the five main cycles, and the possibility of isolating them, particularly through imprinting to various individual objects.

Since the observations on which these chapters are based seem valuable to me not only as illustrations of the views here represented, but in themselves as well, I have not tried to save space in recording them. I am far more firmly convinced of the value of these facts than I am of the interpretation which I have put upon them.

B.   FINDINGS ON THE PROBLEM OF INSTINCT

I should like to record it as a merit of my work that the theories on instinct which were presented as a working hypothesis in Section II have stood the test admirably. I must add that these hypotheses did not act as guideposts in my work, but were gained later, by abstraction, from a method of research practiced earlier, and first of all undoubtedly by Heinroth.

The assumption of a basic dichotomy between instinctive action on the one hand, and learning and intelligent achievement on the other, has at no time caused us difficulties. On the contrary, it has cleared up many an otherwise incomprehensible type of behavior. We have never regretted stating flatly that instinctive behavior cannot be changed by experience, and consistently treating instincts as organs whose individual variability can be neglected when giving a general biological description of a species. This conception is not incompatible with the fact that certain instinctive actions can have a high regulative "plasticity." So do many organs. The conception of instinctive activities as chain reflexes is not intended as an endorsement of either their reflexological interpretation or of mechanistic dogma.

The development of organs and instincts that dictate their use runs parallel. Nowhere is this illustrated so clearly as in the social life of birds. Whatever the factors may be that achieve survival value in the development of organs, the self-same factors surely control the development of instincts. Within a clearly defined group of birds we find sequences of differentiation which distinctly show the connection between an innate behavior pattern and the pertinent organ. In one specific instance we found this connection to be so close that it seemed appropriate to unite instinctive actions and organs with identical functions under one higher concept. We have indiscriminately called all those organs and actions which help to elicit social reactions in fellow members of the species, "social releasers." Very often we find "phyletic" series of releasers: at one end, instinctive actions without a pertinent supporting organ; at the other end, highly developed organs to support almost identical and certainly homologous instinctive movements. The various forms of display behavior and display organs within the family of *Anatidae* are an example of such a series. By intraspecific "agreement," so to speak, releaser and released reaction are particularly resistant to environmental influences within one species of birds, and the possibility of convergences may therefore very likely be excluded. Equality here always spells homology. This means that, by using instinctive behavior patterns as taxonomic characters, we can often ascertain phyletic relationships with an accuracy that the comparative morphologist hardly ever dare hope for.

No one can deny that the phyletic adaptability of an instinctive action resembles that of an organ, and not that of a psychological performance. Its adaptiveness is so very like that of a particularly "conservative" organ that instinctive actions, especially releasing ceremonies, are very valuable taxonomic characters. No one can prove that the individual adaptiveness of an innate reaction is affected by factors irrelevant for the individual adaptiveness of morphological characters. Unless the concept of learning is taken in an immensely wide sense, so that one might even interpret the work hypertrophy of a much-used muscle as learning, there is no justification for maintaining that experience influences instinct.

C. Discussion

In the course of this study, and especially in reporting observations, we have repeatedly encountered facts which appeared decisive for certain controversial questions. Since they are not all directly relevant to the central theme of the paper, I should like to devote a separate section to them.

(a) *Contributions on the Nature of Instinct*

1. It has in no way been proven that instinctive activities can be changed by experience. In the light of all observations heretofore, the contrary seems highly probable. This contradicts the views of Lloyd Morgan and many other students of instinct. Driesch worked out a definition of instinct which is in accord with my own theory. It states that the instinctive act is a reaction "which has been complete from the outset." To be sure, this definition overlooks the possibility of changes due to maturation, which appear only when the act itself is already in use.

2. Ziegler's reflexological definition of instinct does not do justice to the far-reaching regulative processes which Bethe and his followers have found. Bethe attributes all regulation to the plasticity of instinctive acts. We cannot take exception to the term plasticity itself. However, others have interpreted it as implying that adaptive modification through experience is feasible (Alverdes), a possibility which I deny and whose likelihood has been lessened rather than heightened by Bethe's own experiments. In any case, I do not consider plasticity a very happy term to describe the integral regulation that follows immediately after a certain interference.

3. In his "Appetites as Constituents of Instincts," Wallace Craig (1918) makes the significant statement that the readiness for a specific instinctive activity is enhanced when that reaction is not released over a longer than normal period. The threshold of releasing stimuli is lowered, and a behavior which can be interpreted as a search for these stimuli ensues. Craig sums up these phenomena in the term "appetite." Considering the wide usage of this word in English, the choice is doubtless a happy one; but we must bear in mind that the phenomena which it synthesizes are not limited to "positive" reactions, a fact which Craig himself has stressed. The threshold decrease of releasing stimuli is particularly striking in escape and warning reactions. When the threshold value drops to its theoretical minimum, a phenomenon may occur that I have described in this, as well as in an earlier paper, and called "vacuum activity": the motor response is discharged without any external stimulation. These vacuum or explosion activities are of especial

importance to us. They show convincingly that instinctive actions are not dependent on external stimulation (Tolman's behavior supports), and that each behavior pattern is a self-contained unit.

4. William McDougall teaches that specific emotions are subjectively correlated to specific instinctive activities. Years of direct contact with animals confirm the impression that instinctive acts are accompanied by subjective phenomena that correspond to feelings and emotions. No one who really knows animals can fail to see the homologies that exist between them and humans, and one is practically forced to conclude that subjective processes occur in animals. Therefore all real animal lovers and zoologists are followers of McDougall, whether they are aware of it or not. Verwey (1930) writes: "Wherever it is at all possible to distinguish reflexes from instincts, the reflex is mechanical, while instinctive acts are accompanied by subjective phenomena." A somewhat bold definition of instinct, but one which I endorse wholeheartedly! Heinroth, when wrongly accused of treating animals as reflex machines, used to say, jokingly and very much to the point: "On the contrary, animals are highly emotional people with very little brain." These great experts, who know and understand animals better than most people, are in full accord with McDougall's theory, and so am I. However, I do not think that McDougall's comparatively few instinct categories, which were, after all, derived from human psychology, are quite sufficient for animals. Nor do I see how we can distinguish between superior and subordinate instincts in animals, at any rate in birds. Since the individual reactions within a functional cycle are highly independent, even the seemingly less important ones, as autonomous mosaic stones, are as important for the functioning of the whole as any others. If we wish to say anything authentic about the attendant emotions, we must, to be consistent, assume that animals have as many independent types of emotions as they have autonomous instinctive activities. We would have to adopt a far greater number of distinct emotions and feelings for an animal than there are in humans; and again, to be consistent, we would have to assume a simplification and dedifferentiation in the emotional life of humans, corresponding to their instinctive activities. The terms which we use to describe human emotions are entirely inadequate to describe the inner processes of animals. They are too few in number. Heinroth has very properly coined new terms for the emotions of animals, by combining the name of an innate reaction with the word "mood." He speaks of "flight mood," "reproductive mood," and the like, and I have made use of the same terms. Series of reactions, which are coordinated to graded intensities of excitation, and blend into one another imperceptibly, in a flowing chromatic scale, must be regarded as pertaining to one mood.

The double warning-and-escape reaction of hens is a case in point: the animal has two scales of intensities which correspond to only one in a human being. The word "fear" does not cover the twofold emotion of these birds; we must assume a fear of the ground enemy and a fear of the bird of prey, which are qualitatively different. These views represent a criticism of some recent American studies, for instance, H. Friedmann's "The Instinctive Emotional Life of Birds" (1934). Furthermore, they are in direct contrast with what H. Werner says about primitive feelings and emotions in his *Developmental Psychology* (1933).

(b) *The Biology of Mating*

1. Darwin believed that certain conspicuous colors and shapes had developed in the animal kingdom because animals equipped with them were preferred by the opposite sex in the selection of mates. The nuptial plumage of many male birds in particular led him to this belief. Wallace flatly denied natural selection in this narrowest sense, and wished to trace all sexual dimorphisms to mere differences in metabolism. Our exploration of the nature and function of releasers has shown Wallace's hypothesis to be untenable. Although my interpretation differs from Darwin's in many respects, it nevertheless shows once more that his far-sighted genius came much closer to actual conditions than his opponents have been at any time.

2. The data which Noble and Bradley (1933) obtained for a number of reptiles cannot be generally applied to birds, as these authors suggest. Although the nuptial plumage of many male birds has the same threatening and intimidating effect as does the corresponding garb of the reptiles they describe, it is never the only effect of these releasers.

3. A. A. Allen, in his "Sex Rhythm in the Ruffed Grouse" (1934), reaches the conclusion that birds are not conscious of their own sex. This only applies to quite specific, albeit many forms. We have used the term "labyrinthine-fish-type" to denote their manner of mating.

4. In the same study, Allen says that the physiological period of mating readiness is as short in male birds as it is in females, and that successful copulation can therefore only occur if the propagation cycles of both have been "synchronous" from the beginning. Both statements are no doubt true of the species which Allen studied (*Bonasa umbellus*, and a number of small sparrows). But neither, to my mind, can be applied to birds in general, without reservations. I believe with Verwey that the male common heron has a very long period of mating readiness, and I fully agree with Wallace Craig that there is also a subsequent synchronization of propagation cycles.

(c) General Sociology

1. The hierarchy which Schjelderup-Ebbe and others describe exists in many, but by no means all bird societies. There are colony breeders with highly specialized social reactions, in whose social setup no hierarchic order prevails. Herons, cormorants, gannets, and probably many other colony-breeding seabirds belong in this category.

2. Whenever possible, undomesticated species should be used for sociological research. As Brückner says, there is no reason why we should not also study the modified instinctive actions of domestic animals. However, every known source of error which can be avoided must be avoided. One such pitfall is the dropping out of innate behavior patterns in domestic animals. We must not forget that, even in the highest animals, social behavior in particular is largely determined by instincts.

(d) The Structure of Society

In conclusion, may I say a few words on the subject of how, in social forms, the interlocking performances of individuals, the releaser in one animal and the released reaction in the other, make up the complex function of society, of the supraindividual whole.

As a result of the modern tendency to think in terms of wholes, the whole is often studied before its parts, the nature of society before that of the individual. H. Werner says, in his Introduction to *Developmental Psychology* (1933): "It can be shown in every case that a whole can be formed in different ways, that the so-called elements which constitute this whole may vary without affecting its total character. Therefore neither the dots nor a synthesis of them can account for the circle which they form. Any shape or figure can be made up of the same building stones. Conversely, the same figure can be made up of elements other than dots: tiny crosses, for example. Nor is it due to the single human 'dots,' or individuals, that in their entirety they constitute one particular type of whole and none other. A synthesis of individuals never results in a supraindividual totality." Elsewhere, he says: "We can move forward constructively by following the principle of creative analysis rather than creative synthesis." Alverdes repudiates von Uexküll's term "reflex republic" as applied to the sea urchin because of the singular cooperation of its quills, pedicellariae and locomotor tube feet, on the grounds that this term "is incompatible with the fiction of wholeness."

I would say this in answer to both theories: however strongly one may disagree with an atomistic associative psychology, however definitely one may reject the reflex theory, one must not forget that in these cases a conception of wholeness is justified by the presence of a physical whole, which is given in the shape of a higher integrating apparatus, a universal coordination by the central nervous system. To look for such a system of universal interaction where it does not exist physically is, to my mind, and despite my rejection of mechanistic interpretations, an excursion into the metaphysical.

A true, "whole-like" integration of parts can, of course, also create supraindividual wholes. However, in such cases, too, we must search for a real superindividual integrative mechanism. Human society has such an apparatus in its language, which permits a collective accumulation of experiences, supraindividual knowledge and besides, an extensive coordination of the functions of individuals. In an animal society, however, the individuals learn very little about the lives and activities of their neighbors. In this respect they are very much like the several organs in the sea urchin's reflex republic, which are not informed of their neighbor's activities through an integrative network of nerves, but react only when affected by them. I hope I have convinced the reader that the mutual relations of individuals in an animal society are similarly anything but immaterial or imperceptible. I could hardly think of a term that describes the social structure of a species such as the jackdaw more fully and strikingly than the expression "reflex republic."

In the sea urchin, where the functions of the parts are not subordinated to the whole, a synthesis of these part functions brings us closer to an understanding of the over-all performance of the organism than Werner's creative analysis of the whole. For an organism that is more of a whole, and whose parts are well differentiated and subordinated, analysis is the more successful research method. The same applies, of course, to the collective organism of society. But the differentiation and the hierarchy of individuals, even in the best integrated and most collective of animal societies (termites, for example), never exceeds or even approaches that of the single "reflex persons" in a sea urchin, and I am therefore bound to disagree with Werner's statements. I regard them as an undue generalization of principles which may be perfectly valid in the field of Gestalt psychology, but which are not applicable to sociology.

"When a dog runs," says von Uexküll, "the dog moves his legs; when a sea urchin runs, the legs move the sea urchin." A similar relation between the whole and its parts prevails in various, highly organized types of societies. When young people are growing up, they are molded to a great extent by the society to which they belong. When young jackdaws are growing up, they form a jackdaw society which is perfect down to its last details, without any pattern to go by.

"Man," says Werner, "by virtue of belonging to a supraindividual entity, has certain qualities because he belongs to that totality. They can be understood only from its nature." Two entirely different things are thrown together here. An individual has certain qualities because he belongs to a particular society: certain behavior patterns handed down by tradition. A certain language among human beings is a good example. The individual would not have precisely the same qualities if he were a member of another society, another "superindividual" of the same species. But in addition the individual has other qualities. These, too, can only be understood by analyzing the social setup of the particular species; but instead of being traditionally passed on to the individual, they are his instinctive heritage because he is a member of the species, not because he happens to be a member of a specific society within that species. The development of these qualities is not influenced by society.

Innate and traditionally acquired behavior must be kept strictly apart, as two fundamentally different things. To clarify their relative importance in various animal forms, we must observe the behavior of individuals raised in isolation, where the influence of tradition has been eliminated. A human being of this sort would probably be quite different from a normal member of society. The most painstaking study of such an "element" of human society could not, by synthesis, furnish even a tentative picture of that society. A jackdaw, on the other hand, even if deprived of all contact with other jackdaws from earliest childhood, possesses nearly all the qualities and behavior patterns which it would ordinarily have in the normal framework of a jackdaw society. Many of these, of course, will not appear regularly in isolation. But it is all the more impressive when some of them do occur without any goal or object, "*in vacuo*," proving that they are virtually in existence and merely await release. For the rest, the behavior of an isolated bird differs from that of a normal control owing to irregularities in the imprinting process, and not to a lack of acquisition through tradition. Traditional behavior patterns are relatively so insignificant that their absence can only be noticed in very specific cases. Their loss is not necessarily fatal if we try to reconstruct the sociology of a species by synthesis from the behavior of an isolated animal. At times such an attempt is so successful that it continually astonishes the biologist, who is used to more analytical methods. It has ever been a new source of joy and surprise to me when the society of a bird species actually displayed the behavior which I had synthetically reconstructed with fair success from the behavior of a captive young bird.

Werner's simile of the figure which may be formed by either dots or little crosses can only be applied to human society legitimately if we assume that the innate element recedes far behind the acquired in human behavior. I am not at all prepared so to assume; though I must admit that the impact of society upon individual behavior is far greater in man than in animals. The individuals in a social species of animals can invariably be combined into only one, closely confined type of superindividual whole! If we wish to use a simile, we might say that, from the first instant of their lives, they are like the ready-hewn blocks of a stone arch, which can be assembled into only one whole, whose structure corresponds to that of its single elements. The scanty mortar of individually acquired behavior cannot change the form of the structure materially.

Human society is supposedly built up largely on personally acquired or even intelligent reactions. Whenever it has been compared to animal societies in the past, the relations of the part to the whole and the whole to the part were assumed to be so different that it seemed advisable to approach these two types of supraindividual wholes with opposite research methods. It is not my intention, of course, to accentuate such a contrast. It is my considered opinion that sociologists, with the exception of McDougall, have vastly underrated the instinctive element in all human social behavior. It is an essential quality of innate activities that they are accompanied by emotions. But we experience the emotions correlated to our social instincts as something particularly noble and exalted. Far be it from me to imply that they are not so. However, because they rightly estimate the feelings and emotions associated with man's social instincts so highly, many scientists find it psychologically impossible to grant to animals, too, at least some vestige of the exalted and noble, and, on the other hand, to attribute instinctive behavior to humans. Yet this is exactly what we need if we wish to learn to comprehend our own social behavior. Katz says: "In many respects there is a surprising similarity in the social behavior of animal and human groups, so that one may actually foster the hope that animal psychology may be drawn on to reveal laws which govern the social behavior of human groups." This hope can only be realized if we admit that humans also have instincts as such, with their own laws, as something basically different from all other psychological behavior, and if we then endeavor to study these instincts in man.

2

The Nature of Instinct

The Conception of Instinctive Behavior

KONRAD LORENZ (1937*a*)

Whenever any two biologists attempt to discuss the problem of instincts, it soon becomes apparent that they do not understand each other, because they do not speak the same language. Each connects a different meaning with the word instinct. It is, of course, impossible to give a conclusive definition of a biological phenomenon; but many people do not see this. Our problem can only be approached in a purely inductive manner. We cannot make statements about "instinct" without specific experimental study. The fallacy that other methods are possible is responsible for a number of easily refutable statements on instinct by its great theoreticians. It has also led to the formulation of cumbersome instinct concepts, particularly to very *broad* interpretations which, as experience teaches, often hinder analytical research.

I am not trying even to approximate a complete survey of all the concepts that have ever been connected with the word instinct. Instead, I shall analyze some of the views held by great students of instinct theory, which still meet with widespread approval, and try to show in what ways they are faulty or at any rate vulnerable. I believe that from a criticism based on actual facts, a new, more clearly defined concept of instinctive behavior will emerge spontaneously. After all, *practical zoologists,* whether they are zoo keepers, amateurs with some biological background, or field observers, are perfectly well able to discuss the problem of instinct, because they quite obviously think along the same lines, even though they may use different words for their concepts.

One more word about the term chosen. Instinct is a mere word. Statements can only be made about instinctive *action*. Heinroth, to get around the ambiguity of the word instinct, used the expression "species-specific drive-action" (*"arteigene Triebhandlung"*) instead of instinctive action. His is doubtless the better term. If I revert to the expression "instinctive action," I do so because the word "drive" has recently been adopted by the same circles that attempt to deny the very existence of just what we mean by this word, and in order to avoid confusion with the devious drive concepts of certain behaviorists and psychoanalysts.

I shall now give a brief survey of the views under criticism. If, in so doing, I group authors by common errors as it were, this may create the impression of a disparaging attitude, which I am anxious to avoid. I wish to state expressly that I owe a great deal to the authors quoted,[1] and that nothing is further from my mind than to underestimate their merits, which lie mostly in other fields than the one here under consideration.

Some biologists as well as many psychologists believe that instinctive behavior, both phylogenetically and ontogenetically, is a *forerunner* of those less rigid types of behavior which we term "learned" or "intelligent" or, following a more recent American pattern, subsume under "goal-directed behavior."

This view goes back in essence to Herbert Spencer and Lloyd C. Morgan. The latter, in *Instinct and Experience,* suggests that intelligent behavior develops through the gradually increasing effect of experience on primarily purely instinctive processes. The following statement by Spencer is quoted again and again by his followers: "The continuing complication of instincts which, as we have seen, involves a diminution of their purely automatic character, also involves a simultaneous beginning of memory and intellect."

As a mere logical extension of these views, other authors such as Tolman, Russell, Alverdes, and to some extent even Whitman and Craig, say that instinctive action cannot be clearly distinguished from other types of behavior, and regard it, including all part actions in longer, instinctive action chains, as "goal-directed" behavior. This attitude reaches its extreme in Alverdes' formula, $A = F (K, V)$, which is intended to mean that all animal action is the function of a constant and a variable factor.

McDougall's instinct theory follows the Spencer-Lloyd Morgan school in so far as it also classifies instinctive action as purposive behavior. For the rest, it assumes a limited number of superior instincts, thirteen to be precise, which "use" subordinate instincts as means to an end, as it were.

---

[1] This is particularly true of Wallace Craig's views, which will be discussed repeatedly. The greater part of the present paper owes its origin solely to an exchange of ideas in writing with that scientist.

Proof of the purposive character of instincts is seen in this means-end relationship. This theory has numerous followers in America. Many English-speaking writers use the concepts "first order drives" and "second order drives," which replaced McDougall's original ones as the term instinct became obsolete there.

At the opposite end from the Spencer-Lloyd Morgan thesis, and from all the views derived from it, H. E. Ziegler (1920) conceives instinctive action as a *chain reflex*. He gives a histological definition based on the theory of pathways. The chain-reflex theory has gained widespread acceptance among physiologically inclined zoologists.

The "instinct theory" of behaviorists in a narrower sense, with Watson as their chief exponent, need only be mentioned in passing. Only a total ignorance of animal behavior can justify an attempt to interpret all of it as a combination of conditioned reflexes. The behaviorists flatly deny the existence of more highly specialized innate motor coordinations. Since this denial is rooted in a simple lack of knowledge, an extensive refutation of it may well be considered unnecessary.

I. The Spencer-Lloyd Morgan Theory

My criticism of the Spencer-Lloyd Morgan theory is centered on the two above-mentioned axioms: first, that instinctive action can be influenced by individual experience, and secondly, that a flowing transition allegedly leads from highly differentiated instinctive acts to learned and intelligent behavior.

My first objection is perhaps the most serious, because it concerns a matter of principle: the view that experience has an adaptive influence is not based on valid observations. As a typical case of adaptive modification, Morgan adduces the flight-learning of young birds. He overlooks the possibility that the transformation and improvement of motor coordinations might be due to a *process of maturation*. Now, the developing instinctive action of a young animal, like an organ, may begin to function *before* as well as *after* it is fully developed. The development of an organ and that of the innate motor coordinations which dictate its use need not coincide in time. If the action develops before the organ, the situation is easy to fathom. Ducklings of all species, for instance, have very small and quite useless wings. Yet in their fighting reaction, which can be released in the very first days of their lives, they show exactly the same coordination of wing movements as do adult birds: grabbing the enemy with their bill, they hold it at correct striking distance and thresh away at it with bent wrists. But the innately determined fighting posture fits the proportions of grown birds, and the duckling holds its antagonist so far away from itself that it has not the slightest chance of reaching the enemy with its tiny winglets!

If, on the other hand, the organ is fully developed *before* the instinct which directs its use, the relationships are not so clear. In many birds, the wings of the young are ready to function mechanically long before the coordination of their flight movements matures. What happens later, when the maturation of movements overtakes the advanced development of the organs, looks exactly like learning. Beyond the ever identical final outcome, no outward sign betrays that a process of maturation is taking its prescribed course. Experiments are therefore needed in this field. Carmichael kept amphibian embryos permanently narcotized. This did not inhibit their physical growth, but it did suppress all motion completely. When he let them "waken" in late stages of development, he found that their swimming motions were no different from those of normal controls who had been "practicing" them for many days. My student Grohmann made similar tests with domestic pigeons. These were reared in narrow, tubular boxes, where they could not even unfold their wings. At the same time, he plotted a curve on normally raised young doves, as follows: on their first flights, the birds preferred certain perches at varying distances from the dovecot. These were picked out, and the·distance of the perch reached was shown on the ordinate, the dove's age in days on the abscissa. A fairly constant curve was thus obtained for the normal young birds. The confined animals, despite their inevitable muscle atrophy, all showed *more steeply* rising curves. They matched the curves of the controls very soon, often within a few hours. In a borderline experiment the subject was let out of the box 27 days after it would normally have taken to the wing; it flew out of the experimenter's hand straight to the farthest perch registered, thus producing a vertical line as its curve.

These experiments by Carmichael and Grohmann definitely seem to preclude learning for the genetic process under investigation. If, conversely, we should wish to prove that learning prevailed, and exclude maturation, we would have only one criterion: the growing coordinations would have to develop differently under the influence of diverse experience. No such observation has been made in the entire animal kingdom, and particularly not with respect to the flight-learning of young birds. Never has the flight of a fledgling raised in a room developed otherwise than in freedom, in the sense that certain coordinations, in adaptation to given spatial relationships, would have evolved differently. It would be such an adaptation, for instance, if a young peregrine falcon should develop the coordinations of the quivering flight required in confined space better there than in freedom. Nothing of the kind has ever been found.

The assertion that older, more experienced birds build better nests than young ones is another misconception that recurs obstinately in the literature, although Altum disproved it long ago. It is based on a misinterpreted captivity observation. If there is the slightest disturbance in the general health of captive birds, *deficiency phenomena* often appear in the sphere of more delicate instinctive activities, such as nest-building. Such impairments later recede, as the birds' physical condition improves with growing age, especially after completion of an oestrous cycle. This, and not individual experience, explains why the first brood often miscarries in captive birds, whereas later ones are successful. Three pairs of bullfinches that I kept as a young student convinced me of this. The first year, two couples lived in a big flight cage, the third, reared by a friend of mine, in a room cage. The first two couples built very inferior nests, both of which came to grief before the young hatched, while the couple in the room cage did not build at all, although the birds mated. The next year, all three pairs lived in the free flight cage. All of them built identical and adequate nests. I no longer even knew which birds were building for the first time. I venture to state confidently that the same phenomenon accounts for all known cases where older birds supposedly built better nests.

These two instances and a few other, equally contestable ones, are almost invariably quoted to prove that instinct can be affected by experience, with the implication that the author who cites them could produce any number at will. But if one begins to mistrust the stubborn recurrence of the same all-too familiar examples, and then searches the literature and his own experience for other, valid observations, the search remains utterly fruitless.

It requires a certain familiarity with the adaptiveness of instinctive behavior and with the laws that govern its adaptability, to avoid the pitfall of making experience responsible for phenomena which are actually elicited by other factors. I shall therefore discuss these phenomena briefly.

First of all, many instinctive actions, and particularly the simplest ones (such as locomotor patterns), are highly regulative. But regulative plasticity need not necessarily be connected with learning and experience. It is equally typical of many organs, especially of the *less differentiated* ones. Bethe's experiments on the regulation of locomotor patterns in a large variety of animals have shown that, wherever regulations occurred at all, they were available *immediately* after interference. Consequently they were not the results of experience. Bethe repeatedly uses the word "plasticity" for the regulative faculty which he found. There is nothing to be said against Bethe's term; except that Morgan, Alverdes, and others interpret him as saying that instinctive actions are adaptive, although his experiments have not made this appear any more likely. One of his findings even speaks clearly *against* such an assumption. A dog, whose two sciatic nerves were sutured together across its back, walked quite normally once their performance was restored. But there was no regulation with regard to sensitiveness: when pain stimuli were applied to one hind leg, the animal always reacted with the other. The fact that regulation occurred in the motor field, but not in the neuro-sensory, clearly proves that experience has no part in motor regulation. Had it done so, it would have taught this dog precisely the wrong thing.

A second phenomenon often related mistakenly to a regulative effect of experience is this: earlier events, that is, experience in the broadest sense, can determine the *intensity* of a certain reaction to a stimulus of given strength, or even the kind of reaction that a certain stimulus will release.

Let us first consider the differences of intensity in the discharge of instinctive acts. We may say that the opposite of an all-or-nothing law is, so to speak, valid for instinctive behavior. Practically all the instinctive actions of a species, even when reaction intensity is very low, can be noticed in the behavior of the individual as *slight indications* of a specific action chain. These suggestions tell the expert observer what course the animal's actions will take once the necessary intensity is reached. Since they betray the animal's "intentions," as it were, such action initials are often called "intention movements." Aside of the fact that in certain social forms intention movements have acquired a secondary meaning as mood-conveying "means of communication," they have no survival value; and even in that case, their biological function has nothing in common with that of the complete reaction. Now, between the slightest intention movements, which only an expert sees, and the full behavior pattern that fulfills its biological function, there exists *every conceivable transition*. A night heron sitting in the branches in early spring shows the expert the awakening of reactions pertaining to the year's propagation cycle by getting obviously and rather suddenly excited out of the deepest calm, bending forward, grasping a nearby twig with its beak, going through the building-in motions a single time, and relapsing the next moment, "satisfied," into its former repose. If we watch even more keenly, we may perhaps spot the first traces of nest-building even earlier the following year: a fleeting fixation of a twig, together with a suggestion of the bent-over posture that is often adopted in the nest later. From such rudiments, the full sequence of activities that leads to the building of a nest develops in the course of days and weeks, in a smoothly flowing transition.

These scales of intensities are important in answering the question: is the animal conscious of a purpose? That the animal is just as satisfied with an incomplete, biologically meaningless action sequence as it is with the complete action chain that achieves its biological goal, argues very clearly that the goal is not the factor which directly determines the animal's actions, and must not be regarded as a purpose given to the animal subjectively. This is especially clear when reaction intensity is somewhat higher, but still insufficient to attain completeness, and the animal breaks off the action *just short of* reaching the biological end. In many a captive animal, such senseless, incomplete instinctive acts are far more frequent than complete ones. When observing animals, it is this very incompleteness and senselessness that most often indicates the innate character of an action; and nothing could demonstrate the absence of any purpose concept whatsoever more convincingly. It is quite evident that the night heron described earlier has no need, however obscure, for the biological success of its action, but only for the *consummation of the reaction in question,* and at the prevailing low level of intensity this need happens to be satisfied by a single shake of a twig.

In view of these facts, it is hard to understand that many authors still connect the purpose of an action, as given to an animal, with the biological, that is, the species-preserving meaning of an innate behavior pattern, or even identify the two. It is even stranger to me when some-one like Russell says this about instinctive activity in a book published as late as 1934: "It is continued until either the goal is reached or the animal exhausted." The contrary is true. Long ago, an Englishman stressed this fact and estimated its true scope: Eliot Howard made a thorough study of instinctive actions that remain incomplete owing to lack of intensity, and substantiated the view here represented by a wealth of observations, collected throughout the field.

As I have pointed out, the intensity of a process may be determined by what has gone before it. If the same stimulus situation occurs re-peatedly, the intensity of a reaction may be lowered by fatigue or by familiarization with the stimulus, or it may be heightened, in other cases, by a summation of stimuli.

Changes in intensity due to fatigue or to familiarization furnish com-plete, continuous gradations. To a gradual summation of stimuli, on the other hand, the animal mostly reacts as it would to stimuli growing in strength. Phenomena similar to the "creeping in" of stimuli occur; that is, when the slow increase of stimulation finally rises above threshold, an abrupt rise in reaction intensity may be registered. For this reason the complete, gapless series due to familiarization with the stimulus show most clearly that the various intensity levels of a reaction belong together. Two manifestations of a reaction corresponding to two levels of intensity that lie far apart may look very different. Only the existence of all the intermediate stages, and the consequent impossibility of separating one from the other, compel us to treat them as a whole.

The escape reaction of wild animals in the process of being tamed is a case in point. If a human being approaches to within a certain distance, they respond less and less intensely to this stimulation until, instead of making violent escape motions, they merely look about slightly alarmed, and finally no reaction ensues.

Although a repeatedly presented stimulus remains objectively the same, the various behavior patterns which it activates need not necessarily be mere gradations of one and the same instinctive action. In the course of familiarization, the animal behaves exactly as if the intensity of stimulation were decreasing. Thus the same stimulus may release *different* reactions, correlated to stimuli of varying strength. After the intensity of a reaction has been gradually diminishing, a sudden shift into another reaction can sometimes be observed. A pair of wild swans, for example, flee to their nest when a human approaches. As they grow tamer, this escape pattern becomes less intense, until it ultimately yields to the reaction of defending the nest, which it blocked before. We then see a sudden shift from slight escape movements to highly intensive fighting reactions. In the process, the animals not only behave as if the intensity of the stimuli were decreasing, but literally as though the human who emits the stimuli grew smaller. At first they respond to an objectively identical situation as they would react in the field to a human or possibly to a wolf; but later they behave as they would toward a weasel, a crow or, at most, a fox.

In all these cases, the discharge of an instinctive action is in fact affected by individual experience. It may determine with what intensity the reaction will be performed, or even *what* reaction a certain stimulus will elicit. In individual cases this kind of influence may even bear the stamp of adaptiveness. Yet I must repeat that adaptive modification of an action by learning something new, upon which the Spencer-Lloyd Morgan school bases its theories, has never been found. A *new* type of action, not predetermined and genetically established in one specific combination of movements, never occurs. The different intensities of the gradually tamed animal's escape reactions, which succeed each other on a descending scale over many weeks, do not comprise a single motor pattern that is not firmly correlated with a certain level of intensity and elicitable by a certain, stronger or weaker flight stimulus *at any time,* that is, without any previous experience. The reactions corresponding to single intensity levels are photographically identical, regardless of the historical moment of their release.

Similarly, if two different instinctive acts are released by an objectively identical stimulus, no motor combination occurs that cannot be released *at any time* in precisely the same fashion by an adequately selected stimulus, as illustrated in the example of the swans.

Another objection to the Spencer-Lloyd Morgan theory concerns its broad formulation of the instinct concept. It disregards a very definite phenomenon, which necessitates analytical study, inevitably resulting in a narrower formulation of the concept. We owe our knowledge of this phenomenon to careful observation of the developing instinctive actions of young animals, particularly birds.

Instinctively innate and individually acquired links often succeed each other directly in the functionally uniform action chains of higher animals. I have termed this phenomenon "instinct-training interlocking," and emphasized that similar interlockings also occur between instinctive and insightful behavior. Here, where we are dealing with the effects of experience, we must first discuss the interlocking of instinct and training. Its essence lies in the fact that a conditioned action is inserted in an innate chain of acts at a certain, also innately determined point. This action must be acquired by each individual in the course of his ontogenetic development. In such a case the innate action chain has a *gap,* into which, instead of an instinctive act, a *"faculty to acquire"* is inserted. This faculty is sometimes a very specific one. It may apply to changeable living conditions; it may even be an adaptation to an inconstancy of this sort. I would recall the adaptiveness of bees which, as von Frisch was able to show, may be called an adjustment to the blossoming of various plants.

It is, of course, only under natural conditions in the wild life of a species that these "gaps" are filled by the adequate acquired element in such a way that the interlocking parts are fused into a biologically meaningful entity. In captivity, even without deliberate experimental interference, the process of acquisition is often disturbed and faulty. This is what made us realize that functional units of behavior are made up of two fundamentally different components.

Innate and acquired elements of behavior are integrated, for instance, in the fetching and building in of nest materials by *Corvidae.* In common ravens and jackdaws, the following pattern appears as the first step in the intricate sequence of nest-building actions: the birds begin to carry all sorts of objects in their bills, flying with them over long stretches. At first, this carrying is an autonomous reaction, independent of further building motions. Nor do the birds show any preference for suitable nest-building materials while this pattern alone controls their behavior. Both ravens and jackdaws usually carried broken-off pieces of shingles, which they found most often at their dwelling place on the roof of our house, although plenty of twigs and branches, most appropriate for building purposes, were available in the same place. These were only preferred when a further innate component of the nest-building pattern appeared: namely, the peculiar laterally quivering motion with which most birds try to make fast a twig at the site of their nest. Only those materials for which the motion of pushing sideways was phyletically evolved lend themselves to this building-in pattern: twigs, straws and the like. The activity continues until it wanes of its own accord, which is almost always what happens in the early phases of nest-building, or until the object that is to be built in catches somewhere and opposes a certain resistance to the quivering, whereupon the bird lets go. The animals obviously find this ending of the reaction satisfying, and since it occurs only when usable nest materials are brought, they *learn* surprisingly soon to prefer the biologically "right" materials even for the carrying reaction.

No one who has ever watched a training deliberately produced by man, and has then gone on to observe behavior of this type, can fail to see that the two processes are entirely analogous. Experience teaches that in a training devised by humans, the animal must be exposed to certain stimuli, which are termed "reward" or "punishment" stimuli even by those who try to steer clear of subjective expressions. The behavior of animals acquiring the learned component of a complex behavior pattern imposes the question as to what factors operate as reward or as punishment in this situation.

Wallace Craig, in his "Appetites and Aversions as Constituents of Instincts," was the first to point out that the animal achieves or "strives" to achieve the discharge of its instinctive acts by what we call *goal-directed behavior*. In this term we include, with Tolman, all those types of behavior which, *while retaining a constant goal, are themselves variable*. This objective definition of the goal is invaluable for our effort to distinguish conditioned and intelligent behavior from instinctive activity, for it gives us a higher concept that comprises all noninstinctive behavior. But it must be stated right away that neither Craig nor Tolman carry out such a distinction. Rather, as the title of Craig's paper implies, he conceives the purposive behavior by which the animal strives to attain the stimulus situation in which its instinctive act will be discharged as a *constituent* of the instinctive action, whereas we distinguish it from the latter as *something fundamentally different*.

The integration of instinct and training upholds the general correctness of Craig's approach. Indeed, nothing could prove more clearly that instinct consummation is craved than the fact that the "appetite" for an instinctive act can train an animal to a certain, not innate, type of behavior in the same way as the appetite for a piece of meat can train a circus lion! In many cases, the statement that an animal has an "appetite" for an instinctive action or for its releasing stimulus situation hits the nail on the head precisely. Henceforth I shall use the term *appetitive behavior* as a synonym of goal-directed behavior.

We can, and therefore must, analyze functional units of behavior and trace their components: elements that are purposive and subject to change by experience on the one hand, and, on the other, constituents which are not so, but which all the individuals of a species "have got," just as they have organs. The process by which a young shrike acquires knowledge of the thorn cannot be distinguished from training. If we find that in a certain behavior pattern, which we have hitherto regarded as "instinctive," this process is always inserted *at the same point,* while the rest of the behavior remains unaffected, we surely do not have the right to stretch the concept of instinct so far as to include this obviously conditioned behavior. And training undoubtedly is not the sole type of purposive behavior that is interlocked with instinctive actions.

Charles Otis Whitman said, as early as 1898: "There may be mixtures and every possible kind of mutual interaction between habit and instinct, and these may be of great theoretical bearing, but they cannot be precisely defined and are therefore dangerous foundations for theories. Any theory of instinct should, of course, primarily be concerned with the *pure instinctive action.*" In my opinion all those who believe that animals have insight into the purpose of their instinctive acts, and that experience affects instinctive activities, suffer from having chosen unanalyzed "combinations" for the dangerous basis of their theories. That is why instinctive behavior is invested with all the attributes of the learned and insightful behavior patterns interlocked with it, attributes that are not only foreign but downright contrary to its nature.

It is our duty at all times to carry analysis as far as possible, and I believe I must build up a working hypothesis on the fact of interlockings. I believe that those highly complex behavior patterns in higher animals and men, which, though "built up on an instinctive basis," yet comprise "intelligent" and learned components, must equally be conceived as interlockings. These chains of intricate structure defy the few research methods at our disposal, and will perhaps always defy them; but that is no reason why a conceptual separation of their two components should not be strictly carried through. To reject it because there are animal and human behavior patterns in which the components cannot be clearly distinguished, would be like proposing to give up the concept of cotyledons because there are uniformly functioning organs in which, when fully developed, the cells derived from a certain cotyledon cannot be identified. The separation which I suggest has been accused of being "atomistic" and incompatible with the modern biological conception of wholeness. This reproach is no more warranted than maintaining that to distinguish *cutis* and *epidermis* in the skin threatens the same conception. The fact that more than one cotyledon nearly always contributes to the functional unity of an organ cannot constitute an argument against advancing the cotyledon concept. Similarly, we must not be misled by the fact that instinct, training, *and* insight participate in almost all functional units of behavior in higher animals. Behavior patterns in which we can produce one of these three components unalloyed, as Whitman demands, will be especially revealing for our further analysis of action. The student of instinct must therefore be primarily interested in pure instinctive actions and in the simplest, most easily analyzed types of interlocked behavior.

It is important to realize how much more concise the reformulated instinct concept becomes, once the purposive components of interlockings are excluded, as they must be. In many action chains of animals, instinctive actions are combined with *orienting movements,* which direct the animal toward or away from a definite goal in its environment. The turn that orients the animal in space cannot, by definition, be an innate action; its coordinations cannot be predetermined in the specific form of the individual case. The orienting turn is the most primitive form of noninstinctive behavior, and the one reaching farthest down in the system. It is the phyletic root of all appetitive behavior. In certain, particularly simple cases, we are wont to call the orienting turn a taxis. However, it must be understood that this behavior cannot be clearly separated from insightful behavior. If we contemplate the continuous form sequence of homologous behavior patterns that extends from protozoa to man, we must conclude that no sharp distinction is possible between taxis and behavior controlled by the simplest insight. If a frog reacts to a fly by an orienting turn, directing first its eyes and then its body, by corresponding small stepping motions of its feet, symmetrically toward the fly, the eye movements and perhaps the shift of the body too can be described very well in the phraseology of taxology. But the frog's behavior cannot be distinguished from conduct dictated by the simplest form of insight. Anthropomorphically speaking, this insight in the case of our frog would be limited to the realization: "There sits the fly."

In principle, the orienting turn, as well as the taxis in its narrowest sense, must be conceived as purposive behavior, if only for the reason that it typically displays Tolman's requirement of variability while retaining an invariable goal. The goal, the "purpose" given to the animal as the acting subject is, as ever, the attainment of the stimulus situation needed to release an instinctive act. In our example of the frog, the mere symmetrical orientation to the prey achieves this.

The innate readiness to respond to a specific stimulus combination is of the utmost importance in numerous interlockings. Certain sets of stimuli often constitute very specifically effective *keys* to certain reactions. These reactions cannot even be released by very similar stimulus combinations. Thus there exists a receptor correlate to certain key stimuli, which, in the manner of a combination lock, responds only to quite specific sets of stimuli, and sets off the instinctive action. Elsewhere I have called perceptual correlates of this kind "innate releasing mechanisms" (IRM).

Innate releasing mechanisms attain special significance in instinctive actions whose object is a member of the same species. In this case, higher differentiation of IRM's in an animal form may go hand in hand with a corresponding development and specialization of instinctive actions and organs whose sole biological function is to release innate social responses, in the broadest sense. I have called releasing instinctive movements, and the colors and structures supporting them, "social releasers." The entire sociology of many animals, and particularly of birds, is based on complex systems of releasers and innate mechanisms, which guarantee consistent and biologically adequate handling of the sex partner, the young, in brief, of all fellow members of the species.

IRM's also play an important part in many interlockings. An interlocking may begin with the resonance of a mechanism and include purposive behavior later on; or its release may, inversely, be dependent on the acquired component. The aforesaid frog responds to an IRM, and immediately thereafter displays purposive behavior in the shape of an oriented appetent motion. Inversely, an animal may respond to an acquired releasing factor with a pure, undirected innate reaction. For instance, a duck may respond with the innate and undirected motion of submerging to the sight of a gun, for which it naturally has no innate mechanism, but which it must have learned to fear. Thus in an interlocking both the innate and the purposive element may be limited to either the receptor or the effector branch of the reaction.

A consistent analysis of all appetitive behavior shows that the great majority of functionally homogeneous behavior patterns falls into a chain of appetences and endogenous movements for which they strive. We must not forget, however, that in every single complex behavior pattern there is a finite, given number of these successive links. It is a fallacy to think that such an action chain could be split up into an infinite number of infinitesimal purposes and an equal number of appetences. Tolman believes that the chain is dependent at *every* point on a steering by additional directing stimuli, which he calls "behavior supports." He disregards the obvious fact that all complex behavior patterns contain long and highly differentiated motor sequences whose orientation is not variable, which are quite independent of "behavior supports," and within which no appetences can be found; in short, he overlooks the existence of what we call an instinctive act. In his opinion, the innate element is limited to staking out a course by intermediate purposes, toward which the animal strives successively by appetitive behavior; how this is done, is left to the animal. This is quite true of certain behavior patterns in the highest mammals, where the participant instinctive components have indeed become so rudimentary that, to use a simile, they function like a row of lures laid out to entice an animal to follow a certain path. Since Tolman has only studied higher mammals, and has probably observed only this type of "instinctive acts," his definition of instinctive action as a "chain appetite" appears quite plausible. Of course, it misses what we consider the essence of instinct. To be sure, it is essential that an instinctive act may be the goal of appetitive behavior; but not that an integrated behavior pattern results from a repeated succession of these two components, and even less that it must do so. If the possibility of interlocking is neglected, all behavior which contains the slightest instinctive element is inevitably classed as "instinctive," without any attempt at analysis.

Alverdes identifies all interlockings, however intricate, with instinctive action pure and simple. He says explicitly: "Some writers speak of instinctive actions in men and animals, as if they were something basically different. As a matter of fact, an abundant measure of instinct, of striving enters into every intelligent activity; and on the other hand, no instinctive action runs off altogether automatically, for besides the rigid, invariable component it always contains a variable factor, which conforms more or less to the situation." Of this statement by Alverdes, one thing is doubtless true: there are instinctive elements in every intelligent action. But when he says that a variable, situational component participates in *all* behavior, he lapses into the same, to my mind erroneous, train of thought as does Tolman, who assumes that every action is influenced by additional directing stimuli.

The complete independence of the *purely* instinctive act from orienting and, in Tolman's sense, "behavior-supporting" stimuli, is best proved experimentally by a phenomenon which I call the "reaction *in vacuo.*" If an instinctive activity is not released over a long period, the threshold value of the stimuli required to elicit it is surprisingly lowered. The threshold of liminal releasing stimuli may eventually reach a critical value inasmuch as the long-checked reaction finally breaks through *without* a detectable stimulus. *Hardly could a more striking and curious characteristic of instinctive actions be conceived than their tendency to go off in a vacuum for lack of releasing stimuli,* independently of the supporting stimuli which Tolman deems necessary. It is very strange that Tolman, while arguing for the purposiveness of all animal behavior and for its dependence on additional stimuli, should make the statement: "Animal behavior cannot 'go off' *in vacuo.*" In his eagerness to show how absurd it is to contend that nonpurposive actions exist in animals, he stipulates, as proof of their existence, precisely what we are able to produce in the shape of the vacuum reaction.

The vacuum or explosion activity permits very clear conclusions as to what parts of an action sequence are genetically determined. This is especially valuable when highly specialized and long, purely instinctive action chains go off *in vacuo.* I had once reared a young starling who performed the whole behavior pattern of a fly-hunt from a vantage point *"in vacuo,"* with a wealth of detail that even I had, until then, regarded as purposive rather than instinctive. The starling flew up onto the head of a bronze statue in our living room and steadily searched the "sky" for flying insects, although there were none on the ceiling. Suddenly its whole behavior showed that it had sighted a flying prey. With head and eyes the bird made a motion as though following a flying insect with its gaze; its posture tautened; it took off, snapped, returned to its perch, and with its bill performed the sideways lashing, tossing motions with which many insectivorous birds slay their prey against whatever they happen to be sitting upon. Then the starling swallowed several times, whereupon its closely laid plumage loosened up somewhat, and there often ensued a quivering reflex, exactly as it does after real satiation. The bird's entire behavior, especially just before it took off, was so convincing, so deceptively like a normal process with survival value, that I climbed a chair not once, but many times, to check if some tiny insects had not after all escaped me. But there really were none. Especially the way the bird's gaze followed a moving goal that actually did not exist, forcibly recalled the behavior of many a mental patient with optical hallucinations, and made me wonder what subjective phenomena might accompany the bird's vacuum reaction. The behavior of this starling showed that the oriented turn toward the fly is the only appetitive component of the behavior pattern described.

Craig, like Tolman, has the whole process in mind when he refers to "instinctive action" as including the purposive search for the releasing stimulus situation. Since he regards this seeking for stimuli as an essential ingredient of instinctive acts, he also believes that they are purposive. In contrast to others who represent this view, we find in Craig a realization of the utmost importance, namely, *that the "consummation of instinctive action" is the goal of purposive behavior.* This paves the way for a division into appetitive behavior and the subjectively purposeless motor pattern performed for its own sake, which we call instinctive action. Even though, to some extent, Craig shares Tolman's opinion that all action chains can be resolved into "chain appetites," he comes very close to our idea of interlockings, when he says: "If an action is instinctively determined in the highest degree, it has the form of a chain reflex. However, in most allegedly innate reflex chains the reactions at the beginning of the chain or in the middle of the sequence are not innate or not completely innate, but must be acquired by trial and error. *The final link in the chain, the consummatory action, is always innate.*" (My italics.)

To illustrate: the food-getting behavior of a peregrine falcon is made up essentially of innate motor coordinations. Appetitive behavior is limited to a search for a stimulus situation (by trial and error), in which the wonderfully specialized instinctive actions of hunting down the prey, specific to this bird, are released. With this, the *purpose* after which the animal subjectively strives *is already attained.* The motor coordinations that follow, apart from a few orienting movements, are purely instinctive. Quite often they can also be observed as vacuum reactions. In man, contrary to the falcon, the entire motor sector of this species-preserving function is controlled by purposive behavior. What is instinctive, pleasurable, and therefore the purpose of the whole action sequence, are the purely innate processes of chewing, salivating, swallowing, etc. The stimulus situations which are particularly apt to elicit one of these functions are usually the most "appetizing." Thus in humans, too, the purpose of an action quite often is not its biological end, but the discharge of instinctive reactions.

It has been argued that my concept of instinct-training interlockings cannot be distinguished from the Pavlovian notion of the conditioned reflex. Since the two are actually similar in content, I must justify the introduction of a new term. O. Koehler has described Pavlov's terminology as a "watering down of the reflex concept," a criticism with which I agree wholeheartedly. The student of instinct needs a concisely drawn reflex concept. The process of "conditioning" surely cannot be distinguished from real learning. Even if the ensuing process is extremely simple and definitely reflex in nature, as is the salivation of Pavlov's dogs, there is after all no reason to infer that the process of acquisition lends itself to an equally simple mechanical explanation. Frequently such a surmise does indeed seem plausible, for example in the surprising fact that the human pupillary reflex can be "conditioned" to a sound. But to assume that higher, more complex processes, reaching further into the domain of consciousness, do not participate in the numerous experiments made with dogs is surely a mistaken and sweeping generalization. The term "conditioned reflex" tends to make one overlook the scope and the complexity of these processes. Either the process of acquisition involved in the conditioned reflex must be designated as a learning or training process, or else we must speak of "conditioning," instead of learning and training, even in highly differentiated processes (as English-speaking behaviorists actually do). I do not see what is to prevent us from referring to a "reflex-training interlocking," and believe that such a distinction can only be serviceable to both the notions of reflex and training. Pavlov's own disregard for the dual nature of the processes at work can probably be explained by his deliberate and typical avoidance of all psychological inquiry. But it is incomprehensible that he should have overlooked the resulting extension of the reflex concept, which amounts to its downright annihilation.

Before leaving the field of interlockings, I must comment on one more peculiar process of acquiring. Its function, in certain instinctive activities, is to fill their "gaps" with a faculty to acquire. These are various innate responses of birds *to fellow members of their species.* We have known for some time that birds reared in isolation will attach innate social activities in the broadest sense to some object in their environment, mostly to their keeper or to some other living creature or, failing that, even to inanimate objects. Later on, such birds do not react at all to members of their own species.

This process of determining the object of an instinctive act originally coined on a fellow member of the species differs in several essential points from the true learning processes which we have met in filling out the gaps in integrations of instinct and training. These singularities have led me to give the process a special name; in an earlier paper I have called it "imprinting" (Lorenz, 1935).

In the first place, this particular process of acquisition has none of the essential earmarks of training. The animal does not act according to the principle of trial and error, as it does when acquiring an instinct-training interlocking, nor is it led by reward and punishment. Instead, an exposure to certain stimuli, very limited in time, determines its entire subsequent behavior, without—and this is essential—this behavior having necessarily been practiced before the stimuli become effective. It is especially apparent in cases where considerable time elapses between the operation of the object-determining stimuli and the discharge of the instinctive act. Thus, as far as I have been able to observe, the object of the jackdaw's *(Coloeus monedula spermologus)* innate mating behavior is already determined during the young bird's nesting period. Young jackdaws that are taken over by humans around the time they become fledged, will transfer the actions normally directed toward their parents to the humans; but it is too late to transpose their sexual behavior. This cycle only shifts to a human if the animals are adopted much earlier. A musk drake *(Cairina moschata)* hatched with four siblings by a pair of grey geese, and led by them for seven weeks, subsequently proved to be bound to his siblings, that is, to his own species, in all his social activities. But when his mating reactions awoke the following year, they were focused on the species of the foster parents, to whom he had paid no attention for over ten months.

The acquiring process in question has a second characteristic: it is dependent on specific conditions in the young animal's development. This has just been illustrated in the jackdaw and musk duck. The duration of the susceptible period can be determined more accurately for the following reactions of several young autophagous birds. The period during which young mallards *(Anas platyrhynchos)* pheasants *(Phasianus)*, and partridges *(Perdix)* adopt the object which they will follow lasts only a few hours. It begins as soon as the chicks have dried.

Irreversibility is the third essential character of the imprinting process. Once the critical period is over, the animal's attitude toward the object of its actions is exactly as though it were innate. As far as we yet know, it *cannot be forgotten*. On the other hand, as Bühler especially stresses, an essential quality of all learning is that it can be forgotten. Without forgetting, there could be no new learning. Of course, since our knowledge is so fragmentary, we can hardly claim that the process of imprinting is definitely irreversible. We infer that it is so from a few, accidentally gathered observations, all of which, to be sure, point the same way.

By stressing these three properties of the imprinting process I have already indicated the parallels that I am trying to develop. It is influenced by conspecific living material, it is restricted to critical phases in ontogenesis, and it is irreversible: these three characteristics differentiate it from all learning and place it in a, surely not insignificant, parallel with acquiring processes familiar from experimental embryology. One is strongly tempted to resort to the terminology of that science, and to say that the object of an instinctive action is determined by induction.

However these analogies may be evaluated, they nevertheless show that in the ontogenesis of instinctive behavior factors are at work which closely resemble those that operate in the ontogenetic development of *organs,* at any rate far more closely than those which figure in the development of mental achievements. *In this respect, too, instinctive actions behave like organs, and this one fact is the point I wish to make in drawing all these parallels.*

The second main point of the Spencer-Lloyd Morgan hypothesis is the assumption that *phylogenetically* the higher differentiation of instinctive activities has led to learned and insightful behavior in a flowing transition. I should now like to survey the few facts which can perhaps throw some light on two questions: (1) how instinctive action behaves in phylogenesis, and (2) its relations to acquired and insightful behavior.

In attempting to reconstruct the phyletic evolution of an instinctive act, we must depend on other sources of knowledge than in studying the phylogenesis of an organ. Palaeontology fails us; an ontogenetic recapitulation of ancestral types is hardly ever indicated. However, there are a few cases of the kind. For instance, pipits, larks, crows and some other *Passeres* run and walk instead of hopping. This type of locomotion is probably a secondary acquisition in them, not a primitive behavior as compared with the two-legged hopping of most passerines. Since running must be considered the more primitive locomotor pattern in the class of birds, it is an important corroboration of the above view that newly fledged pipits, larks and crows go through a hopping stage before walking matures.

Sometimes the course that the evolution of an instinctive action has taken can be inferred *a posteriori* from the behavior of hybrids. We know that hybrids, in their instinctive behavior as in many a physical trait, often do not represent an intermediate position between the parent species, but a throwback to phyletically older stages. Thus Heinroth was able to show that the mating ceremonies of a hybrid pair of *Tadorna* and Egyptian goose *(Alopochen)* were of the common type that is very widespread among *Anatidae,* and therefore the historically earlier one; yet the introductions to mating in both parent species are far more highly differentiated, and differ greatly from one another as well as from those of the hybrid pair.

In essence, however, the phyletic study of instinctive actions must depend on their behavior in the system. Here we face a field of research whose immensity can perhaps be compared to that of comparative anatomy. Today, this field is practically unexplored. As far as I know, there are four papers, two by Heinroth, one by Whitman and one by Kramer, that deal solely and systematically with the evolution of instinctive behavior in a selected group of forms, and Verwey has studied certain homologous instinctive actions in the group of herons. Ridiculously slight as this literature is in relation to the vast uncharted territory, it has yielded one very important result. All innate behavior patterns that could be followed up over a larger or smaller section of the zoological system can serve as taxonomic characters, exactly as the outward form of any skeletal element or other organ can. The study of certain groups, which we know from elsewhere are systematically related, even reveals that often an instinctive behavior pattern proves to be a *particularly conservative character,* since it occurs in the same form in a *larger* group than any structural trait. The following diagnosis of the highly self-contained group of *Columbae* is taken from a modern zoology textbook: Carinate insessorial, with a weak bill inflated around the nostrils, with pointed wings and low squatting or cleft feet. Not a single one of the characters listed is found in all species. The crowned pigeon *(Goura)* is not insessorial, *Didunculus* has a differently shaped bill. Again, *Goura* has short, round wings, like those of gallinaceous birds, and a whole number of ground forms do not have short legs at all. Thus even a combination of organic characters does not diagnose the whole group. If, on the other hand, pigeons are characterized by the fact that during the brooding period the male sits on the eggs from early morning until late afternoon, the female the rest of the time, we find that no member of the group is an exception. Moreover, I know of no other order of birds that could cause confusion by the same relay hatching behavior. I do not wish to suggest, of course, that we base systematics on instinctive actions alone, but merely to point out that they deserve serious attention as *one* taxonomic character among several.

This is particularly true of a highly specialized group of instinctive acts whose function is to *elicit social reactions* in a fellow member of the species. A comparative study of these particular releasing actions within an extensive systematic unit shows that they are even more constant, more impervious to change, than other innate behavior. The reason is evidently that the releasing and the responding actions constitute a sort of "understanding" within a species, and this understanding or code is especially independent of environmental factors. That the tail-wagging of canine carnivores is an appeasing peace signal, whereas a very similar motion in felines signifies a menace, is only a "convention" between releaser and answering innate mechanism of an animal form. As regards its function, the understanding could just as well be the opposite. Since its specific form, like the signs of a signal code or Morse alphabet, is determined purely historically, the identity of two releasing actions almost *always spells homology.* It is almost infinitely unlikely that an identity of releasing ceremonies in two species should ever have evolved by convergence. This view tallies with the fact that a comparative study of major groups reveals sequences so complete, whose intrinsic relationship is so obvious, as to be more convincing of genetic relations than any sequence known to me from the realm of comparative anatomy. The comparative student of innate behavior is frequently justified in making statements about genetic interrelations that are hardly ever permitted with equal assurance to the phyletic morphologist.

In discussing the different intensities of innate reactions I have already indicated (p. 134) that incipient actions, which are, in fact, incomplete discharges of certain actions, may acquire a secondary meaning through conveying a mood from one individual to another in social species. The primary factor in such cases is doubtless the development of an instinctive "understanding," a "resonance" to intention movements in fellow members of the species. The originally senseless intentive movement may then obviously be further differentiated and develop into a releasing action. Parallel to this evolution of stimulus-emitting factors, resonance readiness develops into a more closely defined releasing mechanism, a perceptual correlate that corresponds to the specific release in an astounding number of details.

The reactions which ensure that all the members of a flock take off together in various social ducks have probably undergone such an evolutionary process. The preparatory actions in a flock of mallards can easily be recognized as preliminary to a take-off which at the last moment does not take place. They will tell even a bird lover who does not know their special significance as releasers that the bird will rise into the air within a predictable time. The mallard crouches as if to jump up from the ground, and from this posture thrusts its head and the front of its body upwards briefly, much as for a real take-off—and yet, curiously enough, in some ways differently. In the greylag goose, on the other hand, the motion has come a long way from the original form of the intention movement, and would not betray the bird's taking-off mood to anyone who does not know its meaning. Here we find a strangely brief lateral jerking of the bill, which looks as if the goose wanted to shake water off it. However, the behavior of other *Anatidae* that display various intermediate forms of these motions makes it seem very likely that the patterns in greylag geese and in mallards are homologous. For instance, the take-off movement of the Egyptian goose (*Alopochen*), like that of *Anser,* is confined to the head, but it "still" goes upwards instead of sideways. The sequence is very impressive. Anyone familiar with the behavior of *Alopochen* would doubtless comprehend the motions of both *Anas* and *Anser* immediately.

Sometimes the age of a motor releaser can be gauged from its distribution in the zoological system, if only in relation to certain structural traits of a species. For instance, several closely related ducks of the genus *Anas,* among them our native mallard duck, have an identical, highly differentiated social courting ceremony. Though their coloring is by no means the same, a connection to this courting ceremony can indeed be detected in the striking colors and markings of the males in some of them: they are all located at points that stand out particularly when the movements common to all species are performed. Since species *without* such colorful markings have the same courting motions, I believe I may draw the conclusion that the innately determined *motions* of the ceremony are, in many forms, *older* than the structures and colors which enhance their releasing effect. In one case we can perhaps even estimate the absolute age of a ceremony. This is a greeting ceremony, specific to all night herons of the species *Nycticorax,* and also to the very divergent South American night heron *Cochlearius,* in the selfsame form. The structures that support this ceremony, namely, elongated and oddly differentiated head feathers, are completely different in *Nycticorax* and *Cochlearius,* and yet so fashioned that the same movement reveals their full effect. Since we can definitely estimate the time when *Cochlearius* was separated from the family of night herons, a conjecture about the palaeontological minimum age of an instinctive action can here be made!

I believe these few examples have made it plausible that comparative behavior study should follow the same lines as comparative anatomy: it should be practiced as a descriptive science. First, we should collect and describe instinctive behavior patterns; and collecting involves the need to experiment. Without this, we cannot know whether or not an action is innate. Field observation, as a rule, cannot tell. This brings us to the necessity of keeping animals, and of taking especially good care of them, since the slightest physical disturbance involves extensive losses in the realm of innate behavior. Merely to collect data on instinctive behavior is very laborious and also very expensive. Besides, it is extremely difficult to describe a behavior pattern so that one can be sure it will be recognized. What we need first is a usable and uniform terminology. The usage that animal lovers have developed spontaneously often suggests morphological usage in its earlier stages. Instinctive actions are named as organs, often even with the name of the man who first described them. We may discuss, for instance, whether the common heron's Verweyan "snapping motion" is homologous with the similar reaction which I have described in the night heron, etc. Moreover, instead of saying: "This or that species customarily acts thus or so," we say: "The species *has* this or that reaction." Even if we develop a usable set of terms, the communication of observations, especially for purposes of comparison, presents the greatest difficulties. It is a sorry sight to watch the vocal and dancing antics in which serious scholars have to indulge if they are to understand one another at all. There is only one way out of this quandary, of course: photography and, whenever possible, motion pictures. I am just now planning to study and film the very similar courting ceremonies of distantly related species of ducks of the genus *Anas,* as well as of crossbreeds between them, so as to gain support for my much-attacked claims concerning the homology of instinctive activities.

All the available facts on the function of instinctive actions in the zoological system point to the conclusion that the evolution of behavior runs parallel to the evolution of organs. We fully agree with Whitman, who said in 1889 that instinctive actions develop in phylogenesis according to the same laws and *at the same intervals* as do organs. We do not know what factors control the phyletic evolution of organs and innate behavior patterns. One thing, however, can be stated: to count individual experience among these factors is unwarranted.

An altogether different problem concerns the phyletic relations of instinctive behavior to learned and intelligent actions. Earlier, we took a very energetic stand against the Spencerian view that the highly complex and differentiated instinctive action is the forerunner of the variable behavior pattern.

A search for the basis of the thesis that instinctive action is the phyletic forerunner of learned and of intelligent behavior yields only the one fact that, among higher vertebrates, forms with higher mental faculties have doubtless developed from ones which, in comparison to them, had more highly differentiated instinctive actions. However, this fact is strictly limited to vertebrates. Even a superficial survey of the system must yield the conviction that no such simple relation exists between higher specialization of instinctive actions and the development of a capacity for learned and intelligent action. Generally speaking, one might say that there is an inverse ratio between the development of both types of behavior, though this only covers extreme cases such as social insects at one end of the line and anthropoids at the other. In forms that are so highly differentiated in one or the other direction, highly developed and specialized instinctive acts undoubtedly *inhibit* the higher development of variable behavior, and inversely, a far-reaching regression of innate activities is obviously the prerequisite for development of the latter. In higher vertebrates the evolution of intelligent behavior has definitely gone hand in hand with a corresponding devolution of instinctive activities. The function of genetically determined behavior is taken over by the plastic purposive action, which easily leads to the assumption that the latter developed from the former. But if instead of vertebrates we were to take insects and proceed as one-sidely as did Spencer, we would arrive at the opposite conclusion. In these animals, species with highly specialized systems of innate behavior patterns have surely developed from more adaptive ones. A cockroach is no less susceptible to training than a bee; in some respects it may even be more so. Should we wish to duplicate Spencer's procedure here, we would infer that instinctive actions had developed from learned and insightful behavior. This idea has in fact been suggested in Lamarckist quarters, to cite only Romanes' "habit theory" of instinct.

If, however, instead of contrasting extremes, such as insects and anthropoids, we compare closely related species with almost identical instincts, we find that their capacity for learned and intelligent behavior can differ astonishingly. I should like to illustrate this by means of the hiding reactions of two closely allied *Corvidae*. Common ravens and jackdaws, which the older classification included in one genus, have exactly the same innate motor coordinations for hiding leftover food. The two species display the following differences in their *application* of these identical movements. If a jackdaw has a morsel of food to hide, he shows appetence for the situation in which he can hide, that is, for a small cavity of some kind. In general, this appetitive behavior is limited to a mere orienting movement, almost invariably directed toward the darkest and deepest of the nooks and crannies accessible. The jackdaw is incapable of learning by experience that the act of hiding loses its meaning if it can be seen by other jackdaws while performing it. Nor does it ever realize that certain places, which can only be reached by flight, are inaccessible to its human friends, and that anything it hides there is safe. The common raven, on the other hand, soon finds out that it can only recover its food if no one watches it hide it. Moreover, if the hidden food is removed several times, the bird will hide objects only in high places that man cannot reach. The motor coordinations of the raven are not a whit less rigid than those of the jackdaw. Furthermore, it is easy to show in an experimental situation that the hiding reaction is its own purpose in both jackdaw and raven. In captivity both will at times perform it *ad nauseam* without rhyme or reason. Finally, it can be demonstrated that the raven has no insight into the essence of "hiding," in the sense of removing what it hides from sight.

Thus the difference between the behavior of jackdaws and ravens is confined to what we call appetitive behavior, in this case to an orienting mechanism inserted into a chain of innate actions. The genetically determined components of these two interlockings with very different functions are *absolutely identical* in both birds. The inserted noninstinctive constituents, on the other hand, have undergone an extensive change.

From a simple oriented motion, which affects the onlooker as a mere taxis, these noninstinctive components have developed into learned, perhaps even intelligent behavior, in so far as we may assume that the jackdaw's behavior should be considered the more primitive of the two. From all we know about the "behavior" of instinctive actions in the system, a very slow tempo must be assumed for their phyletic variability, in analogy to the variability of any highly conservative organ. Learning ability, on the other hand, appears altogether unpredictably and *suddenly* in the system. That startling, leap-like progress in the evolution of the higher mental faculties, to which man owes his prodigious advance beyond his closest zoological relatives, is found repeatedly, though to a lesser extent, in the animal kingdom.

Many authors, as we have seen, formulate the concept of instinctive action so broadly as to include appetitive behavior as one of its constituents. From this they naturally deduce that higher, intelligent behavior develops from what they see fit to term instinctive. Even so, at least from Craig who explicitly divides instinctive action into appetitive behavior and consummatory act, one would expect the statement that only the appetitive component can be compared with learned and intelligent behavior patterns and regarded as their forerunner.

With due emphasis, therefore, I shall now make this statement, to which Craig himself could hardly object. We believe that, in principle, all animal behavior can be regarded as a combination of appetitive behavior and consummatory action, in so far as it constitutes a functional "whole." Both types of behavior together secure the survival value of an action. One or the other may be more highly specialized. Within a certain behavior pattern this may occur to the detriment of the other component, until in some cases it may disappear altogether. Animals with highly specialized innate behavior patterns, such as bees, are born into the releasing stimulus situations to such an extent that, in many of their instinctive activities, there is no trace of appetitive behavior which must first precipitate these situations. At the other extreme, the instinctive act whose consummation constitutes the subjective purpose of an action chain may retreat so far toward the end of the chain that the entire motor pattern, which performs the work that has survival value for the species, is controlled by the purposive component. As the mental faculties of a species grow, the goal of its purposive behavior may be set farther ahead, until ultimately the invariably instinctive end of the action chain is reduced merely to an emotionally accented situation. The mental faculties of a weaverbird are just sufficient to attain the stimulus situation in which its highly specialized innate nest-building behavior is released. The appetitive element of nest-building, aside of a few orienting motions that occur later, is limited to attainment of this particular stimulus situation, in which the presence of suitable nest materials, of a crotch, etc., are effective. A man in a roughly similar biological situation accomplishes the entire work of acquiring a dwelling by purposive behavior. The genetically determined end of his action sequence is the emotionally accented situation of being at home and secure. C. Bühler assumes that with progressive rudimentation of the innately determined motor component, such end situations become more stressed emotionally; that stronger motivation compensates for the greater task set for appetitive behavior.

It is an *essential* quality of instinctive behavior that it copes with tasks to which the mental faculties of a species are not equal. For this reason alone, it seems impossible that an animal should be able to improve upon its own instinctive actions through learning or insight. Strictly speaking, we cannot really decide whether in principle instinctive behavior can or cannot be modified by learning and insight. We can only say that no such adaptation occurs, because the tasks which an animal's environment sets and which it solves instinctively *always* go far beyond the mental capacity of the species. The ability to solve a task of this kind by learning or insight evidently never exists *side by side* with an instinctive motor pattern which fits the same task. The reason is probably that *once* the ability to solve a task by learning or insight appears in the phylogenesis of a species, this solution, with its adaptive plasticity, must have far higher survival value than any mastering of the same task by rigid instinctive actions. This may well be the main cause for the rudimentation of instinctive behavior in mentally high-ranking forms.

Moreover, the existence of an innate behavior pattern seems to hinder the development of a learned or insightful performance with the same function. In man, at any rate, this is so. To test the truth of this statement one has but to observe the conduct of outstanding people, otherwise endowed with good self-criticism, in the surely instinctive reaction of selecting their mates by "falling in love." No doubt the above example of jackdaw and common raven shows that, within limits, mental faculties may develop without a reduction of the innate links in an action chain. But if evolution continues in this direction, the instinctive acts will ultimately recede.

Now I picture this process of reduction as follows: *within* the existing purely instinctive processes, and the genetically determined components of integrated behavior patterns, *new* gaps with inserted appetitive behavior appear. Whitman voiced a similar view, when he said about the easily demonstrable regression of instinctive actions in domestic animals: "In undomesticated species a higher degree of rigidity must be maintained with regard to instincts, whereas in domesticated species they are *reduced* (my italics) to varying degrees of adaptability, so that they display a correspondingly greater freedom of action, accompanied, of course, by a heightened probability that irregularities and so-called 'errors' will occur. These 'instinct errors,' far from being signs of psychic regression, are in my opinion the first signs of a greater plasticity of innate motor coordinations." Elsewhere he says that the intellect shows a tendency "to break up instinctive action," and again, he makes the following statement: "Plasticity of instinct is not intellect, but it is the open gate through which the great teacher, experience, gains access to call forth all the wonders of the mind." If we change "plasticity" to our more clearly delineated concept of a "faculty to acquire," which is inserted into a sequence of instinctive motor patterns, we can agree fully with Whitman's view as formulated in the above statements.

Rudimentation of the instinctive element in the behavior of all animals, and probably of humans, does not go beyond a certain point. I recall Wallace Craig's statement that the end of the action sequence is always instinctive. Instinctive motor processes which constitute the goal of appetitive behavior, and whose releasing stimulus situations are craved, are often retained in humans, too. The most "appetizing" foods are distinctly those which emit the stimuli that release salivating, chewing or swallowing with particular intensity. Some foods are considered delicacies although they activate only one of these functions, but that one they elicit very well: thus, for instance, the easily swallowed oyster, or some pastries which are almost tasteless but whose particularly crisp consistency evokes lusty chewing. In other cases, as shown on p. 153, the instinctive motions disappear completely, the innate goal of the action is rudimented, and there remains a stimulus situation that is pleasurably accented and therefore craved, but in which no further processes are released.

In solving any given task set by the animal's life space, appetitive behavior and consummatory act function vicariously, in the sense that if the one predominates in the work to be performed, the other is naturally unburdened and reduced. In this sense, higher differentiation of the one or the other represents two separate possibilities and *trends of evolution* in animal behavior. On higher levels, specialization in one of these directions is in all likelihood irreversible and exclusive of a later differentiation in the other. It also probably always involves a *reduction* of behavior patterns differentiated in the other direction.

Accordingly, our conclusion regarding the phyletic interrelations of instinctive and purposive behavior contradicts the teachings of the Spencer-Lloyd Morgan school, as do our conclusions regarding the influence of individual experience on the ontogenetic development of instinctive activities.

II.   McDougall's Instinct Theory

McDougall's instinct theory follows that of Spencer and Lloyd Morgan in that it assumes every possible gradation between instinctive actions on the one hand, and learned as well as intelligent behavior on the other. His instinct concept is particularly broad. Any type of behavior that comprises even the slightest instinctive element he terms instinctive forthwith. Thus it is comprehensible that he should regard instinctive action as essentially purposive behavior.

But McDougall's theory is distinguished mainly by the adoption of superordinated "instincts," directed at specific goals, which supposedly employ subordinated "motor mechanisms" as *means to an end.* In America, where the word "instinct" has lately become outmoded, the terms "first order drives" and "second order drives" are used with meanings equal or very similar to McDougall's "instincts" and "motor mechanisms." McDougall and more recent authors regard this alleged means-end relationship as proof that the first order instinct or drive is truly purposive.

McDougall groups the instinctive actions of animals and humans under the concepts of precisely thirteen superior instincts, by purely functional considerations. It hardly occurs to him to consider the evolution of instinctive actions or their distribution in the zoological system, or to take into account the fact that functionally homologous instinctive actions may appear independently of each other in different species. He is not concerned with the phenomena of homology, which are so important for our approach, or, for that matter, with the comparative ethological approach. Therefore function to him is not simply a principle of classification, but the essence of instinct. For the same reason, he never says that the instinctive activities of animals and men can be divided into so and so many functional groups, but rather dogmatically asserts the existence of thirteen instincts.

Let us first examine the notion of higher and inferior instincts more closely. For instance, McDougall adopts a "parental instinct," which employs all the innate motor patterns displayed by any animal in the care of its young, as means to an end. When discussing behavior patterns made up of instinctive and purposive elements, we have already shown how, in normal conditions, each innate part function blends into a functional entity with the appetitive behavior directed toward it, in delicate biological harmony. But we have also seen how easily this unity is disrupted by omission of one seemingly unimportant link in the chain.

Another instance of this: I was able to prove by experiments with ducks leading their young that their diverse fostering reactions are totally independent of each other in their release. They are synthesized into a well-planned functional entity solely by the fact that their releasing cues are found together in ducklings of their own species. The "wholeness" is destroyed as soon as these releasing factors are presented in *separate* objects. Thus a musk duck (*Cairina moschata*) will defend a mallard duckling as one of its own species. But no sooner has the duck "rescued" the newcomer "valiantly" from the experimenter's hands, than the duck treats it in the most hostile fashion. This behavior can be explained from the fact that the duckling's distress call, which elicits the defense reaction as a reflex, is very similar in mallard and musk ducklings, whereas the characteristic designs on head and back, which control other fostering reactions, are rather different in ducklings of the two species. To my mind, the fact that the functional unity of functional part cycles, which are supposedly controlled by one "parental instinct," can be disrupted by the absence of one small organic cue, proves the autonomy and homology of the participant actions. *To assume a "whole-producing," directive instinct superior to all part reactions could evidently be justified only if the effects of a regulative factor, exceeding the experimentally demonstrable regulative faculty of the single reactions, could be observed.* A first order instinct of the kind, that could compensate for disturbances in the integration of component reactions, and restore wholeness by coordinating the single reactions, has never been seen in operation. Nor do we think its assumption warranted. It is our opinion that a great number of autonomous part reactions achieve functional unity only because they are synthesized within the phylogenetically "grown" structural and functional plan of the species. This may appear far-fetched to those who only know instinctive actions in their normal manifestation, which fulfills their biological meaning, and are not familiar with the miscarrying reactions so easily produced in the experiment, which speak so clearly in support of the views here presented.

McDougall speaks of "one instinct" when a system of innate actions appears synthesized into a whole by a common function. From a purely functional point of view, such a classification is no doubt possible. For example, all the instinctive actions that participate in breeding and care of the young can be called "parental instincts." But the term cannot be used in the *singular*. Everything that we term instinctive behavior here would, according to McDougall, be classed as "motor mechanisms"!

Any one of the innate part actions within a longer functional unit of behavior can be conceived as being super- or subordinated to another only from a quite definite point of view. However, as far as I know,

McDougall never adopts this stand; as a matter of fact, we owe it to Wallace Craig. To illustrate it by an example, we shall assume that a blackbird, after long rest, shows appetence for the stimulus situation in which its food-seeking behavior is activated. The bird will next display purposive behavior, by which it strives to attain a situation in which it can successfully perform the rainworm-boring typical of many thrushes. This behavior will include a wealth of instinctive motor patterns such as running, hopping, flying, etc. In its entirety, including the craved end reaction of rainworm-boring, the whole sequence is a typical integrated behavior pattern. Now there is a whole series of instinctive actions, which normally appear almost exclusively in interlockings, and whose purposive end is the discharge of *another* innate reaction. As a rule, this type of action is not the goal of appetitive behavior striving solely for its performance. Most of them are "simple" patterns, as in particular all kinds of locomotion, glancing, grasping, pecking and the like. These coordinations actually function like *tools,* like *organs,* which the animal can apply to diverse purposes. However—and this is a point I wish to stress—they do not function as the means of a "superior instinct." They are *tools of purposive behavior,* even though the goal of this appetitive behavior is the discharge of an instinctive act. Tool reactions, like organs, can be applied in the service of *various* appetences without themselves changing. A bird's beak shows no "adaptive variability" of form, whether it happens to be pecking food, fighting, or building a nest. Nor does the innate motor coordination of these actions ever change. If a flycatcher has young to feed, it goes through the motions of its usual fly-hunt "in order to" discharge his feeding reaction, and not for the sake of eating, as it does in other circumstances. But the motor pattern is identical in both cases. The constancy of motion, its imperviousness to learning, is demonstrated strikingly in the following instance. A female canary that I had not set to breed, carried out the motions of anchoring the foundation of her nest with the green feed handed her: In this motor pattern, the bird steps on the blades that are to be interwoven, and works with her beak on the projecting ends until they are wound around the branch and firmly anchored. Since she was given edible greens, this bird soon learned to hold green food down with her foot and then bite small pieces from it. She thus learned to use a behavior pattern which really serves the biological purpose of nest-building, and in that form does not in the least look like a tool reaction, in the service of another drive, namely, the appetence for feeding. The motions which the bird now made were exactly like those of a titmouse, a raven or any other passerine bird that has the innate reaction of holding down large morsels of food with her foot. It is interesting to note that this female canary "knew" the acquired holding down of her food with her foot only while she was in the physiological phase of nest-building. Toward summer she lost this faculty again, although I deliberately gave her a chance to practice it daily by handing her large lettuce leaves. At this time the bird simply "did not have" the reaction of stepping on the leaf. Her learning ability was not sufficient to reproduce this tool reaction. But it had been sufficient to make use of the motion, while it was available, for other purposes besides its real biological goal. There really is a great difference between learning a new use of an inherited tool, and the free creation of a new tool.

These findings in the female canary show that even instinctive actions, which certainly are not "tool reactions" or "second order instinctive acts" in field life, may occasionally be applied in a new field, subordinated to a different type of appetitive behavior through learning. Conversely, instinctive actions that are normally controlled by striving for another activity may at any time become autonomous goals in an experimental situation, and come to represent the goal of specific appetitive behavior striving solely for their discharge. Only by analyzing the individual case can we claim that one instinctive action is subordinated to another and is only carried out for the sake of the latter. To say that a certain innate reaction is generally a subordinate one is *a priori* wrong, as I shall proceed to show. It therefore seems totally misleading to give the "tool reaction" a different name from the instinctive action "proper." This is what Tolman does, for instance, when he labels what we have called subordinate instinctive actions as "innate skills," thus differentiating them from instincts. Such a clearcut distinction is not feasible. On the one hand, reactions which normally function as the tools of a different appetence may be sought for their own sake; and inversely, autonomous instinctive activities may sink to the status of a subordinate action and be used as the tools of a new purposive behavior, as illustrated in the female canary. In natural conditions, the blackbird mentioned in an earlier example hops and flies only in order to get somewhere. A caged blackbird, on the other hand, hops and flies perplexedly up and down in its dwelling. It does not even take the abnormal conditions of captivity to make locomotor patterns an end in themselves. As soon as their service in the yoke of other appetences is somewhat alleviated, they themselves may obviously become the goal of purposive behavior. It is practically impossible to wear out a temperamental dog or a healthy raven by purposive locomotion to the point where they will not run or fly for the sake of doing so in their free time. If we eliminate the purposive need for such motions completely in the experiment, most animals will perform them as energy-accumulation activities almost as persistently and frequently as under the pressure of a goal to be attained. Typical tool reactions in particular will occur quite independently of the end that normally concludes the action chain meaningfully. The greylag goose spends a large part of the day grass-pulling and "up-ending" (this term, in hunters' parlance, means feeding from the ground with the neck stretched vertically downward and tail up). These motions are quite independent of their biological aim, which is to get food. If a grey goose is brought indoors at night after feeding outdoors all day, it will resume the plucking, feeding movements on every possible or impossible object after just a few minutes. Only if one has witnessed the intensity of these vacuum reactions can he gain an impression of the truly elemental force with which even these simplest of motor patterns demand and attain release. It is equally impressive when a flock of grey geese performs up-ending motions on a pond devoid of all vegetation, almost as persistently as though they had to procure their entire food supply, whereas their only available source of food stands on the shore in a full feeding dish. The lay observer is amazed and wonders what on earth the birds can be finding in the clear water. Up-ending, as well as plucking, can thus be a fully autonomous behavior pattern. On the other hand, beyond the animal's need to perform the reaction for its own sake, the animal may, of course, use the same motor patterns as means to attain a stimulus situation correlated to another instinctive activity. Thus a grey goose may equally well up-end *in order to* achieve the stimulus situation that elicits feeding. Now, to go on with the same example, if the human observer sees the goose first sound and then consume what it has fetched up, he is all too inclined to this interpretation, for the simple reason that *in man* the reactions of eating are instinctive and therefore pleasurable, whereas those of food-getting generally are not. Strictly speaking, even human motivation shows exceptions. For instance, my daughter at the age of five ate berries in moderation if they were set before her in a bowl. But she overate if left to herself, unwatched, in a blueberry patch. One may really say that there she did not pick berries for the sake of eating, but ate for the sake of picking. In other words, she displayed a ratio directly inverse to the usual one between the reactions of acquiring and consuming food. I have found very similar behavior in grey geese. If I sink vegetable food to the appropriate depth, it may happen that the up-ending animals fetch up the plants and, once they have them in their bills, proceed to chew and finally to swallow them, although they are so replete that it would not occur to them to pick up and eat the same plants presented in a dish. In grey geese and humans this relationship between the reactions of getting and consuming food may be regarded as a "captivity symptom"; but in a great many animals it constitutes the scarcely changeable norm. Thus the highly specialized innate food-getting activities of numerous predators are accompanied by intense sensual pleasure. Here they are the real goal of appetitive behavior, while the actual eating motions represent a mere mechanical continuation of an action chain that has once begun. In captivity such animals often do not eat enough, because the stimulus situation that is the real object of their "appetite" is totally lacking. It is an entirely unwarranted anthropomorphism to assume that the goal of appetitive behavior in every animal is an *analogon* of the actions that constitute this goal in human behavior. Yet, explicitly or not, the arguments of all those who believe in super- and subordinated instincts are based on this assumption. We always miss an analysis of the individual case, which alone warrants the assertion that one reaction is subordinated to another in that particular case, and that the animal uses it as a means to the second reaction there.

McDougall does not seem to see the need for an analysis of this kind. The main reason for this is probably that from the beginning, he identifies the biological value of an action sequence with its purpose as given subjectively to an animal. The following thesis on p. 101 of his *Outline of Psychology* would appear to imply that he is completely unaware of the phenomena just discussed: "It is probable that to some extent all instinctive action depends on appetite. The beast of prey hunts only when it is hungry. The satiated cat sometimes lets mice play on its tail." We have seen that this is not necessarily so. The beast of prey does not hunt when its hunting reactions have been thoroughly exhausted and it is satiated besides. If it is hungry, then, provided it belongs to a mentally higher species, it will in certain conditions perform its hunting reactions "for the sake of feeding," although it really "does not feel like hunting." The "hunting mood," however, the appetence for the pertinent instinctive actions, appears quite independently of the animal's nutritional condition. Good nourishment, after all, so long as it does not impair the animal's agility by fat accumulation, has not the slightest influence on the hunting passion of a dog! A mentally lower ranking animal, such as a grebe, hunts only because it has an appetite for the reaction itself, and does not discharge the pertinent actions more intensely if it is hungrier. The grebe, one might say, always feeds only for the sake of hunting, and soon starves to death if its food is presented in a manner that eliminates the innate behavior of chasing its prey.

But what we miss most in McDougall and others with similar viewpoints are definite statements as to how they really picture the relation between instinct and instinctive act. I am equally uncertain about this in modern authors who use the word "drive." It is strange that scientists who strive so radically to limit all their remarks to objective facts should not make animal *behavior* the object of their studies, rather than make statements about "instinct."

Since McDougall was unfamiliar with all the observational facts discussed above, or at any rate ignored them, we may well ask what induced him to adopt super- and subordinated instincts and, in particular, a definite number of the former. We have seen that equality of survival value in a group of instinctive actions cannot lead to this inference. By the same token, one might set up far broader functional categories, as everyday usage does when it refers to an instinct of self-preservation and the like. Similar formulations of ideas are found in psychoanalysis. But this is not how McDougall arrived at his notion of the directive instinct. To suppose so would be to underestimate his importance considerably. It is McDougall's great and lasting merit that he saw the close relationship which exists between instinctive behavior on the one hand, and emotion on the other. He regards these subjective phenomena as correlates of instincts in the subject's experience. From the number of qualitatively distinguishable human emotions he then infers the number of human instincts. The categories of instincts thus obtained are primarily meant to represent the instincts of humans and mammals. For the rest, however, they are treated throughout as the only "first order instincts" existing anywhere in the animal kingdom.

As regards the basic idea that instinctive reactions are accompanied by subjective phenomena and that a specific correlate in the shape of a certain emotion or impulse is coordinated to the single reactions in the subject's experience, all good zoologists and animal lovers are, consciously or unconsciously, in agreement with McDougall. Thus Verwey defines instinctive action as a reflex process "accompanied by subjective phenomena," a somewhat bold, but excellent definition of instinct. Heinroth speaks of the "moods" of animals, which are correlated to certain qualities of excitation, and coins compound words such as flying mood, nest-building mood, etc., by adding the word "mood" to the name of an instinctive activity.

These exceedingly serviceable neologisms of Heinroth's indicate the points where a zoologist cannot go along with McDougall's names for instincts. The number and quality of his superior instincts, as we have seen, follow those of the distinguishable human emotions. Transferring this classification to animals constitutes the mistake that Heinroth ingeniously avoids by means of his newly coined expressions. The seemingly less important links in a functionally uniform chain of actions, as independent mosaic stones, are as essential for the function of the whole as any others, and can be released independently of them. To be consistent, qualitatively distinct and independent emotions and impulses must therefore be adopted for each of these components as well. Consequently, *many more* emotional qualities must in most cases be ascribed to animals than we know in humans, whose emotional life has presumably undergone a similar process of simplification and dedifferentiation as have their instinctive actions. McDougall's categories, which correspond to the human mind, are obviously *too few in number* to describe the subjective processes of animals.

To illustrate: Bankiva hens and domestic hens *(Gallus bankiva)* have two different alarm calls, depending on whether they have sighted a predator in flight or a ground robber. If the excitation specific to the bird of prey reaches high intensity, there ensues an escape reaction downwards, toward the ground into the dark, if possible *under* cover. This kind of excitation is compulsively linked with upward glances. At very low intensities it is conveyed by these eye movements alone. On the other hand, if the other quality of excitation, which corresponds to the alarm call for a ground enemy, reaches a high level of intensity, the hen generally rears, takes off, but does not flee over long stretches. Surely one cannot correlate the same experience to these two, mutually independent reactions without committing an inexcusable anthropomorphism. The word "fear" surely is not enough to cover the bird's two clearly distinct qualities of excitation. Now if we adopt uniform qualities of excitation, we cannot, by McDougall's own procedure, infer a comprehensive "instinct of escape" as he does. As I have said before, such instincts can be referred to in the plural—but the singular is a mere word, without meaning.

As names for reactions grouped together from a functional viewpoint, McDougall's instinct categories are extremely serviceable, for, of course, instinctive actions that lead to escape from danger, care for the young, etc., occur in most animals. Still, all these expressions involve the danger that mere words may be accepted as concepts, if we forget that each of them can only be used as a *plurale tantum*.

III. The Reflex Theory of Instinctive Behavior

Ziegler's hypothesis of instinctive behavior contrasts sharply with that of the Spencer-Lloyd Morgan school. H. E. Ziegler says about instinctive action: "I have defined the difference between instinctive and intelligent types of behavior thus: the former are dependent upon innate pathways, the latter on individually acquired ones. Thus a histological definition is substituted for the psychological."

We shall overlook the fact that this definition contains a statement about "intelligent" behavior with which we cannot fully agree. It is a statement that can perhaps be suggested as a working hypothesis. For the time being, however, it can be neither proved nor disproved. But I should like to point out the interesting and by no means self-evident fact that radical mechanists are practically the only ones who look upon instinctive actions as chain reflexes. Biologists who are not mechanists usually adopt a somewhat emotionally tinged attitude against the suggestion that instinctive actions might be explained as reflex processes. McDougall in particular argues against the reflex theory of instinct as though it meant identifying the organism with a machine. This is understandable, since the authors to whom he rightfully objects attempted to carry through this leveling too dogmatically. Since instinctive activities most certainly constitute only a part of animal behavior, the animal will not be "degraded" to the status of a machine if we should succeed in interpreting instinctive processes in terms of reflex physiology. Such a procedure does not stamp an animal as a machine any more than, roughly speaking, the fact that we can explain fairly fully in mechanistic terms how a part of the human organism (for instance the elbow joint) functions, makes man a machine. The circumstance that mechanists have stood for the reflex theory and vitalists for the other views has had a disastrous effect on the discussion.

Before we can discuss whether our concept of instinctive action is comparable to the reflex, and if so, to what extent, we must clarify what we mean by reflex. It would be a fallacy to think that the word reflex is always applied to a notion of identical content, even though linguistic confusion has not gone so far here as in the case of the word instinct. For purposes of comparison, it is advisable to use the *narrowest* reflex concept possible. Identifications that involve *broadening* either concept are bound to be pseudo solutions. Bechterev's reflex concept is so broad that it includes all the motor processes of living organisms. It comprises the motions of protozoa, tropisms of plants, and even growth processes. With such a broad concept, our statement that instinctive action is a reflex process, while undeniably correct in form, would at the same time become worthless. A category superior to instinctive action and the current reflex concept can evidently be formulated. But by applying the term reflex offhand to this superior category, we become guilty of broadening the reflex concept, and may be accused of destroying the formerly achieved conciseness of the original, narrower concept, grounded in legitimate research, without substituting anything adequate for it. The damage thus done is surely not repaired by gaining a new viewpoint for classification. This criticism is directed solely against Bechterev's general terminology. What he says specifically about "hereditary organic reflexes," as he terms instinctive actions, is on the whole very much to the point.

For these reasons, we shall use the *narrowest* of the practicable reflex concepts in the following discussion of Ziegler's reflex theory, interpreting as "reflex" only a process based on an anatomical substratum in the shape of a "reflex arc." This reflex arc consists of a centripetal and a centrifugal pathway, together with an interposed minor or major sector of the central nervous system, which, as the "reflex center," transfers the excitation from the afferent to the efferent leg of the arc. Ziegler actually believed that instinctive activities were built up of such reflex processes with tangible anatomical correlates.

The most obvious objection to a reflex theory of instinctive behavior in this extreme formulation lies in the *regulative phenomena* which can be demonstrated in many instinctive acts, particularly in the simpler ones. I refer the reader to Bethe's experiments, whose main purpose was to point up that the theory of pathways and centers was untenable. Bethe was able to show in his amputation experiments that the locomotor coordinations of diverse animals are susceptible to numerous regulations. In polypods, such as crawfish, the number of possible stepping coordinations was so great that Bethe rightly pointed out how unlikely it was that each should depend on a separate "pathway." One can hardly suppose that a crawfish has a special "reserve pathway" available "to provide against" each experimentally produced combination of losses of feet! It is doubtful, however, whether the organism must actually react as a whole to effect these "whole-like" *(ganzheitlich)* regulations, or whether highly complicated systems of reflexes in the narrowest sense might not possibly explain them. A decerebrated frog surely cannot be considered a whole organism. All physiologists regard its reactions as mere reflex processes. Yet in its "wiping reflex" the frog reacts integrally. With its hind leg it always hits the stimulated spot with true aim, wherever the stimulus is applied, and if the colateral hind leg is confined, the frog will immediately use the other leg. Bethe's scruples concerning a neurophysiological interpretation of instinctive behavior are thus equally valid in the case of processes which physiology generally regards as reflexes.

Only in the simplest cases could the anatomical correlate in the shape of a reflex arc be traced with some precision. All the reflexes that neurologists have analyzed as to their pathways, such as a tendon reflex, the diaphragm reflex and so forth, are only known accurately as they operate in isolation from what goes on in the organism as a whole. Their neurophysiological explanation can therefore only be regarded as valid for a specific case. Now there exists every conceivable transition from these simplest processes, which can be rather fully defined in neuro-physiological terms, to "reflexes" which, like the wiping reflex of the frog, have the regulative faculty characteristic of instinctive actions.

If regulation constitutes an argument against the reflex theory of instinctive behavior, this argument applies equally to the neurophysiological interpretation of many processes which are generally regarded as reflexes. Consequently we cannot use regulation as a criterion to distinguish instinctive action from the reflex, unless processes like the frog's wiping reflex are also to be separated from the reflex as "instinctive actions." There is, in fact, something to be said for such a separation. Very few of the reflexes, whose anatomical foundations have been fairly well identified, can pass for behavior patterns with survival value if experimentally isolated. Important as they are to the neurologist, the biologist must really evaluate them as random phenomena. Nevertheless, their relationship to processes with survival value is so obviously close that, although the latter are barely accessible to analysis at present, no physiologist would seriously contemplate drawing a line between the two. Verworn's definition of the reflex even includes its survival value as an essential character. He says: "It is the essence of the reflex that an element which perceives the stimulus and one which responds to it *purposively* [my italics] are joined by a central connecting sector so that . . ." To separate instinctive action from the reflex as outlined above would mean defining both concepts according to the *tangibility* of their anatomical foundations and would thus be rather meaningless, since every new discovery in analytical research could bring processes hitherto regarded as instinctive actions under the reflex concept.

Finally, I believe that the regulative phenomena described *do not* preclude the possibility of explaining instinctive behavior in neuro-physiological terms. It seems quite feasible to construct mechanical models capable of imitating the regulations of locomotor patterns observed by Bethe. The structure of such a mechanical model of a reflex system would have to be exceedingly complex. But then, it would not occur to a reflexologist familiar with the facts that an instinctive act could be built up on anything but a very highly differentiated system of reflex pathways. Ziegler certainly did not think so. The phenomenon of regulation does not itself argue against the pathway theory in general, but only against the assumption that an instinctive action depends on a single pathway, or on a very few pathways.

If I defend the reflex theory of instinctive action and even follow it with some reservations, this does not mean that I rate it particularly high as a working hypothesis. In our study of instinctive behavior we rely on factual material derived from other sources than those of reflex physiology. To study instinctive actions with the methods of reflex physiology does not seem very promising. Since highly differentiated instinctive actions drop out immediately as a result of the slightest organic damage, we cannot draw any conclusions from the loss of a function after vivisectory interference. This purely technical difficulty greatly diminishes the value of the reflex theory of instinctive behavior as a working hypothesis.

The *different intensities* in the discharge of innate reactions (p. 134) constitute another objection to the reflex theory. We have seen that one and the same reaction may be very different in form, depending on the level of excitation. Since these manifestations merge into one another imperceptibly, it may be contended that they exist in an infinite number, and this number may be adduced against assuming an anatomical correlate for the process. On the other hand, these intensity scales reveal a regularity so compulsory, one is tempted to say, so "machine-like," that physical similes unwittingly flow into one's pen, suggesting expressions such as a "pressure of excitation."

Another attribute of instinctive action which, while not actually arguing against the reflex theory, yet cannot be explained from the reflex nature of instinctive processes, is the lowering of the threshold to releasing stimuli (cf. p. 143). We have seen that the threshold is lowered if the stimuli normally required to elicit a reaction are withheld for a long time. As a result, the instinctive action ultimately erupts independently, without any stimulation. We have termed this phenomenon "vacuum activity." None of these phenomena can be deduced from the stimulus-reaction pattern of the reflex. Therefore, to a follower of the reflex theory of instinctive behavior, they require additional explanation.

Such an explanation may possibly have something to do with the relations between the threshold decrease of releasing stimuli and the striving for these stimuli represented by appetitive behavior. Aside of their purely functional interdependence, we may look for relations between threshold decrease and appetitive behavior in the fact that both are connected with the subjective phenomena which accompany all instinctive behavior and the intensity of which undoubtedly increases greatly when an instinctive activity has been "dammed up" for some time. I should like to add this about the subjective aspect of the phenomena in question: apparently modification of a reaction usually strikes at the perceptual part of the "reflex arc." "Soon, with this draught in thee, Helen in every woman thou'lt see," says Goethe. Or, to quote a more prosaic example, the human salivating reflex, after prolonged starvation, will even respond to the odor of food from which we ordinarily turn in disgust. Eliot Howard says that the animal's perceptual field changes with differences in the intensity of a reaction. By this, he quite obviously means the same thing that I am trying to express here.

Craig evaluates the threshold decrease of releasing stimuli as a part phenomenon of "appetite," whose chief outcome is a purposive quest for these stimuli, that is, appetitive behavior. Since he includes this stimulus-seeking in the concept of instinctive action, as part of it, it appears quite consistent for him to do so. In fact, both *function* in unison, in that they heighten the animal's *readiness* for the reaction in question. But since our narrower formulation of the instinct concept compels us to go further in analyzing such functional units of behavior, we must distinguish the threshold decrease of releasing stimuli, as a quality of instinctive action, from stimulus-seeking appetitive behavior which, even at its most primitive, must be looked upon as an instance of higher, goal-directed behavior. The relations which may possibly exist between both do not affect this separation of concepts, nor do they contradict it in any way.

In the examples cited earlier and discussed in their subjective aspect the phenomenon in question is not only a lowering of the threshold to releasing stimuli, but also a reduced selectivity by the organism, a readiness to respond to not quite adequate stimulation. In object-directed behavior the reaction may, as a result, "make shift" with another, not entirely appropriate object, if the biologically adequate one is absent for a long time. Just like a biologically meaningful process, an instinctive action discharged at a substitute object immediately raises the abnormally low stimulus threshold again, even though the threshold value may not return to normal. As a result of this rise in threshold, of this heightened selectivity on the perceptual side of the reaction, the response to inadequate stimulation vanishes again after a very brief discharge. Consequently an instinctive action that is discharged long and repeatedly at the normal object will be activated only quite briefly or only a few times by the substitute object. Lissmann was able to show that the fighting reactions of singly kept male fighting fish *(Betta splendens)* could at first be elicited by very clumsy clay dummies, but were very soon exhausted. If he presented a series of dummies whose resemblance to a conspecific fighting partner diminished, the reaction was exhausted sooner. A night heron, whose chick we took out of the nest and set free in a meadow, responded to this abnormal stimulus situation by hovering the fledgling for an instant, only to rise again at once and go away from it. Shortly thereafter the bird defended the fledgling *once* against a peacock, but then, although this bird continued to menace the chick, the heron immediately turned its attention once more from both to the nurse who stood nearby quietly, and begged her for food. When the young bird was put back in the nest, the parent greeted it at great length and with intense "joy," immediately hovered it at great length, and defended it against me most furiously and indefatigably.

I am, in general, no great lover of physical symbols for biological processes. They lull one all to easily into the belief that a process has been causally analyzed and comprehended, whereas in truth only a very crude model of it has been understood. Yet I believe it is permissible, with this in mind, to use a model to symbolize how an instinctive action and its releasing stimuli work during and between discharges. Several times we have referred symbolically to "excitational pressure." And in fact, during the time that a certain activity remains undischarged, the animal behaves exactly as if some reaction-specific energy were being *built up*. It is as though a gas were constantly being pumped into a container, where the pressure is therefore continually growing, until, under quite specific circumstances, a discharge occurs. I should like to symbolize the various stimuli which lead to discharge of the accumulated "excitational pressure," by taps, which allow the piled-up gas to stream from the container once more. The adequate stimulus, or more precisely, the adequate stimulus combination, corresponds to a simple tap, which can reduce the pressure in the container to the level of the pressure outside. All other, more or less inadequate stimuli are represented by taps before which a block is inserted in the shape of a spring valve, which allows gas to escape only beyond a certain internal pressure. Consequently these taps can never completely relieve the pressure inside the container. The stronger the spring of the inserted valve, that is, the less the substitute stimulus resembles the normal, adequate situation, the less its power to relieve the internal pressure. The quick exhaustibility of inadequately released instinctive reactions can be symbolized very well in this way. But our model is imperfect in one important point: it cannot, or can but poorly represent vacuum activities. The elemental, downright explosive eruption of the reaction, which "pumps out" the animal to the point of exhaustion, cannot possibly be pictured as a blowing off of pressure through some sort of security valve. At best, it might be symbolized as a bursting of the whole container.

This nature of instinctive behavior, which renders the idea of endogenous processes of accumulation so plausible, is easy to fathom in all the reactions that cover an organic *need:* thus the innate reactions of absorbing food and water, of depositing feces, excrements and sexual products. In many of these we know exactly how the internal motivation, by way of more or less complex systems of indicators, grows into a subjective need, and relieves external stimulation of a major or minor part in releasing the reaction. However, I wish to emphasize that the animal's behavior is quite similar in a great many, possibly in *all* instinctive reactions, and even in those where there is no evidence of such internal stimulation. This independence from palpable internal motivation is particularly striking in the so-called negative reactions, the escape and defense reactions of many animals. These reactions best illustrate the lowering of the threshold to releasing stimuli, which occurs almost regularly in captive animals, especially in those that have grown up under human care. I was able to show that in birds raised from infancy the threshold of escape reactions was lowered particularly in species where the fledgling's escape is not released by the sight of instinctively "recognized" enemies, but rather by the warning call or, in general, by the fright-and-flight of the parents. In human care, such young birds are deprived of *all* adequate release for their escape behavior, and cannot get rid of it, as it were. As one would expect, the slightest substitute stimulus is liable to put them into quite a dangerous panic; they will even dash off suddenly, without any evidence of one—a most irksome habit when you are keeping animals. Many ungulates behave similarly, especially some antelopes. Here again, as Antonius informs me, individuals brought up in isolation by humans are particularly apt to dash themselves to death at the fence of the enclosure.

I have pointed out that the vacuum reaction is generally distinguished by a high level of excitation. In many innate behavior patterns, as for example in the escape reactions just discussed, it is perhaps always of *maximal* intensity. The intention movements and incomplete reactions described on p. 134 occur typically if the need for a certain reaction is slight and external conditions for its discharge are optimal; whereas, if internal motivation is high and environmental stimulation weak or even nonexistent, miscarrying behavior patterns of another kind appear. In the first case, incompleteness prevents the reaction from attaining its survival value. In the second, the reaction is complete, but its rigidity hinders fulfillment of the biological meaning, if the slightest adaptation is required of the action chain. *Both extremes clearly prove that there is no connection between the biological meaning of an instinctive behavior pattern and the goal toward which the animal subjectively strives.* In the one case, the survival value of a reaction is not attained because, although all the external prerequisites are available, the animal's internal "excitational pressure" is not sufficient to "drive it through" all the links in the chain; in the other, the animal carries out the full sequence with the utmost zeal, although all the stimuli allegedly needed as "behavior supports," and often even the purely physical conditions of the reaction, are lacking.

The completeness of action chains discharged *in vacuo* may at first tempt one toward a reflexological interpretation. The lowering of the stimulus threshold, however, which must rate as the process at the root of all vacuum activities, is something entirely foreign to the simple stimulus-response schema of the reflex. At least, as I have already pointed out, it requires a special explanation. Like the regulative phenomena, the threshold decrease does not necessarily mean that a reflex theory of instinctive behavior must be fundamentally wrong, but only that it is insufficient as an explanatory principle.

If we now ask whether the lowering of threshold can be used for a clear-cut conceptual separation of instinctive action from the reflex in its narrowest sense, the answer must be, No. After all, every change in excitability can be expressed as a change in the same process, but of opposite sign. While recovering from long and strenuous activity, diverse tissues that serve organic functions show a gradually rising excitability, a lowering of the threshold to releasing stimuli, which may vary greatly in quantity, but is unmistakably analogous. We are therefore certainly not dealing with a phenomenon restricted to the anatomical correlate of instinctive processes.

The most important character of the instinctive motor process which the S-R schema of the reflex cannot explain is that the behavior elements which we discussed fully on p. 139 as *purposive or appetitive behavior strive for it*. The fact that the goal of purposive behavior is the discharge of an instinctive act does not necessarily mean that its motor coordinations are not chain reflexes. But at present we have no idea why an animal craves the consummation of these particular chain reflexes, whereas he certainly has no such desire to discharge *all* his reflexes! It would not occur to anyone to crave the stimulus situation in which his patellar reflex is activated, solely for the sake of discharging the reflex. It is inherent in the nature of the reflex that, like an unused machine, it is ever in readiness, and enters into activity only when certain key stimuli affect the animal's receptors. That the reaction, as it were, announces itself spontaneously, that it causes restlessness and makes the animal *seek* these key stimuli actively, is not essential to the reflex. However, it does not argue *against* the reflex nature of the final process. In the simplest case, this seeking is a mere motor unrest, though even this operates as a search by the principle of trial and error. At the opposite extreme, it may be directed by the highest achievements of learning and insight ever encountered in the animal kingdom. The process that spurs the animal on to search, directedly or at random, for a specific stimulus situation (the only one in which the innate releasing mechanism of the craved reaction will respond) is what I should like to call "drive" (*Trieb*). I am fully aware that this drive concept is even more remote from the conventional than my notion of instinctive action.

There are undoubtedly two factors which move the animal directly to strive for the stimulus situation that releases the consummatory act. The first of these is what we have just named "drive." The second, after previous experience, are the pleasurable subjective phenomena which accompany the discharge of an instinctive act. Although we may never succeed in explaining these subjective phenomena causally, it is natural to put a finalistic construction upon them—merely, of course, in the sense of species survival. The animal is "driven and lured" to perform the motor patterns needed to maintain the species. We have already discussed (p. 138) how, when an animal is acquiring an instinct-training integration, the wish to function acts as a lure, inducing him to enter the path mapped out by species survival. Without this dual motivation of all appetitive behavior, there could be no assurance that instinctive acts would be performed often enough. One might say that, without it, a species would be doomed to speedy extinction.

Whereas upon closer inspection neither regulation nor the lowering of threshold proved an adequate criterion to distinguish instinctive action conceptually from the reflex, the fact that it is craved, that it is the goal of appetitive behavior can definitely be used to define instinctive activities and set them apart as reflex processes of a special kind. It might seem disturbing at first sight that such a definition of instinctive behavior should draw upon subjective factors. Let me therefore emphasize once more that we can give a purely objective definition of purposive behavior in Tolman's sense, from the standpoint of behaviorism (p. 138). The definition of instinctive action as a "reflex process for which the animal actively strives" is a more precise formulation of the instinct concept which Verwey states as follows: "Where reflexes and instincts can be distinguished from each other at all, the reflex functions mechanically, while instinctive activities are accompanied by subjective phenomena." A definition of purpose in the terms of objective behavior study and from its standpoint is, of course, valuable. But I believe it would mean deliberately ignoring an essential factor if we omitted to state that the *subjective* phenomena accompanying instinctive activities constitute the *immediate* purpose of appetitive behavior.

I realize that the definition of instinctive action as a craved reflex process is not entirely devoid of its philosophical difficulties. The combination of striving, an essentially psychological process, with the physiological concept of the reflex, has about it something of the naïveté of Descartes' notion that the pineal gland is the point of attack for psychological influences on organic processes. Yet this very fact clearly indicates the philosophically difficult, but for that very reason important and perhaps even revealing position of instinctive motor patterns in the theory of animal and human behavior; perhaps in this way a question which the nature philosopher has to ask the biologist is formulated more concisely.

Summary

This criticism of nearly all the established beliefs concerning the instinctive behavior of animals, and my formulation of a new concept of instinctive action, were prompted almost exclusively by *new observations*. The facts are by no means all gleaned from my own investigations. Yet they come from the studies of so narrow a circle of like-minded zoologists, and one so well known to me, that I may well assume they have never yet been taken into account in trying to get an idea of what an instinctive action really is. I should mention that I have been acquainted with most of these facts far longer than with the theories here criticized by means of them, and that I had developed the views presented in this paper, if not in their scientific formulation, nevertheless in all their basic essentials, before I had so much as heard the names of the great instinct theoreticians.

Since each of these observations occurs *repeatedly* in this paper, and has been discussed in different places in its bearing upon different issues, I believe my meaning can be conveyed most clearly by going over the facts in abridged form. In so doing, I propose to present them, not in the order in which they have appeared before, but in a sequence which, I think, reflects a gradation by their importance and scope.

With this in mind, I must definitely give the first place to the *instinctive action that fails to achieve its biological meaning*. Instinctive acts that remain incomplete from insufficient motivation (p. 134), and those that become biologically senseless through lack of external stimulation (p. 143), may both be observed very frequently in captive animals. At a very early age, they convinced me that the biological meaning of a reaction and the subjective purpose given to the animal had nothing in common and must on no account be identified. The extreme type of reaction that is senseless owing to lack of external conditions is the *reaction in vacuo,* which is discharged without an object. The truly photographical identity between its motor pattern and that of the normal process with survival value proves that the motor coordinations of instinctive activities are generically determined down to their smallest details. The vacuum activity makes it possible to study instinctive action in a pure culture, as it were, in captive animals reared in isolation. It must be accepted as an incontrovertible basic fact, which refutes a way of thinking that still has followers in America and attempts to derive all animal and human behavior from conditioned reflexes. Since the motions encountered in vacuum activities and normal, biologically meaningful reactions are the same, we cannot conceive instinctive action as a type of purposive behavior. It is a fallacy to maintain that any changes have ever been found in an instinctive behavior pattern in relation to a specific goal subjectively comprehended as such by an animal.

As a second basic fact I should like to recall the *distribution of instinctive actions in the zoological system* (p. 144), which shows that innate motor patterns behave exactly the same as organs in their phyletic variability, and that, like organs, they can and must be approached with comparative methods. A systematic comparison of innate behavior patterns shows forcibly how senseless it is to make statements about "instinct." Our statements can at all times refer only to innate motor patterns, to instinctive *actions,* and then only to those of a specific, larger or smaller taxonomic group.

Both facts, the completeness of motor patterns discharged without biological meaning, and the parallel evolution of organs and instinctive actions in the zoological system, must, in view of their inherent nature, make us suspicious of all allegations concerning adaptive changes of instinctive actions through individual experience. On the basis of our studies on the evolutional history of innate motor patterns, and of our experiments on their ontogenesis, it seems highly likely that, wherever individual experience has wrought an adaptive change in an instinctive action, a confusion with maturational processes has occurred.

The ontogenetic development of instinctive actions resembles that of organs in another way, the significance of which I would gladly let others judge. I have in mind the singular acquiring process which we have termed *imprinting* (p. 102). Its dependence on conspecific living material, its restriction to brief critical periods in individual development, and particularly its irreversibility, present distinct parallels to the process of inductive determination familiar from the field of experimental embryology.

Finally, I must mention the integrations or *interlockings* of instinctive and purposive behavior (p. 139). The fact that, in a functional unit of behavior, rigidly innate and adaptively modifiable components may alternate in direct succession, is of the utmost importance in two respects. In the first place, our accurate analysis of such motor sequences has saved us from assuming a gradual transition between instinctive action and purposive behavior and thus lapsing into the error of adopting an instinct concept that is much too broad because it includes appetitive behavior.

Secondly, the ontogenetic development of a certain type of integrated behavior pattern, namely, the instinct-training interlockings, has furnished proof of what Wallace Craig discovered and stated long ago: that in all goal-directed behavior, consummation of the instinctive act is the goal, and the purpose subjectively given to the animal (pp. 138-139). This gives us the only criterion for distinguishing instinctive action as a "craved reflex process" from other, "pure" reflexes (p. 144-145).

It may seem that this relatively small number of findings does not warrant such a fundamental departure from most of the prevailing beliefs. But I can see no danger in formulating my views concisely, so long as we bear in mind that they are in part mere working hypotheses, and that new findings may at any time compel us to change them.

I do, however, hope and trust that I have proved one thing conclusively: that the study of instinctive behavior is not a field for extensive philosophical speculation, but one in which, at least for the time being, experimental analysis of each individual case is the only legitimate procedure.

3

Taxis and Instinct

Taxis and Instinctive Action in the Egg-Retrieving Behavior of the Greylag Goose[1]

KONRAD LORENZ AND NICHOLAS TINBERGEN (1938)

Introduction

The experiments which we have carried out this year, dealing with the way in which the greylag goose retrieves eggs displaced from the nest, are by no means complete. Our subjects are not of pure wild strain but have some blood of domestic geese. We have made many control experiments with geese of pure wild strain and expect soon to report those experiments together with a more accurate analysis of the present data by study of motion picture films. However, in spite of such limitations, we feel that publication of the material in its present form is essential. Recent discussions of the theoretical position expressed by Lorenz in two papers (1937a and b) reveal several misunderstandings which should be cleared up as soon as possible. Our findings on the egg-rolling of the grey goose should help to accomplish this.

I. Theoretical Aspects of Taxis and Instinctive Action

However one may wish to interpret the word "instinct," the existence of certain "motor patterns," rigidly innate in the individual, will always have to be recognized. These movements may have great taxonomic

[1] This research, which was carried out with the support of the "Het Donderfonds" foundation, is the outcome of talks between the authors in Leiden and later in Altenberg about the concept of instinctive action formulated by Lorenz (1937a). Although our individual contributions can hardly be distinguished, we wish to say nevertheless that the theoretical arguments should largely be attributed to Lorenz, while the invention and execution of the experiments generally represent Tinbergen's share.

value for a species, a genus, or even for a whole phylum. Since they constitute the very core of what earlier students of animal behavior regarded as the manifestations of instinct, we have used, or rather, retained the expression "instinctive action" for them. Instinctive actions are remarkably independent in form from all receptor processes; not only from "experience" in the broadest sense of the word, but also from the stimuli that affect the organism during their operation. In this, they are clearly distinguished from the taxis or orienting reaction, although both types of reaction share a purposiveness in the sense of survival value, as well as an independence from individual learning, and are therefore often merged under the concept of "instinct." When Driesch defines instinct as "a reaction that is complete at its first appearance," this applies equally to motor patterns whose form is genetically determined, and to all innate orienting processes, regardless of the radical and fundamental difference between instinct and taxis. To convey an understanding of the approach that guides our work, the differences and relationships between taxis and instinctive action will have to be discussed in brief.

A. The Topotaxis

Most of the processes which, with A. Kühn, we shall call *taxes* and more particularly *topotaxes,* contain rigid instinctive actions in addition to orienting reactions; they "use" certain motor patterns, above all the locomotor ones. Nevertheless, the essential motor component of the topotaxis, which is specific to it alone, is that *turning* of the whole body or of one of its parts, such as the eyes or the head, which as a unit is steered by external stimuli in relation to the environment. This does not apply to the phobic reaction or phobotaxis in Kühn's sense. The latter reaction is related to the automatisms which we term instinctive actions. Its motor pattern is rigid, and independent of the kind and direction of external stimulation. Thus the phobotaxis is a very different kind of reaction from the topotaxis. The analogies between phobic reaction and instinctive action may be only superficial, and causally the two probably have but little in common, considering the dependence of instinctive actions on a central nervous system. Yet in developing our working hypotheses we would not wish to draw as sharp a contrast between these two types of behavior as we do between topotaxis and instinctive action.

K. Bühler called the turning which is typical for taxes in their widest sense, and which directs the animal in space, "oriented movement" *("orientierte Bezugswendung").* This very broad concept includes every change in the motor state of the organism that relates to the spatial conditions in its world. It comprises the simplest turning "toward" or "away from," as well as the most complex activities directed by environmental stimulation. The veering "away from" in phobic reactions, which is not wholly directed in relation to the environment, is thus included in this heading. We must therefore state that our concept of orientation refers to only part of the processes summarized by Bühler as oriented movements, namely, the turn which is directed throughout by environmental stimuli and characteristic of the topic reaction alone. Since, in the following comparison of taxis and instinctive action, we are concerned only with the topic reaction, we shall, for the sake of brevity, call it alone a taxis. It is, after all, only a question of expediency what terms one adopts, and our selection of terms for the briefest statement of the facts we wish to present is in no way intended as a criticism of other usage.

Even if a taxis as a whole contains motor patterns that are rigid in themselves, its total form nevertheless depends on the dimensionally stimulus-directed turn. It is essential to a taxis that its over-all motor pattern is adapted to spatial conditions in the environment, and this is achieved by the pattern of reacting to external stimuli. Without going into the purely metaphysical question of whether the animal steers subjectively by these stimuli or is passively guided by them, we may say that, objectively, movements with survival value are molded by stimuli from the outside. In the simplest and best analyzed cases this process is assuredly a reflex in the true sense of the word. But even in orienting reactions controlled by "higher mental faculties," what the central nervous system does is essentially to answer and utilize external stimuli, a process which, functionally at any rate, is reflexive.

B. The Instinctive Action

Instinctive actions are also related to reflexes, since they, too, are released by certain, often highly specific external stimuli. Closer investigation shows, however, that only the release is a genuine reflex, not the further course of the motor pattern. Once the movement is released, it seems to be quite independent of the animal's receptors as well as of further external stimulation. Unlike taxes, which are innate reaction patterns, instinctive acts are innate motor patterns.

It may appear unlikely at first sight that well-coordinated motor sequences with high survival value can be executed without participation of receptors, like the movements of a tabetic; in other words, that they are not built up of reflexes. However, there are many weighty grounds for assuming that such is the case. E. von Holst has found evidence of automatic-rhythmical processes in the central nervous systems of various completely deafferented organisms. The nervous impulses are integrated in the central nervous system, so that an impulse sequence with survival value emerges and is dispatched to the muscles without participation of receptors. Nearly all the centrally coordinated motor sequences which have been analyzed to date are locomotor patterns. And precisely these were almost universally regarded as chain reflexes, in which each motion was supposed to release the next one by a circuit through the peripheral receptors!

The motor patterns studied by von Holst must in all respects be regarded as instinctive actions in our interpretation of the term. This does not necessarily imply that, conversely, everything hitherto called instinctive action is based on identical processes in the central nervous system. However, a series of facts derived from observation and experiments (1937) indicate that basically the receptors, in the widest sense of the word, probably do not take part in the genesis of movements with survival value even in more highly differentiated instinctive activities. It may seem premature today to identify the motor mechanisms investigated by von Holst with instinctive action. Yet it may be pointed out that two of the most important and distinctive aspects of instinctive action, which present insurmountable difficulties to any other explanation, can be interpreted quite simply by adopting a hypothesis of automatic-rhythmical generation and central coordination of its impulses. These phenomena are the decrease in threshold to releasing stimuli, and the discharge *in vacuo* of instinctive acts, which may as a result occur even in situations where the action has no survival value.

An instinctive movement released by an unconditioned reflex, which normally appears only in response to a very specific set of external stimuli, is at times quite evidently independent in form from the releasing stimuli. If these stimuli are absent longer than they would be under ordinary conditions, the instinctive response becomes less selective in its stimulus requirements. The animal now responds with the same motor pattern in stimulus situations which only resemble the usually adequate one. The similarity of effective stimuli to those which normally alone release a reaction decreases with the length of time that it has been "dammed up." In cases where the nature of stimuli that release a specific instinctive act allows some quantification, we find that the intensity of the liminal stimulus required to elicit the reaction sinks continually with the length of the quiescent period. Since both phenomena are obviously based on one process in the central nervous system, Lorenz summarized them by one term: "lowering of threshold" (1937*a* and *b*). Now in very many, perhaps in all instinctive actions, the threshold may decrease until it literally attains a minimum value of zero. After being dammed up for a shorter or longer time, the full motor sequence is carried out perfectly without any demonstrable external stimulus. We usually term this phenomenon a reaction *in vacuo*. Lowering of threshold and vacuum reaction furnish a twofold argument for assuming automatic-rhythmical generation and central coordination of impulses.

The phenomenon of diminishing thresholds lends plausibility to the idea of an internal accumulation of reaction-specific excitation—von Holst speaks of excitational substances—which is produced continually by the central nervous system and rises in proportion to the time during which discharge of a specific instinctive action fails to afford relief. The higher the state of tension attained, the more intensely will the instinctive act be discharged when it finally breaks through, and the more difficult it will be for the higher "centers" in the central nervous system to prevent the instinctive act from erupting in the "wrong" place. These ideas, roughly simplified here, were evolved in ignorance of von Holst's findings. But now we actually know, owing to him, that discharge of the continuous impulse flow from "automatic centers" is constantly blocked by the activity of higher or more centrally located parts of the nervous system, and that release of the reaction simply means that these central checks are lifted. Left to themselves, the lower centers (in the case of von Holst's experiment a spinal preparation) carry out the movement incessantly, in keeping with the automatic rhythm. If, in the spinal preparation, certain additional stimuli are substituted for the checks otherwise supplied by the activity of higher centers, there ensues a phenomenon which Sherrington called "spinal contrast." The longer and the more intensely this inhibition is applied, the more violently will the inhibited motion break forth when it ceases. This conformity between the automatic rhythms studied by von Holst, and instinctive actions in our interpretation, is apparent down to the smallest details, which we do not propose to discuss in this place.

The lowering of threshold and the heightened intensity, which can be observed in almost all instinctive activities that have been dammed up for some time, clearly argue for assuming an automatic production of impulses. Similarly, the ultimate, spontaneous eruption, the vacuum activity, suggests that the impulses sent out by this mechanism are centrally coordinated. It is surely significant that the form of a behavior pattern which is often literally performed "in a vacuum" resembles in every detail the reaction displayed under normal conditions, where the action has biological value. This is particularly striking in actions which normally have mechanical work to do; that is, the movement ordinarily ensues against a resistance which is lacking in the case of an "empty run" reaction. This will be discussed in more detail later. The complete independence of the motor pattern from environmental conditions and stimulation can be explained only by assuming that the impulses for the single muscular contractions emerge from the center ordered in form and sequence. Otherwise it would be inexplicable that, for example, a starling should carry out the sequence of actions required for catching, killing and swallowing small insects when there are no such insects present, or that, as Lorenz recently witnessed in the Berlin Zoo, a hummingbird should fasten "nonexistent nesting materials" to a twig with a wonderfully coordinated weaving motion.

Vacuum activities show that instinctive motor patterns do not depend on exteroceptive processes. The part which proprioceptive reflexes may play in the discharge of highly differentiated instinctive acts, on the other hand, is uncertain as yet. We do find, however, that even very coarse mechanical interference, which temporarily prevents the discharge of an instinctive movement, or forces the animal's body into an unnatural posture, entails no change in the later phases of the action. Once the mechanical pressure ceases, the reaction runs its typical course. Yet changes would have to occur if proprioception of each partial movement determined the form of the following one, as the chain reflex theory of instinct assumed. No such modification has ever been seen yet.

For these reasons we may adopt as a working hypothesis the assumption that instinctive actions, in the coordination of their constituent motions, are independent of all receptors and cannot be affected by them. This may be an oversimplification of the facts. Perhaps it also restricts the concept of instinctive action excessively, since we know from experiments by von Holst that an impulse emitted by a centrally coordinated mechanism and one delivered by a reflex may be superimposed on one another in a single muscular contraction. Nevertheless, we may neglect this possibility for the present in view of another circumstance which further complicates the analysis of animal behavior, in particular of instinctive action, and which requires that we make our conditions as simple as possible for the time being. This complicating circumstance is as follows.

C. The Interlocking of Taxis and Instinctive Action

An intact higher organism in its natural environment hardly ever performs only a centrally coordinated movement. It almost always does "several things at a time." While performing an instinctive act, for instance, it gives way to an orienting reaction. In the effort to distinguish instinctive activity from the "reflex," a most misleading statement keeps cropping up: that instinctive behavior is a reaction of the "organism as a whole," whereas in the reflex, only some part is involved in the activity. If we may ever say that only part of an organism is involved in a reaction, it may confidently be said of instinctive action. With its automatic rhythm and central coordination, instinctive action is far more autonomous than the reflex. Owing to them, it is functionally independent of the receptors. The mechanism of an instinctive action is a closely self-contained system. It is subordinated to the whole central nervous system only in so far as the latter may inhibit it. Yet, although the mechanism of instinctive action is highly independent and though it may be insubordinate to the higher nervous centers of man (the "ego"), it is still very restricted in its control of the motor apparatus of higher animals. It sends its impulses only to specific groups of muscles and never, save perhaps some possible exceptions, involves the whole muscular system of the organism at one time. Thus it is always possible that other muscles and groups of muscles may, during an instinctive activity, carry out other movements caused by fundamentally different processes in the central nervous system. For a study of instinctive action itself we must therefore concentrate on processes in which only the centrally integrated impulse sequence of the instinctive action is translated into movements that can be seen and described, without any disturbing secondary effects from nervous processes of another kind. Or we must select behavior patterns in which the effects of noninstinctive motor processes can easily be distinguished from the instinctive action proper.

All instinctive activities of higher animals are accompanied by certain noninstinctive motions that are particularly easy to identify. The tropotactically directed mechanism of balancing operates all the time, even during instinctive activities. With the sole exception of the male rabbit's mating reaction, we know of hardly an instinctive behavior during which an organism normally directed by gravity would lose this orientation and fall over! But even instinctive actions accompanied only by postural reflexes are rare. For our comparative and genetic study, we had to find an instinctive action whose discharge could be plotted with some precision, and registered for comparison. In this quest, it was not at all simple to find a centrally coordinated motor pattern free of simultaneous orienting mechanisms! We finally selected the courting behavior of certain species of ducks, which occurs almost purely in the erect swimming bird's median plane. If these motions are filmed exactly from the side, the motor curve can be reconstructed rather fully from the motion picture, and represented in a graph. In this projection the only simultaneous orienting reactions, the lateral balancing motions, can be completely neglected. In many similar instinctive actions of the same birds, which have the selfsame biological function, a second orienting mechanism operates: the courting drake continually directs his motions in such a way as to make the visual releasers which they disclose most easily seen by the courted bird.

The effect of these instinctive actions is purely optical or in part acoustic: they serve to emit stimuli. The importance of simultaneous orienting reactions is, of course, far greater in behavior patterns whose survival value lies in manipulating some environmental object. Naturally, only a very few of these mechanically effective motor processes can function without an orienting mechanism which directs the organism toward the object of its instinctive act. The tactically steered turn "toward" or "away from" can rarely be dispensed with in mechanically effective actions, unless the animal is dealing with a homogeneous medium. Only for plankton-eating animals is their food itself sometimes a homogeneous medium. Consequently, we find the most taxis-deficient free-moving organisms among these inhabitants of free water spaces. In the world of solid objects, however, no animal capable of locomotion can hold its own without oriented movements. However highly differentiated or delicately adapted to the environment a mechanism of centrally coordinated motor patterns may be, it cannot function adequately unless the animal is also adjusted spatially to the object of each action.

This change of posture, which is always steered by a taxis, an orienting mechanism in the broadest sense of the word, may be completed before the instinctive act is discharged. We may then observe a purely taxis-steered act followed by a purely centrally coordinated motor pattern. The snapping reaction of the sea horse (*Hippocampus Leach*) is a case in point. This fish assumes, no doubt by a very intricate orienting reaction, a posture in which the prospective prey is exactly in the central plane of its head, in a definite direction and at a definite distance, obliquely in front of and above its oral slit. This may take a long time to achieve. The fish often follows a small crab back and forth for minutes, turning and twisting as far as its stiff armor will let it. The stimulus situation that releases the muscular play of snapping is effective only when the aforesaid postural relationship has been perfectly attained. Such an orienting reaction, which precedes the discharge of an instinctive action, constitutes the simplest case of what, with Wallace Craig, we call "appetitive behavior."

Psychologically the most important and striking quality of instinctive action, and at the same time the one least open to causal explanation, is that its purely automatic performance, while not directed toward a goal after which the subject strives, represents such a goal as a whole: the organism has an "appetite" for discharging its own instinctive activities. Disinhibition and consummation of an instinctive action are accompanied by subjective phenomena. For the sake of the latter, animals and men actively strive to attain the stimulus situations in which these processes occur. We believe that every organism which performs instinctive actions experiences them pleasurably. In part, we arrive at this conclusion through reasoning by analogy. Moreover, we regard this type of experience as one of the most important factors that contribute toward maintenance of the species. Experience, as Volkelt in particular points out, is not a fortuitous side effect, an "epiphenomenon" of physiological processes! Without the "sensual pleasure" represented by the subjective aspect of probably all instinctive acts, they would be discharged only when the organism happened by mere accident upon the releasing stimulus situation. What makes an instinctive activity a goal to be craved is undoubtedly the subjective experience that goes along with it. The insertion of a subjective element into a causal chain of physiological processes that have survival value presents great philosophical difficulties; it must in fact be viewed as an essential point in the problem of body and soul. It is especially remarkable that these largely proprioceptive pleasurable sensations accompany motor processes to whose form and integration the proprioceptors do not contribute.

Appetitive behavior is adaptive and variable. It strives for the release of an instinctive action. In the simplest case, it can be one of the commonest and best analyzed topic reactions. From these, however, every conceivable transition leads up to the highest learned and intelligent achievements known. In the aforementioned papers (1937a and b), Lorenz discussed in some detail the curious fact that, from the standpoint of objective behavior study, no sharp line can be drawn between the simplest orienting reaction and the highest "insightful" behavior.

Some taxes precede the release of an instinctive act in time; they lead up to it, and so clearly have the nature of appetitive behavior. Others, as in the example of tropotactic orientation to gravity, continue to operate during the discharge of an instinctive motor pattern. In mechanically effective behavior patterns, an orienting reaction, which comes under the heading of appetitive behavior, establishes a postural relationship between the animal and the object of its action. The role of the taxis here is to maintain this orientation. Psychologically speaking, this postural relationship often corresponds to an emotionally accented stimulus situation. Consequently the orienting mechanisms that are linked simultaneously with an instinctive activity can also very often be conceived as a sort of appetitive behavior. A grazing cow, for instance, steered by correcting mechanisms, constantly holds her head so that a certain spatial relationship is maintained between her mouth and the grass. Objectively, this makes the purely instinctive motions in the muscles of the cow's jaw, tongue and lips mechanically effective and gives them biological meaning. To the cow as a subject, on the other hand, it means a pleasurable stimulus situation, whose continuance is a goal to be striven for.

Such simultaneous combinations of a taxis and an instinctive pattern are evidently very frequent among the integrated motor sequences of higher organisms. It is equally evident that these "simultaneous inter-lockings" may be infinitely complex and present all but insurmountable difficulties to analysis with the few methods at our disposal. But our research optimism—which we certainly need, considering the immensity of the task we have set ourselves—is enhanced by one fact: as there are pure, taxis-free instinctive actions, and easily analyzed time sequences of instinct and purposive behavior, so there are others in which especially favorable circumstances make it possible to distinguish between motor pattern and orienting reaction despite their simultaneous operation.

II.   The Problem

It is the task of this paper to investigate the interaction of an instinc-tive pattern and a simultaneous orienting mechanism, in a very simple case. The simplest conceivable situation would be one where the cen-trally coordinated impulses yield a movement in one plane, while the motions elicited by the taxis occur perpendicularly to this plane, that is, cause receptor-steered deviations from the plane of the instinctive action. We shall devise a simplified model to illustrate such a process. Let us imagine a skeletal unit which pivots in a socket-joint, like a sea urchin's quill, and is moved by two pairs of muscles arranged perpendicu-larly to one another, one pair pulling vertically and the other, the an-tagonistic pair, pulling horizontally. For reasons of species survival, the skeletal element would have to move back and forth in a certain spatial plane, say, the vertical. This swinging of the organ can be accomplished by a centrally coordinated mechanism, transmitting its impulses to the approximately vertical muscles. But to ensure that the motion will occur exactly in the vertical plane (in spite of variations in the animal's posi-tion), a taxis steered by a gravity-receptor will have to be introduced. Without affecting the posture of the entire organism, it can induce con-tractions in the second, horizontally pulling pair of muscles through the orienting mechanism. These contractions cause the skeletal section to deviate from the swinging plane of the central mechanism as far as is required to secure the exactly vertical motion necessary for survival of the species. This particular case, where an instinctive movement occurs precisely in one plane, and is steered, like a horse between two reins, by antagonistic muscles arranged perpendicularly to that plane and governed by an orienting reaction, is probably quite a frequent one. Similar conditions seem to prevail in the chewing motions of humans, in the thrusting motions of copulating male mammals, and in many others.

The above requirements are fulfilled especially well by a motor pattern that can be observed in the brooding birds of many species. Expressed in terms of survival value, this movement is the retrieving of eggs that have rolled from the nest. This behavior pattern includes motions directly recognizable as maintaining balance, which must therefore be classed as orienting reactions. But in addition, it contains motions that clearly bear all the traits of real instinctive actions. Since, moreover, these diverse motions ensue simultaneously and in perpendicular planes, we considered that we had a particularly favorable object for study and attempted an analysis of the interaction of taxis and instinct. When the geese of Altenberg brooded in the spring of 1937, we took the chance to use them for observation and experiments on this problem.

The observational approach and the planning of the experiments started from a very simple consideration: if, as presumed, the taxis is dependent on external stimulation and the instinct is centrally determined, it follows that, when taxis and instinct govern different groups of muscles, the movements dependent on the orienting mechanism will be omitted in the absence of steering stimuli. Therefore, in the case of a vacuum reaction, only the instinctive behavior pattern should occur, without the orienting reaction that normally accompanies it. Moreover, any change in the stimuli typical of the total situation should entail changes in the taxis-controlled motions, because of their dependence on these stimuli. These changes would be adaptations to the new spatial conditions. On the other hand, the instinctive action, which is impervious to the receptors, should always be performed in exactly the same manner, whether it is discharged entirely without an object, with a substitute object greatly differing from the norm, or with the biologically adequate object. Furthermore, any environmental change that requires the slightest adjustment of the motor pattern should cause an immediate and complete breakdown of the instinctive action. Finally, it seemed plausible to use the specific exhaustibility of the instinctive action in an attempt to eliminate the central mechanism through exhaustion, in order to see how this would affect the appetence for the normally releasing stimulus situation and the orienting reactions that lead up to it.

III. Observations on the Egg-Rolling Movements

We shall first present our findings in nonexperimental observations because, as "unintentional" experiments, they are free from many sources of error in the experiment, and because we made them before the experimental studies.

The normal process, which fulfills the survival requirements of the reaction, is approximately as follows. When the brooding goose first catches sight of an egg outside the nest, but not too far from it, the egg-rolling pattern does not ensue at once or "determinedly." Rather, the bird merely glances toward the egg swiftly, and then looks away from it. The next time she fixates it longer. She may also point her head slightly toward the egg. After a short series of intention-movements that gain rapidly in intensity and may vary greatly in number, the goose stretches her neck as far as she can toward the egg, but still does not move otherwise (Fig. 1a). In this posture she often remains for several seconds, "as if spellbound." At last she rises from the nest slowly and hesitantly, without altering the posture of her neck and head, and approaches the egg with the peculiarly careful gait that characterizes all her locomotion in the vicinity of the nest. The early stretching of the neck toward the egg looks as if the bird did not "place" it correctly in space and "hoped" she could reach it without getting up. This surely mistaken impression grows when the bird approaches the egg laboriously, begrudging every step. The reluctance to leave the nest is justified: the instinctive pattern does not really "fit," and cannot roll the egg into the nest by a single discharge, unless the goose advances to the elevation at the edge of the nest and no farther.[2] When the goose is close enough to the egg, she first touches it with the tip of her bill at the point of its surface nearest to her (Fig. 1b), and usually pushes against it with her bill slightly opened. Then the undersurface of the lower bill, maintaining constant contact with the egg, glides over its upper surface so that, overreaching the egg, it approaches the ground on the side away from the goose (Fig. 1c). At this instant a peculiar tension envelops the bird, her neck tautens and her head begins to quiver noticeably. This delicate trembling continues while, with a flexion of the neck, singularly stiff and clumsy in appearance, the egg is slowly rolled or pulled toward the goose and thereby toward the nest, so that it finally comes to rest on her toes (Fig. 1d); or, if by then the highest point in the edge of the nest is crossed, it rolls down

---

[2] If she is forced to go beyond this, a second, altogether different reaction is added to the egg-rolling movement here under discussion. Studies on this second reaction have not been completed, and are to be reported next year.

Fig. 1
Normal egg-rolling reaction

to the other eggs in the nest depression. The tension and the delicate quivering are caused by relatively strong co-innervation of the antagonists to the muscles that do the actual work of rolling. A similar phenomenon may be observed in voluntary human movements, if they act against a resistance of unknown size, or one that is subject to sudden and incalculable fluctuations. In such cases, together with the muscles that do the real, mechanical work of the motion, their antagonists are also activated. In this way the heightened internal resistance to the motion, known and subjectively controllable in its extent, greatly lessens the impact of unpredictable fluctuations in the external resistance, since the latter now constitutes only a small part of the total resistance to be overcome. Although, as a result, far more muscular energy is consumed than is needed for the work that actually has to be performed, yet divergent movements are reduced to a fraction of what they would otherwise be. This form of force, controlled and curbed by extravagant use of the antagonists, is the only means to safeguard the form of an intended motion against fluctuations of external resistance in cases where they occur too fast for our receptors, so that receptor-steered braking of the divergent motion would come too late. In instinctive actions, too, we should like to attribute the co-innervation of antagonists and the resultant tension in the organ involved, as well as the often distinct quivering motion, to the necessity of foregoing a regulation by the receptors. The centrally coordinated movement as such cannot be influenced by receptors. Therefore, wherever it works mechanically against resistances in the environment, these are always, as it were, unknown. Wherever the resistance is subject to fluctuation, the instinctive movement needs internal control much more than does an arbitrary one. The states of tension described, with antagonistic quivering, are indeed found in many a mechanically effective instinctive action. An especially clear example is the lateral pushing motion with which herons and related birds fit a twig into the nest. Another fact that substantiates the co-innervation of antagonists is that in occasional vacuum reactions, where the normal conditions of external resistance are absent, the form and speed of the instinctive reactions remain unchanged.

Besides the motion described, which occurs fairly accurately in the bird's median plane, additional movements may be observed. These are lateral, normally very slight oscillations of the head and bill. Their obvious function is to prevent the egg, which is being rolled up the nest rampart, from deviating to the right or left and rolling down past the bill. They hold the egg in balance on the underside of the bill. This is especially noticeable if the pathway along which the egg is rolled slopes very steeply upwards, so that a considerable portion of the egg's weight rests upon the goose's lower bill. The amplitude of these oscillations increases as soon as the egg is in danger of losing its balance, and only a cruder compensating motion can save it from rolling down. Figures 1e and 1f show the average amplitudes of this motion.

After the egg-rolling pattern has been completed, and prior to resuming the posture of tranquil hatching, there ensues a peculiar instinctive action which we shall term nest-molding movement. By stretching the elbows slightly, the goose lowers her bent wrists and moves them forward until they press against the front of the nest. At the same time her feet, with alternating backward raking motions, propel the whole bird forward, so that her breast and wing joints exert strong pressure against the front of the nest and the surrounding mound, while the feet themselves push nest materials toward the back wall of the nest (Fig. 2). This motion is used to hollow out the nest when it is first built, and also to remove the down cover which protects the clutch during the bird's absence from the nest. It always precedes resumption of the ordinary brooding posture.

FIG. 2
Nest-molding pattern

The discharge of the reaction in the normal situation, where it has survival value, indicates right away that two fundamentally different motor processes are involved. Various unmistakable characteristics of true instinctive behavior, such as the state of tension with antagonistic quivering, the identical repetition of the retrieving movement, and several other factors, indicate the presence of centrally coordinated motor patterns. On the other hand, the lateral balancing movements are directly dependent as to their direction, amplitude, and general form on tactile stimulation from the egg as it deviates more or less to the right or left. They must therefore be regarded as the effects of a taxis. This view is further strengthened by a number of other facts derived from observations which, although pre-experimental, were nevertheless made with an eye to the problem under discussion.

The most important of these observations, strictly speaking, comprises all that we could later confirm by our experiments. It is as follows. An egg that has been brought back to the nest by the movement as described does not necessarily reach its goal. Quite often—more than half the time, if the nest has a steeply sloping edge—the egg slips from the bill, and rolls back down. If such a miscarriage occurs, the rolling movement does not always break off, but often continues in a curious way. The flexing motion of head and neck goes on exactly as if it were pushing an egg under the goose's abdomen, but there are no lateral balancing movements when the activity runs on *in vacuo*. Since the goose is standing in the nest, the continuing motion in the median plane finally brings the bill in contact with the eggs in the nest. This contact stimulus seems to give the rolling reaction renewed impetus. In such a situation all the eggs are almost invariably rolled around pell-mell, very intensely and thoroughly, which is not usually the case if the retrieved egg lands properly in the nest. It looks as if the brief motor segment traversed without an egg left the goose somewhat "dissatisfied," and she were now "enjoying" the contact of her bill with the eggs with heightened appetence. After uprooting the clutch in this fashion, the goose settles down on it, performs the nest-molding pattern described earlier (Fig. 2), and then sets—as long as she feels some eggs under her—quite content, until her gaze again falls on the egg that has just escaped her. At this point the goose seems astonished—to use an involuntary anthropomorphism—that there should be "another" egg outside the nest. In any case, one cannot safely say that the goose knows whether or not her rolling pattern has actually brought the egg back into the nest. After a pause of varying length and a further summation of the stimuli coming from the egg, a new retrieving reaction ensues.

The absence of balancing lateral motions when the reaction goes off *in vacuo* shows that these are dependent on contact stimuli from the egg, and are therefore orienting reactions. This does not necessarily mean that the rest of the reaction is totally free from taxis control. However, even if additional orienting mechanisms should be linked simultaneously with the reaction, they are surely not essential. At any rate, while rolling the egg, the bill does not follow every little deviation which the egg makes in the vertical plane because the ground is uneven. Instead, the bill touches the egg near its upper contour when it is rolling through a slight depression, and very low down when it is on top of a rise. The stretching of the neck toward the egg before the retrieving reaction is probably the only activity that makes the rolling movement more or less parallel to the pathway of the rolling egg. In other words, the adaptive process for this component is not an orienting reaction that operates simultaneously with the instinctive act, but the preceding telotaxis, which should be classed as appetitive behavior in its narrower sense. At times the movement may even deviate considerably from its parallel direction to the pathway. The egg-rolling pattern seems to be adapted quite specifically to the case where the goose stands exactly at the edge of the nest. In the natural life of the species this is no doubt what usually happens. First, the goose is very reluctant to go beyond the edge of the nest. Secondly, this is usually far enough for the bird to reach an egg, if it is not deliberately placed farther away, but allowed to roll freely down the outside of the nest mound, so that the most natural spatial relationship between the goose and the egg-to-be-retrieved is obtained. Since the nest generally lies amid rough-stalked plant growth, the egg does not roll beyond the area covered with nest-building materials, so that a fairly constant limit of excursion from the center of the nest is assured. In these conditions, the sagittal motion appears well adjusted to the path of the egg. Owing to its form, the upward component of the bill-push becomes the strongest precisely where it is most needed, namely, toward the end of the reaction, when the egg has to pass over the last and steepest rise of the rampart. Now the nest of our experimental bird was made of pine needles, a very unnatural nesting substance. Moreover, it was not nearly so high or steep as any nest that we found in the field. Figure 1d suggests vividly that the motion really requires a somewhat steeper barrier. A real disturbance in the retrieving reaction ensued if the egg lay nearer than it would do in natural conditions. In that case the goose did not step forward, but remained standing above or even behind the eggs in the nest. As a result, the bill gave the egg the strongest lift at a point where the ground had already begun to drop again, because the egg had passed the summit of the rim. It was then frequently lifted off the ground, balanced on the underside of the bill, often for several seconds, and dropped on the rest of the clutch from a considerable height, with the result that many eggs were cracked.

Accordingly, no taxis-directed motion seems to occur in the sagittal plane of the egg-rolling reaction, except, of course, for the stretching of the head toward the egg. This, however, must be classed as appetitive behavior. It merely determines the general angle at which the goose's neck and body are bent forward, and occurs at a different time from the centrally coordinated motor pattern. Nevertheless, the possibility that other taxes may function during the instinctive activity must be more closely investigated. This, if at all feasible, we plan to attempt next year, by taking motion pictures of the retrieving movements directly from the side and varying the profile of the pathway as much as possible. Such pictures will enable us to plot the motor curve, and to determine how the contact stimuli from the egg affect the reaction.

IV. Experiments

In this year's experiments we wished to demonstrate, first, that the sideways balancing motions depend on tactile stimuli, and second, that the sagittal motion is rigid and unaffected by receptors. This we must postulate if the sagittal component is to be conceived as a pure instinctive pattern. First we had to find objects which, while releasing the goose's retrieving reaction, were so different from a goose egg that they did not present the stimuli required to elicit the thigmotactic orienting reaction, or presented them in greatly modified form. Next we looked for objects that required receptor-steered adaptation of the sagittal movement, that is, ones which literally had to jam if this motion was independent of receptors and purely centrally coordinated. In our search for dummies we found out a great deal about the requirements for release of the egg-rolling reaction. We shall next discuss this hereditary combination of sign stimuli provided by the object, the innate schema of the egg.

A. The Innate Releasing Mechanism

By innate releasing mechanism we mean the innately determined readiness of an animal to respond with a certain action to a certain set of environmental stimuli. It is an innate neurosensory correlate to a specific stimulus combination. Despite its relative simplicity, it fits the biologically adequate situation clearly enough to prevent erroneous releases by other, accidentally similar external stimuli. The releasing of motor processes by the response of an innate mechanism corresponds in every essential way to an unconditioned reflex, and forms a continuous gradation with the simplest unconditioned reflexes. This, however, holds only for the releasing mechanism proper, and does not imply any inferences for the motor sequence which it sets off or disinhibits. On the contrary, the latter may be of a fundamentally different nature. The response of an innate mechanism may directly release an undirected instinctive action or, on the other hand, the appetence for an instinctive act. This appetence may in turn lead to anything from a simple orienting reaction to the highest purposive achievement. Again, an innate mechanism may activate a pure taxis which, instead of introducing an action-releasing stimulus situation, leads to a state of repose free of stimuli.

In the case of the egg-rolling reaction, the innate response to the situation "egg outside the nest" releases appetitive behavior in the form of the orienting reaction described: protrusion of the neck. The sign stimuli of the "egg" in this case are very few and simple; it is downright astounding that they distinguish the object clearly enough. We have known for some time (Köhler and Zagarus, Tinbergen, Goethe, Kirkman, and others) that in the incubation and retrieving of eggs, many birds will make shift with objects that bear little resemblance to the eggs of their own species. Silver gulls incubate polyhedra and cylinders of any color and almost any size, laughing gulls seem to be even less selective. Our greylag geese at first did much the same, but later they showed a notable shift in behavior, conditioned by individual learning. Moreover, thoroughbred specimens might perhaps react differently from the hybrids which we studied. It is especially true of innate releasing mechanisms that cues have often dropped out in the process of domestication, with the result that the range of effective stimuli is broader and the reaction less selective. Control experiments with thoroughbreds must prove whether such was the case with our experimental subjects.

The purely visual release of the appetitive orienting reaction, the directed neck-stretching, depends on a single cue: continuity of the object's surface. Practically any smooth object with approximately rounded contours attracts the goose's attention and causes her to stretch out her neck. The next instant, however, tactile cues come into play. Even before the goose overreaches the egg with her bill, she explores the hardness of its surface by tapping it lightly (Fig. 1b). A roundish toy dog made of white rubber clearly arouses her appetence for the rolling reaction. The goose rises, reaches toward it with her bill, but abandons it after a single, very slight tap. A yellow balloon inflated to the size of a goose egg receives the same treatment. A hard-boiled and shelled musk-duck egg is nibbled at greedily after the tapping test. In our experience, the color of the object makes no difference to the goose. In this she differs somewhat from gulls and plovers. Size matters only within such a wide range that when the reaction breaks down with objects too large or too small, it is hard to say whether perceptions or purely mechanical circumstances set the limit. On the other hand, the demand for continuity of surface, which has existed from the beginning of the appetitive behavior, grows quite considerably as the reaction progresses. Visual or tactile perception of any angles or peaks that stand out from the object interrupts the motor pattern at once. The goose will immediately retrieve a wooden cube open on one side, but only until it comes to lie with this open side up; this ends the rolling reaction, which shifts to intensive nibbling at the free edge of the opening. A white wooden toy hen the size of a goose egg is not retrieved. Instead, the goose pecks at the very short projections glued to the egg-shaped body, such as eyes, bill and feet. A large cardboard Easter egg is treated the same way: the goose nibbles at the paper fringe around its seam (Fig. 3). On the other hand, the rectangular edges of a cube, or the edges of a plaster of paris cylinder do not interfere with the rolling reaction.

This intensive response to anything that stands out is not a fortuitous phenomenon. It appears as described only if the peaks that release nibbling are attached to an object which otherwise fills out the schema of the

FIG. 3
Nibbling at free edges

egg satisfactorily, and rouses an appetence to retrieve and incubate. The behavior in question is probably typical of all *Anatides*. Its biological purpose is to dispose of broken eggs. These, as we have confirmed in various ducks as well as in the African goose (*Alopochen*) are demolished and consumed, starting at the edge of the fracture, before the other eggs could be soiled and their respiration impaired by the exuding contents. The reaction must, of course, be inhibited before the young begin to hatch, else the mother would kill the emerging goslings. When grey goose eggs of pure strain, which had been incubated by a turkey hen, were just beginning to hatch, we wished for technical reasons (because the goslings' down coat must be greased on the plumage of an old goose) to let the actual act of emerging take place under our experimental goose. This, however, proved quite impossible. The brooding goose immediately began to nibble at the edges of the punctured spots, greedily and furiously. She hacked away so ruthlessly that the shell was at once deeply indented and blood started to flow from the torn egg membranes. The goslings would all undoubtedly have perished, had we not quickly removed the eggs. But when, only two days later, her own goslings hatched, the pattern of nibbling at edges and points was totally extinguished in the same goose. We could not even persuade her to nibble at the edges and protruding points of the eggshell by holding the pecked spots directly in front of her. To be sure, she bent her head excitedly and attentively toward the peeping egg, and even touched it with her slightly opened bill, but always without biting at it. This same motion of the head and bill is often seen in mother geese leading their tiny goslings, where it is a gesture of tenderness. We have the impression that acoustic stimuli from the hatching egg may suddenly change the brooding mother's reaction. Even an egg that has only just been pipped is normally treated "as a gosling." Thus eggs that are pipped are seemingly not turned over again, since the first punctures in the shells are found at the top and remain there so long as the goose is undisturbed. Moreover, the mother no longer treads on the eggs, as she does in the earlier phases of incubation (see also Fig. 5). She does not even rest her weight on the pipped eggs, but squats as she later does in brooding the goslings. Unfortunately we neglected to test whether a pipped egg would be retrieved from outside the nest.

An attempt to release the rolling reaction by presenting goslings that were just dry but could not yet walk had curious results. The goose at first behaved exactly as at the beginning of an ordinary retrieving reaction. She rose, bent toward the gosling and touched it tentatively with her opened bill. A few times we even saw her reach over the gosling with her lower bill. But the pulling-in movement never ensued; instead, she invariably pulled back her neck very suddenly, as if "disappointed." It seemed as though the goose "wanted" to get the gosling back into the nest and were trying to accomplish this by the rolling movement, which failed because the gosling was so unlike an egg. Her excitement was quite obvious; a few seconds after her reaction had failed she stretched her neck toward the crying gosling again. We do not wish to discuss this behavior in more detail, since corresponding experiments with pure-bred greylag geese have not yet been made. Perhaps the constant back-and-forth motion of the mother's head might ultimately guide a gosling to the nest even though it can hardly crawl as yet; or perhaps, due to domestication, our experimental goose lacked some specific reaction to such a young gosling outside the nest.

Long before the brooding period of our subjects was over, our experiments on the innate releasing mechanism of the egg-rolling reaction came to an unexpected and remarkable end. About the middle of the incubation period, after an interval of several days, we tried to make the tamest of our geese retrieve various objects once more, but now she did not react. We found that henceforth her retrieving reaction could only be elicited by real goose eggs! All the objects that we have mentioned as substitutes for eggs remained unheeded. Even a small intact hen's egg did not elicit a reaction. With goose eggs, on the other hand, the egg-rolling movement was performed at once, and was not easily exhausted. Our surmise that the central process might have lost in intensity thus proved to be groundless.

FIG. 5

Retrieving a wooden cube

B. Experiments to Distinguish Taxis from Instinctive Action

The rough innate mechanism of the egg depends on relatively very few sign stimuli; dummies of very different size and shape can activate it. Consequently, by presenting suitable objects of specific form and size, we were able to create situations which made it easier to break up the total behavior pattern into its directed and released components.

First we wished to confirm experimentally that the lateral bill motions, which balance the egg while it is rolled, are elicited directly by steering tactile stimuli, as we had assumed after the observations reported on pp. 190-191. For this purpose, we had to find a dummy that would not, like the rolled egg, swerve continually from its path, thus furnishing tactile stimuli to the lateral edges of the lower bill. First we tried to make the goose retrieve a plaster of paris cylinder along a smooth pathway, by presenting it on a wide wooden plank propped up against the rim of the nest. This experiment was unsatisfactory; the goose, disturbed and apprehensive because of the strange plank, tired after a few reactions. Moreover, unlike egg-shaped objects, she often caught the cylinder, not in the middle but so far over toward the side that it again veered sideways from its path and induced lateral head movements. Yet these movements were very different from the customary ones and, since the cylinder swerved more slowly and rarely than an egg, the connection between the deviating motion of the object and the compensating motion of the bill was far more evident than in the normal process.

The lateral balancing motions could be eliminated far more simply and effectively by presenting an object that would not roll, but slide, on the ground. A small, very light wooden cube, which did not slide back from the rim of the nest, proved to be the best object for our purposes. One mechanical factor may have been of some importance here: the cube usually tilted over and then found a relatively broad and level rest for one of its surfaces on both branches of the goose's lower jaw (Fig. 5); this must, of course, have contributed toward keeping it in the right direction. The cube was always pulled straight into the nest without the slightest lateral motion.

With these two experiments we believe that we have proved the lateral motions of the bill to be released directly by tactile stimuli from the deviating motions of the object retrieved.

Besides this evidence and in contrast to it, we had to investigate whether the movement in the median plane, which we have regarded as centrally coordinated only, could not be changed by supplementary orienting reactions so as to achieve closer adaptation to spatial conditions. After the observations described, this seemed highly unlikely; yet we wished to see if a slight change in the fixed pattern of the sagittal neck and head movement could not be induced. The largest of the dummies used in our experiments, the oversize cardboard Easter egg, seemed suitable for this purpose. Since its diameter required entirely different flexions of the neck from a goose egg, it would be revealing to see how the reaction coped with these modified conditions. Right at the beginning of the movement, the size of the object and its radius of curvature created a disturbance. The overreaching of the egg, as seen in Figure 1c, is followed by a motion of the head alone. It is bent at a sharp angle toward the neck, without the latter changing its outstretched position. In this typical initial phase of the sagittal movement, a real goose egg is pulled nestward. But not the dummy in our experiment. The bill reached the surface of this object at so unfavorable an angle that it slid off, and we had to give some assistance before the reaction could proceed (Fig. 4a). In other ways, too, all the details of the movement showed that it was rigidly adapted to a far smaller object. Even before the intensive flexion of the neck could occur (as in Fig. 1d), the dummy got stuck between the goose's bill and breast, so that in our filmstrip the position illustrated in Figure 4b continued unchanged for over 5 feet of film, until the reaction broke off and the goose straightened up. This, significantly, was never followed by the nest-molding pattern which characterizes a "satisfying" discharge of the reaction. Instead, the goose continued to stand "perplexedly" erect in the nest (Fig. 4f). Such breaking down of an instinctive action by brute force thus appears to cause a most unpleasant sensation. The goose showed an "aversion" for the large Easter egg sooner and more intensely than for any of the other dummies. This was expressed in diminished readiness and rapid exhaustibility of the reaction. It never occurred to the goose to move the egg into the nest without the normal excessive flexion of her neck, by merely stepping backwards.[3]

In a number of our experiments, as in the one from which Figures 4a to 4e are taken, there occurred another solution, more satisfying to the goose. The dummy, like a cherry stone between two fingers, suddenly shot off sideways between the bird's bill and breast. Figure 4c shows clearly how the bill follows the egg to the right in an "attempt" to maintain balance. Four film squares later the sagittal motion is distinctly running on *in vacuo*. In Figure 4d the head is still pulled to the right by the last, excessive and thigmotactically directed movement. In later

---

[3] Rolling the egg while stepping backwards occurs as a special reaction if the full flexion of the neck is not enough to get the egg to the rest of the clutch. While rare in the greylag goose, it is the main behavior pattern for salvaging outlying eggs in many short-necked ground breeders, and probably the only one in many of them.

FIG. 4

Miscarrying reaction with oversized dummy

pictures its motion no longer has any relation to the object that lies far in the foreground. Next came the intensive rooting among the eggs described on p. 191 (Fig. 4e), followed by settling and nest-molding. Whenever the large but light pasteboard egg slipped aside, depriving the reaction of its object, the discharge *in vacuo* could be observed particularly well: the object was eliminated suddenly and completely, without disturbing secondary stimuli.

The form of the motion in the median plane, in the light of all our observations and experiments, proved highly rigid. There remained another question: could its intensity be modified by the receptors in accordance with resistance to be overcome? The simultaneous innervation of antagonistic muscles and the identity of vacuum activity and functional achievement, reported earlier, might suggest the possibility of adaptation to the weight of the object by interaction of antagonistic reflexes. In the case of greater external resistance, for example, the tension of the muscles inhibiting the motion might be diminished. According to the results obtained with dummies heavier than a goose egg this does not seem to be the case. These findings were at first involuntary: the egg-rolling reaction broke down in the face of resistances which we had presumed would naturally be overcome. In the case of the plaster of paris cylinder, the force exerted by the bill was just enough to set it in motion on a smooth surface, but the slightest obstacle immediately brought the rolling to a standstill. At the same time, the force applied was evidently a mere fraction of the potential force; moreover, it was not all applied in the direction in which the dummy was to roll. On the contrary, the play of the antagonists proceeded as described. This feeble and unsuccessful trying out of the reaction on an object only slightly too heavy seemed stupidly mechanical, especially to the expert who knows what astounding strength there is in the neck of a grey goose. When playfully performing the grass-pulling movement, for instance, she can tug a heavy oaken chair across a rough surface or pull a tablecloth from a table set for several people. The fact that, in the retrieving reaction, only such a disproportionately small fraction of this tugging force can be applied to slightly overweight objects, substantiates the assumption that the force of the sagittal motion cannot be essentially affected by receptors.

With dummies lighter than a goose egg, such as the wooden cube, the sagittal motion was practically identical with a reaction *in vacuo*. Toward the end of the reaction, as described on p. 192, a goose egg itself may be lifted up and balanced on the goose's bill. This lifting occurred regularly with the hollow cube, which was often raised to the goose's breast and jammed for a second between it and the bill (Fig. 5). The easy and regular lifting of the light cube definitely suggests that the state of tension of the muscles involved in the sagittal motion was predetermined, once and for all, for the normal weight of an average goose egg. On the other hand, it implies that, in addition to the centrally coordinated impulses, slight reflex processes may also be at work in the muscles performing the sagittal motion. When this reaction goes off completely *in vacuo*, when the bill has absolutely nothing to carry, the head should go up even more than when it moves a cube, and such is not the case. On the contrary, in a vacuum reaction the head is held particularly low, often even scraping along the ground (Fig. 4d). The tactile stimulation from the object rolled probably does not have a directive effect in the true sense of the word, but does have a tonic influence on the flexor muscles of the neck and especially of the head. Such a tonic reflex effect would, of course, be dependent on receptors, but could only be regarded as an orienting mechanism if its force were found to increase with the weight of the object rolled. For the time being, we consider this highly improbable. On the basis of our observations we believe rather that the force applied in the case of light and heavy objects is identical, though it may be very slightly greater in both cases than in a vacuum activity.

C. Appetitive Behavior in Oversatiation of the Instinctive Action

Finally, two more observations will be discussed. While both can be used indirectly to separate taxis from instinctive action experimentally, their prime importance lies in their bearing on another question. The compulsory release of "instinctive" actions has repeatedly been stressed as one of their important characteristics. Orienting reactions have naturally often been included in the term. An instinctive action in our sense cannot, of course, always be elicited with such compulsion as is shown in a tendon reflex, since its release at any time only amounts to disinhibition and its discharge depends on central conditions of excitation. Any exhaustion of the central nervous impulse flow renders the normally activating stimuli ineffective. In many instinctive activities this fatigue ensues uncommonly soon and is reaction-specific. It occurs long before the organism as a whole or the participant effectors are exhausted. Many a behavior pattern, such as feigning lameness to lure enemies from the vicinity of the nest, can be performed only a very few times in succession. The action is not repeated, even though the releasing situation continues to exist. Instead, the bird, in the presence of a human being who but a little while ago elicited a reaction, turns to some indifferent pursuit: it begins to search for food, to groom, etc. The situation is quite different in the case of a taxis. An orienting mechanism can, generally speaking, be activated an almost unlimited number of times in succession. A beetle turned on its back will turn right side up more perseveringly than a human is capable of doing. The same is true of an ant oriented to the incidence of light, if we try to divert it from its line of march.

We now ask whether those orienting mechanisms which, in the form of appetitive behavior, effectively relate an organism to the object of its instinctive activity, are equally inexhaustible. In general, this is not assumed to be the case. The prevailing opinion is that appetitive behavior, even where it consists of a simple taxis, ceases to be elicitable owing to satiation when the instinctive act is discharged. Jakob von Uexküll writes: "The functional cue always extinguishes the perceptual cue—with this, the action is completed. Either the perceptual cue is objectively destroyed, if it came from the food, which was eaten, or it is subjectively extinguished, in satiation, in which case the selective action of the sense organ terminates." It seems to us, however, that this extinction of releasing stimuli is not always quite complete, especially if the appetitive behavior which they initiate is a relatively simple orienting reaction. Numerous instances could be cited where, after repeated discharge, the introductory, orienting reaction can still be elicited, even though the instinctive action itself cannot. As a rule, the satiated organism continues to be aware of the normally activating stimuli, to glance in their direction or otherwise orient itself toward them, even after the instinctive action proper has been totally exhausted by repeated discharge.

It is most remarkable that an orienting mechanism, which by definition is only meaningful as appetitive behavior, should be elicited even when real appetence, in the sense of active striving by the subject, is completely eliminated. Such a release appears decidedly compulsive or reflex-like. Furthermore, it is curious and perhaps essential that the reflex release of such "appetiteless appetitive behavior" is evidently not pleasurable to the subject. We, too, turn in disgust from the most savoury foods when we have had enough, and push the dish far from us; in short, we withdraw from the stimuli which come from the object of an instinctive action that has just been consummated. But this very fact argues for the compulsive, reflex character of reactions to such stimuli. We would not need to withdraw from them if they really were quite "extinguished subjectively," as von Uexküll puts it, that is, if their continued presence did not compel us to repeat the response with repugnance, despite our lack of appetite. Although von Uexküll's statements surely have a general validity, there are numerous exceptions. In a great many cases an organism does not at any stage of satiation of an instinctive activity become totally indifferent to the stimulus situation that releases its appetitive behavior, but responds with an averting reaction as soon as the adverting one has been extinguished.

The perseveration of the initial orienting reaction after the instinctive process had been exhausted could be studied very well in the retrieving reaction of the greylag goose. The instinctive component of the movement is soon exhausted. This is not surprising, since the rate of the central nervous impulse-flow, and with it the frequency of dischargeable processes, are fitted to conditions in the natural environment, where the eggs are certainly not displaced from the nest as often as we took them out in our experiments. There was no need to set up special experiments on exhaustion, for without any interference on our part we became more familiar with all its phenomena than we would have wished. In this connection, the differences of behavior evoked by a real goose egg and by the large pasteboard Easter egg were striking and perhaps significant. Since the observations about to be described were made shortly before the goose rejected all substitutes, the contradictions in them might be attributed to the fact that, from her own experience, she knew the goose egg as a full-valued object for retrieving and hatching, and the dummy as a substitute object that would not give full satisfaction.

Toward the goose egg, the goose's adverting ("turning to") taxis persevered even when the instinctive pattern was completely exhausted. The directive outstretching of her neck (Fig. 6a), or at least an attentive glance toward the egg, could almost always be evoked. It seemed as if the stimuli from the egg would not let her come to rest, again and again she reached out toward it, and finally showed a behavior that appears very interesting to us theoretically. A different instinctive action was suddenly substituted for the exhausted rolling pattern. As soon as she had stretched forth her neck toward the egg, the goose performed the settling movement which is otherwise used in nest-building, a motor pattern common

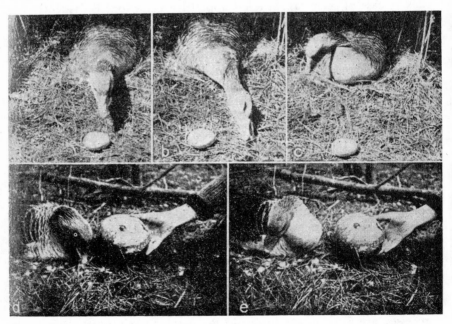

FIG. 6

a-c: Settling-back motion, generally used for gathering and arranging nest materials

d-e: "Gesture of humility"

to all *Anatides,* and one which results in gathering nest materials and keeping them together on the site of the nest (Figs. 6b, 6c).

Such substitutions of one instinctive act, in this case a biologically meaningless one, for another, are known in birds in various situations. Birds that get very excited if a foe appears close to their nest or young, often display the patterns of food-seeking, grooming, or even falling asleep, alternating with threatening motions and the familiar luring-away reactions. Plovers stirred up from their nest peck at the ground; ravens, not quite daring to attack, hack with all their might into the branch on which they perch, etc. It appears that these "erroneously" exploding instinctive actions can be initiated in two different ways. Small birds defending their nests sometimes begin to preen their feathers suddenly after a few, very intensive reactions of pretended lameness or the like. Here we are inclined to assume with Howard that, once the specific motor pattern adequate to a situation has been exhausted, the receptor-conditioned state of excitation may overflow "into other pathways" and lead to the eruption of "some" other instinctive action. In other cases, as in the instance of the raven hacking at its perch, we lean to the assumption that two conflicting instinctive actions, in this case those of flight and attack, mutually block each other, and the prevailing general excitation finds an outlet in a third one. A third possibility is the following. In some mammals we find senseless applications of instinctive actions, which at the same time are "insightful" in certain respects. In *Equides,* the cart-horse as well as the wild horse in the Zoo, everyone is familiar with the pattern of "begging" by pawing the ground with a front hoof. Dogs which, after painful experience, dare not snap after a wasp or a hedgehog, regularly dig in the direction of the exciting object with scratching motions that fall just short of it, so that a rolled-up hedgehog may end up lying on a mound, surrounded by a ditch. Monkeys in intelligence tests sometimes throw sand at the goal they are supposed to reach, etc. In all these cases we are probably faced with a quite primitive insight into the direction in which "something should be undertaken."[4]

It may be overestimating the mental faculties of a grey goose to assume that her behavior as described above is probably closely comparable to that of the mammals mentioned. However, this interpretation seemed the likeliest to us when observing the process. It looked as though the goose "could not bear" the sight of the egg outside the nest without doing something about it. This subjective interpretation is perhaps less

---

[4] This same phenomenon is the basis of the following statement by McDougall: "The animal in which any instinctive impulse is excited does not suspend action, even though the object be remote; the impulse probably always expresses itself in action."

naive than it may appear at first sight, since we have comparable experiences in just such situations where, as in the grey goose, innate releasing mechanisms and instinctive actions play the lead. We believe that, after the fiasco of the retrieving reaction, the strongly motivated goose sought to control the unpleasant situation quite purposefully by "applying" another instinctive pattern in her repertoire. We even venture to suggest that it was by no means accidental that this was done by another motor pattern which also moves something toward the nest. A high mental achievement of this kind—just about the highest of which we think a bird capable—is the kind of phenomenon best suited to show that the animal is controlled by innately coordinated motor patterns.

While a grey goose egg near the nest drove our goose to the behavior just described, even after the retrieving pattern was exhausted, a cardboard egg placed there left her completely indifferent, as soon as the rolling reaction was even slightly fatigued. She continued to brood quite calmly with the dummy right in front of her. If the Easter egg was thrust upon her, however, as in Figure 6d, she drew in her bill as shown there, as though to avoid contact with the egg. If we continued to hold the dummy out to her, she turned her head far away (Fig. 6e). This motion of her head was not the one used for "storing" nest material, but the so-called "gesture of humility," which brooding geese adopt whenever they are roughly molested in their nests by hierarchically superior members of their species, whom they dare not chase away. Even the close approach of a human being, stroking or patting the setting goose, was never answered with this gesture. It evidently did not cause her quite such an offensive sensation as having the literally "revolting" dummy thrust upon her. Although this motion, too, is innately determined in form, it was uncommonly expressive in this application (Fig. 6e). It created in the observer the subjectivistic impression of a state of mind which well-mannered children often convey to aunts urging them to have another piece of cake, by the words: "Thank you, it makes me shudder!" It is surely significant that this behavior was most prominent toward a nonadequate object of the instinctive act.

Summary and Conclusions

The object of our study has been the interaction of a centrally coordinated instinctive motor pattern, independent of receptors, with one or more receptor-controlled topic taxes, and their integration into a functional unit of behavior with survival value. In the motor sequence with which the greylag goose (*Anser anser* L.) retrieves an egg that has rolled from the nest, instinctive actions and taxes participate both consecutively and simultaneously. A directed outstretching of the neck, as the initial orienting reaction, creates the stimulus situation in which the instinctive action is released and, at the same time, the spatial relationship required for its biologically effective discharge. This is a typical case of "appetitive behavior" in Craig's sense. The instinctive action which it activates is a breastward flexion of the neck and head, which pulls the egg, resting against the undersurface of the bill, toward the nest. From beginning to end, an additional orienting reaction accompanies this motor pattern which runs in the sagittal plane throughout. Thigmotactically controlled lateral motions hold the egg in balance and in its proper direction on the undersurface of the bill.

Our assumption that the sagittal movement is a purely instinctive action is based on the following findings:

1. It is sometimes performed as a vacuum activity, which characterizes the independence of instinctive actions from receptors (p. 186).

2. The form of the movement is always the same. We did not succeed in producing noticeable receptor-steered adaptations to changing environmental conditions in it. Neither the characteristics of the path along which the egg traveled, nor the shape of the object rolled, caused perceptible changes in the motor pattern. Where we tried to force such a change through mechanical conditions (by presenting an inordinately large object, p. 192), the movement jammed and broke down.

3. The force applied to the sagittal motion is constant within very narrow limits. Although the tactile stimuli from the object exert a slight tonic influence on the muscles that carry out the motion, this effect seems to be constant despite varying weight of the objects. Consequently, the reaction breaks down if the object is even slightly overweight.

4. The motion shows the reaction-specific exhaustibility which characterizes instinctive actions in contrast to taxes.

The assumption that the lateral balancing motions, in contrast to the sagittal motor pattern, are orienting reactions controlled by tactile stimuli, is based on the following facts:

1. There are no lateral motions when the sagittal movement is performed without an object and goes off *in vacuo* (p. 186, 191).

2. They are absent when rolling objects do not swerve from their pathway (p. 192).

3. With objects whose lateral deviation differs from that of a goose egg, the balancing motion is fully adapted to the object's motor character (p. 191).

As incidental results, we should like to mention the following findings:

1. The appetitive component, an oriented stretching of the neck, is elicited by any object so long as it has an unbroken surface and approximately continuous visual outline. Size may vary within wide limits (Figs. 4, 5).

2. If the object substituted for the egg has any protruding points or corners, the rolling reaction is discontinued and another reaction, that of destroying and devouring it, ensues. This reaction, which serves to dispose of broken eggs, is eliminated before the young hatch, probably by acoustic stimuli (p. 196).

3. The object of the retrieving reaction is at first determined by a very simple set of innate attributes. But during the brooding period, acquired characteristics are added, and the selectivity of the reaction is greatly increased by learning.

4. If the instinctive pattern is eliminated through the easy exhaustion of its central mechanism, the preparatory orienting reaction continues to be elicitable.

5. If the rolling reaction is exhausted, the goose seeks to eliminate the stimulus situation presented by an egg outside the nest by applying a different instinctive action.

6. If an object has releasing value, but the goose knows it to be unsatisfactory, she withdraws by turning aside.

4

Feeding Behavior in Young Thrushes

Releasing and Directing Stimulus Situations in *Turdus m. merula* L. and *T. e. ericetorum* Turton

NICHOLAS TINBERGEN AND D. J. KUENEN (1939)

I. *Introduction and Statement of the Problem*

In the food-begging reaction typical of all passerine birds (Fig. 1), a young thrush gives a sudden upward thrust of its head, at the same time opening its bill wide, so that the orange-colored lining of its mouth is revealed. The gaping bill remains in this position for several seconds and is closed only after the adult bird has fed the fledgling. If this fails to occur, the gaping subsides after not more than fifteen seconds. While it lasts, the neck is fully stretched. In the first days of life the head is not altogether stationary, but wavers to and fro, as though it were too heavy for the neck muscles; later on these wavering motions disappear. While gaping, the animals make a high whimpering sound, which becomes stronger day by day.

The direction of the neck is not the same throughout the nesting phase: at first the animals gape straight upward; later on they turn toward the parent bird's head. From the age of about one week, other movements accompany the gaping response: the animals stand up and make twitching motions, and later (after they have made their first flights from the nest), they also flutter with one or both wings.

The gaping of young thrushes, as that of other sparrows, is affected by sensory stimuli in two different ways. In the first place, it must generally be released. Except for rare "reactions *in vacuo*," that occur only under abnormal conditions (prolonged hunger), nestling thrushes gape

Fig. 1

Thrush *(Turdus m. merula* L.); male feeding the young

only when the adult bird comes to the nest. Continuous begging, as known for example in herons, does not occur.

Secondly, the gaping movement is directed. The animals always turn their gaping throats in a specific direction. As stated above, in the species studied by us this direction changes with growth. During approximately the first ten days, they gape straight upward. Thereafter they aim at the parent bird's head.

We have attempted to analyze the releasing stimulus situations through dummy experiments. To the best of our knowledge, no analysis of this kind has been undertaken before. During our experiments, Lorenz' momentous study on companionship in bird life was published (Lorenz, 1935). In discussing the role of the parent companion, Lorenz makes several statements that bear on our problem. We shall have to return to this paper again later.

After preliminary experiments in the year 1935, our main experiments were made in the spring of the years 1936 and 1937. Tinbergen corroborated and broadened some of the experiments on visual orientation in the blackbird during a visit with Lorenz at Altenberg.

II. Material and Methods

For the 1936 and 1937 experiments we borrowed 8 broods of black-birds (*merula*) (31 birds) and 3 broods of song thrushes (*ericetorum*) (11 birds), mostly at the age of 5 days. They were raised on a mixed food made of boiled eggs, worms, meal worms and "Sluis' Lijstervoer." In the first year (1935) the food had apparently not been fully adequate, and pathological symptoms appeared in the fifth week of life. When we fed them more fresh earthworms, the young birds grew normally. The results obtained with the defective young birds were not included in this paper.

Each brood was kept in its original nest in a wooden crate covered with glass or cardboard, and fed ten to five times a day. Before each feeding, we made the following experiments.

In order to identify the releasing stimuli, it was essential that gaping be elicited solely by the test stimulus. When the experimenter came to the nest before the experiment, the animals usually gaped for a second as a result of removing the lid or other preparatory motions. However, they soon settled down again. After about half a minute, the stimulus was presented (Figs. 2a and 2b) and the reaction observed. When the birds had settled down once more, the same stimulus could again be presented one or more times. However, we did not repeat this very often without feeding them soon afterwards, so as not to condition the animals against gaping in response to originally effective stimuli.

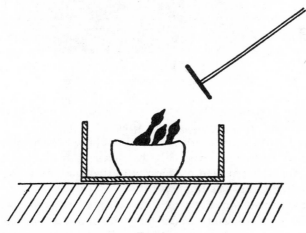

Fɪɢ. 2a
Directed gaping toward a cardboard dummy

FIG. 2b

Presentation of a cardboard dummy

Moreover, the development of eventual positive associations was prevented by varying the stimuli all the time.

In the case of negative results, we always offered other stimuli, which we knew from experience were highly effective, to check on reaction readiness. Since we attempted only a qualitative analysis, accurate dosage of the control stimulus was unnecessary.

In the experiments on directing stimuli, once the gaping was elicited, the particular sign stimulus under investigation was moved by itself, so that the effect of this motion on the direction of gaping could be observed. Since, starting with the 10th to 11th day, gaping is directed toward the parent bird's head, an artificial head often had to be moved in relation to a "body." This could best be done by rotating a circular "body," to which the "head" was attached; the head then revolved around the body which remained stationary. When we wished to distinguish between reactions to two different heads, these were presented in an entirely homologous situation on the same body, or even without a body.

To forestall objections that might arise because the animals were kept in captivity, many experiments were repeated in the field with undisturbed broods reared by their own parents. For this purpose, 5 broods (16 birds) of blackbirds and 3 broods (10 birds) of song thrushes were used.

III. The Release

Jarring the Edge of the Nest. Slight jarring of the nest always elicits gaping, except right after a feeding when the animals are completely satiated. This reaction was so dependable that we used it constantly in other experiments as a control for sufficient reaction readiness. If the birds did not react to a light nudging of their support, a negative result previously obtained with another stimulus was disregarded.

Only a slight jarring, approximately as it is caused by the adult bird alighting on the nest, evokes gaping. If a more violent shock is applied, the nestlings often duck.

Some illustrative protocols follows:

May 8, 1936. Song thrushes, 8 days old. Lid lifted, hand moved to and fro above the nest, no reaction. Edge of the nest jarred slightly; all three gape at once, vertically upward. After they have settled down again, no response to moving hand.

May 9, 1936. Same animals. The experiment is repeated with identical results, then: knocking or pushing against the wooden crate that contains the nest elicits gaping. A percussion of similar strength, soundless to our ears, is also followed by immediate gaping. If we tap without first lifting the lid, so that the birds are in total darkness, their bills can be heard knocking against the lid. Light, therefore, is not an indispensable condition.

June 28, 1936. Blackbirds, 8 days old. Lid lifted. Removal of feces with a forceps does not elicit gaping. Then, a very slight tap against the nest: immediate vigorous reaction.

May 22, 1937. Blackbirds, 5 days. Strong, immediate response to very slight tapping of the nest. Intensive rocking of the nest checks the gaping.

May 23, 1937. Same animals. A heavy object is set down on the table supporting the birds. The shock does not release gaping. Immediately afterwards, slight tapping on the table elicits a vigorous reaction.

Touching the Edge of the Bill. Like many young *Passeres*, thrushes have a thick yellow bulge at each corner of their beaks, which vanishes only after they have started to feed themselves. If this protuberance is touched with some object, a gaping response often follows. This stimulus, however, is not as effective as the percussion stimulus. The ensuing reaction is not stronger to touch by small wooden, glass or metal sticks coated with the juice of earth-worms or with juice pressed from the food used, than it is to touch by clean glass rods. The stimulus is therefore purely tactile, not chemical. Illustrative protocols:

May 9, 1936. Song thrushes, 9 days. The nestlings gape twice when we jar the edge of the nest. After they have calmed down, a tap against the rim of the beak gives a good reaction; in the smallest animal, it comes only in response to the second tap. Similar taps on back, head or wings elicit no reaction in any of the three nestlings. Then: tap against the corner of the beak, immediate gaping. Wings tapped, no response.

May 10, 1936. Song thrushes, 10 days old. At the first feeding, when the birds as usual are not easily stimulated, they react only to the second jarring of the nest. When the beak bulges are poked, they gape immediately.

May 13, 1936. Same animals. After visual stimuli cease to evoke gaping, the reaction follows immediately when the corner of the beak is tapped.

June 26, 1936. Blackbirds, 5 days. Tapping the margin of the beak elicits immediate gaping. Similar taps applied to other parts of the body do not release a reaction.

Puffs of Air. Whenever the parent bird alights on the nest, the young are exposed to a rather feeble local movement of air. To test the releasing value of this factor, we used a small bellows, with which all sorts of air movements could be produced. We succeeded in eliciting gaping very often, although not as frequently as with the stimuli discussed earlier.

The most effective puffs of air are locally very restricted, sudden, not too violent ones, and they must be directed at the young bird's head. The duration of the puff is irrelevant. This is plausible, since the nestlings gape as soon as the air starts to move.

During the earliest phase, when the birds lie in the nest with their eyes closed, a puff of wind can easily be presented while all other effective stimuli are eliminated. But later, when their eyes remain open all the time, we always took care, first, to make the operation of the bellows as inconspicuous as possible, and secondly, we moved the bellows in the same fashion, but without blowing. In this way we succeeded very well in demonstrating that the puff was effective, whereas the slight visual stimulus was not.

Unlike the stimuli discussed before, puffs of air are not equally effective in all phases of growth; older animals do not respond to them. The oldest birds still responsive were 16 days of age.

Fluctuations in Intensity of Illumination. According to Lorenz (1935, p. 194), " a great many young cave breeders" gape if their environment is darkened. This might be equally true of thrushes, whose nests are usually concealed; there, too, the arrival of the parent probably diminishes the light. Conversely, the increase of light when the mother bird rises to make room for her mate could also be an effective stimulus, though the behavior of both species of thrushes around the nest makes this appear highly unlikely.

Since, under natural conditions, the shadow produced by the alighting parent bird is probably always accompanied by movements, all motion must be eliminated in the experiment, and an even change in illumination brought about.

We used two different setups. Either the light came through a pane of opaque glass above the animals, or two incandescent light bulbs, invisible to the animals, illuminated a wooden board suspended above the nest. The light switches could be operated noiselessly.

All these tests had negative results. We could never observe a gaping response to diminished or increased illumination. However, if motion was not sufficiently eliminated, the birds often gaped. Considering the aforesaid statement by Lorenz, it would be worth while to analyze this problem carefully in a cave breeder.

Fluctuations in Temperature. Besides an increase in light intensity, the rising of the adult bird also causes a change in temperature. Lorenz (1935) surmises that a sudden drop in temperature releases gaping in various young passerines. Although, judging from the behavior of grown birds in our species, the effectiveness of this stimulus was equally questionable, we did test the influence of different temperature fluctuations in a series of experiments. The radiation from an electric heater suspended about 50 cm. above the nest was directed onto the nest. A pane of glass suddenly placed over the nest cut off the radiant heat; when suddenly removed, it admitted the rays. Intensity could be controlled by moving the heater upward.

The results were clearly negative: the birds did not respond to either rise or fall in temperature. One example from the protocols may suffice:

May 9, 1936. Song thrushes, 9 days. Heater turned on, glass pane removed, no reaction; tap at the nest edge: immediate gaping. When they are settled, the glass pane is slid over the nest: no reaction. Upon slight tapping, immediate gaping. Glass plate removed, no reaction; slid back, no reaction. Tapping again elicits gaping, etc.

Sound. Observations in the field show that adult thrushes have no specific feeding call. But there are some pairs of blackbirds in which the male approaches the nest with a short strain of song. We had such a pair, and were able to observe that this call released gaping in about ten-day-old birds. Since, owing to the particular situation, visual or vibratory stimuli were excluded (the nest was on a thick elm trunk and the nestlings could not see the parent bird singing down on the ground), the song itself evidently had a releasing effect. This connection, however, was certainly not innate but individually acquired, since most of the young birds whom we examined could not be induced to beg by any single sound. Times without number, in addition to all sorts of arbitrary sounds, we studied sounds that might be classified as releasers (vocalization of adult birds, as well as flight and other noises), all with negative results except in one instance. This exception occurred in a brood of blackbirds, which gaped temporarily, but only in response to the blackbird's warning cry ("tyuktyuk-tyuk-tyuk").

Otherwise, both in the blackbird and the song thrush, any warning cry of the adults immediately extinguishes gaping. Even a feeble imitation of the warning cry, or slight sounds made by knocking hard objects together, have the same effect. This circumstance hampered our experiments in the open not a little. As soon as the adult birds warned, the young ducked, and even with optimal stimuli the gaping response was hard to elicit.

The brood of blackbirds that gaped abnormally on hearing the warning cry was brought into the institute at the age of 5 days, on May 22, 1937. A few nonexperimental feedings were followed by some experiments with tactile stimuli at 6 P.M. Then: they gaped very vigorously in response to "tyuk-tyuk," and also to various other sounds that we made. Later at night we got the same results.

May 24, 1937. Same animals, 7 days. Our imitation of the warning cry elicited gaping. On the other hand, shouting or other sounds did not.

May 29, 1937. Same animals, 12 days. When we imitate the warning cry, the birds now duck instead of gaping. Later the same day we get sometimes a gaping reaction, sometimes ducking.

On the days following, the birds always reacted by ducking down. Thus these animals, singularly enough, have a selective sensitivity to the warning cry, but they answer it with the wrong reaction. In our opinion, the subsequent "correction" has nothing to do with experience. Our protocols do not in any way indicate that we might, even inadvertently, have brought about a training in this sense. We therefore wish to interpret this finding as resulting from abnormally late maturation of the normal nervous connection between warning cry, as the adequate sensory stimulus, and ducking down as the reaction. The strange fact that the warning cry initially releases another reaction naturally raises a new question, which cannot be answered by this one observation.

Visual Stimuli. As already stated, the nestlings first open their eyes on the 9th or 10th day of their lives. Prior to that, it is impossible to elicit gaping by visual stimuli. But even after optically released reactions have appeared, the importance of visual stimuli is still slight, for the birds still keep their eyes closed most of the time. Only after tactile warning do they open their eyes and respond to visual stimulation. From the protocols:

May 26, 1936. Blackbirds, 9 to 10 days. Lifting and moving the cover to and fro elicits no reaction. When the edge of the nest is tapped, they gape at once. When the gaping subsides somewhat, we move our hand to and fro above the nest, and the animals again beg vigorously.

Later the same day: tapping the closed box releases gaping, subsequent removal of the lid does not, eyes are closed. Tap evokes gaping. After the reaction ceases, the animals lie with their eyes open. We display successively above the nest, a white cardboard disc of 20 cm. diameter, a black disc of identical dimensions, a small white wooden stick 25 cm. by 0.75 cm. and a black stick of the same size. The birds respond to all these objects with strong gaping.

May 10, 1936. Song thrushes, 10 days. Cautious lifting of the lid elicits no reaction, slight tapping does. After they have settled down again, a finger shown above the nest immediately releases gaping. In the evening of the same day, one of the nestlings responds to the black stick without previous tactile warning. When the same stick is shown once more, none of the young respond; however, control by tapping is positive.

After the 10th (blackbird) and 11th (song thrush) days respectively, the eyes of satiated and resting animals remain open for longer periods, and correspondingly the gaping can be elicited more often by visual stimuli. In the light of the above records, the visual pattern must be very broad and poor in perceptual cues, for the reaction is quite unspecific. But continued analysis showed that certain conditions must, nevertheless, be fulfilled. The following factors were investigated: elevation, size, color, form, motion.

Relative height. If a gaping response is to be elicited by visual stimuli the releasing object must be above the horizontal line passing through the nestlings' eyes. If objects which otherwise release a reaction are not situated high enough, the birds, though following them with their eyes, do not gape at them.

June 19, 1936. Blackbirds, 10 days. A black disc is moved to and fro just under the rim of the nest. The birds stretching their necks and heads far out of the nest see it, but do not gape.

A black cardboard disc of 8 cm. diameter is moved toward the nest at about eye level. The upper edge of the disc is about 4 cm. above eye level. One young bird opens its beak once, but does not gape. The next time, one nestling gapes.

May 27, 1937. Song thrushes, 12 days. A stick presented below eye level does not elicit gaping. However, the birds fixate it steadily. At a tap against the nest edge they gape immediately.

June 8, 1937. Song thrushes, 8 days. A small black stick moved forward at eye level is fixated without gaping. As soon as it is moved a few centimeters higher, the birds gape vigorously.

Protocol 1 shows that larger objects may be quite far above eye level before gaping occurs. For smaller objects, the borderline between effective and ineffective stimuli often lies with amazing precision at the nestlings' eye level.

Portielje (1922) describes how young orioles (*Oriolus o. oriolus* L.) at the age of 30 days only accepted food if he presented it above their beaks. Food offered lower was fixated but not eaten. When they began to feed themselves, they again heeded only fruits hanging above them. Since an adult male behaved similarly, it may be that Portielje's observations do not concern the gaping response. But the behavior he describes is dependent on "objects situated above eye level" as strictly as it is in the gaping thrushes.

Size. The young birds gape at objects of greatly varying sizes. Initially at any rate, there is no upper limit. A smooth board 20 cm. by 40 cm. presented at a distance of 20 cm. elicits strong reactions. Later on, surprisingly, the animals no longer react to very large objects; the upper limit, therefore, is shifted in the course of development. We believe that a learning process may definitely be excluded here. Since the animals see the experimenters themselves before each feeding, the only possible effect of an eventual conditioning would be to extend the releasing value to objects of human size. In other words, the upper limit should be shifted upward rather than downward. We seem rather to be dealing with a kind of maturation; not a maturation of motor form which is the usual meaning of the term, but a maturation of selective stimulus dependence, of the releasing mechanism.

May 17, 1936. Song thrushes, 17 days. Lively gaping at white and at black cardboard discs of 20 cm. diameter.

May 19, 1936. Same animals, 19 days. No gaping at black discs of 18 cm. or of 16 cm. diameter; the animals even duck a little.

As the last protocol indicates, the shifting of the upper limit could be due to the fact that the dependence of crouching on certain visual stimuli is just being established.

A lower limit of size can be determined fairly well. It lies in the vicinity of 3 mm. However, the reactions to objects so small were rather vacillating, and no definite conclusions could be drawn.

May 27, 1937. Song thrushes, 12 days. A green clay globule of 3.5 mm. diameter, suspended by a thread, elicits gaping. Wire of 0.7 mm. diameter does not elicit gaping. Nor does white sewing thread, though it is fixated.

May 29, 1937. Same animals, 14 days. No response to white thread, slight gaping at the 3.5 mm. clay globule. When a similar clay globule of 8 mm. diameter is presented, the birds gape vigorously. Later the same day: 3.5 mm.: slight reaction; 12 mm.: vigorous reaction.

Color. In general, color seems to be irrelevant for the releasing value of an object. We do not know to what extent animals of gaping age are able to distinguish colors. We know no reaction of these thrushes that would be innately dependent on a specific color. Moreover, it would be extremely difficult, if not impossible, to build up any kind of color training during the nesting period. Nevertheless, we endeavored to find out how far the birds we reared would be trained to our color cues. We always worked in white laboratory coats. Consequently, their white color was one of the few properties studied in which we differed from the adequate parents, and we had a good opportunity to determine whether or not our experiments linked the gaping reaction in any way to naturally ineffective stimuli. We therefore limited our question to whether fledglings reared solely by people clad in white would perhaps prefer white.

A black and a white object, homologous in all other respects, were presented either simultaneously or in succession. In these experiments black was always distinctly preferred, not only by the blackbirds, but also, though to a lesser extent, by the song thrushes. This becomes plausible if one considers that the feeding parent will in most cases stand out as a silhouette against the light surroundings.

May 27, 1936. Song thrushes, 11 to 12 days. Two cardboard discs of 8 cm. diameter each, one white, one black, are presented side by side. Each dummy is shown three times on the right and three times on the left, so as to avoid any left-right preference. The birds gape five times at black and once at white.[1]

The dummy illustrated in Figure 3, as well as its mirror image, were presented to several broods of blackbirds. If we were careful to hold both "heads" at the same height, the animals always preferred the black half.

[1] Strictly speaking, only the orienting, not the releasing value of colors is investigated in this experiment. But for various reasons we believe it best to mention this discrimination experiment, too, at this early stage.

FIG. 3
Dummy for testing white-black preference

Form. As may be seen from the foregoing, form has no demonstrable influence on the intensity of the reaction. We found no form which, moved above eye level, could not release the gaping. There is no point in corroborating this by protocols; the correctness of the assumption is evident from the protocols given earlier.

From this last finding we infer that free-living thrushes must have the ability to narrow down the releasing stimulus situation by training. If the innate stimulus situation, which consists of very few sign stimuli, were to remain fully effective, the slightest breeze would constantly release reactions in these forest birds, as there are usually fluttering leaves, swaying branches and the like around them. However, we did not go into this question any further; but it is certain that moving leaves in their environment do not stimulate young thrushes living in the field to beg. How this training is accomplished, we do not know.

Motion. We have found that motion has a releasing value in two respects. First, the adult bird must move; motionless objects are never able to release gaping. Secondly, if a motion diagonal to the axis of the eye has no effect, motion toward the young may evoke the reaction.

To study the influence of the diagonal movement, we originally used the following setup: we placed one of our dummies on a stand above the brood under observation. Then we carefully removed the lid of the box and observed whether the motionless disc released a reaction. If it did not, we moved the disc and evaluated the reactions that followed this motion as positive. With a motionless disc, reactions were observed in only a few cases. Moreover, as we discovered later, these responses had been released by the moving lid and not by the disc, for sometimes removal of the lid elicited begging even if no dummy was present.

We next worked with silhouettes (Fig. 4). By operating an electric switch noiselessly, these could be presented at any time without any

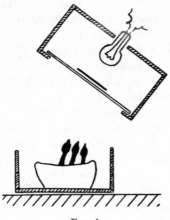

FIG. 4

Setup for projecting silhouettes

motion being visible to the birds. With this kind of presentation, no reaction ever followed motionless shadows; on the other hand, even a slight motion released gaping.

May 26, 1936. Song thrushes, 10 to 11 days. No light in the box. Cover-board removed, waited until the birds were settled again. Then the light in the box was switched on and off four times. At each change, the nestlings looked upward a little, but did not gape. Then the disc was moved lightly to and fro behind the opaque glass by a thread: begging ensued at once.

That motion in line with the axis of the eye has a considerably stronger releasing value can best be shown by feeding the birds so long, or exhausting the gaping response so thoroughly, that they cease to react to motion oblique to the eye axis. If the dummy is then moved toward the animals, they often beg again. The decisive factor here is not the growing size of the dummy (mere projection of the movement of its outline); the difference continues to exist if, in the control experiment, the diagonal motion is made much more extensive than the projected movement. The reaction to moving dummies is most intensive if they approach obliquely from above.

IV. Orientation

Gaping is always directed in relation to the environment. This orientation is not the same throughout the nesting phase. Two successive stages may be distinguished. In the first, the neck is stretched straight upward; in the second, neck and throat are directed toward the parent bird's head. It is remarkable that the transition from the first to the second phase does not coincide in time with the taking over of control by visual releasing stimuli. Not until 1 to 3 days after gaping can first be released visually does visual steering appear as well. This means that, if both release and steering are used for classification, three successive stages must be distinguished: orientation to gravity with mechanical release, orientation to gravity with visual release, and visual steering with visual release. Before returning to this theoretically important fact, we shall first substantiate the threefold division in more detail.

Orientation to Gravity with Mechanical Release. This phase, as already mentioned, lasts 9 to 10 days. That the reaction is directed by gravity is inferred from the following facts: changes in illumination do not affect the direction of neck-stretching. The direction of light incidence, moving light or dark objects, or even total darkness, are wholly ineffectual. Repeatedly presented mechanical stimuli, such as tilting the nest, or even interposing an object that impedes normal motion, are equally without effect. For instance, the animals hit the lid with their beaks again and again if one taps on the closed container. This steering by gravity was therefore not analyzed further.

Orientation to Gravity with Visual Release. This phase is of greatly varying duration in different individuals; though usually no longer than 1 day, it may sometimes last as long as 3. On the average, it begins on the 9th day in blackbirds, on the 10th day in song thrushes.

At this stage the nestlings still keep their eyes closed much of the time and, as we have said, only vibratory or tactile stimuli elicit begging. But after their eyes are opened upon tactile warning, visual stimuli, although they can release gaping, have not the slightest influence on its direction; the birds gape vertically upwards, often past the releasing object. Figure 5 illustrates this in a young bird fostered not by us, but by its own parents. An extreme case follows as an example:

May 24, 1937. Song thrushes, 9 days. Eyes closed, visual stimuli ineffective, jarring the edge of the nest elicits a vertical reaction. Later the same day: I move my fingers slightly above eye level. One animal is lying with its eyes open; it starts up at once, and gapes beyond the finger. The others are stimulated by his movements and also gape straight upward.

In the two days following, the birds became increasingly sensitive to visual stimuli; however, the first indication of visual steering could not be observed until the 12th day.

Visual Steering with Visual Release. As we have said, the young birds begin to direct their gaping motions toward the adult bird's head 1 to 3

FIG. 5

Visually released, gravity-steered gaping reaction

FIG. 6

Visually released, visually steered gaping
reaction

days after their eyes have opened (Fig. 6). This orientation is entirely
dependent on visual stimuli, as shown by the following experiments.

The transfer to the parent bird's head is a gradual one. At first the
nestlings continue to gape almost vertically, turning to a hardly noticeable extent toward the adult bird. Slowly, in the course of 12 to 24 hours,
this deviation becomes so perfect that the young bird's neck is really
pointed toward the parent bird's head. The visual schema of the directing component thus matures and, during this maturation, it is superimposed on the mechanical orientation, so that the gaping response as
a whole is a gradually changing resultant of the mechanically and the
visually directed reactions.

Simple preliminary experiments in 1935 drew our attention to some
of the cues provided by the head. The experiments described below followed quite naturally. To gauge the effectiveness of a sign stimulus, we
first let the nestlings choose between two dummies which differed in the
one character under investigation. Secondly, we moved one part of the
parent dummy, to see whether the moving part was effective as a head,
that is, whether the fledglings begged from it.

Relative height. If a cardboard disc of moderate diameter (e.g., 8 cm.)
is presented, the animals gape toward its upper edge, not toward the

center. In this, as in the following experiments, we always took care to show the whole disc above eye level, so that every single part had a releasing value. Of two optically identical objects, the one situated higher was always chosen. The experiment was made with two small sticks (Fig. 7), two cardboard discs, or with fingers. In order to eliminate possible

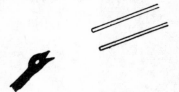

FIG. 7

Presentation of two sticks at equal distance
but at different heights

differences of shape or color, one or the other object was presented alternately as the higher. Orientation proved to be exclusively dependent on height. The higher dummy need not be above the other in its entirety; it is enough if a piece of it extends above the highest part of the other object. A difference of only a few millimeters is enough. In this subjective sense, the model whose upper portion is situated so far above the other as to attract gaping will henceforth be called the higher dummy.

May 16, 1936. Song thrushes, 16 days. Two small black sticks at equal distance; one above the other. Gaping directed at the higher (Fig. 7).

May 19, 1936. Song thrushes, 19 days. Black double disc (Fig. 8). As soon as one disc is presented about 3 mm. higher than the other, gaping is directed toward it.

June 19, 1936. Blackbirds, 16 days. One of two small sticks held up at identical distance is presented 3 mm. higher than the other. The nestlings gape toward the higher stick.

FIG. 8

Black double disk

Relative distance. If two optically identical objects are presented at the same height, the birds gape at the one closer to them. This experiment can also be made with widely varied dummies. But since distance is not as effective as height, the two dummies must be precisely on the same level in these experiments.

May 16, 1936. Song thrushes, 16 days. Two optically identical small sticks are shown at equal height and equal distance. Upon repeated presentation, the animals gape sometimes at the left stick, sometimes at the right one. If the one is held at a distance of 3 cm., the other of 2.5 cm., they immediately gape at the one nearer to them.

We also made numerous observations like the following:

May 30, 1936. Blackbirds, 10 days. The nestlings gape at each other's heads as soon as our dummy is farther away than the head of a sibling. Often the gaping response is released and directed by our dummy, and is then deflected toward the siblings during the experiment. We ascribe this to the circumstance that the dummy is held fairly still, while the siblings' heads move briskly. Often the bird in the middle of the nest gaped toward the dummy, while the two on the side gaped toward the central bird's head. It may be that the latter did not gape toward its neighbors because, in our setup, the animals on the side always had to gape obliquely, so that their heads were automatically situated lower than the central bird's head (Fig. 9).

FIG. 9

The fledgling in the center gapes at the dummy, the ones on the side gape at the head of the central one

If distance and height are pitted against each other, the height cue directs more accurately than the distance cue.

May 14, 1936. Song thrushes, 14 days. Two small black sticks are shown at equal height: the nearer one is always chosen. Now one stick is presented at a distance of 3 cm., while the other is held 3 cm. higher and 2.5 cm. farther away than the lower. Nevertheless, it is still preferred. Then the lower stick is shown at a distance of 4 cm., the upper 4 cm. farther away and 4 cm. higher. The birds gape toward the higher one.

Relative size. If two cardboard discs of different sizes are presented at "equal height," the birds orient themselves toward the smaller. If one is considerably smaller than the other, they gape at the smaller one even if it stands below the larger. A certain ratio of magnitude between head and body therefore seems to be decisive. In order to compare heads of varying sizes, we always presented a circular body with a circular head in its normal position, that is, with the head at the top. We then rotated the dummy in its own plane. The birds turned with it, continuously aiming for the head. If the dummy's head got too far down, it lost its meaning, and all at once the birds oriented themselves toward the currently highest part of the body outline. The measure of rotation tolerated varied for different head sizes. When the presentation of the dummies was standardized to some extent, the angle of rotation could be roughly measured. In experiments with a body of 8 cm. diameter, the nestlings followed a head of 3 cm. diameter the farthest. Both larger and smaller heads were abandoned at lesser rotation (Fig. 10). We next presented

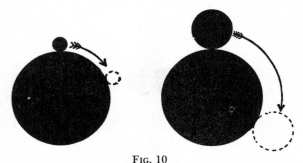

Fig. 10

Maximum rotation tolerated for two heads of different sizes

bodies of various sizes with heads of various sizes, and obtained the findings given in Figures 11 and 12. They show that the size of the optimal head varies with the size of the body. In other words, there is no absolute optimal head size, but only a relative one. The optimal head has a diameter about one third that of the body.

This finding can also be demonstrated in another way. We presented a body with two heads of different sizes, whose upper edges were held at exactly the same height. The animals then "chose" one of the two heads. Of the two head sizes used, the nestlings preferred the one of 3 cm. diameter on a body of 8 cm., and the head of 1 cm. on a body of 4 cm. diameter (Fig. 13).

A further question is this: how small can the head be before it loses its directive value altogether? Since, as we shall show, the shape of the head is largely irrelevant, the series of dummies used for this purpose may vary greatly in form. First we let a head of 1 cm. diameter disappear

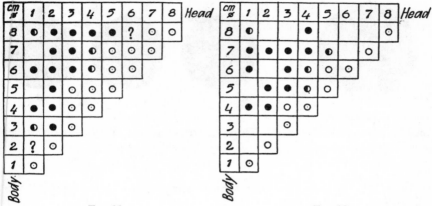

cm ø	1	2	3	4	5	6	7	8	Head
8	◐	●	●	●	●	?	○	○	
7		●	●	◐	○	○	○		
6	●	●	●	◐	○	○			
5		●	○	○	○				
4	●	●	○	○					
3	◐	●	○						
2	?	○							
1	○								

Body

Fig. 11

cm ø	1	2	3	4	5	6	7	8	Head
8	◐			●					○
7	●	●	●	●	◐		○		
6	●		●	◐	○	○			
5		●	●	◐	○				
4	●	●	○	○					
3		○							
2		○							
1	○								

Body

Fig. 12

Ratio of head to body in nestling thrushes. White circle: the higher is always chosen. Black-and-white circle: the smaller is preferred, even if it is "lower" than the larger. Black circle: the smaller is greatly preferred, and followed far to the side. ?: doubtful result

Ratio of head to body in nestling song thrushes. Although these observations are incomplete, it is possible to conclude that there is an optimal relative head size

gradually behind a body of 8 cm., to find the smallest distance the head must stand out to retain any perceptible steering influence. The critical point was reached when the head protruded only 2 mm. (Fig. 14).

In a second series of dummies, the two tangents to the body circle were drawn from a point coming closer and closer to the body, so that the angle enclosed by them grew increasingly wider. The minimum

a   b

Fig. 13

Two double-headed dummies
Body in a: 4 cm.; in b: 8 cm.
Head in a: 1 cm.; in b: 3 cm.

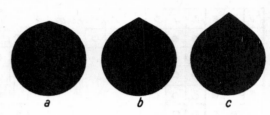

FIG. 14

Smallest effective size of a
head circle which protrudes
by 2 mm.

FIG. 15

Three "head" dummies; on the left the widest
effective angle

break in the outline that was still heeded in this setup is given in
Figure 15a.

With this method, we discovered a gradual change in the effectiveness
of directing stimuli: as the animals grew older, they reacted to more
obtuse angles. We have not ascertained whether this was due to learning
or to maturation.

Form. The preliminary experiments with fingers, small sticks, etc.,
already indicate that the shape of the "head" may vary considerably
without losing its directive effect. To substantiate this conclusion more
fully, a number of identical body circles with heads of varying shapes
were presented (Fig. 16). All the heads were approximately equal in area

FIG. 16

Five different heads, all equally effective

to the circular head which had an optimal effect above the circular body used.[2]

As far as could be ascertained with our crude method, the birds gaped with equal intensity at all the heads reproduced in Figure 16. Nor did the body rotation method reveal differences in the measure of rotation tolerated. Choice trials were not given. No growing selectivity with increasing age could be found in this instance.

According to these experiments, then, the fledglings seemed to regard all interruptions of the body outline as heads. To test the influence of concave breaks in the outline, the model illustrated in Figure 17 was presented. To our surprise, the nestlings followed this "head" quite

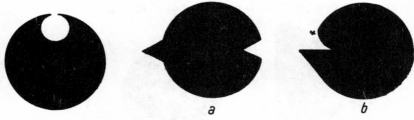

FIG. 17
Concave break in outline

FIG. 18
Concave and convex breaks in outline are pitted
against one another

intensely. We found later that these concave interruptions gained a directing influence about one day later than the optimal convex heads. Upon observing the gaping motions more closely, we also saw that the parts of the body to the right and left of the indentation acted as goals of orientation, not the concavity itself. If the hole was rotated from right to left, or vice versa, over the zenith of the body, as soon as it passed the zenith the birds changed their orientation with a noticeable jerk to the point which now appeared higher. As far as the animals were concerned, therefore, our model was a body with two heads. The fact that the body was then flattened, not circular, apparently did not diminish its value as a body. This explanation would be wholly satisfying if it could be proved more conclusively that convex breaks are more effective than concave ones. This we actually succeeded in doing with the models shown in Figure 18. With (a) the nestlings always gape at the protruding

2 Since we did not know by what properties the birds judged the size of a "head" (area, outline, and so forth) and since we had found, in the above experiments, that the optimal relative head size was not too clearly defined, it would have been superfluous and even unwarranted to make the diversely shaped heads "equal in size" by a definite, arbitrarily selected "objective" scale.

head; but if this is lowered by rotation, they transfer to the point above the indentation. In model (b) the indentation has two advantages over the protruding point: it is higher, and it deviates a little more from the contour. Nevertheless, the birds gape toward the point; if it is rotated farther down, the gaping is directed at the point indicated with an "x."

A convex break in outline is therefore a characteristic of the sign stimuli provided by the head.

On the other hand, the bird's outline has a significant concave interruption. This serves to separate the head from the body, as a "neck" indentation. If the nestlings have to choose between two heads, the one with, the other without a neck indentation, they always gape toward the head marked off by the indentation. The smallest indentation that is still effective in a body of 8 cm. is one of 2 mm. (Fig. 19).

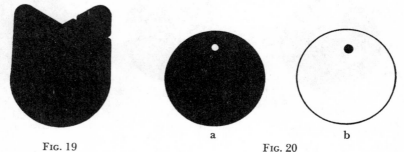

FIG. 19   a   b
Two-headed dummy, one with, the   FIG. 20
other without neck indentations   Two dummies with color spots

Color. If a black disc with a small white spot near its edge was shown, the birds gaped at the spot (Fig. 20a). A black dot in a white circle (Fig. 20b), however, worked just as well in both species of thrushes. If the discs were rotated, the nestlings followed the spot exactly as they did a break in contour.

May 14, 1936. Song thrushes, 14 days. Upon rotation of the discs (Fig. 20) the birds follow either spot down about 90°, but no farther.

May 17, 1936. Song thrushes, 17 days. Results as on the 14th day, except that one of the fledglings repeatedly follows the black dot on the white disc all the way down (180°).

May 30, 1936. Song thrushes, 14 to 15 days. We rotate white and black discs of 8 cm. diameter with black or white spots respectively. The spots vary in size (1 and 2.5 cm.). Almost without exception, the birds follow the spot all the way down. But if the spot is at the bottom when first presented, the animals gape at the upper rim of the disc.

Since the color of the head in both species hardly differs from that of the body, it is hard to fit the ascertained effect of the color spot into the pattern of the food donor. It might possibly correspond to the beak which, at least in the blackbird, is of a different color. Should this be true, then there might be an optimal size for the beak, as there is for the head. This, however, should be considerably smaller than the optimal head size in relation to the same body. In the following experiments two color spots of different sizes were therefore presented in one body (Fig. 21). No definite optimum size could be discovered; rather, the gaping was always directed at the larger spot.

June 23, 1936. Blackbirds, 14 days. Two white spots, of 0.8 and 2 cm. diameter respectively, are painted on a circular body of 8 cm. diameter. The nestlings always select the large spot, even when it is presented somewhat lower than the small one.

July 29, 1937. Blackbirds, 12 days. Same experiment with white disc. Same findings.

Fig. 21

Large and small color spot, at
equal distance from the rim of
the circular body

Fig. 22

The large spot is farther from
the rim than the small one

Hence, the preferred size would in no way fit the actual size of the beak, and the assumption that we were dealing with a cue to the beak became unlikely. However, we had a slight suspicion that the birds might be gaping at the upper edge of the spot rather than at the spot itself. At times it seemed to us as if they were gaping at the "horn" between the spot and the edge of the disc, exactly as in the concave contour breaks, where the point between hole and disc-contour functioned as a head. Figure 21 shows that, for the human observer at any rate, the bigger spot cuts out far more conspicuous "heads" than does the smaller, at least so long as both spots are at equal distances from the outline. Should this hypothesis prove correct, we could expect the effect of a spot to diminish in proportion to its distance from the outer edge, since the effect as a "horn" (as a convex contour break) is strongest when the spot is closest to the outer edge.

We next presented the model shown in Figure 22, and now the smaller spot was in fact more effective.

This finding was obtained with both black and white discs. In the experiment with the white disc the blackbirds reacted somewhat differently from the song thrushes. They gaped quite frequently at the smaller spot even when it was rather far from the outline. This could perhaps be explained by the predominance of black, which we had found in blackbirds at the outset. Next to the larger black spot, the smaller one might have been taken for the large spot's head, and the white disc disregarded. To verify this possibility we presented, instead of two black spots on a white disc, two circular black discs identical to the spots in relative size and distance. If in the first experiment the white disc was merely considered as a background, the experiment with the two black discs should turn out exactly the same as did the one with the black spots. The results were not conclusive. The gaping was in fact sometimes directed toward the smaller disc, sometimes, however, toward the larger. Thus we cannot account fully for the divergent choices: the ones directed at the small spot by blackbirds. Possibly the experiment is too complex; it seems to us that the two discs may have been regarded once as two segregated objects (two adult birds of different size), another time as a single body-with-head.

Judging from the results of the experiments reported (save occasional divergent choices in blackbirds), the color spots apparently owe their effect to the fact that, together with the proximal outer edge of the body, they constitute two "heads," and these heads have the same directive value as convex breaks in the contour. Consequently there seems to be no reason to regard interruption in color as a different perceptual cue from a break in outline.

V. Control Experiments in the Field

For several reasons, our experiments needed supplementation by control experiments in a natural habitat. In the first place, the inadequacy of our feedings might have lowered the threshold of the gaping reaction. This would account for its unspecificity. Secondly, in the course of our experiments the fledglings might have been trained to stimuli derived from the experimenters. This would have been reflected directly in differences of reaction readiness between laboratory animals and wild specimens. Finally, it should be considered that inadequate nourishment might have involved phenomena of disintegration or loss in specificity of the reaction, a possibility stressed especially by Lorenz (1935).

The critical experiments were therefore repeated with a number of wild birds (16 blackbirds and 10 song thrushes) reared entirely by their own parents and only used for experiments occasionally, between two feedings. The animals were never removed from the nest, and care was taken that no parental warning cries disturbed the gaping tendency during our experiments.

The following experiments were repeated in the field:

Release: jarring the edge of the nest; touching the rim of the beak; sound; visual stimuli (fingers, small sticks, black, white and brown cardboard dummies of widely varied shapes and sizes, choice between black and white discs, relative height).

Orientation: distinction of the three phases; relative height; relative distance; relative size (choice trials); irrelevancy of the shape of the head; the head as a convex break in outline; neck indentation; discrimination experiments with color spots of varying size and location.

The outcome of these field controls is easily described: all experiments had almost precisely the same results as the laboratory ones. Only the following differences, which in our opinion are not critical, were found. One brood, as already mentioned, reacted to the father's call. Furthermore, the naturally reared fledglings in general seemed less hungry than our birds; they did not gape so vigorously. But this affected the threshold of the release so little that no difference in reaction readiness was found with our method.

The experiments performed in a natural environment thus refute the contention of abnormality, whether due to lowering of threshold or to damage caused by deficient nourishment. They also preclude the possibility that, owing to training effected unwittingly by the experimenters, the stimulus dependence of the laboratory animals' gaping response differed from the mechanisms of wild birds. Whether the innate mechanisms of the gaping reaction are modified by learning processes, and if so, to what extent, is a question that has not been answered as yet. We shall attempt to answer it in what follows.

VI. Evaluation and Summary

Our original intention was to make a thorough study of an "innate mechanism." We wished not only to prove that there are "simple" mechanisms built up of a few perceptual cues, but also to analyze these cues as fully as possible. We soon found, however, that there is no such thing as "the pattern of the parent companion," or even a mechanism of the food donor. Two schemata are effective side by side for this one reaction alone: a directing one and a purely releasing one. The motor as well as the receptor components of both are subject to maturation.

The effective stimulus situation for the releasing mechanism is initially mechanical (tactual-vibratory); later on, the visual factor is added.

For visual release, three perceptual cues are indispensable: an object that is larger than 3 mm. in diameter, must move, above eye level. The form of the motor component released also changes: the neck is stretched more vigorously and, as described, wing and leg movements are added.

The effective stimulus situation for the directing mechanism is also mechanical to begin with: the nestling orients to gravity. Later on, visual steering is added, and the gaping is directed toward the parent bird's head. The head bears the following main perceptual characters, which are therefore part of the directing mechanism: it is above the rest of the body, it is nearer, it is a convex break in outline, and it is separated from the body by an indentation. The motor element of the response to visual directing stimuli is more complex than orientation to gravity, for here the force of gravity does not function in line with the direction of gaping, but operates obliquely on the neck. In the case of mechanical directing stimuli, the same muscles that effect orientation also compensate for the direct mechanical influence of gravity, whereas in visual steering, compensation for the effects of gravity is undoubtedly controlled by muscles other than those which determine orientation toward the head.

The gaping response remains complex throughout the nesting period; it is always an integration of two mechanisms. We are thus compelled to make the same distinction that Lorenz (1937) made between "instinctive action" ("hereditary coordination") and "orienting mechanism" ("taxis"). As in the egg-retrieving reaction of the greylag goose, analyzed by Lorenz and Tinbergen (1938), the two components are simultaneously interlocked. It seems to us methodologically important that in the present paper we have made the distinction between instinctive action and taxis differently than was done in the case of the egg-rolling reaction. In the first place, the change from mechanical to visual stimulus control occurred sooner in the releasing than in the orienting mechanism. Secondly, the optimal stimulus situations are different for the two mechanisms in regard to both mechanical and visual stimulation.

It is evident from the foregoing that a mechanism can pertain equally well to a taxis and to an innate coordination. This impels us to point out a certain misuse in nomenclature of the word "mechanism," due to an inaccurate formulation of concepts. It is customary to refer to "the mechanism of the sex partner," "the mechanism of the parent companion," etc. This does not always mean the same thing. Sometimes it indicates the mechanism of a certain reaction directed toward the sex partner, the parent companion, etc., and sometimes it refers to the sum total of key stimuli correlated to various reactions directed at the sex partner, etc. A mechanism, however, pertains to one reaction. Since the action system of an animal often comprises several reactions to the sex partner, etc., each of these reactions may presumably have its own mechanism, and each of these mechanisms may consist of different perceptual cues. More than one "mechanism of the sex partner" will then be found. This is indeed the case. In the first place, the actions are often successively interlocked so as to form a chain, in which each link has its own mechanism responding to a special set of key stimuli. Instances of this are found in the mating behavior of many animals (birds, fish, insects). Proof of the chain character is the fact that, whenever certain responses of the partner fail to occur, the behavior breaks off at specific points. The gaping reaction itself is the first link in a chain consisting of at least two: the next link is swallowing, which occurs only if something really reaches the throat. The tactile stimuli that are effective here pertain to the "mechanism of the parent companion" as do the above analyzed stimuli which release the gaping reaction. But they fit an entirely different component of the behavior, and therefore belong to the mechanism controlling this component.

Our experiments further disclose that, besides this successive type of interlocking, a releasing and a directing component may also be linked simultaneously within "one" reaction. The releasing mechanism pertains to the innate coordination, the orienting one to the taxis component.

It must be emphasized that, in distinguishing the two components of the gaping reaction, it is irrelevant whether and to what extent conditioning of any kind may modify the mechanisms. Yet whether we have here examined innate mechanisms is a question important enough in itself to be summarized and discussed once more in this place, for very few schemata which we definitely know to be innate have been analyzed so far.

Since our laboratory and field experiments yielded similar results, a training to specific cues in which we differed from the normal food donors cannot be assumed. In many other characters, however, there was a rough conformity between ourselves and the adult birds. An eventual modification of these perceptual cues by some kind of training would work out similarly in the field and in the laboratory, and the difference would therefore not show up in our control experiments. However, during our laboratory experiments we gained several pointers which, together with the field trials, allow us to judge with certainty whether learning processes had changed the optimal stimulus situation or not.

The mechanical releasing stimuli certainly operate without any previous experience. Moreover, it is impossible to break the animals of their gaping response to vibratory stimulation. Certain components of the visual releasing situation, such as size, are also assuredly innate. The specific sensitivity to these cues was present as soon as the nestlings opened their eyes, before they could have learned anything. We have described how the upper limit of the sign stimulus "size" is shifted during growth, and shown that this is not due to learning.

Since both experimenters and adult birds always pushed the food into the fledglings' throats from above, it is of course questionable whether the cue "above the horizon" was not conditioned by learning. We therefore tried to teach nestlings to gape at moving objects below eye level as well. We released their gaping response regularly by jarring the nest, and then put the food into their mouths from below. However, the birds did not learn to beg from an object moving below eye level. Moreover, the preference for black in our experimental subjects also argues against a learning effect: we always fed them in white laboratory coats and yet they did not develop a preference for white.

As we have said before, we believe that learning processes do occur which render certain stimulus combinations ineffective; that is, in some measure they cut a small section out of the originally broad innate mechanism. For instance, the birds do not gape at branches and leaves in motion, which have all the visual characters of the optimal stimulus situation. This can only be the result of negative conditioning. How this negative training is accomplished in the field might be discovered by long-range observation of a few broods; we unfortunately neglected to do so.

In the light of our observations, we doubt whether similar, but positive "excisions" also exist, inasmuch as the thrushes, for instance, learn to gape at the forceps more intensely than at the other dummies. We wish to state emphatically at this point that our conclusions refer only to the two species which we studied, and only to the one reaction we investigated. Differences between species as well as between different reactions of one and the same species are naturally to be expected.

Of course, the young of many other song birds learn to gape at specific stimulus combinations more vigorously than the innate mechanism "prescribes." For instance, various species certainly learn to know their parents, or their foster parents, more or less personally (Lorenz, 1935); but this learning process probably influences the gaping response only toward the end of the nesting period, or even later. The innate mechanism has then already been in operation for some time. If such learning processes occur in the species of *passeres* which we studied, this too happens only after they have left the nest.

Finally, in many cases an essentially different learning process can create the illusion of a change in the releasing mechanism. Recently caught young birds often duck in the presence of humans. This mood of escape or of crouching suppresses the gaping reaction. Once the animals have become accustomed to the new situation, the "block" to gaping is lifted. It is then usually maintained that the nestlings have "learned to gape at the forceps." It does not seem in the least unlikely, however, that in many passerines the forceps fits extremely well into the innate pattern of the gaping reaction. In that case, however, we cannot assume that the releasing mechanism of this reaction has been affected by learning. In consequence of habituation, the threshold of the escape reaction is merely raised, but this does not alter the fact that flight inhibits gaping.

As for the steering, the tendency of young birds to orient themselves to gravity is, of course, innate. The newly hatched young already show this tendency, though at that stage the motions are still very immature. Of the visual directing stimuli, relative height is a character of the innate mechanism. Even our birds, which were not fed from the highest point of our bodies, developed a preference for the highest. Thus they could not possibly have acquired the character of height from us; on the contrary, even our different method of feeding never taught them that the food did not come from the highest point. We cannot make a positive statement concerning relative distance, since both the field controls and the laboratory animals always received their food from the part of the dispenser nearest to them, and could thus have been trained to this characteristic in both cases. The cue of relative size, however, must be innate; our experimental subjects could never have learned this from us, since the ratio of human hand and body is not 1 to 3. Form undoubtedly has no part or, at most, an utterly negligible one in the innate pattern. We did not investigate to what extent a training to specific forms is feasible. In any case, learning of this kind never goes so far as to impair the sensitivity to other forms within the range of the mechanism.

These facts seem to demonstrate conclusively that the optimal stimulus situations, as we found them, correspond to the innate mechanisms, and normally are not affected in any essential way by learning processes.

In the fragmentary data on learning and its modifying effects on the mechanism to be found in the literature, definite proof that we are not dealing with changes due to maturation is lacking. As we said in the descriptive section, there is not only a maturation of motor form; the stimulus dependence of a reaction, its releasing mechanism also matures. This has been discussed in reference to changes in the upper limit of the "size" cue in the releasing mechanism. The extent to which the maturation of a mechanism is due to growth in the receptor or in the nervous system or in both, will probably differ from case to case.

The most complete study on the release of the gaping response is probably the one by Kuhlmann (1909). He describes changes in reaction readiness in various passerine birds *(Agelaius ph. phoenicus* L. and *Hylocichla mustelina* GM.), which he attributes sometimes to learning, at other times to growth, but without substantiating his interpretation of each individual case.

We conclude: (1) The releasing and the directing mechanisms of the gaping reaction, which we found in the two passerine species, are in fact innate. (2) Many of the identifiable changes in the readiness of song birds to beg are not due to learning processes affecting the mechanisms correlated to the gaping response, but either to maturation or to learning processes of another kind.

We know of only one other instance in the literature where a reaction directed at the partner's head has been examined as to its releasing as well as its directing stimulus situation. This, too, is a case of a pattern segregated into a "head" and a "body" (Portielje, 1926).

If surprise prevents a bittern from taking flight, the bird will adopt a posture of defense and peck with lightning speed at the enemy's head, as soon as it ventures too close to the bittern. But no pecking occurs if the antagonist has no "head." When Portielje drew his head deep down between his shoulders and covered himself with a cloth, the bird did not peck at him. As soon as he then placed a roughly head-shaped cardboard disc over his covered head, the bittern pecked at the disc. He concludes from his experiments: *"Botaurus stellaris* in a posture of fright, face to face with an enemy-*in-toto* and prepared for defense, reacts to a complex of cues, which probably consists of something like a smaller head shape or head outline above a larger torso shape or torso outline" (p. 11). To be sure, Portielje's experiments do not appear to prove conclusively that the head must actually be smaller than the body and be situated above it. But they do show that the shape of the head itself needs to present only a few key stimuli and, moreover, that a head is required not only to direct the pecking response, but also to release it. In this respect the bittern's reaction differs from the gaping reaction of *passeres*. An even more exhaustive study of the bittern in the light of our results would be desirable.

5

Comparative Study of Behavior

KONRAD LORENZ (1939)[1]

I. *The Evolution of Instinctive Behavior*

Taxonomy is at present generally disparaged as a branch of science that has become static and obsolete. We tend to disregard the fact that the idea of evolution, which has done more than any other in giving science a dynamic outlook, was developed in this field. Comparative morphology arranges the living world according to rising and waning similarities. Owing to it, we have gained insight into the evolutionary change of species, which rules our personal and social thinking and doing. Comparative morphology may already have made its greatest and handsomest gift. However, combined with genetics but with a slightly different emphasis, it may yet yield important discoveries on the causal factors underlying evolution. Moreover, in a vast area of biological research the comparative approach has yet to do what it has done in morphology. This is the study of animal and human behavior. Psychology, human as well as animal, has recognized the need for comparative phylogenetic research ever since Wundt. Psychologically as well as organically, all living creatures are historical entities, and it is impossible to understand all their traits without a historical perspective. Even a complete typology of what is present cannot satisfy the quest for causal explanation so long as its development is neglected. In a purely typological system of classification there is no place for yesterday's adaptation, for the rudiment, for things that no longer exist and whose purpose can only be interpreted historically. This is what the student of behavior misses most. It is one of the worst oversights which the current teleological outlook involves. The "dystelic" effects of obsolete psychological structures are theoretically important. Moreover, in man, who changed his entire ecology and sociology in less time than any other species before him, they present one of

[1] Report given at the Zoological Convention, Rostock, 1939.

the most pressing practical problems today. Many an inherited taxis and instinct "no longer fits"; they conflict with the growing social demands on the individual. This is so disturbing that the layman assumes the influence of an "evil fiend," a devil, while psychoanalysis, in a manner no less naive but less excusable, postulates a specific "death drive." Yet, with even an inkling of the conservative character of instinctive actions in evolution, and the physiology of their endogenous impulse production, these phenomena are not only understandable, but obvious and theoretically necessary.

There are several reasons why the comparative method was not applied to our problem until quite recently. It seemed hopeless to search for constant behavior patterns accessible to a phyletic approach while a general belief in the Protean variability of all animal behavior prevailed. Such an approach was equally foreign to mechanistic behaviorists and teleological vitalists. To the former, the conditioned reflex was the sole explanatory factor, while the latter were barred from admitting constant elements by their dogmatic faith in the purposiveness of all animal action. But there is another, far simpler reason for the absence of a comparative method in psychology: it can be acquired neither from books, nor by speculation, but only through experience and observation. Only the naturalist in close touch with the object of his studies can get a true picture of animal behavior and evaluate phyletic facts. The appraisal of phyletic relations not only requires contact with the animal, but a flair for selecting the processes to be investigated, as well as analysis of the reasons for choosing those items. Though judgments based on unanalyzed complex qualities can hardly be assessed scientifically, an intuitive grasp is indispensable when it comes to determining the direction in which analytical research is carried out.

It was in fact a zoologist, not a psychologist, who first tackled the problems of animal behavior with a truly comparative method. He discovered something which many psychologists still deny: the hereditary invariable in behavior. On the one hand, this makes a phyletic comparison of different species possible; on the other hand, it is necessary to account for their specific forms. Charles Otis Whitman wrote in 1898: "Instincts and organs are to be studied from the common viewpoint of phyletic descent." Not content with this theoretical statement, he made a thorough comparative study of a well-defined group, the pigeons. In this study, innate behavior patterns are considered as one taxonomic character among many, along with the morphological ones. Instinctive action stands out as a particularly conservative character in evolution, and therefore has great taxonomic value. If only morphological elements are used to distinguish the group of pigeons, a complicated combination of these characters is needed: carinate, insessorial, with a weak, soft-skinned, inflated bill, medium-length pointed wings, low squatting or split feet, etc. There are exceptions to every single one of these characteristics. *Goura* is no nest squatter and has rounded, henlike wings; *Didunculus* has a totally different bill, and so forth. If, on the other hand, the family is described by the single behavior element that when drinking, they pump water by peristaltic movements of the oesophagus, no exception will be found within the family. At the same time, this doubtless very ancient behavior pattern brings the only other group that shows the same behavior, the *Pteroclidae* (sand grouse), closer to the pigeons than many an organic character pointing in the same direction.

Shortly after Whitman, though quite independently, Oskar Heinroth also made early comparative studies of behavior. His paper "On Certain Types of Movements in Vertebrates" extended this viewpoint to far larger systematic groups. In it he shows that a motor pattern, such as the dog's familiar scratching of its head with a hind leg, has equal taxonomic value with the earliest morphological traces of the kladus, e.g., of the structure of hind limbs consisting of femur, tibia, and fibula. The fate of this behavior pattern within the class of birds shows that its particulars are determined by historical, not by functional motives. A great many birds perform the movement in the manner typical of amphibia, reptiles, and mammals. The scratching hind leg wanders toward the head laterally, past the front limb, so that the wing must be brought back into the position typical of quadrupeds before the motion can be carried out. This procedure, understandable historically from the—*sit venia verbo*—change of class of the reptilian arm, was abandoned by certain groups in the course of evolution in favor of the functionally natural method: the bird leaves its wing, which in any case does not hamper the scratching leg, on its back, and scratches "round the front." The distribution of forward and backward scratching within the system is not related to functional traits, long- or short-leggedness, shape of foot, etc., but follows group allegiance only. *Chionis* documents its mysterious and isolated position in the system by displaying an intermediate pattern between forward and backward scratching. It spreads its wings as though to scratch around the back way, but follows this up by carrying its hind leg to its head medially past the wing, a behavior that can only be interpreted historically. Other motor patterns, such as yawning, stretching, shaking, etc., are equally widespread in the system.

Besides this study, which traces the entire phyletic course of certain homologous characters, Heinroth also carried the second method of comparative research into the study of behavior. Like Whitman, he analyzed all the taxonomically appraisable innate behavior patterns in a restricted group of animals, in his case the order of *Anatides,* on the basis of extensive observations. Heinroth's taxonomic conclusions have been impressively confirmed by Poll, who made the measure of barrenness in hybrids the criterion of phyletic relationship. Wherever both scientists departed from the traditional classification, they coincided with each other.

Neither Whitman nor Heinroth ever use the term "homology." Yet both their studies are based on the assumption that this concept, so widely used in morphology, applies to innate, genetically determined motor patterns as it does to organic characters. The compelling force of their findings proves the correctness of this working hypothesis. The problem now is: what is to be compared and considered homologous? While neither of the two scientists defines instinct precisely, both regard all innate behavior patterns as its effects. Today we distinguish between two physiologically different types of innate motor processes with survival value: internally motivated automatisms, to which alone I apply the term instinctive action, and orienting reactions dependent on external steering stimuli, which Kühn called taxes. The two pioneers of comparative behavior study did not expressly separate these two components. Yet, with an intuitive grasp of the system, both realized the importance of the physiological difference between them. The motor character of an instinctive action, whose form is centrally coordinated and independent of environmental stimulation, naturally has greater taxonomic value than the stimulus-dependent orienting reaction. For taxonomic purposes, both Heinroth and Whitman almost exclusively employ endogenous movements, and particularly the taxis-free courting ceremonies. It is important to stress this point because their comparative phyletic reflections were the first to point out that instinctive actions are invariable. Without comparative-descriptive confirmation of this striking fact, which so many psychologists have denied, we should never have found out that instinctive action, as an endogenous automatism, is causally and physiologically different from all individually variable behavior.

Very few studies have been made since Whitman and Heinroth. Most of these deal with birds. I shall mention only the names of Verwey, Tinbergen, Goethe, and Makkink. Mammals are practically unexplored to date, for Carpenter's studies on platyrrhine monkeys have few comparative aspects, and Goethe's research on Mustelides is incomplete.

This being the situation, I planned a comparative research program to investigate a well-defined animal group thoroughly. My intention was to make the fullest possible inventory of the system of actions in each of the member forms, and to attempt a complete representation of all taxonomically important forms, so as to tabulate the single behavior characters and the single species. This would make it possible to follow up a cue in its presence or absence throughout the group, and to compare the species-specific complex characters with each other in a statistical survey. I did not, of course, intend to confine my study to behavior cues, but meant to include all morphological characters that are in any way accessible. Only a very small systematic group could be considered as a topic for such detailed research. To begin with, purely technical considerations entered into its selection. I wanted a group which had been systematically and morphologically studied, and which comprised a wealth of forms with many and varied degrees of relationship, that is, as many gradual transitions between variety and species, species and genus as possible. It had to be rich in taxis-free instinctive actions; and these had to lend themselves to motion picture photography, the only objective and reliable method for recording complex movements. The group of *Anatinae* fulfilled all these requirements better than any other. Moreover, a number of "good species" in this group form fertile hybrids with each other. This indicated that the largest possible number of characters might be investigated from the genetic as well as from the comparative viewpoint. I was mainly interested to see whether obviously homologous behavior patterns in two species would always prove homogenetic in crossing experiments. If they should behave like organic characters, this would justify applying the concept of homology to innate motor patterns. Sixteen clearly distinguishable and recorded courting actions were selected. They are undoubtedly homologous patterns in most species, and occur in such varied stages of development and differentiation, that the direction of their evolution can be gauged with some probability. The distribution and differentiation of these characters tallies with that of the morphological characters (as illustrated by the structure of the drake's bone drum). To be sure, the taxonomy derived from these characters departs somewhat from Hartert's generally accepted one; for one thing, it renders his genus of *Anas* vulnerable. I shall confine myself to two examples. In the group of wild ducks, *Anas platyrhynchos, poecilorhyncha, melleri, obscura, superciliosa, undulata*, etc., as in many other *Anatinae*, the males display an action called "chin-lifting." Comparative research teaches that this is a phylogenetic derivative of a symbolic drinking movement. The females have an even more widespread "teasing" or "goading" pattern, a symbolic threatening motion backwards over the shoulder. Functionally, both actions together constitute a "ceremony": they mutually release each other, and well-adjusted couples most often perform them simultaneously. Widgeon couples, *Mareca penelope* as well as *sibilatrix*, differ from the group of wild ducks in that both partners display a movement corresponding to that of the mallard drake; the female teasing over the shoulder is missing. The stimulus situation in which the chin-lifting is performed by both partners always occurs after a fight with other lake dwellers, especially with other widgeon couples. It resembles an analogous (not homologous) ceremony in *Anserinae:* the so-called "triumphal calling." The chin-lifting, as compared with the same pattern in mallard ducks, is more differentiated, and its connection with the earlier drinking motion is no longer noticeable, whereas drinking is "still indicated" in the mallard drake by a brief pecking at the water surface. I would not dare pronounce both forms of chin-lifting to be homologous, were it not for the fact that the gadwall *(Chaulelasmus streperus)* offers an unmistakable connecting link. Although in this species both sexes display the chin-lifting, the female also has the mallard duck's teasing over the shoulder. The chin-lifting of both partners occurs simultaneously, as in the widgeons, but approximately every second time the female substitutes the teasing pattern for it. This results in a peculiar motor rhythm, with a corresponding rhythm in the calls that accompany the ceremony. In contrast to the mallard ducks, the gadwall's reaction distinctly has the meaning of triumphal calling, although not so explicitly as in the widgeons. Moreover, the downy fledglings already have the pattern. This would seem to indicate brooding care by the male, and a close-knit family life, as we find it in geese and *Casarcinae.* If reaction intensity is high, the adult male gadwall, like the mallard drake, pecks at the water surface before raising his chin. It seems to me that what we know of the gadwall corroborates the homology of chin-lifting in the mallard drake with that of both sexes of widgeons. This assumption is further confirmed by the gadwall's definitely intermediate position between mallard and widgeon, both morphologically and in the fertility of its hybrids with both other species. *Anas-Mareca* hybrids show "tritophyle steironoty" (Poll): their spermatogenesis is checked before the first maturational fission. Gadwalls, on the other hand, produce physiologically fertile hybrids with both other species! It is astounding how the study of hybrids confirms our inferences from the facts described earlier. A hybrid pair of mallard and widgeon *(Mareca sibilatrix),* made available to me by the Berlin Zoo, displayed precisely the same synthesis between the behavior characters of the parent species which is found in the gadwall as a phyletically developed differentiation! A second example: two courting actions, which mallards perform separately and independently, are linked together in the gadwall. Various circumstances suggest that the mallards' behavior is the historically earlier of the two. Now I possess a brood of domestic ducks, so-called Kaki-Campbells, who link both patterns into one as a mutation due to domestication. Crossing experiments are to follow.

Before concluding the chapter on the phyletic trend of innate behavior, I must mention a second source of comparative morphology which is available to it. This is the temporary appearance of phyletically old characters in ontogeny. An undoubtedly original behavior pattern, which is typical of a group, is often found in the young of forms whose adult specimens no longer have it. For instance, in some *Passeres* which walk, instead of hopping, as do most members of the family, the young pass through a phase of the hopping characteristic for the family. This is particularly clear if nestlings that cannot yet fly are made to move on foot. Quite recently, Ahlquist has published an important observation on *Laridae*. The genus *Larus,* which may be regarded as a typical representative of the group, has a specific motor pattern of fishing from the water surface. In the two species of laughing gull, *Hydrocoloeus* and sea hawk, *Stercorarius,* both diverging from the general and surely older type of sea gull in different directions, the adult bird lacks this instinctive action; but it appears in the "play" of the young in its typical, group-specific form.

II.   The Physiology of Instinctive Behavior

The findings of comparative research unanimously indicate a stereotypy of instinctive actions. The constant element is the form of motor patterns, not their effect, as a mistaken generalization of the laws valid for orienting reactions and purposive behavior leads some people to believe. In view of the variety of releasing stimuli, this stereotypy is remarkable. It raises the question of the physiological causes underlying it, and suggests a dependence of instinctive movements on internal structural factors of the central nervous system. The first theory was one of reflex chains, presented by Ziegler.

Various objections have been raised against the chain-reflex theory, among them the regulative faculty of innate motor coordinations studied by Bethe. One difficulty in assuming simple reflex chains consists in the varying intensity of instinctive actions. The opposite of an "all-or-none" law prevails for them. If the excitation coordinated to an instinctive action is so slight that its full discharge, which alone has survival value for the species, cannot develop, the movement does not fail to ensue, but occurs in a meaningless, incomplete form. There is every conceivable transition from the slightest incipient actions, termed "intention movements" as they betray the direction of an impending action, to the full, effective process. Statistically, meaningless discharges are more frequent than effective ones. Thus a greylag goose or a silver gull performs incomplete nest-building activities all year round; but only at a certain season, when internal motivation is at its height, do they achieve their biological purpose. The actions pertaining to a single sequence of rising intensities may appear very different at times. When its flight intention is rising, a wild goose first stretches its neck far forward, produces a certain call, and performs circular shaking motions with its bill. Then only do the flying motions proper begin: the goose unfolds its wings and prepares to jump into the air. This is followed at last by the actual jump and the wing-beat of the take-off. However, all these variants in the form of the activity do not argue basically against its reflex nature. In fact, it might conceivably be interpreted on this basis. Von Holst's investigations have shown that the law of all-or-none is valid for the motor element of centrally coordinated patterns, differences of intensity being based on the number of partaking elements, which fluctuates up or down with the level of excitation. The differences in form at various levels of intensity are due to the different threshold values of diverse motor patterns for the same form of excitation. The goose's bill-shaking happens to be elicited by lower values than its preparation for the jump. The results could be exactly the same if reflexes were the basis of instinctive actions.

However, the chain-reflex theory cannot explain certain fluctuations in the intensity of instinctive behavior patterns which obey a definite rule. This rule may be very roughly worded as follows: the longer the time that has passed since an instinctive action was released, the greater the intensity with which it will respond to a given stimulus situation. Looking at it from the side of the stimulus, the same rule reads like this: the stimulus capable of releasing an action will be lesser in proportion to the length of time elapsed since its last release. Reflexes do sometimes behave similarly, when a state of repletion in hollow organs (bladder, spermatocyst) aids external stimulation in the work of releasing, by proprioception, which lowers their thresholds. Deficiency conditions often supply proprioceptive stimuli by means of complicated indicators, such as thirst through perception of dry mucous surfaces. But without such additional mechanisms to accumulate internal stimuli, the reflex lacks the regular fluctuation in intensity and elicitability described, and so does the orienting reaction composed of reflexes. If we turn an insect on its back, thus releasing its tropotactic turning reaction, this experiment can be repeated any number of times, until the organism as a whole, or at any rate its effectors are exhausted. The same is true for the menotactic light-compass reaction of a migratory ant. In all these cases the experimenter will tire before his object. Similarly the reflex, like a machine out of use, can lie inactive over long periods without the least change, ready to be released at full intensity. The patellar tendon reflex does not respond more readily if it has not been elicited for a long time.

In instinctive actions, the state of affairs is entirely different. If one releases the grasshopper's reaction of "pretended lameness" by approaching within threatening distance of its nest, the provocation may succeed once, twice, distinctly less strongly the third time, and only after a short interval or not at all the fourth time. This specific exhaustibility, a common basic trait of all instinctive behavior, suggests the idea of a reservoir for reaction-specific energy. After this is exhausted, the motor pattern "ceases to be at the disposal" of the organism, long before the organism as a whole or its effectors are tired out. This same idea of an accumulation of excitation emerges even more impressively in the reverse experiment, if the instinctive action, instead of being "pumped out," is "dammed up," that is, subjected to long stagnation by withholding all releasing stimuli. Then an instinctive action does something which the reflex, in keeping with its nature, cannot do: it "strains to break through." This causes a lowering of thresholds to releasing stimuli, and a motor unrest of the total organism. Objectively, this unrest raises the likelihood that the releasing stimulus situation will ensue; in the subject's experience it appears as a "seeking" for these situations. Finally the "internal pressure" of accumulating excitation reaches such a high level that it breaks through all inhibitions. The threshold value for releasing stimuli sinks to zero, and the motor pattern "goes off of itself" without any traceable outward stimulus. Such explosions of highly differentiated movements in a complete vacuum often enable us to isolate the instinctive component from the complex and partly taxis-steered sequence into which it is built. Moreover, it is of great theoretical interest that highly differentiated behavior patterns with survival value should be utterly independent of the animal's receptors. Purposive psychologists, who regard all animal behavior as the pursuing of a goal after which the subject strives, go so far as to make the dependence of an action chain on additional steering stimuli the critical proof of their outlook. It affects one very strangely when Tolman, for instance, while arguing for the purposive nature of all animal behavior, says, "Animal behavior cannot go off *in vacuo*." While thus endeavoring to carry the assumption of non-purposive behavior patterns *ad absurdum*, he stipulates for their existence the very evidence which we are able to furnish most convincingly in the shape of vacuum activities. Even an expert is impressed and surprised again and again when, for instance, a hand-raised young starling, who has never in its life caught a flying insect, suddenly carries out the pertinent motor patterns in all their minute details, including the killing and swallowing of the nonexistent prey, or when a *Kolibri* in its cage intricately winds nonexistent nest-building fibers around a stick. Lashley, who seeks the basic explanation of all innately purposive motor patterns in the perceptual field, wonders that rats are still able to carry out complex instinctive actions after they have been deprived of all their essential sense organs. We shall see that the coordination of instinctive behavior patterns is not affected by such peripheral "deafferentation," or even by one of a central kind.

The accumulation of action-specific energy and its consumption through discharge of a motor pattern have long been familiar to physiology, though under a different name. I refer to the phenomenon of spinal contrast studied by Sherrington. To give an instance: a sea horse *(Hippocampus)* is decapitated, and the spinal preparation artificially respirated. After some time the dorsal fin takes on a certain, semierect position of balance. If tactile stimulation is now applied in the shape of pressure on the cervical region, the fin lies down entirely, only to rise higher than before when the inhibiting stimulus ceases—hence the term "contrast." If the inhibition is prolonged, upon its extinction the fin not only spreads to its maximum extent, but also starts to beat laterally for a short time. This soon stops, and the fin sinks back to the position of balance. The lateral beating motion occurs only at a higher level of the same quality of excitation that causes the erection of the fin. Both movements consume the same action-specific impulses. Normal generation of these impulses is just balanced by spending them in the "half-mast" position of the fin; any blocking of this consumption causes accumulation, and as a result the erection is intensified when the obstacle is removed. Prolonged inhibition raises the level of excitation to the threshold value required for the lateral beating motion. It is probable that even more complex processes, of the kind described in the greylag goose, may lend themselves to a similar interpretation.

All these facts argue against the reflex nature of instinctive actions. Causal analysis has been greatly advanced by the work of von Holst, with which I was not acquainted when first describing them. Von Holst showed that many complex and biologically meaningful movements, which until then were generally regarded as chain reflexes, continue undisturbed in their form and coordination when the central nervous system of an animal has been completely deafferented and consequently cannot receive stimuli that would release and direct reflexes. In the ventral cord of earthworms and the spinal cord of various teleosts, motor impulses are generated automatically and, like the endogenous stimulus production of the heart, in rhythmic continuity. Moreover, they are coordinated into purposeful movements in the center itself, independently of receptors, including proprioceptors. The mechanisms analyzed by von Holst, which effect this central integration, may here be disregarded. However, owing to the far-reaching parallels between instinctive activities and von Holst's automatic rhythms, I believe that the following may stand as a well-substantiated and legitimate working hypothesis: wherever species-specific motor patterns show the characters of threshold decrease, vacuum activity, and action-specific exhaustibility, processes of endogenous impulse production are at work.

This assumption opens up a vast field to causal explanation. Not only does it offer an explanation for phenomena that appear enigmatic to any other approach; it postulates them theoretically. In an even larger group of phenomena, we must allow for rhythmic fluctuations in the "actual level" of action-specific excitation to avoid a source of error. The effect of every stimulus is quantitatively and qualitatively dependent on the level of one or more reactions which it can release. A mallard duck may once treat the same dummy of a flying bird "as a bird of prey," and another time "as a male of her own species," depending on whether her threshold for certain courting actions or flight movements is particularly low at the time. Without a knowledge of the laws underlying it, this state of affairs might create the impression of utterly arbitrary "intracentral" shifts. The tremendous subjective variability of things in the worlds of animals, and of their different "moods" (von Uexküll) has an objective physiological correlate in the processes described.

III.   Automatism and Reflex

If we assume that the central nervous mechanism of instinctive actions is an autonomous process and that it differs fundamentally from the reflex, we are obliged to clarify their relations to each other as well as to various as yet unanalyzed achievements of the central nervous system. What processes must we continue to interpret from the reflex element? Functionally, any regular response of the organism to some feature in its environment, to a stimulus from without, is a reflex. This broad formulation includes all orienting reactions, which direct the organism in space, from simple, obvious reflexes to the highest complex achievements of the central nervous system. It also comprises all those releasing processes through which the automatic nervous impulses, that are normally blocked by the higher centers, are allowed to take their proper course at the biologically proper moment. Such a "coat of reflexes," as von Holst expresses it, is interposed between the rigid automatisms and the equally hard conditions in the environment. Sometimes the reflex is superimposed on the endogenous movement, rounding it off very slightly, as a blanket of snow softens the outlines of a roof. No one would say that the snow changed the shape of the roof. For the same reason, there is no reason to assume a plasticity of instinct.

A. TAXIS AND INSTINCT

The indiscriminate use of the term "instinct" for both taxis and central mechanism has caused much barren argument in the literature. Russell says of innate behavior in general that it is "continued until the goal is reached or the animal is exhausted." This applies only to the taxis. McDougall, arguing against the slogan *"Animal non agit, agitur"* says, "The healthy animal is up and doing," in constant activity from an inner drive. This is true of a dog, a raven, or any other organism with many instincts, but not of a reflex animal with few automatisms, such as an ant lion, a toad or other animals that lie in wait for their prey.

The essential innate element in a taxis is not, as in the case of instinct, a centrally controlled movement, but one that responds to external stimuli. In all analyzed cases it is a system of ready-made reflexes. In order to separate the reflex and spontaneous components which make up all innate behavior, the concepts of both must be narrowed in somewhat more than has been customary. By saying that a tadpole, when short of breath, is "positively phototactic," we have already indicated a system of movements: a directing reflex combined with an instinctive action. The undulating locomotion of the tail (though it has only been studied in fish and not, to the best of my knowledge, in amphibians) is undoubtedly due to an endogenous mechanism, while the steering turn toward the light, as well as its correction whenever the animal veers from the right direction, are essentially reflex in nature. This turn, steered by environmental stimuli, is what I consider the essential feature of a taxis, more particularly of the topotaxis. When in the following pages I shall, for briefness' sake, refer to a taxis in general, this is what I mean.

On close inspection, therefore, even a "pure" orienting movement, that is, one aiming at the optimal stimulus situation, is a combination of taxis and automatism, a system creating the impression of a unit but welded together out of two causally different components. Probably most types of complex and highly differentiated innate behavior are built up on the same plan, though only the simplest cases are accessible to analysis for the present. Tinbergen and I studied one of these: the retrieving reaction of the greylag goose (see pp. 176-208).

Another, equally typical case of interlocking presents more complex relations between taxis and instinctive pattern. A high level of excitation specific to a certain innate action is reflected passively in a lowering of the threshold for releasing stimuli and a greater readiness to respond. It also affects the higher centers actively; more and more energy may be needed to block its discharge. In the simplest case such internal tension causes motor unrest and a random "search" for the releasing situation.

As a rule, however, very specific taxes are built into the system of innate behavior patterns at this point. These taxes are only activated if excitation is at a high level. As the tadpole's specific response to otherwise unnoticed light stimuli only occurs in oxygen deficiency, certain, generally very complex stimulus situations only elicit a strong positive taxis when action-specific energy is highly accumulated. Once the desired spatial relationship is established, the activating stimulus combination may also go on to release an instinctive action. Taxes of this kind, which depend on the level of excitation pertaining to a certain instinctive activity, are usually termed "drives."

From a subjective angle we may say that in such cases the goal of the orienting reaction is a stimulus situation and the discharge of the specific behavior pattern which it releases. This type of interlocking is extremely frequent and familiar. To put it colloquially, the animal has an "appetite" for a certain instinctive act, such as eating, mating, etc. Wallace Craig was the first to recognize this goal-function of the action, which is tremendously significant for our understanding of motivation in the behavior of animals and men. In his "Appetites and Aversions as Constituents of Instincts" he distinguished clearly between the two components of such action chains, the more or less variable purposive behavior initiated by a drive, and the purely instinctive, satisfying "consummatory action." With Craig, we call purposive behavior which strives toward a stimulus situation that releases an instinctive act, "appetitive behavior." The relative role of each function in apparently analogous behavior patterns of various animals differs quantitatively according to their mental capacity. The higher the organism, the more variable its behavior in relation to a goal. Let us take, as extremes, the food-getting of a predatory bird and of a human being. In the bird, appetitive behavior is confined to a primitive search, at best containing some self-training, until the prey is sighted. Aside from the simplest guiding taxes, only instinctive actions follow, and they represent the emotional goal for which the animal strives subjectively. The behavior of a man motivated solely by bread-winning, on the other hand, includes practically all the higher psychological achievements of which he is capable. The motive, the consummatory action of "breaking and biting" which is the subjective goal, has retreated far toward the end of the action chain, without, however, renouncing its instinctive nature in any way. Indeed, the optimal releasing stimuli for the instinctive activities of chewing, swallowing and the like can be inferred from the qualities that make foods "more appetizing." In men, as in animals, the subjective goal at which appetence aims is in no way identical with the objective biological success of the action chain. Since Craig developed these concepts clearly as early as 1918, it is really amazing how obstinately some teleological-minded animal psychologists still play havoc with them.

The aforesaid "recession" of an innate behavior pattern probably parallels the phyletic procedure whereby a species reaches a "mentally higher level." Spencer, Lloyd Morgan and others held the long-prevalent opinion that "instinct" is the ontogenetic and phylogenetic forerunner of higher mental achievement. It must be made quite clear that appetitive behavior, the sole root of all "variable" behavior, is intrinsically different in its physiological causation from the spontaneous instinctive act. Moreover, both processes may function vicariously, the higher development of one rendering that of the other unnecessary and ousting it. Whenever a higher mental achievement is mastered in one of two functionally identical motor sequences, the participant automatisms are reduced.

From a subjective point of view, an instinctive action may appear in complex interrelations once as a means (as in the case of the optimal taxis, or in appetitive behavior), another time as an end. This has led some authors to believe that there are two different kinds of instinctive activity (first order drives, second order drives, etc.). But the objective difference between them lies only in the proportion between their rate of impulse accumulation and the probability or frequency of their release. Some activities, such as mating, nest-building and the like are rarely activated in the life of an organism. Others, like the pectoral fin-beat of a parrot fish, the hopping of small birds, etc., are translated into motion almost continually. Even in homologous actions, the accumulation of action-specific energy varies from species to species and is adapted to biological needs. The fin-beat of the freely floating parrot fish continues practically uninterrupted even in the deafferented spinal preparation, while in the sea horse, which is anchored most of the time, it must be "saved up" by inhibition before it shows itself through spinal contrast. Of course there are even greater quantitative differences between functionally divergent instinctive actions, for instance, between a locomotor pattern, the extreme of everyday "tool reaction," and mating, the extreme of consummatory action. There is a close correlation between the varying rate of impulse accumulation in these two "types" of instinctive behavior and the selectivity of their releasing mechanisms. Not only are the common tool reactions set off by comparatively unspecific and frequent stimulus situations, but every single one of them is controlled by numerous and varied central nervous mechanisms, ranging from the simplest unconditioned reflex to the least analyzed "voluntary" disinhibition. Accordingly, these simple motor elements are widely applicable. The seldom "used" instinctive act, which is the goal of a motor sequence, on the other hand, nearly always has only a single highly specific function, and correspondingly only one releasing mechanism which unerringly selects the unique biologically adequate situation. This so-called "innate releasing mechanism" is usually a system of unconditioned reflexes. Such instinctive actions can never be disinhibited "at will." The differences discussed are merely differences of degree in every respect. They account easily for the most extreme contrasts between instinctive actions that are a means and those that are an end. The motor impulses of tool reactions accumulate rapidly, but they are easily released; therefore they do not usually cause action-specific drives and appetitive behavior. A dog can easily find the chance to run, a mouse to gnaw on something. But highly selective and rarely activated behavior patterns are preceded by an appetitive action. Though theoretically possible, it is generally improbable that such a response should be released accidentally, before an accumulation of specific excitation has activated the drive for it. Conversely, every tool action can at any time be turned into the goal of a drive, simply by depriving the animal of every chance to translate the endogenous excitation of the pattern in question into overt movements and so to "get rid of it." In such a case the threshold of the motor pattern is lowered almost immediately, or the reaction goes off *in vacuo*. Moreover, it becomes the goal of a truly elemental subjective drive, as any instinctive action that is a goal in normal conditions. Schaff demonstrated in excellent experiments that mice who were given a chance to discharge their accumulated locomotor patterns on a running wheel made no attempt to leave their narrow enclosure by gnawing through an obstacle, but did so as soon as the wheel stopped. The running of dogs, the flight of ravens, etc., illustrate the same principle.

Tool reactions, especially all the locomotor patterns "available" in a practically unlimited supply to orienting reactions or to appetitive behavior in general, are currently regarded as voluntary acts. This is a source of error even in cases where the release of a response is directly controlled by the highest centers. As I have said, there is no sharp borderline between frequent, unspecifically elicited instinctive actions and rarer, more specifically released ones. Similarly, "the same" homologous motor pattern of two species may be closer to the first type in one and to the second in the other species. The flight of a small sparrow bird on one hand and that of a grey goose on the other may serve as an illustration. If a sparrow is faced with a detour problem which calls for flight, the momentary level of specific excitation can safely be ignored. The excitation is maintained at an approximately constant, very high rate, and we may assume that the higher centers almost always have the movement at their disposal. But if we give a similar task to a grey goose in whom flight is rare, the actual level of the reaction must be carefully weighed to prevent totally misleading conclusions as to the bird's higher mental achievements. In a detour experiment requiring use of its wings, the goose will indeed show its "insight" into the situation after an approximately constant period, by going to a spot best suited for taking off and making intentional flight movements there. But when the goose will take off is no longer determined by the highest nervous centers. The goose wants to fly, it "tries to work itself into a flying mood," and an expert can easily foretell when it will fly from the intensity of its intention movements. But this point of time is not a voluntary one; it depends on the current level of action-specific excitation. Immediately after a long flight, which lowers this level considerably, a goose that has to fly over a fence will often show "insight" and a flying intention after only a few seconds. But it may not take off for several hours, perhaps not until the next day. Experience and familiarity with the obstacle make no difference: the same bird that has just mastered the task will fail, once the reaction is exhausted. Since similar processes are widespread in the animal world, the "degree of voluntariness" or the actual level of the instinctive act must always be taken into account in analyzing learning and intelligence.

B. The Releasing Mechanism

The "coat of reflexes" has another distinct function besides spatial orientation. It releases innate behavior patterns in specific situations where they fulfill their biological function. The boring behavior of the common tick responds to the interaction of a heat stimulus of 37° C and the chemical stimulus of butyric acid. A very simple combination; but since the motor pattern responds selectively to it alone, the biological situation which it "fits" is clearly determined. In natural conditions it is almost inconceivable that any object besides a mammal (the suitable host) should emit both these key stimuli and elicit the boring reaction in the "wrong" situation. Such a neurosensory correlate to a set of stimuli that release an unconditioned reflex characterizes a certain biological situation by simplified reproduction of its outstanding features. We shall therefore call it an innate schema or mechanism. Instinctive actions, taxes, and intricate combinations of both may all depend on innate releasing mechanisms to select opportunities. Tinbergen showed that the releasing and directing mechanisms which take part in the gaping reaction of nestling thrushes are activated independently, by utterly different stimulus combinations. The stimuli inducing the young bird to reach up and open its beak wide are easily separated experimentally from those that guide this gaping response toward the parent bird's head. When dealing with an objectively homogeneous object, we are usually concerned with a whole series, a system of taxes and automatisms. Actually it is a misuse of the term to refer to "the innate mechanism" for a fellow member of the species, for the sex partner, for the prey, and so forth, a practice that I myself have, alas, encouraged in part. We cannot really maintain that the sum of an object's perceptual correlates equals a "total mechanism" for that object. Each reaction is dependent on its own releasing mechanism and independent of all others. The stimuli specific to a response release it independently of all other reactions coined on the same object.

The method for studying innate mechanisms is the dummy experiment. As O. Koehler has shown, two courses are open: a systematic elimination of effective stimuli, starting from the natural, adequate object, and the reverse procedure of a synthesis from the simplest models to the most realistic dummy possible, whose releasing value equals that of the natural object. Since visual stimuli are the easiest to control in an experimental setup, most studies of highly differentiated innate mechanisms are concerned with visual releasers. Thus Goethe found a reaction in young heath hens to a fake predator moved by wires, which could be quantitatively distinguished from their response to other, hardly simpler models. In twenty-day-old chicks this behavior already varied according to sex: the hens sought shelter, whereas the cock took up a defensive posture. Tinbergen and I tried to develop this type of experiment further. In the spring of 1937 we tested just about all the young birds available in Altenberg with fake predators that we moved along a rope stretched between two tall trees. Grey geese start to react spontaneously from about their eighth week of age. Up to then they display similar actions in response to the parents' warning call. Although they had a chance to learn the mechanism of the predator, the reaction matured at a certain time, unaffected by experience or the parents' example. The properties that a model must have to release the fully intensive reaction of taking cover indicate that it is coined on the image of a specific predator, the white-tailed sea eagle. Shape is of little significance; it is essential, on the other hand, that the object silhouetted against the sky should move slowly in proportion to its size, that is, measured in self-lengths. This is interesting because we also judge the size of a bird flying high in the sky in the same way. Grey geese often fixate slowly floating feathers despite their small size, but never small birds flitting past swiftly. A model symmetrical in back and front, and about the size of a starling, that could be moved back and forth any number of times, evoked intensive covering, warning and marching off to the shelter when dragged past slowly; but on being brought back swiftly the next instant, it did not attract a single glance, although the geese were all still gazing skyward. It was particularly striking that the birds perceived the slow model as something projected high into the air, and the fast one merely as a low-flying small bird. Doves soaring slowly in the sky against a strong wind released a sea-eagle response, but only if they did not flap their wings. As soon as they did, the geese calmed down. Slow soaring must therefore definitely be evaluated as a cue to the innate mechanism. Ducks behave differently. In the spring, they react again and again to the newly arrived common swift by showing alarm, or even by a negative phototaxis of seeking cover, whereas geese pay no attention to this bird. On the other hand, ducks are far less afraid of airplanes than are geese. It appears very likely that the releasing mechanism of escape reactions in geese is coined primarily on the sea-eagle, that of ducks on the falcon. Our experiments with the geese came to a premature, though amusing close owing to undesired conditioning. They began to display the sea-eagle response as soon as Tinbergen or I swung ourselves up on the lowest branch of the rope tree. In fact, the swinging up itself, on any tree, sufficed to make them guard suspiciously against the sky and run to the nearest shelter. Actually, experiments on innate mechanisms should always be made with fresh young birds, who are sure to be "blank pages."

While the form of the model is indifferent, or at any rate does not have a statistically reliable effect on grey geese and ducklings (for technical reasons we were unable to experiment with adult hand-raised ducks), the contrary could be proved in young turkey hens. These experiments were based on Heinroth's observation that domestic hens are more alarmed by short-necked, long-tailed birds than by long-necked ones. Our model had wings symmetrical in front and back and, on the longitudinal axis, a short continuation at one end, and a long one at the other, functioning as its head or tail respectively. The young turkey hens actually reacted much more vigorously when the model was propelled with the short end forward. This was well quantifiable in the number of alarm calls uttered.

Innate schemata attain their highest differentiation where the adequate object of a reaction is a fellow member of the species. Elsewhere the number and kind of key stimuli sets a limit to differentiation of the mechanism. The lock cannot be developed beyond the key, and the latter is generally something fixed in the environment, and not subject to the evolutionary development of the species. But when a reaction responds to a member of the same species, the object that emits the stimuli and the innate mechanism activated by them can be differentiated simultaneously, woven into a significant functional system. To put it bluntly, the pike cannot "make an additional signal develop" in its prey to safeguard its catching reaction from responding "by mistake." But, phyletically speaking, *Poephila gouldiae* could develop a small sign-lantern at the corner of the young bird's beak, and at the same time a corresponding perceptual correlate in the responding parent bird. We call stimulus-emitting devices of this kind "releasers" or, to specify that they affect a fellow member of the species, "social releasers." Social releasers may be organic properties (shape, color, etc.) or conspicuous motor patterns. Most of them are composed of both. Social releasers may operate in any sense modality. The love-shaft of pulmonates has a tactile effect, many scent organs have an olfactory one, and the effect of all the vocal differentiations is acoustic. For reasons stated earlier, visual releasers are the best for experimental purposes. The entire sociology of higher animals is built up on social releasers and corresponding innate mechanisms. They should be the main building stones of all sociological research, because the thin coating of acquired behavior amounts to very little in proportion. Mr. and Mrs. Peckham made the first good studies in this field with spiders, as early as the middle of the last century. Though they used spiders of diverse species as models, their discussion of the effectiveness of single cues shows a great deal of insight. By now we have a good many studies: a number of valuable observations by Heinroth, the detailed analysis of sticklebacks by Pelkwijk and Tinbergen, experiments with silver gulls by Goethe, with the fighting fish (*Betta*) by Lissmann, on breeding in *Sepia* by Tinbergen, etc.

Among the social releasers, endogenous movements claim a particular interest. They are the only innate behavior patterns of whose phyletic development we have some knowledge. Comparative research shows that they are almost invariably derived in one of two ways from actions that originally had a mechanical effect. One group developed from intention movements. In so doing, they underwent a peculiar ritualization to heighten their effect, and a "mimical exaggeration," which has at times changed them beyond recognition. I have termed releasers of this type "symbolic actions." The second way in which motor releasers have evolved phyletically is based on a different phenomenon. In high general excitation, certain behavior patterns, especially the locomotor ones, are easily disinhibited. An excited lecturer, for instance, paces back and forth on his platform. Now an excitation specific for one instinctive activity will at times shift or spark over regularly and predictably to the disinhibiting mechanism of another. This phenomenon, discovered independently by Tinbergen and Kortlandt, has added much to what we know about the development of social releasers. The movements activated by displacement of an excitation may become excessively formalized, as have the so-called symbolic actions. This descent from displacement activities explains the curious change in meaning of many an action. Thus a formalized preening behind the wings is an introduction to mating in the domestic pigeon, but a menace in the crane, etc. According to Makkink, even the sleeping posture has become a threatening gesture in the scooper!

The systems of innate mechanisms are a wonderful field for comparative phyletic research because in studying them the phenomenon of convergence may almost certainly be excluded. The specific form of such fixed, overaccentuated movements cannot be interpreted from their function, but solely from their historical evolution. Therefore a similarity of ceremonies in two different and allopatric groups always spells homology as, for instance, in the signal code of human speech symbols. If this were not so, any such identity could only be brought about by pure chance, which is highly unlikely. These circumstances often make it possible to clarify phyletic relations with a degree of probability hardly ever granted to purely morphological research.

The interaction of social releasers and innate releasing mechanisms is of great interest for a discussion of the Darwinian views on sexual selection. As in the courtship of many a bird, reptile and bony fish, striking colors and forms also participate in other releasers. This can easily be explained by their function as cue stimuli. It is entirely wrong, however, to infer from the effect of these nonsexual releasers that such conspicuous differentiations were not bred through sexual selection in the strictest Darwinistic sense. On the contrary, we now know that the most sumptuous nuptial markings occur in animals whose males do not fight, but have a social courtship, and are selected actively by the female. The most colorful of all ducks in its nuptial attire, the mandarin duck, is precisely the species where social courting is most developed and the females' choice of their mates the most active. The same holds for birds of paradise, the gamecock, the peacock, etc. All these "exaggerated" cases of nuptial apparel surely owe their origin to sexual selection.

It is a psychologically interesting question whether innate mechanisms should be described as Gestalten (configurations). The functionally constant and adequate reaction to an object characterized by innate mechanisms, for example, to a fellow member of the species, very easily misleads the observer into overlooking the fact that this uniformity is not grounded in the subject, but in a combination of releasing sign stimuli in the object. The subject displays each of the component reactions just as readily in response to a dummy which emits the stimuli pertaining to the releasing mechanism of one particular reaction in isolation.[2] In

---

[2] Gestalt is, of course, not any totality but some decisive relation, a form-quality that can be isolated, transposed, by definition. [Translator's note.]

sharp contrast to stimulus situations whose releasing value depends on acquired cues, on conditioned reflexes, the stimulus combinations that elicit unconditioned reflexes, and whose perceptual correlates we call innate mechanisms, are never complex qualities. Even the most primitive self-training of mentally low-ranking animals usually depends on a practically boundless number of single cues in the releasing situation. It is perpetually astonishing how an infinitesimal change, which one would not even expect the animal to notice, alters the complex quality of the total situation so greatly that his training fails to respond. The slightest change in the habitual environment of birds results in total disintegration of all behavior patterns dependent on their habits. If a familiar path is strewn with a different kind of sand, cranes or grey geese will not take it. In the innate mechanism, on the other hand, cues that to us appear the most essential in the total situation may drop out. As long as the few sign stimuli "provided" in the mechanism are present, the intensity of the reaction to the simplified dummy is the same as in the normal situation. This is even true of organisms whose response to conditioned releasing situations shows the sensitivity described above in perceiving complex qualities. A jackdaw can recognize about twenty other jackdaws by minute physiognomic differences. Yet it immediately responds with an equally intense social defense reaction whether one of these personal friends or a pair of black bathing trunks is attacked before its eyes! The statement which Demoll made more than twenty years ago, that "In view of its hereditary nature, instinct can presumably only be released by the simplest of stimuli," is still fully valid today, if we substitute our concept of the mechanism for "instinct."

Verbal description of an object offers a good analogy for the functioning of an innate mechanism. It follows from the nature of description that it cannot convey the complex quality of the sensory impression, but only a sum of single characters. Assuming that an object which must be identified from verbal description has a limited number of characters, and that the receiver of the description is somewhat slow, so that he can recognize very clear, absolute cues but cannot make relative and quantitative distinctions: this is a model of the way in which the innate mechanism functions. This model, applied to reality, coincides fully with the facts. Suppose we have to describe a female garganey teal to someone unfamiliar with the bird, so that he may be able to distinguish her from all other female ducks. This can only be done by picking out the few cues that have been developed into releasers by the species and consequently display the conspicuousness and simplicity typical of such organs. In the teal, these are solely the colors of the wing speculum and their distribution. If this single releaser is removed from sight, and we think of the bird swimming with folded wings concealed beneath her wing coverts, it is well-nigh impossible to describe her. Even a mentally underprivileged person can easily be trained to recognize the complex quality of a swimming garganey. But it is just as hard, indeed impossible, to impart this faculty to him by additive description. Even a nature lover who has no trouble in identifying the teal can hardly name the cues that lead him. Animals in whose appearance social releasers play an important part, on the other hand, are always easy to describe by summation. This was what called our attention to the relative simplicity of stimulus combinations typical of all true releasers, and to the limitations of the innate mechanisms under discussion. If the innate mechanism could respond selectively to complex qualities, as does the conditioned reflex, there would be no need for social releasers! We next conducted experiments with mallard ducks to find out how much the releasers determine innate recognition of a member of the same species. The results were as follows. A female whom I raised from the egg in company of pintail ducks, isolated from her own species, never showed the slightest sexual reaction to a pintail drake. But when, without any intention on my part, she first sighted a mallard drake in the neighboring enclosure through a crack between two boards, a most impressive, explosive outburst of female courting actions ensued. A mallard drake raised with pintail ducks in isolation from his own species, on the other hand, became transposed to the other species in his mating behavior, though interestingly enough he mated with male and female pintails indiscriminately. For social courtship he sought out wild drakes, which shows that he had an innate response to the releasing nuptial garb, but not to the complex quality of the female plumage. Seitz analyzed the same phenomenon far more thoroughly in the cichlid fish *Astatotilapia*. In a male of this species, raised normally in company of his own kind, fighting reactions can be elicited simply by counterfeiting the releasers of another male of his species. The essential sign stimuli (in analogy to Pelkwijk and Tinbergen's findings in male sticklebacks) are: the blue of the nuptial markings, the bejewelled scales, and even more, the display of threat behavior. But, contrary to the stickleback, courting cannot be elicited in this fish by a dummy. Only if the female is imitated in every detail, and the threshold of the reaction lowered, can a few feeble initiatives to courting be evoked. Contrary to the female stickleback, the female of *Astatotilapia* has no specific releasers. The courting reaction is so extremely selective because it responds to an acquired complex quality of the female. A male raised in isolation courted practically all dummies, but was no different from normal controls in his reaction to stimulus combinations that release fighting. This proves that in *Astatotilapia*, too, innate receptor correlates correspond only to the conspicuous, simple stimuli of the releasers, while the response to complex qualities must be acquired by conditioning. All these findings flatly contradict Jung's so-called archetype doctrine, to which Alverdes resorted liberally for an explanation of innate behavior, and which, starting out from an assumption of innate, organized ideas, in analogy to perceptual images, goes so far as to assume that such images can be "projected" into the motor sphere!

Perhaps the single characters of an innate mechanism can, with certain reservations, be regarded as "configurations." The "short-necked-ness" of the turkey hen's mechanism for the bird of prey, the relative head size that can be transposed into diverse absolute magnitudes in the young thrush's gaping mechanism, have certain configurational features. But there can be no doubt that the integration and correlation of the various cues that characterize a stimulus situation or an object is neither uniform nor configurational. Above all, their releasing effect is in fact additive, as Seitz has demonstrated in his unpublished study of cichlids.[3] In this paper he speaks of a law of heterogeneous summation (*Reizsum-menphänomen*, Tinbergen's translation). This law simply says that no single component of a releasing stimulus combination is qualitatively indispensable for its effect, but that the powerful total effect of the adequate object, or of a dummy that sends out all the essential stimuli, is based on additive cooperation. Within this total, the effect of single cues can be studied quantitatively, if only roughly and relatively. If the blue shine is omitted in a model intended to elicit fighting in *Astatoti-lapia*, certain motor releasers must be better imitated. For the following reaction of the female stickleback, the effectiveness of red approximately equals that of all the other morphological characters. Without red a very accurate model is needed, but a clay globule suffices if it is red. If the releasing values of single sign stimuli are thus weighed against one another, motor characters, especially all endogenous movements acting as releasers, greatly outweigh all others quantitatively. In certain conditions they may even become "indispensable." In the mating of sticklebacks, if the male omits a certain behavior pattern which Leiner has named "zigzag dance," the female does not follow him, or follows only at very low intensity. The same is true of releasing motions in *Astatotilapia*.

Owing to the phenomenon of heterogeneous summation in innate mechanisms, the release of any instinctive action can be quantified in two ways. The duration of a reaction can be taken as the measure of a

[3] Three papers on cichlids have since been published by Seitz (1940, 1941, 1950). [Translator's note.]

dummy's effectiveness. Lissmann followed this procedure with *Betta splendens*. The animal continues to react until the threshold of release has risen above the value needed to elicit a response. After showing the dummy, the fully adequate stimulus situation is then presented, to ascertain "how much specific energy is left," for the current level of this excitation depends on many factors and cannot be predicted from the length of the accumulation period alone. For example, in the case of scarcely perceptible organic disturbance, it takes much longer to accumulate. Bearing in mind these sources of error, it is also possible to quantify by the reverse process, by measuring the releasing value of a dummy in terms of the time required to "dam up" a reaction until it will respond to the dummy. Both methods can be used to study the relative rate of energy accumulation, either in different individuals or species, or in a single individual at various temperatures, etc. Thus correlated, the two phenomena: the relative effect of releasing stimuli, and the continuous decrease of thresholds for specific reactions, create the impression of being governed by definite laws. Without knowing both laws underlying the behavior of an animal, the variability of its reactions to constant stimulus situations seems altogether chaotic and haphazard! Indeed, these very phenomena have been cited by various sources as instances of what cannot be rationally explained. I frankly admit that there are technical sources of error. But despite them, the effects of the phenomena discussed are so consistent that Seitz succeeded in inferring a third law from certain inconsistencies in the two superimposed regularities. This is the so-called "inertia" of instinctive action. Let us take an animal that temporarily does not respond to a certain object, because the momentary level of some action-specific energy is too low. Let us leave the animal with the object, and wait until the threshold sinks to the point where it elicits a response. Theoretically, we should expect that, once the threshold value corresponding to the object in question is reached, the activity would begin to "trickle out" at minimum intensity. This is actually the case in the spinal preparation of the sea horse discussed earlier (pp. 248-249). In the intact animal, however, once an instinctive activity has been set off, it continues to run on for a longer period than would be expected. This causes the level of specific excitation to sink beneath the threshold value at which the reaction began to respond out of a state of quiescence. The more intensely the action "comes into full swing," the greater this span. Seitz was able to show this in the differences of time that passed until the next wave of activity set in. Other details of these phenomena also suggest a thought model of "initial friction" and "inertia of the reaction."

It cannot be the purpose of this report to convince its readers that the views here presented are correct. They should all be regarded as working hypotheses. We are fully aware that they represent gross simplifications of reality. Nor do we in any way pretend that we can "formulate a system" to explain "everything" with the aid of the few phenomena which we have attempted to analyze. We have due respect both for the proven findings of others, including the students of conditioned reflexes, and for all that is yet unanalyzed. In the foregoing, I have myself repeatedly used the word "arbitrary," a both comfortable and dangerous collective term for things as yet unanalyzed and beyond the power of rational explanation in the realm of animal and human behavior. But I hope I have conveyed one fact to some extent. Comparative ethology offers a boundless field for true causal analysis in relation to the whole, in the truest sense of the phrase. In this field, both descriptive-comparative study and the hardly initiated experimental approach must begin to restrain the mass of speculation still prevalent. Neither philosophical speculation, nor preconceived principles of solution, such as Buytendijk's "vital fantasy" or Jung's "archetypes" will advance our knowledge appreciably. Only the modest and, in our case, unfortunately most time-consuming and costly day-by-day work of inductive research can do so. The subject matter of this research comprises the deepest and oldest structures of the human mind as well, which we have a crying need to know.

6

Innate Motor Action as a Basis of Learning

Manipulative Patterns in the Chimpanzee

PAUL H. SCHILLER (1949)[1]

The analysis of stereotyped behavior patterns, originally discovered in insects, has been extended in the last fifteen years to various classes of vertebrates. Behavior studies on birds and fish by Lorenz (1935, 1939) and by Tinbergen (1940) initiated a comparative analysis of apparently unlearned movement patterns. Recently Schenkel (1947) has reported on social responses inherent in a mammal, the wolf. However, so far little attention has been drawn to that type of response in primates. The wide range of adaptability in the anthropoids, in particular, has directed research to the analysis of learning responses rather than to unlearned patterns of behavior. The apparently immediate adaptation to problem-solving situations in the gorilla (Yerkes, 1927) and chimpanzee (Köhler, 1921; Yerkes, 1925) suggested that there is a special higher type of learning by ideation or insight in apes. Attempts to reduce these performances of apes to conventional learning doctrines have not yet been successful. It is quite possible, however, that the wide range of behavior adjustment in apes may have a basis in innate organization. Instrumental behavior, for example, seems not to be based on an understanding of its usefulness but on the activation of a generalized play activity (Schiller, 1952).

There is some evidence (Schiller, 1937) that human manipulative forms evolve from purposeless motor patterns in handling objects. The learning of useful manipulations in other primates might, therefore, be traced back to some of its native constituents. With this idea in view, I

1 This study has not been previously published.

have studied the problem-solving manipulation of sticks, and compared it with the spontaneous manipulation of various objects, in fifty chimpanzees of the colony founded by R. M. Yerkes of Yale University.

Since learning is a modification of the original behavior repertoire, this original inventory of available movement patterns, which becomes modified in consequence of learning, should be analyzed with some care. Studies of detour problems in lower vertebrates, fish (Schiller, 1949) and rats (Bakay and Schiller, 1947), have shown that the immediately adaptive movements appear as generalizations of unlearned locomotor responses. The orientation toward food behind an obstacle and around the surfaces of the obstacle produces a sequence of responses that can be readily transferred to various novel situations of a range of similarity defined by the receptor-effector equipment of the organism. The fish or rat finds his way to the food by displaying a sequence of turns around obstacles in whatever direction as long as they can be followed. Similarly, once established, a tool-using pattern of a primate can be maintained even if a shift to a nonpracticed effector is involved. Such facts of response-generalization raise the question whether the primate did not have the response available in his original repertoire, before learning.

I. Development of Problem-Solving

The classical instrumentational problems solved readily by an ape are the pulling of strings, drawing in food with a stick, and stacking boxes under an elevated lure. Although adult animals show clever primary solutions of such problems, it has been emphasized (Guillaume and Meyerson, 1934) that young animals have to learn how to perform such tasks. The question now is whether the readiness of adaptive behavior in adults is due to some generalized experience or perhaps to a maturational factor that prepares prefunctionally for establishing the patterns utilized. In a first study of this kind Birch (1945) found that chimpanzees 5 to 6 years of age were quite clumsy in their first attempts to use sticks as implements, but the same animals, after having had access to sticks to play with for three days, showed remarkable improvement in problem solutions.

I have repeated Birch's experiment with younger animals, 2 years old, and found that they did not benefit from a three days' period of experience, and that even two weeks of free play with sticks did not improve their problem-solving capacity. This shows that at the age of 2 the experience cannot be incorporated in their not yet matured repertoire of manipulative patterns. After this test, the same animals were given a full year's opportunity to play with twigs, etc., in an open enclosure.

Three of four such animals made a spectacular improvement. Although none of them had previously adjusted the position of the stick to the food so as to be able to draw it in when the food was presented behind the stick, after one year's life in the open they not only picked up the stick from any place on the same platform where the food was, first placing the stick behind the food and then sweeping it in, but even took the stick from some remote place, from another platform, although they never could see the stick and the food in the same visual field. In addition, they learned with ease to use two sticks of different lengths, one too short to get the food but sufficient to get the other one which in its turn was long enough to pull in the food.

Two control animals of the same age were kept the whole year in a living cage where they had no access to sticks or any elongated solid objects whatever. These two animals had to learn the simple sweeping-in pattern anew and did not progress beyond this stage; they did not manage to use sticks on two different platforms, and only one of them mastered the task of adjusting the position of the stick so as to get its end behind the food on the same platform. It is obvious, then, that the lack of opportunity to play with stick-like objects definitely retarded their development in manipulation.

The fourth experimental animal who lived in the open enclosure, Alfalfa, was an unusual case. This was a chimpanzee reared for her first 20 months of life in a dark room. She learned, however, to use the stick, if the food was within the range of a simple sweeping movement, though she took more time to learn this task than did a normal animal. This individual did not improve at all in the open enclosure, and retesting after a year yielded worse rather than better results as compared with her own achievements at the age of 2 years. An animal, thus, who had visual difficulties, did not benefit by the general experience provided by life in the open, but behaved like normal animals kept in isolation from manipulative objects. This fact suggests that her original handicap was not due to the lack of visual experience so much as to the lack of actual visual guidance which still seemed to prevail more than a year after release from the dark room. The paradoxical finding that this female, Alfalfa, regressed rather than developed in manipulation might be ascribed to the greater discrepancy of her vision with general motor skill at the age of three than at the age of two. The same lack of improvement was found in another dark-reared chimpanzee, the male Snark, who, as a control, was kept alone in a living cage ever since his release from the dark room. These two visually handicapped animals were not differentiated by the radically different opportunities for practice that they were given.

The improvement of the three successful animals was, of course, limited. They certainly did not reach the level in manipulation of the 7- to 8-year-old animals who represent the earliest age group in which the most difficult varieties of the stick problem can be tested with quick success. This highest level, beyond which no adult chimpanzee can be brought without extensive specific training (approximation training or drill), includes the use of three sticks on three different platforms, and the joining of two sticks, one narrow, the other wider and hollow, so that the end of the narrow one can be fitted into the other and an elongated tool produced by insertion or connection. These highest achievements obviously require, beside the general experience of open-air life, a maturational factor that enables the animal to manipulate several objects with reference to each other. This is accomplished with the two elements at the age of 4 to 5 years. But, as I have said, it is only reached if general experience is provided on both the sensory and the motor side. This experience alone, however, is not enough to bring about the level of adjustment which is reached at puberty. (Even the inexperienced adult does not immediately solve the rake problem.) As to the more-elements problems, they are not strictly solved at once by the older animals. After testing several adults, it was found that none of them succeeded in joining sticks or even sweeping in a longer stick with a shorter one at the first trials. Though well adapted to experimental situations, they were clumsy in such problems. They reached for the food across the stick with an empty hand, then pulled in the stick when they could not reach the food, and started playing with the stick, chewing it and turning it around, poking with it in cracks and corners. Soon they would thrust the stick outside the cage, wave it, and shake it, and scoot or throw it in the general direction of the food. It is necessary at first to give the simplest problem: food within the range of a simple sweeping movement. While grabbing for the food, the chimpanzee will hit upon the stick, grasp it, and while pulling it in, chances are that the food will come nearer also. One such lucky coincidence, and the chimpanzee discovers what to do. He repeats the same trick faster, with less hesitation, and in two to three trials he has learned how to use the stick as a tool.

Sometimes it is difficult, even for an adult, to master the next step, when food is placed behind the stick. This is learned whenever the chimpanzee, in his restless attempts to grab the food, pushes the stick ahead and then pulls it in when it is behind the food. As soon as this twofold pattern of push-and-pull is mastered, it is easy to elicit it when the stick has been placed in a different direction from the food. The adults will sooner or later omit to reach in vain for the food with the naked hand and pick up the stick at once, bring its end behind the food and sweep, draw or angle in the food. Young animals, as stated, have such difficulty in this situation that they never learn it before 3 years of age, and then after considerable training. The adults, however, develop this pattern readily in some twenty trials, in such a way as to fetch the stick from distant places without attempting to reach by hand for food beyond their grasp. They learn the two- and three-stick problems as fast as, or maybe somewhat faster than the 8- or 9-year-old chimpanzees entering puberty.

Once a complex pattern is mastered, the chimpanzees develop a liking for it. They perform the trick even in situations in which the complex pattern is not necessary for adaptive behavior. If a sufficiently long stick is given as the nearest one, they use it to angle in the other stick—which is no longer than the first—to secure the food with this second one. The same is true if the stick-joining pattern has been developed. If two short sticks are given and a third long one at an equal distance, they neglect the one that is long enough, take the two fitting parts, perform the connection with great patience, and then use this double stick instead of the simple one. If sufficiently activated, a chimpanzee may even prefer to connect two very short sticks and try to sweep in the food with this inadequate implement, although the amply long simple stick is available all the time.

These results show that there is an inclination to develop stereotypes for problem solutions. These stereotypes are, of course, not rigid in any spatiotemporal sense, they have a wide range of equivalence as to direction, succession, etc., but the general manipulative pattern seems to be fixed. I am, therefore, inclined to separate the tool manipulation from its cognitive aspect, and analyze its motor constituents.

Such a program of research is, furthermore, encouraged by the fact that I have not found any difference in the way of learning the various stick problems in chimpanzees that had the prefrontal regions of their cerebral cortex removed. Five operated chimpanzees were tested at least one year after bilateral prefrontal lobectomy, and their performance was compared with that of twenty-five normal animals in all age groups. The operated animals were 2, 2, 8, 8, and 24 years old. The first two were at the level of infants; of the 8-year-old chimpanzees one was average and one exceptionally skillful; the adult, unusually quiet and successful in learning. The brain regions essential for adaptive instrumentation are certainly not located in the prefrontal areas, allegedly responsible for highest coordination of adaptive behavior.

II. Free Play

The importance of a maturational factor that can be facilitated but certainly not replaced by general experience and specific training, suggested a study of spontaneous behavior, of the manipulative patterns with implements which are used in giving problem situations to primates. Therefore, practically all chimpanzees of the Yerkes colony were tested in situations with no incentive whatever, in their natural handling of objects. Some observations on the play of apes have been reported earlier, but as curiosities rather than as a subject of systematic study. Köhler has described how some chimpanzees would throw away the stick if frustrated in getting in the food, how they would poke at chickens, explore ant hills or pools of water with sticks, place covers (garlands, cloths) over their shoulders or tramp in a circle around a pole.

These careful descriptions, however, did not induce his followers to check upon the contribution these playful patterns made toward problem-solving. My original plan was to provide the chimpanzees with facilities for play and see whether they would derive any benefit from their acquaintance with tools in subsequent problem situations. This would have been, if positive, a demonstration of latent learning of instrumentation. Learning, without any specific motivation, how to handle a stick would, as I hoped, enable them to use the stick for some purpose, as a tool. This plan had to be abandoned, for I have found just an opposite relationship. With no incentive the chimpanzees have displayed a higher variety of handling objects than under the pressure of a lure which they attempted to obtain. The previous play did not facilitate problem-solving, but rather impeded it, or, at least, the problem situation impeded the play. All these activities occur more easily when not motivated. This is shown in the figures on joining sticks (Figs. 1a-1c).

Let me start with the end. Fifty-two chimpanzees were given the double stick, in two parts, to play with (in the cage, the animal alone, about one hour after feeding). Of the twenty adults thus tested, nineteen performed the insertion of the peg into the hole, a complete connection of the two sticks, within a fifteen-minute test period, the majority of them right at the beginning. The one who did not perform this pattern was a pregnant female. It is interesting that half a year later another female, now pregnant, did not perform this pattern although she had done so at her first test. The rest of the adults carried out the connection the second time, too, and all of them repeatedly in any one session.

Of the younger animals, between 5 and 8 years of age, only about half performed the joining of the sticks; of the infants and children up to 4

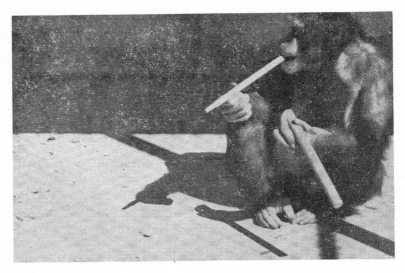

FIG. 1a

years of age, not one. This fact points obviously to a correlation with the ability of the chimpanzee to handle several objects at a time. It is clear that a maturational component is present in the spontaneous play activity of connecting sticks that can be fitted together. There is some suggestion of a correlation with sexual factors, inasmuch as males are faster

FIG. 1b

in performing the connection, and females less inclined to do so in their sexually inactive periods.

The act itself shows some primitive appearances in the poking and exploring activities of the younger animals: if they do not place the peg into the hole, they explore the latter, pushing a finger as deeply as can be into the hole, pressing their lips and tongue into it, and so forth. They also use the peg as something to explore with, in holes in the ground, in the fence, in cracks, and the like; but not so readily in the other stick, which they have to hold in one hand while the other hand is

FIG. 1c

Figs. 1a-1c: Successive phases in "unmotivated" joining of two fitting sticks
Subject Karla, 6 years

performing the activity of poking. This coordination of the two hands needs to be developed before the active connecting or joining can take place. In the adult act this poking and exploring is most obviously the basic pattern that results in a connection. In this sense, inasmuch as it does not require any external reinforcement, it is not a product of specific learning, but of maturation facilitated by general functional experience of the capacities of the effectors. It is in this sense that I have chosen to use the adjective "innate" or "prefunctional."

The same animals who performed the stick-connecting in play were not all able to solve a pulling-in problem by connecting the same sticks. The youngest animal who connected the sticks in play was 6 years old, the youngest one who did it in the work situation was 8. Those who used the stick connection for work took much more time to develop this habit than to join the sticks in play: in repeated trials, of five minutes each, it took them eight to ten trials or many times the maximum time in which they carried out insertion when there was no problem to solve with its aid. The problem of joining sticks was never solved, of course, by animals who had not performed the connection previously in play: chimpanzees under 5 or 6 years of age, and monkeys (five spider and five rhesus were tested) never do it and are helpless in the problem situation requiring the joining of two sticks. Those who were slow in performing connection in play were more retarded in utilizing it for work than the ready players. It is obvious, then, that presence of the play-performance is a prerequisite for the solution of the stick-joining problem. The pattern must be readily available before it can be utilized, and it is not the pressure of a need that makes it emerge, but, on the contrary, such a pressure represses it, if it is not highly available.

This rather unexpected state of affairs led me to search for pre-problem patterns in less complex tool-using situations. An analysis of the very first attempts to use the stick when a lure is offered along with the stick has shown the following. The stick is accepted as a secondary or as an equivalent lure by practically all chimpanzees. Many of them are more interested in the stick than in the food. This is invariably the case with the youngest ones, especially after a few frustrating experiences or when they have obtained enough food for the work involved. They will not work any more, though they eat readily when food is offered. The stick is then taken immediately, without any attempt before or after to bring it into relationship with the food. The stick is only used to play with.

I had one male adult, a castrate, who was so fond of playing with the sticks that he snatched one away as soon as it was presented and fled to a far corner, ignoring the "bait." Several hours of fasting did not improve the situation, until he was conditioned to expect food: whenever he touched the stick a piece of food was thrown to him. By this technique he was brought to look around for food after he had touched the stick and the food could then be placed in such a way that a straight pull on the stick would bring it in to him. Even then he kept the stick for play after consuming the food and would not part with it. When bait was placed in front of the grill, he, Don, soon tried to put the stick in front of it, but became involved in placing the stick across the bars. This activity fascinated him so much that as soon as half of the stick was outside, he grabbed the outer part with his free hand and pulled the stick back. This alternate pushing out and pulling back in another gap is a characteristic pattern that can be observed outside problem situations as well: I call it the *weaving* pattern (Fig. 2). Don performs it in play by preference on the top mesh of the cage, and if he has the stick thoroughly entangled, he swings on the free end, with the frequent result of breaking it. Now, in the problem situation, he is attracted to the grill-window by the bait and the experimenter and, sitting in front of it, displays his favorite games there. He cannot resist "weaving," though it obviously does not bring him closer to his "goal," which he certainly devours eagerly, if he by chance gets it.

FIG. 2
"Weaving" a stick through the wire mesh
Subject Jenny, 9 years

A few repetitions of the "weaving" pattern seem to exhaust his reservoir of this specific pattern, and he suddenly shifts over to another form of activity. This is the *pointing and shaking* pattern. The stick is thrust through the grill and pointed toward the food, or equally frequently, toward the experimenter (the camera, if present, is a favorite "goal" too). With outstretched hand the stick is pointed in the air, often lowered to the ground or lifted as high as it will go. If the bars are vertical, a waving movement develops with an angle of 90° or more, and even the top of the cage, if accessible, is hit regularly above the chimpanzee's own head. If the bars are horizontal, this same pattern is dominant too, but naturally restricted to a mere shaking. A frequent alternative is a free side movement in a horizontal plane, dragging the stick back and forth on the ground: this pattern is the predecessor of adjusted sweeping.

By placing the food carefully, the pointing and shaking can be utilized to develop it into sweeping or angling. The latter is a pattern of hitting the fruit closer with the stick hanging in the air and leaning from above with its point on the ground; it was well described by Guillaume and Meyerson (1934). Yet this attempt at a reinforcement has to overcome another natural tendency of the younger chimpanzees (and of Don). As soon as the shaking hits the fruit so that the latter moves, this distant effect of an action fascinates the animal and he repeats it with the most likely result that the food is pushed aside and often out of reach. For this reason, students of stick-using behavior in primates build side-frames on their platforms. This precaution pays because the angling pattern has better chances to become correlated with moving the food, if both the food and the point of the stick are prevented from skidding away and are forced to move along the straight line of an edge. This way only two alternatives remain: to pull the food in or to push it away.

To be sure, these two alternatives are originally equally frequent. In a few monkeys and chimpanzees I have tried to develop the push-away rather than the pull-in pattern, and the result was easy learning of a very well-adjusted and generalized pattern; even two sticks could be used to produce a very intricate double push (if food was dropped from elsewhere after performance). There is no indication that the congruent activity is preferred to the incongruent one of pushing food beyond any possible reach or even sight (cf. Schiller, 1950, 1952). The struggle with stick and food frequently results in throwing the stick away, mostly toward the food or other frustrating objects, like the experimenter or the camera. Sometimes it is thrown in the air, sometimes scooted along the ground.

This pattern has been observed by Köhler, and interpreted as a "good error," expressing the general direction of a desirable activity but not attaining its end. I am inclined to believe that this type of activity contains no intention of obtaining the food by a pseudo-logical act, but is simply the emotional outburst of a pattern which otherwise has a higher threshold. The stick is sometimes just placed quietly out in front of the grill, somewhere between food and experimenter, and the animal gives up work and play, resorts to rocking himself like a baby and making grooming sounds. He is giving up and turns his back to the scene of frustration. Later, he turns back and then he suddenly picks up the stick again and points or shakes it toward the "goal." If there is no effect on the goal, the stick is scooted or thrown away .

Comparing this sequence to the free play with sticks, it is clear that the throwing is an end-member of a series of activities which seem to induce one another. The exploratory activity, *poking and sounding* in holes and meshes with the stick, easily develops into waving and shaking if there is open space behind the crack or hole. This waving goes over into "weaving" if there is nothing on the other side, but it turns into a distant poking if there is something to bring the stick into relation with. This poking and hitting is likely to be directed toward a social partner, if there is one. The hitting of the food and subsequent pulling-in is a modified, usefully adapted form of the social challenge of exploring companions behind a partition.

This interpretation is derived from the fact that the shaking of the stick toward a partner is directed as a *challenge*: as soon as the other chimpanzee or man attempts to seize the offered stick, it is violently withdrawn and the free hand of the challenger grabs at the accepting hand of the naive victim. This play is invariably produced, though more often by vicious females than by males and only from puberty upward. It has the appearance of a trade offered but not meant seriously, as if to deceive the partner. Several repetitions are enjoyed. If the grabbing does not succeed in striking the challenged animal, the challenger yells in a high tone and escapes, turns his back and runs two or three steps, or swings to the next pole, and looks back (as if he would be followed). This "escape" or "evasion" is often accompanied by losing the stick or giving it to the partner. If not followed, the animal comes back and *presents* himself to be scratched, pressing back or belly against the mesh (males and females equally lift their genital areas toward the partner). This play is mostly performed by females in heat, and looks as if the presentation of the stick might serve as some sort of sexual challenge. Such an instinctive pattern seems to be at the basis of placing a stick out across a network of bars, shaking it there and pulling it back or throwing it away: the elements of problem-solving. Whichever components are reinforced by the responses of the outside world, those will be produced in the proper sequence, omitting repetitions, and develop into a unified pattern that the human observer calls a problem solution.

The fact, described by Köhler, that chimpanzees try to perform changes in the sticks as if they would construct implements (Klüver found similar attempts in a Cebus monkey) is also due to native patterns of handling movable objects. That a chimpanzee breaks off a branch if excited, has nothing to do with his desire to get at the food. Once he has the stick in his hand, he will use it sooner or later. Such a sequence can easily be reinforced in a couple of trials and then it appears to be a coherent, continuous pattern. All problem-solving patterns look like this, but they are really composites of originally independent reactions, just like the detour performances of lower vertebrates.

The same pertains to breaking off branches from fork-shaped sticks that are not easily placed across bars. If frustrated, the animal resorts to a different activity from the one in which he was actually engaged and displays aggression, bites or breaks the stick (Fig. 3). Once he has it this way, he again returns to his previous activity, and now gets the stick smoothly through the grill and sweeps in his food. It was anger that made him a good craftsman, not an intention, ideation, or insight.

FIG. 3
Breaking a stick
Subject Karla, 6 years

The same happens if the sticks that are to be joined do not fit exactly. Köhler describes how his Sultan pulled out a peg and then chewed the peg smaller "in order to" achieve better fitting. This is benevolent interpretation. Chimpanzees only too often chew at sticks, and more at their ends than in the middle. The stick is turned end for end almost always with the help of the mouth (Figs. 1a-1c), which is also utilized in getting it through the bars and the like. If the animal has a set developed to join sticks, everything impeding him in doing so makes him angry. Take away one of the sticks, and the chimpanzee will furiously bite into the other one, making it less rather than more fit to be used. If there is difficulty in connecting them, the chimpanzee will chew the ends of the sticks, the socket as well as the pin; if there is a stopper, it will be removed; if there is a too-thick peg, by splitting off a splinter it now stands a better chance to be fitted. This is accident, but once the sticks fit, the chimpanzee uses the double stick when he sees the food. It happens, though, that after fitting, the stick is pulled apart and refitted, and this goes on in series (Fig. 1). The first observation of this kind (Köhler's) points out that the joining was made in play, but then was immediately utilized for work. My chimpanzees learned it rapidly after a few trials, but they played a lot with the double stick before incorporating it into the problem solution and in the latter situation frequently disconnected the sticks while grasping with an empty hand, meanwhile, for the food. Play and work for food were separate spheres of activity, that became correlated with repeated experience. The complex stick-handling is a pattern that develops independently of its external utilization. Learning connects this pattern with certain external situations (not S with R), like perceiving food beyond reach, and then it gradually develops into a skill that is applied with a large range of generalization, once the association is established, and the action sequence can become elicited by a perception associated with the commencing act of the chain (stick pointed to the experimenter). Repetition condenses the chain, to a unified skill pattern.

The breaking of the stick is a pattern that also occurs without any frustration in play activity. The longer the stick, the greater are the chances that it will be used as a lever. The same way as a piece of food is angled in, another stick will be rotated so as to reach its end. The same way as the end of the stick is placed in a corresponding opening, it will be thrust into any cavity and then tilted until the rim is touched. The stick is often used as a lever in cracks, so its point breaks off. It is used as a rod that is pounded into a crack or corner, at a preferred angle of about 60° to 70°. This is often accompanied by "weaving" if displayed on the upper or lower rim of a fence. After performing this lever-and-pounding activity, almost exclusively in a sitting posture, the chimpanzee will sooner or later roll over on his back and place the stick under his neck or shoulder, lift it up in his feet and, bracing the middle part against his soles, pull with both hands on the ends, so that thin and already misused sticks break (Fig. 3). Now the parts are collected around the still lying, or again sitting chimpanzee and he rubs his back and head against them. The collection of the stick fragments into a pile is invariably performed in a corner, and the place is usually carefully chosen. I shall presently describe this activity in some detail.

While the social challenge, etc., was considered in some obscure relationship with sexual functions, this fragmentation of the sticks and piling the pieces into a corner suggest some correlation with nest-building activities in nature. Chimpanzees in the field often build day nests for a rest, and invariably build a sleeping nest for the night in the branches of big trees. Nissen (1931) describes how the wandering group of chimpanzees settles every night in a different tree, and every individual builds himself a small sleeping berth in the course of several minutes by bending and breaking lots of branches. Yerkes (1925) has observed the same activity in captive chimpanzees living on a farm. The colony chimpanzees do not perform this activity; they have comfortable sleeping nooks in their indoor cages, and few building materials available. No study has yet been carried out as to whether chimpanzees born in the colony and exposed to cool nights in the open air and provided with nest-building opportunities would display such an instinctive act. But it is likely that the elementary motor patterns are present and ready to be displayed as soon as objects that lend themselves to such handling are presented. I certainly have observed that all youngsters in the open enclosure collect leaves in their laps while rocking at a post or in a corner. This happens especially if there is reason to believe that they are *insecure*. Other patterns in similar situations are lifting the hand vertically above the head (especially frequent in the dark-reared animals), and clinging to each other with a peculiar embrace: one has his arm around the other's shoulder, and the other embraces his mate under the armpit. They even walk rapidly along in this posture if the threatening thing (usually a human being) is approaching them. Such common defense is present, of course, between mother and child, where the dimensions of the bodies produce a carrying in the lap or on the back rather than the apparent couple of Siamese twins.

III.   *Play with Boxes, String, etc.*

The nest-building pattern is more clearly observable in the case of handling boxes. After having found a possible reduction of stick problems to native handling patterns, I was interested in seeing the origin of the box-stacking problem solutions. In the literature (Köhler, Bingham, Yerkes and Spragg) it is obvious that lots of play precedes the problem solution, accompanied by what the authors consider "good errors." I am inclined to believe that the intention expressed in the random activity is more of a "bad instinct" than a "good insight" clumsily performed. (The behavior which has been described as adaptive in the problem situation appears when there is no "problem.") The fact that a too-short box is often placed on its point under the suspended fruit certainly does not express the idea that a diagonal is longer than a side (Fig. 4): cubes and blocks are lifted, carried in the lap, and placed carefully with one corner or point to the ground most of the time. This is the natural way of manipulating large-sized bodies, just as it is the natural way of carrying sticks wherever they can be grasped so as to leave all extremities free for climbing; in the lap or between neck and shoulder. Cubes are carried in the lap between the palms so that the sides are flat to the half-bent-in palms and thus the *point* is downmost (rather than one of the sides on which it can rest on the ground or on the surface of another box).

FIG. 4
Placing a box on its point over another box

Placed somewhere on a point, the box is carefully balanced until it heels over on one side. Then it is pushed back and forth, or dragged along the floor, invariably to a preferred corner. In the corner a peculiar ritual activity is performed. The animal places the cube at a distance of, say, two feet from either wall, stretches one leg toward the lower edge of the wall, the other toward the cube, and pushes lightly at the box, moving it an inch or two. Then he turns around and does the same with the feet reversed. Often the arms are also used in this "measuring" rite, or they do it alone after the feet have done their own part. The arm is used on the dorsal side, the hand bent up as high as it will go, the palm facing up, and the lower arm brushing back and forth a few times against the lower edge of the wall or alternately against the box. This activity suggests a careful selection of a place for the box. Soon the animal rapidly turns over on his back on top of the box and rests there briefly or turns around, scratching his back. Down he tumbles, and if the box has been pushed aside by this, the animal again starts measuring (Fig. 5). Sometimes only the back of the neck is placed on the box, the head held high as if on a hard pillow. If there are two boxes, either of them is measured, and the chimpanzee rolls down between the two, tossing them around his shoulders while on his back. All extremities are lifted high in the air and usually the smaller, but sometimes the larger box (5 and 10 lbs.), is lifted on the belly and thence with the feet

FIG. 5
"Measuring"
Subject Jojo, 9 years

and hands in the air, where it is rotated like a large ball for many minutes. This play resembles the fighting games between companions. Actually the box is carried like an infant in the lap while swinging, or on the back while walking, in the neck and on the shoulder. The placing of the box on the head is analogous to putting branches or leaves there. Whether this play has any sexual significance is an open question. Bingham (1928) saw decoration in this connection, since masturbation with leaves, etc., occurred after the animal placed such articles on his head. On the other hand, he regards play with boxes as recreation after work. In howling monkeys, Carpenter (1934) describes tumbling at the forks of trees after coitus. One young virgin female in heat actually placed the box in a corner, some two feet high, and braced her rear against it, performing characteristic pelvic movements and panting associated with the

mating activities of experienced females, over a period of several minutes. Much of the showing off, drumming, clapping and the like in the
male has sexual invitation or jealousy-dominance character: exploration
of feet, skin, and grooming, licking; pasting feces on poles, vomiting.
Spitting water, often on feet or face, is a challenge, as is urinating. Smack-
ing the lips and rhythmic tongue movements in many primates (Zucker-
man) are invitations to mate.

The two boxes are often stacked one on the other. Each of the older
animals performs this construction of a tower, and then does one of two
different things with it. The animal either drags the tower into the
corner and "measures" its place, rolls on it, or beside it, lifts both boxes
on his belly and plays until they fall apart, and then either places them
back on each other or plays with the two boxes alternately (Fig. 6). The
other game with the double box is to climb on it very carefully, sitting
and rocking on top, as if balancing, standing up with all fours on the
top surface (like a circus bear on a sphere), standing erect and, if this does
not topple the boxes, stretching the hands high, clapping and jumping
in the air (Fig. 7).

This pattern was observed in half of all animals tested. It is exactly
the pattern utilized in the problem-solving situation, where two (or
three) boxes are dragged under the lure, the animal climbs up and jumps
for the food suspended from above. There is no doubt that this solution is
based upon the chimpanzee's natural inclination to carry out all these

Fig. 6a
"Measuring" with piled boxes

FIG. 6b

Rolling over on back with "tower" tilted over belly

complex instances of patterns in this very way (when they have no relation to a goal). The lure produces only a concentration of activity near to it, and the agitated animal performs his play patterns or native manipulative forms, which incidentally lead him to success. Reinforcement asso-

FIG. 7a

Mounting a "tower" of boxes

ciates the pattern with a place characterized by specific perceptual features, and repetition makes the skill a smooth unit.

Originally the patterns are displayed with no reference to any external perceptual situation, except the material itself, with which the animals play. But even the perceptual qualities of the objects of manipulation themselves are not specific in determining the kind of activity evinced. The same motor patterns that are displayed toward boxes can be observed with sticks also. In the case of the sticks, however, that have far fewer manipulative surfaces than the boxes, the measuring is less conspicuous and the possibility of manipulating them across the fence

FIG. 7b
Jumping high in the air from the box

lends them a type of appeal that is lacking in the boxes which are far too big for that.

The "weaving" is displayed, of course, with any suitable objects, such as strings or a cloth that can be twisted into a bundle and pressed through the mesh, only to be pulled back through the next opening. The chimpanzee may make a loop and hang on it in a way which closely resembles the hanging from the stick "woven" into the ceiling mesh. The "leash" is then pulled in quite as in a problem task. The loose structure of a string or cloth makes it more likely that it will be placed around the body in varied ways, put around the neck and shoulders or the hip. These objects are placed carefully before or behind the animal; he sits or lies upon them, stretches them flat on the ground, or between his feet and hands, while he is rolling over on his back (Fig. 8). The cloth is used as a scarf, very frequently placed on the head and held against the light to peep across it. This covering of the head is performed in sitting and lying postures as well. Both string and cloth are often chewed and pressed into the mouth (calling to mind the manipulation of the umbilical cord), dragged or pushed, scrubbed, stretched, strained, and so forth. Sitting on a pile of leaves or sticks is often associated with eating leaves picked up while walking with objects (as if nesting were associated with peeling of bark and stripping twigs of leaves). Challenging offer and sudden withdrawal, shaking, and throwing are displayed with these objects just as with sticks.

The removal of outstanding particles, such as the bark of a twig, or a splinter of wood, is a characteristic pattern in handling objects. A thread getting loose from the cloth is invariably picked up, pulled and twisted, a spot on the box is scratched and groomed like any small unevenness on a fellow's skin. The poking with a stick is frequently directed toward circumscribed rough spots on the ground. The mouth is used to turn and twist, to help objects through bars and so forth. Having a chimpanzee scribble with a pencil on a patterned background, the figural parts are preferred, and explored, or groomed, covered with lines more than any other section of the drawing surface (Schiller, 1951). The poking toward eyes, mouth, etc., shows intense interest in holes, ridges, cracks. The peeling of fruit and the grooming of the skin can be repeated in the peeling activity displayed with twigs, as described by Guillaume and Meyerson (1934). Poking with a stick into liquid or dirt and licking off these substances is a common play form; the animals do it with the hollow stick and do the same with cavities in the boxes, which they fill and empty repeatedly.

Conclusions

The fact that such radically different objects as the three-dimensional box, the thin sticks, and the loose texture of a two-dimensional cloth or a string are handled in essentially the same way, suggests an independence of the manipulative patterns from their actual releasers. This independence is, of course, limited to the dimensional properties of the objects. Much larger things cannot be handled the same way, and are explored cautiously; much smaller things again are scrutinized in detail and placed into anything that has the qualities of a container. The investigation of new objects, if they fit a certain range of manipulability, soon turns over into the gross handling, carrying them to various places and placing them into relation with various portions of the body.

FIG. 8a
Pulling and extending string with all four extremities
Subject Flora, 8 years

FIG. 8b
Starting "measuring" with a piece of cloth
Subject Banka, 8 years

I am inclined to believe that a certain order of magnitude of objects is their sole criterion for being used as described in this paper. Thicker sticks are preferred by older animals; bigger boxes, too, broader leashes, in correlation with the size of their manipulative effector organs. Not specific innate schemata but matured motor patterns that fit the objects determine their native manipulation; the rest is association with opportunities; "insight" is the chance occurrence of this manipulation in a situation where it is appropriate. The chimpanzee seems to have a certain repertoire of manipulative patterns, not specifically learned, and this is displayed whenever the animal is ready to play (not overexcited, frustrated, etc.) in essentially the same manner whatever the detailed nature of the plaything might be. One or another pattern has, of course, better chances with one object than with another, according to its structural qualities. Besides this immediate selection of possible patterns it is the consequence of the activities that helps to reinforce certain patterns more than others and to establish a certain sequence of native patterns more than any other sequence. The mechanism of generalization of responses in adaptation to actual, nonassociated situations is a most puzzling subject of learning theory (Lashley, 1930). The genesis of it is certainly independent of expectations, purposes, and is due rather to inhibition of repetitions of activated patterns.

As the ultimate units of which adaptive patterns are composed, individual or elementary patterns of grasping, pointing, shaking, carrying, placing, pulling, pushing and so forth can be conceived as being at the chimpanzee's disposal as his sensorimotor capacities develop in the course of maturation and connecting general experience. In this sense these motor elements, rather than stimulus-response connections or unconditioned reflexes, are the basis of adaptive behavior. Their organization is serialization or rather condensation, not selection (Schiller, 1952). They can be connected with very different perceptions. Since no external stimulus is definitely correlated to the response, it is fair to replace the term "response" with that of "emittence" of patterns determined more by the internal state of the organism than by the external stimulus (Skinner, 1948). There is some indication that certain varieties of play with a stick are evinced more often in a hungry state and again others more in a socially deprived situation, and so forth, than otherwise. To follow up this point is the topic of a separate investigation.

An analysis of the competition of learning with the unlearned display of spontaneous play forms is a further subject amenable to experimental study. In this paper it is only attempted to draw attention to the fact that even the highest vertebrates, primates, have certain peculiar manipulative forms of activity available, without specific training to develop them. They are present uniformly in all individuals of the same age group, and are invariably displayed if the general condition of the animal favors them. They bear all the criteria of instinctive activities, and can be correlated to known patterns of functional cycles such as nesting, mating, social activities, and so forth. These internally coordinated manipulative patterns are not derived from experience but, on the contrary, the adaptive learned performances seem to be derived from them, by a mechanism of association with external and internal cues in consequence of repeated and consistent occurrences.

7

The Past Twelve Years in the Comparative Study of Behavior

KONRAD LORENZ (1952a)[1]

Almost thirteen years ago, I had the privilege of reporting on the status of comparative behavior study at the Convention of this Society in Rostock. Today I am giving a condensed account of recent findings in our science, and in particular of any changes that our earlier views have had to undergo. Jakob von Uexküll once said: "Today's truth is tomorrow's error," and Otto Koehler countered: "No, today's truth is the special case of tomorrow." I am proud to say that literally every important erroneous statement I made at Rostock thirteen years ago and that I must rectify today, illustrates this principle. Certain specific cases of animal behavior led to simplisms and premature generalizations by their relative simplicity; but these simplifications and generalizations have their heuristic value even where they now call for modification. The first step toward discovering a natural law has been to find the most easily analyzed case.

To begin with, I shall restate briefly the results of comparative ethology as I presented them in 1939. C. O. Whitman (1898) and O. Heinroth (1910) had discovered, independently of each other, the existence of genetically determined behavior patterns that are highly constant in form, and which are as characteristic of a species, genus, order, etc., up to the highest systematic categories, as are any morphological taxonomic characters. The concept of phyletic morphology, and the methods of comparative morphology may therefore be applied to these behavior patterns. A species, a genus, or even a whole class has a certain instinctive movement, as it has certain structural devices.

Neither of these two scientists attempted a causal analysis of instinc-

[1] Report at the Zoological Convention, Freiburg, 1952.

tive activities or made any statements about their physiological properties. Both of them simply used behavior as a taxonomic character. All the motor patterns which they described and evaluated systematically are purely instinctive movements unaccompanied by orienting mechanisms. The common physiological characters of these movements were incompatible with all the prevailing theories on instinctive behavior. According to McDougall's vitalistic "purposive psychology" (1933), instinctive behavior must at all times be adaptively plastic, and only its end result constant. In the opinion of the mechanistic schools, behaviorists as well as Pavlovian reflexologists, innate behavior patterns are chains of unconditioned reflexes, completely rigid, and devoid of all spontaneity. The motor patterns which Whitman and Heinroth discovered were as rigid as could be expected on the basis of the chain reflex hypothesis. At the same time, however, they had a remarkable spontaneity of their own. All these behavior patterns respond more readily if they have not been released for some time. The threshold value of releasing stimuli decreases during quiescence. Moreover, an instinctive movement that is not "used" over a long period literally becomes a "motive." It causes motor unrest in the organism as a whole, and induces it to search actively for the releasing stimulus situation. Wallace Craig called this phenomenon appetitive behavior.

The purposiveness and adaptiveness of behavior does not reside in the instinctive movement, but precedes it. An instinctive act is not purposive; it is the goal toward which the organism actively strives. The survival value of an action, to either an animal or a man, is not its subjective goal: I have a desire to eat, not to gain weight. This discovery of Craig's is one of those commonplaces which, as Goethe says, are "the hardest of all" to see.

All these phenomena—spontaneity, lowering of threshold, discharge at inadequate objects, periodic-rhythmical occurrence, appetitive behavior—suggest a process of accumulation. "Something" is accumulated (generated) rhythmically and continually, and used up by the consummation of an instinctive act. This is incompatible with the conception of instinctive movements as chain reflexes.

In view of these facts, it would have been plausible to argue as follows: instinctive actions are rigid; they are evidently dependent on genetically fixed structures of the central nervous system, yet they are not reflexes. Are there other processes, equally rigid and structurally determined, but spontaneous and independent of external stimulation? Yes indeed, we know such processes, in the stimulus-producing centers of the heart, in the respiratory mechanism, and in the spinal cord (Sherrington). Unfortunately, neither Craig nor I myself posed this question.

E. von Holst (1939) found the answer in the course of his experiments on automatic-endogenous stimulus production and central coordination in the ventral nerve cord of earthworms and the spinal cord of fish.

Most instinctive actions are accompanied by orienting mechanisms. If we disregard these, then afferents, including proprioception, are of negligible importance in the emergence and the coordination of instinctive movements. It would be premature to identify instinctive reactions with the endogenous automatic movements discovered by von Holst. Even so, the latter are surely the essential and dynamic elements of all true, spontaneous instinctive behavior.

This sheds a new light on the release of innate reactions. So long as we conceived instinctive actions as chain reflexes—as did Craig (1918) and I myself originally—the first link in the chain did not stand out much from the rest. Now, however, we have a picture of a spontaneous, constantly maintained process, under permanent central inhibition, and disinhibited only by certain, very specific stimuli. The releasing mechanism does not respond to a complex of all the stimuli given in the biologically adequate situation. It responds to specific, simple but outstanding sets of stimuli, which act as "key stimuli." It "schematizes" the total situation; hence our original term of "innate releasing schema" (or "mechanism"). Each of these key stimuli also has a releasing effect by itself. The effectiveness of a total situation (for instance, of a dummy) corresponds to the sum of key stimuli realized in it *(Reiz-Summen-Effekt,* A. Seitz 1940, translated by Tinbergen as "law of heterogeneous summation"). There is a basic difference between an innate reaction that is activated by an innate releasing mechanism (IRM), and a learned reaction. The latter may also respond selectively to the complex quality of very intricate Gestalten, but these configurations cannot be dissected into summative parts.

Instinctive behavior thus consists of at least three components. First, appetitive behavior motivated by internal accumulation of readiness for a specific action. Second, activation of an IRM, which disinhibits the innate reaction. Third, discharge of the "consummatory act" (Craig, 1918), which is the purpose of the behavior. The model shown in Figure 1 symbolizes the interaction of endogenous energy accumulation, IRM and instinctive movement. The stream flowing from tap T corresponds to the endogenous accumulation of action-specific energy, the spring S, connected to the cone-valve V, represents the central inhibition that must be overcome, the valve itself the IRM, the weights on the scale-pan SP, which contribute toward opening the valve, represent the releasing key stimuli. The instinctive movement itself is symbolized by the stream of liquid spouting from the lower tap. This model, which should not be taken too seriously, shows that the intensity of an instinctive reaction always depends on two factors: the effectiveness of the stimulus situation and the level of internal motivation. It also shows that the effectiveness of a key stimulus can only be determined if motivational level is known, and vice versa. Therefore, we must work with the so-called method of dual quantification.

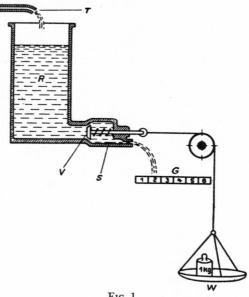

FIG. 1

So much for the standing of our analysis of instinctive behavior in 1939. What has changed since then, and what has been added? There are innate behavior patterns which consist of the three links of appetitive behavior, attainment of the releasing stimulus situation by activation of the IRM, and consummatory action. Moreover, the examples which we were then able to give for this simplest form of instinctive action are right. But these cases are exceedingly rare, much rarer than behavior patterns of far more complicated composition. The ratio is about the same as that of simple genetic characters which split up according to the Mendelian law and more intricate genetic processes met in the course of blindly conducted crossing experiments. However, the elementary processes which we—meaning Wallace Craig and I—isolated from the simplest cases are actually the same ones that we meet again and again in more complex structure.

I shall now tell, first, what new knowledge we have acquired on the three elementary processes, and then what we have found out about different and more complex types of interaction between them.

As for appetitive behavior, there is little to be said, for it may comprise practically all types of learned and insightful behavior, and a detailed discussion of these would go beyond the scope of this report. I wish only to mention the studies of the Swiss psychologist G. Bally (1945), who conceives play as an appetitive activity "in a relaxed field," as he expresses it.

Now for the innate releasing mechanism. This is in fact a self-contained "apparatus" with laws of its own within the receptor sector in the central nervous system. It was discovered originally as the disinhibitor of a consummatory action; but this is not its sole function. An IRM may set off an orienting reaction, or it may effect a block. For instance, the numerous IRM's which respond to the so-called gestures of humility displayed by fellow members of the species block the already activated instinctive motions of attack. It is particularly important for experimental techniques that orienting reactions may have their own IRM's. In some homogeneously functioning behavior patterns, which are made up of orienting reactions and instinctive movements, the orienting component may have an entirely different IRM from the one that disinhibits the consummatory action. Where such a state of affairs may be surmised, choice trials should be excluded. In the female of the grayling butterfly *Satyrus semele,* mating behavior is released by the scent substances of the male, the attendant orienting reactions by visual and tactile stimuli. Tinbergen (1942) presented intact males to the females simultaneously with males deprived of their scent emitting organs. The females turned toward both with equal frequency. But if no scent-emitters were present, the females showed no reaction to the males. Prechtl (1951) found similar behavior in salamanders.

Our knowledge of the functioning and the limitations of IRM's has been greatly enriched by the experiments of Tinbergen (1938), Tinbergen and Kuenen (1939), Baerends (1950), Perdeck (1951) and many others on the so-called releasers. Releasers are differentiations which have developed solely in the service of a single function: they emit key stimuli to which an IRM of another animal responds. This is why, to distinguish them, Tinbergen calls them social releasers. In most cases this animal is another individual of the same species (social releasers), but sometimes a symbiont, or even the host of a social parasite. Many synechthra of termites and ants live by copying the social releasers of their hosts. So do breeding parasites among birds. Releasers occur in all sense modalities, but the visually effective ones lend themselves best to an analysis of

IRM's. At first, there was much skepticism concerning the existence and the function of releasers from various sides (G. K. Noble, Hingston, Rand and others). Meanwhile, however, all that I said in 1935 simply on the basis of random observations—albeit very numerous ones—has been fully verified in exact experiments by a large number of scientists.

The negative statement that an IRM does not respond to complex qualities, but to very simple configurations, has gained a probability amounting to certainty. A very large number of stimulus-emitters (stimulus-emitting devices) has been found, and they all have the qualities of simplicity and conspicuousness. It stands to reason, after all, for instance to a cybernetic way of thinking, that it must be easier to construct a receiving mechanism which responds selectively to such simple, outstanding sign stimuli, than one which can distinguish diffuse complex qualities. On the other hand, the path that leads to structural differentiation of visual releasers is a difficult and intricate one for analysis. The mating organs of the horned pheasant, *Tragopan satyrus,* when fully developed, display an exactly regular blood-red circle in an ultramarine blue field. Such simplicity and symmetry of form meets perception halfway— it is "easy to retain." However, both phyletically and genetically it is doubtless hard to produce. It follows that if an IRM could be tuned so as to respond selectively to a random, diffuse complex quality, the evolution of species would never have trodden the path toward differentiation of conspicuous releasers!

Dummy experiments on IRM's correlated to releasers have revealed a theoretically important property of the IRM. It is often possible to offer dummies which are more effective than the biologically adequate situation. Tinbergen and Perdeck (1950) studied the IRM of the pecking reaction in herring gull chicks, which normally respond to the lowered bill of the feeding parent bird. The following sign stimuli were found to have releasing value: A) the red color of the patch on the lower mandible, B) the contrast of this patch with its yellow background, C) the narrow form of the bill, and D) its sloping position, which is maximal at the moment of regurgitation. Except for A) (absolute stimulus), all these key stimuli had a higher releasing value if they were exaggerated. The most effective dummy was a small stick with several dark red rings on a white background (exaggeration of sign stimulus B), very thin (exaggeration of sign stimulus C), held almost vertically (exaggeration of sign stimulus D), which, judged by standards of human Gestalt perception, bore practically no resemblance to the natural releaser. There are key stimuli which the IRM "fits" exactly, and which therefore cannot be exaggerated, for instance the configurational stimulus "head diameter 30 per cent of the body diameter," which orients the food-begging reaction of nestling thrushes toward the parent bird's head. But as a rule the IRM is, as it were, "open toward one side." It need not, after all, have a sharp boundary in the direction where no harmful exaggeration need be feared in natural conditions. Many alimentary IRM's, both in animals and men, "aim" at a possible concentration of nutritive substances, in other words, at the utmost poverty in slag substances. In natural conditions, the survival value of such behavior is evident. In the civilized conditions of humanity, however, it results in the obstipation of whole nations that are rich enough to live on concentrated foods alone. Where the IRM's of sexual behavior patterns are "open" in this manner, they cause acute sexual selection in the direction specified. Steiner (unpublished manuscript) was able to show that the female dwarf cichlid fish *Nannacara annomala* selects her mate mainly by his size. He put an enormous but senile male into a large tank with three young, well breeding pairs. From then on, only unfertilized clutches were laid, for all the females fetched only the impotent giant for the purpose of spawning. The same results were obtained when the experiment was repeated. It seems most significant to me from the point of view of selection that the natural object of a reaction need not necessarily be the optimal one. The key stimuli of certain human sexual IRM's can no doubt also be unnaturally exaggerated ("supernormal").

Prechtl (1952) has recently discovered a functional property of the IRM which is unwelcome in the sense that it complicates experimental technique. If a single key stimulus is applied frequently, the part of the IRM coordinated to it tires: an "adaptation" to that stimulus takes place. Other key stimuli of the same IRM are unaffected by this very limited exhaustion. For instance, if a young chaffinch's gaping reaction is exhausted by means of a percussion stimulus, it can still be released later by an acoustic stimulus and vice versa. Curiously enough, the number of elicitable reactions increases if we use one key stimulus to "pump out" almost, but not quite down to the threshold of complete adaptation, then switch to another key stimulus of the same IRM, etc. This is the same principle which a sophisticated gourmet follows in choosing his menu—*variatio delectat*—and which seems to be very widely applicable. The exhaustibility in the IRM, that is, in the afferent sector of the total pattern, complicates experimental procedure, because instead of a "method of dual quantification" it calls for a threefold one. Moreover, we know today that in some cases the exhaustibility of the receiving apparatus was mistaken for fatigability of the motor response, for instance in the gaping reaction of several young passerines.

Drees (1950) has recently demonstrated a very important relation between the IRM and the general state of the organism as a whole. In jumping spiders the function of the IRM changes with the physiological state of hunger. The object which releases the motions of prey-catching in these animals is of a certain size. The optimal size for releasing the pounce upon the prey has been ascertained with accuracy. Pumping out the reaction in a constant, standardized state of nutrition does not alter the optimum. However, the optimal object became smaller if the animals were fed more before the experiment, and bigger if they were hungrier. Prechtl found that, if young *Passeriformes* were very hungry, the IRM's of their gaping reaction became less selective and responded to formerly ineffective stimuli; while the speed of their adaptation to a single releasing stimulus did not change.

And now for the recent findings that have slightly changed our ideas on instinctive movements. Many years ago, when I devised the model shown in Figure 1, it was surmised that the "something" which accumulates during the quiescence of an innate reaction and is used up when that action is discharged, is material in character. Several students of hormones, especially of neurohormones, still think so. In the meantime, however, certain facts have come to light which clearly indicate that the way in which the accumulated "something" is specific for a certain instinctive action is not based on the specificity of an excitational substance. What is action-specific is apparently not that which is accumulated, but the "reservoir" in which it is accumulated. In certain circumstances a reaction different from the one normally correlated can be fed from this "pot." At any rate, this is how we would today like to interpret the fact of displacement activities, which were discovered by Tinbergen (1940) and Kortlandt (1940).

If certain conditions prevent an action-specific excitation of high intensity from activating the correlated behavior pattern, it often "flows" into the path of another instinctive action. Tinbergen lists three typical situations in which displacement activities occur. In the first and most important case an action-specific excitation which has already been activated is blocked by activation of an antagonistic drive. For instance, in innumerable cases the fighting drive is blocked by the drive to escape. This results in the displacement activities of threat behavior, in which the phenomenon was first discovered. In the second type of situation the releasing object is not quite adequate. It activates the impulse to a certain innate reaction, but does not quite allow its full discharge up to the satisfying consummatory act which is its goal. This case is very frequent in the courtship of fish and birds. The female releases mating intentions in the male, but she herself is not fully motivated, and the further sign stimuli which are needed to continue and complete the male's mating behavior are lacking. In the third typical displacement situation the appetence for a certain instinctive goal "reaches this goal so swiftly that after consummation there is still energy left over that the animal must get rid of" (Kortlandt, 1940). Here it is due to the so-called "inertia of the reaction" (Seitz, 1940) that the activated drive continues to function for some time after the goal has been reached. As Tinbergen (1940) has shown in many instances observed, the suddenness with which a stimulus situation is objectively or even subjectively extinguished is of great importance here. Many instances of this type of displacement activity are found in the so-called mating-afterplay of birds.

It is a common feature of all displacement activities that a certain, often highly specialized instinctive reaction is elicited by a type of excitation other than the "autochthonous" one (Kortlandt, 1940) that normally activates it. The "allochthonous" reaction thus always occurs in an environmental situation where it in no way displays its original survival value. It is completely senseless. It would be far-fetched to surmise an adaptive process when a cock in a conflict situation between attack and escape suddenly picks at the ground as if he were feeding, a heron in a similar situation preens itself, a sparrow whets its bill, or an avocet assumes a sleeping posture, etc. At most, we can say with Tinbergen that in a certain sense displacement activities act as outlets through which a surplus of motivation "blows off." They have a cathartic soothing function, as every smoker knows, for smoking itself is basically a displacement activity.

However, displacement activities may develop a secondary survival value. The autochthonous excitation never "sparks over" unpredictably into any old "track." It always initiates only a very specific allochthonous behavior pattern. Consequently, to someone who is thoroughly familiar with the behavior of a species, it can indicate unerringly the type of excitation that is going on in the organism. It can and does act as a signal to fellow members of the species, and in this way many originally purposeless displacement activities have developed into expressive movements. This process is usually connected with ritualization, a phenomenon of which I shall say more later.

Some other properties of displacement activities may arouse certain conjectures as to the physiological process underlying them. First among these is the so-called "decrease of potential." The intensity of any displacement activity is always incomparably lower than that of its "own" activating drive. It must be stressed, however, that this intensity is in direct proportion to that of the blocked, autochthonous drive. A male stickleback facing his rival in strong fighting motivation at the boundary of his territory, and yet not daring to attack, performs the nest-digging pattern as a displacement reaction of very low intensity. In fact, the intensity is so low that even an expert like Tinbergen (1940) originally regarded this activity as feeding behavior. But when Tinbergen and van Iersel (1947) greatly heightened the conflict situation by overstocking a tank with nesting male sticklebacks, displacement digging became so intense that real nest pits were dug.

Another characteristic of displacement activities is their relation to the concomitant orienting reactions. Even if an autochthonously activated instinctive action is discharged at very low intensity, it is always accompanied by spatial orientation to key stimuli. Frequently this orientation is the salient feature, the one that betrays the presence of a very slight intention to the observer. A bird whose feeding intention is barely suggested, first fixates edible objects, etc. However, an innate pattern of allochthonous motivation at a low level of intensity is not accompanied by orienting reactions. A male stickleback who is digging as a displacement activity in a threat situation fixates his rival, not, as he would in "genuine" digging, the sand which he has to remove. A displacement feeding domestic cock in a similar situation behaves the same way. Due to the lack of "attention," these motor patterns then appear "absentminded." Very early ornithological observers were struck by this characteristic of displacement activities. Eliot Howard (1929) spoke of "sham reactions," Heinroth (1910) of "sham preening," "sham pecking," etc. Tinbergen first believed that in the case of displacement activities the concomitant orienting reactions were not co-activated at all. Later, however, he found that under strong "pressure" of the blocked and sidetracked excitation, that is, if the motivation is very strong, the displacement reaction may be complete, including all orienting reactions.

There is a remarkable relationship between the animal's posture in the displacement situation and the direction of the displacement. The autochthonous excitation seems to spark over with particular frequency and ease into the nervous path of the behavior pattern whose initial phase the animal's posture fits at the time. Cocks threatening to attack perform intention movements of leaping into the air against each other. In the course of this behavior, they assume a position where their bills are held close to the ground, and they then perform displacement pecking. Many analogous instances are found in fish. Anatides in the conflict situation created by the difficult decision to take off often shake their heads, a reaction which as a "genuine" activity serves to throw off dirt or water. In various forms of anatides this displacement activity occurs more frequently if the autochthonous intention movement of taking off resembles the bill-shaking pattern.

An important property, probably common to all displacement activities, is that the innate reactions which function as displacement reactions are always the ones which "are available" in the greatest endogenous abundance. In an overwhelming percentage of cases observed, the excitation sparks over into the paths of very "common" motor patterns, such as preening, shaking, scratching, pecking in birds, gnawing in rodents, locomotion, etc. Even where more specific instinctive actions are involved, they are always the ones whose source flows freely in the organism at the time. The autochthonous types of excitation which result in displacement activities when blocked also seem to have certain qualities in common. Here again, in a vast majority of cases, the drives that cause displacement reactions if blocked are fighting, escape, and mating. These activities have two features in common: the animal is in a state of "general motor excitation," and the reactions are seldom fully discharged. I do not know a single case of displacement where one of those "common" activities that are performed all day long, at a low level of general excitation, is blocked.

In explanation of the term "blocking," which I have used here as does Tinbergen, it should be added that all displacement effects amount to a reblocking of the autochthonous excitation which was previously disinhibited by an IRM. If a readiness to action remains blocked, no matter how strongly it is dammed up, it never leads to a displacement activity, but to appetitive behavior, discharge at inadequate objects, and in rare extremes to vacuum activities. Expressed in terms of the model in Figure 1, it might be said that in displacement activities the cone-valve V must be open, and the spout in full flow. If the excitation is "shunted" into a different track, this occurs distally from the valve. It is essential to distinguish clearly between the dammed-up, still latent readiness, and an already activated "mood" (Heinroth, 1910 and elsewhere) for a given instinctive activity.

One of the striking parallels between innate reactions and learned, kinesthetically "ground-in" motor patterns is that the latter can also be activated by an allochthonous drive. It is a well-known fact that, besides genuine instinctive reactions, such as scratching, acquired ones such as lighting a cigarette, straightening one's tie, etc. occur in human conflict situations.[1] In these cases, too, it is often clear that the allochthonously activated action "goes off" first, and orients itself toward an object afterwards. In descriptions of human displacement activities one often reads that a person does something "absently," "with a vacant look" and the like. In smoking, which, as I have said, often has a displacement character, both acquired movements and the innate ones of sucking play a part.

In some processes which resemble genuine displacement activities,

[1] See Paul H. Schiller: Purposeless Manipulations. XI. Cong. Internat. Psychol., Paris, 1937. [Translator's note.]

with one instinctive action obviously occurring as a substitute for another, the blocking of a drive nevertheless results in an allochthonous action of full intensity. For instance, if a breeding pair of the cichlid fish *Hemichromis bimaculatus* is induced to fight by presenting a dummy, and then, after fighting has attained its fullest intensity, the sham rival is suddenly removed, in a few seconds the fish will begin to court with equal intensity. Fighting and courting lie very close together in the system of the reproductive instinct and are both dependent on the same superordinated center. The underlying physiological process in such cases is probably an entirely different one from that at the base of displacement activities. One might assume that a growing irradiation from the direction of fighting excites this higher center, which then in its turn activates another center subordinated to it. Tinbergen has suggested the term "alternative movements" for these activities, which must be clearly distinguished from displacement reactions.

Displacement activities are a typical case of the exception that proves the rule. They strengthen rather than weaken the hypothesis that an excitation is basically specific for a quite definite action. Without assuming a quality of excitation that is in general specific for a definite innate reaction, the concept as well as the term "displacement" or "oversparking" would be utterly meaningless. It must be admitted, however, that no quantitative studies have as yet been made concerning the "cathartic" effect of displacement activities. In other words, we do not know to what extent their discharge actually uses up blocked energy specific to the autochthonous instinctive action. We are still looking for an object that lends itself to such a study.

The expression "action-specific" must not be interpreted too narrowly. We have long known that very different behavior patterns with different response thresholds are elicited by the same quality of excitation. Seitz (1940, 1949) has studied such scales of intensities in the fighting behavior of cichlid fishes very accurately. There, the various behavior patterns belong together functionally, despite all differences in their form. Recently, however, cases have come to light where functionally incongruous behavior patterns are fed from a common source of excitation. Drees (1950) found that in jumping spiders such different behavior patterns as prey-catching and courtship could be fed from the same "reservoir." If he "pumped out" one of these two behavior patterns, the threshold value of the other also rose, or, in total exhaustion, it was made impossible. Both reactions begin with the same introduction: the animal turns toward the object, fixates it and creeps toward it. Moreover, they occur in the same general situation. Both these factors have evidently favored this highly interesting "special structure" in salticides. But "everything" does not come from the same reservoir of instinctive excitation in these animals either. By exploiting their phototactic reactions, the spiders can be made to turn and run dozens of yards an almost unlimited number of times without changing the threshold values of hunting and mating in any way.

Drees made another extremely important discovery concerning the physiology of instinctive movements. He was able to prove in his spiders that the metabolic-physiological state of hunger vitally affects the recharge rate of an innate reaction. The hungrier the animal, the more rapidly the readiness to pounce on the prey builds up after being pumped out. According to recently published studies by Prechtl (1953) on the gaping reactions of young passeriformes, there is no connection in these birds between hunger and the recovery of action readiness.

So far, we have discussed behavior patterns in which only one type of instinctive movement is activated. We used to think that this was the general rule. Julian Huxley once said that the central nervous system of most animals is like a ship skippered by many captains, only one of whom is on the bridge at any one time; when another appears, the first yields his place. In man, on the other hand, all the diverse motives are in charge in conflict-creating simultaneity. I myself used to agree with this statement and quote it repeatedly. It is by no means wrong, but it describes a special case. That it struck both Huxley and myself so strongly is due to the naturalist's above-mentioned fingertip-feeling, which infallibly finds the simplest cases even where more complex ones are incomparably more frequent. As a matter of fact, reciprocal inhibition of instinctive excitations is far rarer than simple superposition, that is, addition of analogous movements and subtraction of antagonistic ones. Even at very elementary levels of the central nervous system, real "conflicts" are found, and solved by compromises. Von Holst (1937) has demonstrated this convincingly in his studies on central generation of excitation and relative coordination. Similar phenomena exist at the higher integrative level of innate reactions. They are found surprisingly often since Tinbergen's student van Iersel opened our eyes to this phenomenon by analyzing the simultaneous cooperation of the mating and fighting drives in the courting behavior of sticklebacks. Another instance of such superposition is this: if territory-owning pairs of various species of cichlids threaten each other at the boundary line between their territories, the following behavior can often be observed, particularly clearly in *Etroplus maculatus.* One fish faces the other exactly—as a rule male faces male and female, female—and slowly advances toward him, while the rival retreats. The caudal fin movements are remarkably strong and, as the fish advances, the incongruence between their intensity and the slowness of the forward movement grows. It looks as if the fish were swimming against a current that increases in strength as he pushes further and further into enemy territory. This impression is further enhanced when the fish—mostly in response to a slight counter-advance by the hostile territory-owner—begins to beat a retreat. At this point, if the tail-fin movements which propel the fish forward become just a bit weaker, the fish stands still and, as soon as the motions cease altogether, is driven backwards with growing speed. Before this backward drive has reached its peak, the tail-fin resumes its propelling movements, with the result that the fish continues to swim backwards for quite a bit after the tail-fin has once again begun to work "forward." This behavior pattern has quite a stunning effect on the onlooker. Its explanation is that the pectoral fins beat "backwards" throughout the entire process, and the intensity of their beat grows as the animal pushes ahead into hostile territory. Undoubtedly the fighting drive controls the motions of the caudal fin, while the drive to escape controls those of the pectorals. The intensity curves of the two antagonistic drives do not by any means mirror each other, as would be the case in reciprocal inhibition. Instead, the backward intention culminates shortly before the attack comes to a standstill. To put it into drastically anthropomorphic words: the fish is afraid of his rival all the time, but his fear reaches its height in the seconds when his fury has driven him farthest into enemy territory.

The superposition of instinctive actions is an important factor in the genesis of expression, to which it may lend high apparent variability. Canines, for example, whose expressive motions have been studied in great detail by Schenkel, convey their intention to escape by drawing back the corners of their mouths, and their ears (Fig. 2c). Their fighting intention, on the other hand, is expressed by opening their mouths slightly, raising the upper lip, and knitting their brows and snouts (Fig. 2g). These two expressive motions can be superimposed on each other at any level of intensity. Figure 2 represents a square. If we take only three intensity grades for each instinctive movement, we get nine distinguishable "physiognomic expressions." In many cases more than two innate expressive motions may be superimposed on each other. The result is a seemingly unlimited variability, which is actually based on a quantitative variability of only a few invariables.

We used to think that mutual inhibition of instinctive actions was the general rule. Actually, this appears to be a very special case, and seems to occur only in cases where a simultaneous initiation of two instincts could be harmful for survival of the species. It is, of course, vitally important that in defenseless animals, for instance, no other instinctive movements should be superimposed on the patterns of escape behavior and thus lower their effectiveness. The far more general rule, however, is that every instinctive reaction can be superimposed on every other one, in so far as this is at all feasible mechanically. Above all, however, autochthonous and allochthonous impulses can obviously be superimposed on each other in displacement activities, a fact which often makes analysis extremely difficult.

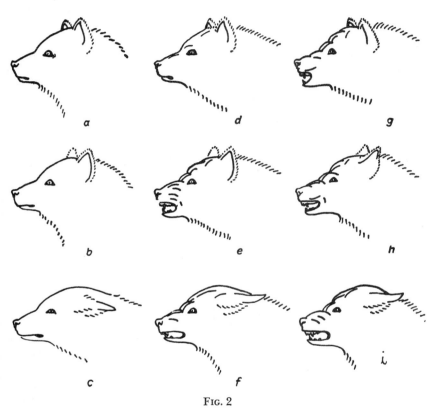

FIG. 2

One field in which our knowledge of instinctive actions has grown greatly in the last few years comprises the phenomena of so-called ritualization. Huxley (1914) and Selous (1933) spoke of ritualization or formalization of instinctive motor sequences. Their choice of these terms was undoubtedly influenced by the analogy of these phenomena to certain types of human behavior. This analogy consists, first, in the fact that a sequence of movements has forfeited its original, everyday meaning and acquired a new one as a means of expression, and secondly, that an originally variable sequence of actions has become a rigid, unchangeable "ceremony." Heinroth briefly called these ritualized behavior patterns (Huxley, 1914) "ceremonies."

Tinbergen (1940) considers expression the most important function of ritualized motor patterns. However, some decidedly ritualized behavior patterns, instead of becoming expressive motions, have retained their primary function. These are the "symbolic fights," of which more later. Here, I should like to stress the second characteristic of ritualization: a behavior pattern of variable composition becomes a rigid, single, and as such innately determined motor pattern.

The so-called teasing or baiting (urging attack) of several anatides is a good example of a process of ritualization, and one that can be followed up in a fine series of differentiations. In its original form, the female, after a slight advance against a real or imaginary opponent, takes alarm, hurries back to her mate for protection, gains new courage as soon as she reaches him, and again threatens in the direction of the enemy with outstretched neck. In *Casarcinae* this behavior of the female is thoroughly functional; as a rule the male actually takes on the rival designated by the female, and drives him away. In these forms the motivation of each behavior component is variable within itself, and they are clearly separable. The components are: (1) the welling up of the fighting mood, (2) predominance of the drive to escape when approaching the opponent and seeking protection from the mate, and (3) renewed threatening. The interplay of the directive components toward the enemy and toward the mate most often results in a spatial relationship wherein the female stands with her breast turned toward the male, and threatens the enemy backwards, over her shoulder. The angle between her neck and body, however, is highly variable. The females of the Egyptian goose, *Alopochen,* and the ruddy sheldrake, *Casarca ferruginea,* often run in a circle around the male, threatening toward the enemy at the same time with a constantly changing angle between their body-axis and the direction of their menacing, until they finally stand next to their mates, threatening straight forward. But in a certain sense, a ritualization is initiated in *Casarca.* The female visibly favors the orientation: head toward the male —tail toward the enemy, and accordingly the threatening gesture backward over her shoulder. This is especially clear when the entire motor sequence is carried out by a pair kept in isolation, in the absence of an "enemy"; in that case the female invariably "supposes" that the enemy, who exists only in her imagination, is directly behind her. In surface-feeding ducks *(Anatinae),* baiting has been ritualized to an almost completely rigid behavior pattern. In this group, it has lost all its meaning for settling questions of territorial ownership, and developed into a pure courting movement of the female. Yet there can be no doubt as to its phyletic homology with the behavior patterns described in *Casarcinae*. Here the threatening gesture of the head is completely rhythmic, and it always goes backward over the shoulder; the motion has become almost, yet curiously not quite independent of orienting factors: even if the foe, whose meaning here is purely "symbolical," is straight in front of the duck, her head still goes backwards over her shoulder when she is teasing, but to a distinctly lesser extent than when the rival is in the "expected" direction behind her. Moreover, the duck looks sharply toward the enemy, so that, if he stands in front, her glance follows an entirely different direction from the one in which the rigid instinctive movement draws her head. The location of the sham opponent also determines the side toward which the baiting is directed. In several divers the baiting pattern has been ritualized along entirely different lines, which can be followed just as distinctly.

In this and a great many other cases, the form of a behavior pattern, which was primarily dependent on two or more orienting reactions, each of them variable, has developed into a single, rigid and, in this new form, hereditary reaction. If I regard the development of a new hereditary coordination as the essence of ritualization, this is confirmed by the changes which both intention movements and displacement activities undergo in the course of evolution. After all, these two types of behavior are the most frequent source of ritualized expressive motions. To the extent that a ritualized motor pattern becomes an autonomous instinctive reaction, it acquires all the properties of such a one. Intention movements lose all connection with the instinctive action whose forerunners and indicators they were primarily. For instance, the numerous expressive motions which were originally mating intention movements in the females of *Corvidae*, cormorants, baboons and others, no longer have anything to do with the quality of excitation specific for mating reactions. In their new form, they have gained a purely social "meaning." The expressive movements that have developed by ritualization from displacement activities have become utterly independent from the displacement situations discussed earlier. They no longer provide an outlet for a drive, as does the primary displacement activity, but are in many cases self-stimulating, as are autochthonous intention movements. Makkink describes how the displacement preening which introduces mating in the avocet, *Recurvirostra avocetta*, has a self-stimulating effect, and gradually grows more intensive. Probably the same is true of the displacement shaking which, in courting swimming drakes, has a self-stimulating function; it results in a reciprocal "see-sawing up" of excitation by transmitting the mood.

A remarkable group of ritualized motor patterns are the so-called "symbolic fights," which are quite frequent among bony fish (teleosts), reptiles, birds and mammals. These innate reactions originally served to harm rivals of the same species. They have developed along one of two lines of differentiation. Some have turned into perfectly harmless, rigid "ceremonies" (sham fighting in mandarin ducks and gamecocks), which serve to allure the female rather than to drive off a rival. Others are so changed that, although the rival is exhausted and finally "gives up," he is not annihilated. Lines of differentiation as well as ontogenetic development leave no doubt that symbolic fighting has evolved by ritualization from primary destructive fighting. Its survival value is evident: it must be of advantage to the species if the strongest animals are selected for reproduction without involving an unnecessary sacrifice of individuals.

I must emphasize that a Lamarckist interpretation of the ritualizing process is far from my thoughts. The development of a new connection between two instinctive reactions, which is so important in the evolution of a ritualization, is a very frequent occurrence. My own studies on the courting movements of *Anatinae* have brought to light many such instances. One of the main differences between very closely related species consists in the fact that the same motor elements occur in different combinations. Some breeds of domestic ducks differ from the wild strain only by the appearance of new, fixed connections between certain instinctive movements. It would seem, therefore, as if only relatively slight mutative steps were needed to develop these connections.

The possibility that we are dealing with ritualization, or at any rate with a ritualized behavior pattern superimposed upon a primary one, must always be kept in mind when observing displacement activities and intention movements, especially where they function as expressions. It is often extremely hard to decide whether we are dealing with a primary displacement or with a ritualized pattern. It is equally hard to determine whether and to what extent a behavior pattern composed of two superimposed antagonistic instinctive reactions is ritualized. The answer can only be supplied by comparative phyletic study of as many related species as possible. Once again, in the ultimate analysis, the good old comparative-descriptive method must give analysis a lift.

After this brief discussion of the most important recent findings on appetitive behavior, innate releasing mechanism and consummatory action, let us now turn to the fairly new realization that these three elementary processes do not necessarily always occur in the same successive connection which we originally thought was the only possible one.

First, an instance of a different, simple type of "connection": Prechtl and Schleidt (1951) and Prechtl (1952) found an instinctive activity in newborn kittens, which is literally discharged continually as long as the animals are awake. The head swings from side to side at great amplitude all the time, whether the animal is lying down or crawling forward. This pattern, the so-called "seeking automatism," has no central inhibition which needs to be removed to release it, nor an IRM which would accomplish this. It continues until certain orienting reactions which determine the kitten's crawling create a quite specific stimulus situation: the kitten's nose must find a bare spot, the aureola of the nipple, in a furry surface. The IRM coordinated to this stimulus situation blocks the "seeking automatism," which until then has been running continually, and this inhibition enables the kitten to react directedly to the nipple and grasp it. The inhibition is now maintained by the sucking motions which it releases, and then by the sleep that follows. In this case, therefore, the most essential IRM is found not before but after the instinctive reaction; it has a blocking, not a releasing function.

Another, more complex possibility of linking the familiar elements is the following: appetitive behavior, as in the old Craig-Lorenz diagram, achieves a stimulus situation, in which an IRM is activated. This IRM, however, does not at once release an innate behavior pattern which constitutes its goal, but next initiates appetitive behavior of a new, more specialized kind for another releasing situation, and the consummatory act, which is its goal, comes only after a whole series of such links. Baerends (1941) and Tinbergen, who discovered these "chain appetites," speak of a hierarchic organization of the nervous mechanisms underlying instinctive behavior. Besides displacement activities, I consider this principle of hierarchy the most important discovery that has been made in our field of science in the last twelve years. We know today that hierarchically organized instinctive behavior is far more frequent than the type which consists only of appetitive behavior, IRM and consummatory action. If all our earlier examples were taken from the latter type, this again is due to our legitimate quest for the simplest, the most easily analyzed case.

Two examples will suffice to illustrate the principle of nervous hierarchy. A peregrine falcon, in whom the drive to strike a prey awakens, leaves its perch and begins to range through its hunting ground, more or less at random, perhaps with a certain preference for places that have recently brought it success. The bird's further hunting behavior depends on the kind of prey it then finds. The falcon may pick out a starling, a plover, or a teal from a flock, a sick gull from the water, or a mammal from an open field. The main point is that the sight of one of these potential preys does not lead directly to a consummatory act, but to appetitive behavior of a more specialized kind. For instance, if the falcon sights a flock of teal, it will not react at once by swooping, but first with a certain form of sham attack, which aims at isolating a single bird from the flock. Only when the falcon has succeeded in this does it actually swoop down, and only when this has brought the bird into the appropriate spatial relationship does it finally pounce on the prey, performing the consummatory act which represents the goal.

Tinbergen (1950) interprets the physiological process underlying such behavior as follows. Activation of a center on the highest level of integration induces appetitive behavior of a very general nature. This continues until a new stimulus situation of more restricted effect elicits appetitive behavior of a subordinate nature, which again continues until the next releasing situation is attained, and so on down to the final consummatory action which is its goal. We are already aware of the facts which indicate that the releasing stimuli do not affect a reflex mechanism, however complex, but rather remove a block and thereby allow the motor impulses coming from the activated center free passage. At best, the IRM, which removes the block under which the continually self-recharging centers of the instinctive action generally stand, may be related to the "reflex." If there were no such blocks, all the centers would discharge their motor responses simultaneously and perpetually, and a "motor cacophony" of chaotic impulses would result. The orderly succession of individual instinctive reactions is ensured by the IRM's, which activate one after another in response to adequate sign stimuli. Each center, at each level of integration, has its own block with a coordinated IRM, and so long as the block is not removed by stimulating the IRM, the center cannot "get rid of" its motor impulses.

On the basis of the three-spined stickleback's *(Gasterosteus aculeatus)* reproductive behavior, Tinbergen (1950) developed a graphic model of the hierarchy of instincts, which is reproduced in Figure 3. The "centers" are symbolized by circles, causal influences by arrows, blocks by crosshatched rectangles, IRM's by a schema of the nerve cell, and motor pathways by continuous lines. The highest center has no coordinated block of its own. This state of affairs seems to be typical for centers of the highest level of integration, and stems from the fact that activation of such a general drive always leads directly to appetitive behavior of the most general nature. In the stickleback it is the greatly increasing length of days in early spring which, by affecting various other endocrine glands, brings about an increase in the gonadal hormones. This in its turn evokes an excitation in the highest "center." The impulses generated by this center can flow in two directions: first, to the next lower center, secondly, however, into the path of appetitive behavior. Since, for the time being, the lower center is still blocked toward the periphery, they activate a first

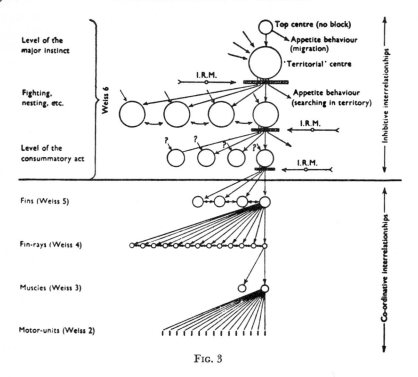

FIG. 3

and most general appetitive behavior: the spring migration of the fish. This takes the fish from the sea or from deep fresh water into shallow fresh water, and is continued until a stimulus situation is reached to which the first IRM responds and lifts the block beneath the second center. The essential sign stimuli for this are: a rise in temperature, and visual stimuli received from water plants. Removal of the block frees the path to the next more specialized appetitive behavior, while that of the first order ceases. This seems to imply that the response of appetitive behavior at a relatively low level of integration always has a lower threshold value than at a higher level. The stickleback does not go on migrating; it "becomes territorial." What happens next is, in principle, the same thing that we have just described about the highest level of integration. The impulses from the "territorial center" may flow either into the path of appetitive behavior or into the next lower centers, and they do the former as these centers are blocked. Appetitive behavior at this level means that the fish, within his territory, searches for those more specific stimulus situations which, by way of the pertinent IRM's, unblock the centers of fighting, nest-building, courting, etc. This behavior consists in an excited, jerky swimming around within the fish's territory, and continues until, for instance, it meets a trespassing rival. This lifts the block to the fighting center, all impulses flow toward the latter, the fish immediately ceases swimming about aimlessly, and attacks. What type of fighting pattern will now break through, in other words, which of the five next lowest centers is activated, depends on the opponent's behavior. Each of the five types of innate reactions which it can release represents a "consummatory act," an end response which is the goal of the entire behavior pattern.

The most important aspect of these results and hypotheses of Tinbergen's is undoubtedly the bridge which they build toward the physiology of the central nervous system. Tinbergen's concept of the "center" is purely functional and comprises no statements concerning localization or the possibility of localization. Yet the number of centers can be clearly determined, since that of the blocks and of the IRM's which remove them has been ascertained experimentally. The concept of an endogenous generation of impulses, as Tinbergen attributes it to his "centers," corresponds fully to those which von Holst, Weiss and others have developed in their studies. In his "Self-Differentiation of the Basic Patterns of Coordination," Weiss (1940) demonstrated a quite analogous hierarchic organization of central nervous mechanisms, all of which lie below the level of integration of the goal, the consummatory act. His "level of behavior" includes everything that is above it. Accordingly, Tinbergen (1950) was able to include in his diagram the one drafted by Weiss (1940). There are close relationships with Hess' (1948) results, too. The specific instinctive impulse patterns which Hess succeeded in obtaining by electric stimulation in the hypothalamus undoubtedly correspond in most cases to an activation of centers which belong to the highest level of integration. Sometimes, however, if the location of the stimulus was shifted very slightly in a caudal direction, Hess no longer got the whole, integrated instinctive behavior pattern, but dissociated, single motor patterns of the same system. Since one would expect the higher centers to be located cranially from the relatively lower ones, this part-finding appears to be particularly significant in the light of Tinbergen's beliefs.

It may be seen that our ideas on the central nervous mechanisms underlying instinctive behavior have grown considerably more complex in the years since my report in Rostock. Those who think that simplicity is always a sign of truth may mourn over this development in our hypotheses. We believe, however, that we have come a good bit closer to conditions as they actually are. We have learned to realize how very intricate the relationships are in actual fact, and what sources of error lurk everywhere. Perhaps a certain sadness overcomes the zoologist, who dwells in a world of tangible phenomena, at the realization that the growing complexity of our ideas will soon lead to completely intangible statistical, perhaps even to cybernetic methods. Max Hartmann once said that no biologist would ever have tackled a problem if he had imagined at the outset that it would be as difficult and complicated to solve as it subsequently proved to be. I will admit that this is perfectly true as far as I am concerned. But I find consolation in the thought that plenty of descriptive-comparative work has yet to be done. For one thing, many "simplest cases" that are easy to analyze are no doubt still swimming unrecognized in the nearest ditch. Moreover, to recall what I said earlier about the study of ritualization, countless analytical problems can only be approached through the comparative-phyletic method.

Bibliography

Allen, A. A. (1934): Sex rhythm in the Ruffed Grouse *(Bonasa umbellus* L.) and other birds. *The Auk, 51,* 180-199.

Allen, F. H. (1934): The role of anger in evolution, with particular reference to the colors and songs of birds. *The Auk, 51,* 454-469.

Alverdes, F. (1925): *Tiersoziologie.* Leipzig.

────── (1932): Die Ganzheitbetrachtung in der Biologie. *Sitzungsber. d. Ges. z. Förd. d. ges. Naturw.,* Marburg, 67.

Baerends, G. P. (1941): Fortpflanzungsverhalten und Orientierung der Grabwespe *Ammophila campestris* Jur. *Tijdschr. Entomol., 84,* 68-275.

────── (1950): Specializations in organs and movements with a releasing function. *Symposia. Soc. Exper. Biol., 4.* Cambridge: University Press.

────── and Baerends, J. M. (1950): An introduction to the study of the ethology of Cichlid Fishes. *Behaviour,* Suppl. *1,* 1-242.

Bakay, E. and Schiller, P. H. (1947): Detour experiments with rats. *Psychol. Stud. Univ. Budapest, 9,* 26-30.

Bally, G. (1945): *Vom Ursprung und den Grenzen der Freiheit.* Basel.

Bechterew, W. (1926): *Reflexologie des Menschen.* Leipzig und Wien.

Bethe, A. (1931a): Anpassungsfähigkeit (Plastizität) des Nervensystems. *Bethe's Handbuch der normalen und pathologischen Physiologie,* Berlin, *15,* II, 1045-1130.

────── (1931b): Plastizität und Zentrenlehre. *Ibid., 15,* II, 1175-1222.

Bierens de Haan, J. A. (1933): Der Stieglitz als Schöpfer. *J. Ornithol., 81,* 1-22.

────── (1935): Probleme des tierischen Instinktes. *Die Naturwissenschaften, 23,* 711-717.

Bingham, H. (1913): Size and form perception in *Gallus domesticus. J. Anim. Behav., 3,* 65-113.

────── (1928): Sex development in apes. *Comp. Psychol. Monog., 5,* 1-161.

Birch, H. (1945): The relation of previous experience to insightful problem-solving. *J. Comp. Physiol. Psychol., 38,* 367-383.

Brown, T. G. (1913): Die Reflexfunktionen des Zentralnervensystems mit besonderer Berücksichtigung der rhythmischen Tätigkeiten beim Säugetier. I. *Erg. Physiol., 13,* 279-453.

────── (1916): Die Reflexfunktionen des Zentralnervensystems mit besonderer Berücksichtigung der rhythmischen Tätogkeiten beim Säugetier. II. *Erg. Physiol., 15,* 480-790.

Brückner, G. H. (1933): Untersuchungen zur Tiersoziologie, insbesondere zur Auflösung der Familie. *Z. Psychol., 128,* 1-3.

Brunswick, E. (1934): *Wahrnehmung und Gegenstandswelt, Psychologie vom Gegenstand her.* Leipzig und Wien.

Bühler, C. (1927): Das Problem des Instinktes. *Z. Psychol., 103,* 46-64.

Bühler, K. (1936): *Zukunft der Psychologie.* Wien.

Carmichael, L. (1926): The development of behaviour in vertebrates experimentally removed from the influence of external stimulation. *Psychol. Rev., 33,* 51-58.

Carpenter, C. R. (1934): A field study of the behavior and social relations of howling monkeys. *Comp. Psychol. Monog., 10,* 1-168.

Coburn, C. A. (1914): The behavior of the crow. *J. Anim. Behav., 4,* 185-201.

Craig, W. (1908): The voices of pigeons regarded as a means of social control. *Am. J. Sociol., 14,* 86-100.

—— (1909): The expression of emotions in the pigeons: 1. The blond ringdove *(Turtur risorius). J. Comp. Neurol. Psychol., 19,* 29-80.

—— (1912): Observations on young doves learning to drink. *J. Anim. Behav., 2,* 273-279.

—— (1914): Male doves reared in isolation. *J. Anim. Behav., 4,* 121-133.

—— (1918): Appetites and aversions as constituents of instincts. *Biol. Bull., 34,* 91-107.

—— (1921): Why do animals fight? *Int. J. Ethics, 31,* 264-278.

—— (1922): A note on Darwin's work on the expression of emotions, etc. *J. Abn. & Soc. Psychol., 16,* 356-366.

Crane, J. (1941): Crabs of the genus *Uca* from the West coast of Central America. *Zoologica N. Y., 26,* 145-208.

Doflein, F. (1916): *Der Ameisenlöwe, eine biologische, tierpsychologische und reflexbiologische Untersuchung.* Jena.

Drees, O. (1950): Verhaltensphysiologische Untersuchungen über instinktive Verhaltensweisen bei Salticiden. *Verh. Dtsch. Zool.,* Marburg.

—— (1952): Untersuchungen über die angeborenen Verhaltensweisen bei Springspinnen *(Salticidae). Z. Tierpsychol., 9,* 169-206.

Eibl-Eibesfeldt, I. (1950a): Über die Jugendentwicklung des Verhaltens eines männlichen Dachses *(Meles meles* L.) unter besonderer Berücksichtigung des Spieles. *Z. Tierpsychol., 7,* 327-355.

—— (1950b): Beiträge zur Biologie der Haus- und der Ährenmaus nebst einigen Beobachtungen an anderen Nagern. *Z. Tierpsychol., 7,* 558-587.

—— (1951): Beobachtungen zur Fortpflanzungsbiologie und Jugendentwicklung des Eichhörnchens *(Sciurus vulgaris* L.). *Z. Tierpsychol., 8,* 370-400.

—— (1953a): Vergleichende Verhaltensstudien an Anuren: Zur Paarungsbiologie des Laubfrosches *(Hyla arborea* L.). *Z. Tierpsychol., 9,* 383-395.

—— (1953b): Zur Ethologie des Hamsters *(Cricetus cricetus* L.). *Z. Tierpsychol., 10,* 204-254.

Engelmann, W. (1928): Untersuchungen über die Schallokalisation bei Tieren. *Z. Psychol., 105,* 317-370.

Friedmann, H. (1928): Social parasitism in birds. *Quart. Rev. Biol., 4,* 554-569.

—— (1934): The instinctive emotional life of birds. *Psychoanal. Rev., 21,* 242-271, 381-407.

Goethe, F. (1937): Beobachtungen und Untersuchungen zur Biologie der Silbermöwe *(Larus a. argentatus* Pontopp.) auf der Vogelinsel Memmertsand. *J. Ornithol., 85,* 1-119.

Groos, K. (1907): *Die Spiele der Tiere.* Jena: Gustav Fischer (2nd ed.).

Guillaume, P. and Meyerson, I. (1934): Recherches sur l'usage de l'instrument chez les singes. III. L'intermédiaire indépendant de l'objet. *J. de Psychol., 31,* 497-554.

Hediger, H. (1935): Zur Biologie und Psychologie der Zahmheit. *Arch. f. Psychol., 93,* 135-188.

Heinroth, O. (1910): Beiträge zur Biologie, namentlich Ethologie und Psychologie der Anatiden. *Verh. V. Internat. Ornithol. Kongr.,* Berlin, 589-702.

—— (1918): Reflektorische Bewegungsweisen im Lichte der Stammesverwandt-schaft. *J. Ornithol., 33.*

—— (1930): Über bestimmte Bewegungsweisen bei Wirbeltieren. *Sitzgsber. Ges. naturforsch. Freunde,* Berlin, 333-342.

—— and Heinroth, M. (1924-1933): *Die Vögel Mitteleuropas.* Berlin-Lichter-felde.

Herrick, F. H. (1935): *Wild Birds at Home.* New York, London.

Hess, W. R. (1948): *Das Zwischenhirn.* Basel.

Hinde, R. (1952): The behaviour of the Great Tit (*Parus major* L.) and some other related species. *Behaviour,* Suppl. 2, 1-201.

—— (1953): The conflict between drives in the courtship and copulation of the chaffinch. *Behaviour, 5,* 1-31.

—— (1954): Factors governing the changes in strength of a partially inborn response, as shown by the mobbing behaviour of the chaffinch (*Fringilla coelebs*). II. The waning of the response. *Proc. Royal Soc.,* B, *142,* 331-359.

Hingston, R. W. G. (1933): *The Meaning of Animal Colour and Adornment.* London.

Holst, E. von (1935): Alles oder Nichts, Block, Alternans, Bigemini und ver-wandte Erscheinungen als Eigenschaften des Rückenmarkes. *Pflüg. Arch. ges. Physiol., 236,* 515-532.

—— (1936a): Versuche zur Theorie der relativen Koordination. *Pflüg. Arch. ges. Physiol., 237,* 93-121.

—— (1936b): Vom Dualismus der motorischen und der automatisch-rhyth-mischen Funktion im Rückenmark und vom Wesen des automatischen Rhythmus. *Pflüg. Arch. ges. Physiol., 237,* 356-378.

—— (1937): Vom Wesen der Ordnung im Zentralnervensystem. *Naturwiss., 25,* 625-631, 641-647.

—— (1948): Von der Mathematik des Nervensystems. *Experientia, 4,* 374-381.

Howard, H. E. (1929): *An Introduction to the Study of Bird Behaviour.* Cam-bridge.

—— (1935): *The Nature of a Bird's World.* Cambridge.

Huxley, J. S. (1914): The courtship habits of the Great crested Grebe (*Podiceps cristatus*); with an addition on the theory of sexual selection. *Proc. Zool. Soc., London,* 491-562.

—— (1934): A natural experiment on the territorial instinct. *Brit. Birds, 27,* 270-277.

—— and Howard, H. E. (1934): Field studies and Physiology: A further cor-relation. *Nature, 133,* 688-689.

Iersel, J. J. A. van (1953): An analysis of the parental behaviour of the male three-spined stickleback (*Gasterosteus aculeatus* L.). *Behaviour,* Suppl. *3,* 1-159.

Jennings, H. S. (1923): *The Behavior of the Lower Organisms.* New York.

Katz, D. (1931): *Hunger und Appetit.* Leipzig.

—— und Révész, G. (1909): Experimentell-psychologische Untersuchungen an Hühnern. *Z. Psychol., 50,* 51-59.

Kirkman, F. B. (1937): *Bird Behaviour.* London.

Klüver, H. (1933): *Behavior Mechanisms in Monkeys.* Chicago: The University of Chicago Press.

Koehler, O. (1933): Die Ganzheitsbetrachtung in der modernen Biologie. *Schriften Königsberger Gel. Ges. 9,* 7.

—————— und Zagarus, A. (1937): Beiträge zum Brutverhalten des Halsband-regenpfeifers (*Charadrius hiaticula* L.). *Beitr. Fortpfl. biol. Vögel, 13,* 1-9.

Koenig, L. (1951): Beiträge zu einem Aktionssystem des Bienenfressers (*Merops apiaster* L.). *Z. Tierpsychol., 8,* 169-210.

Koenig, O. (1951): Das Aktionssystem der Bartmeise (*Panurus biarmicus* L.). *Oesterr. Zool. Zs., 111,* 1-82.

Köhler, W. (1917): Intelligenzprüfungen an Anthropoiden. *Abhandl. Preuss. Akad., Phys.-mathem. Kl.,* 213.

—————— (1921): *Intelligenzprüfungen an Menschenaffen.* Berlin: Springer.

—————— (1925): *The Mentality of Apes.* New York: Harcourt Brace.

Kortlandt, A. (1940a): Eine Übersicht der angeborenen Verhaltensweisen des Mitteleuropäischen Kormorans (*Phalacrocorax carbo sinensis* [Shaw and Nodder]), ihre Funktion, ontogenetische Entwicklung und phylogenetische Herkunft. *Arch. néerl. Zoöl., 4,* 401-442.

—————— (1940b): Wechselwirkung zwischen Instinkten. *Arch. néerl. Zoöl., 4,* 442-520.

Kramer, G. (1930): Bewegungsstudien an Vögeln des Berliner Zoologischen Gartens. *J. Ornithol., 78,* 257-268.

Kuhlmann, F. (1909): Some preliminary observations on the development of instincts and habits in young birds. *Psychol. Rev. Monog. Ser., 11,* 49-85.

Kühn, A. (1919): *Die Orientierung der Tiere im Raum.* Jena.

Lashley, K. S. (1930): Basic neural mechanisms in behavior. *Psychol. Rev., 37,* 1-24.

Lissmann, H. (1932): Die Umwelt des Kampffisches, *Betta splendens Regan.* *Z. vergl. Physiol., 18,* 65-111.

Lorenz, K. (1927): Beobachtungen an Dohlen. *J. Ornithol., 75,* 511-519.

—————— (1931): Beiträge zur Ethologie sozialer Corviden. *J. Ornithol., 79,* 67-120.

—————— (1932):Betrachtungen über das Erkennen der arteigenen Triebhand-lungen der Vögel. *J. Ornithol., 80,* 50-98.

—————— (1934): A contribution to the sociology of colony-nesting birds. *Proc. VIII. Internat. Ornith. Congr.,* Oxford, 206-218.

—————— (1935): Der Kumpan in der Umwelt des Vogels. *J. Ornithol., 83,* 137-213, 289-413.

—————— (1937a): Über die Bildung des Instinktbegriffes. *Die Naturwissen-schaften, 25,* 289-300, 307-318, 324-331.

—————— (1937b): Über den Begriff der Instinkthandlung. *Folia Biotheor., 2,* 17-50.

—————— (1939): Vergleichende Verhaltensforschung. *Zool. Anz. Suppl., 12,* 69-102.

—————— (1941): Vergleichende Bewegungsstudien an Anatinen. *J. Ornithol., 89,* Sonderheft, 19-29, 194-293.

—————— (1950): The comparative method in studying innate behaviour patterns. *Symposia, Soc. Exper. Biol., 4.* Cambridge: University Press.

—————— (1952a): Die Entwicklung der vergleichenden Verhaltensforschung in den letzten 12 Jahren. *Verhandlungen der Deutschen Zoologischen Gesell-schaft in Freiburg,* 36-58.

—————— (1952b): *King Solomon's Ring.* London: Methuen.

—————— and Tinbergen, N. (1938): Taxis und Instinkthandlung in der Eiroll-bewegung der Graugans I. *Z. Tierpsychol., 2,* 1-29.

McDougall, W. (1921): *An Introduction to Social Psychology*. New York.

—— (1922): The use and abuse of instinct in social psychology. *J. Abn. Soc. Psychol., 16*, 285-333.

—— (1923): *An Outline of Psychology*. London (6th ed., 1933).

Makkink, G. F. (1932): Einige Beobachtungen über die Säbelschnäbler (*Recurvirostra avosetta* L.). Ardea, *21*, 38-43.

—— (1936): An attempt at an ethogram of the European avocet (*Recurvirosta avosetta* L.) with ethological and psychological remarks. *Ardea, 25*, 1-60.

Morgan, C. Lloyd (1909): *Instinkt und Erfahrung*. German transl. by M. Semon, Leipzig and Berlin; German transl. by R. Thesing, Berlin, 1913.

Moynihan, M. H. (1950): Physiological mechanisms in animal behaviour. *Symp. Soc. Exper. Biol., 4*. Cambridge: University Press.

—— (1955): Some aspects of the reproductive behaviour of the Black-headed Gull and related species. *Behaviour*, Suppl., iv, ix + 201.

Nice, M. M. (1933/34): Zur Naturgeschichte des Singammers. *J. Ornithol., 81*, 552-595; *82*, 1-96.

Nissen, H. W. (1931): A field study of the chimpanzee. *Comp. Psychol. Monog., 8*, 1-105.

Noble, G. K. (1934): Experimenting with the courtship of lizards. *Nat. Hist., 34*, 1-15.

—— and Bradley, H. T. (1933): The mating behavior of lizards: Its bearing on the theory of sexual selection. *Ann. N. Y. Acad. Sci., 35*, 25-100.

Peckham, G. W. and Peckham, E. G. (1889): Observations on sexual selection in spiders of the family *Attidae*. *Occas. Papers Nat. Hist. Soc. Wisconsin, Milwaukee, 1*, 1-151.

Peracca, M. C. (1891): Osservazioni sulla riproduzione della Iguana tuberculata. *Boll. Mus. Zool. Anat. Comparat. Reg. Univ. Torino, 6*, 1-8.

Portielje, A. F. J. (1922): Eenige merkwaardige instincten en gewoontevormingen bij vogels. *Ardea, 11*, 23-39.

—— (1926): Zur Ethologie, bzw. Psychologie von *Botaurus stellaris* (L.). *Ardea, 15*, 1-15.

—— (1927): Zur Ethologie bzw. Psychologie von *Phalacrocorax carbo subcormoranus*. *Ardea, 16*, 107-123.

—— (1930): Versuch einer verhaltungspsychologischen Deutung des Balzgebarens der Kampfschnepfe (*Philomachus Pugnax* L.). *Proc. VII. Int. Ornith. Congr.*, Amsterdam.

Prechtl, H. F. R. (1951): Zur Paarungsbiologie einiger Molcharten. *Z. Tierpsychol., 8*, 337-348.

—— (1952a): Über Adaptation des angeborenen Auslösemechanismus. *Naturwiss., 39*, 140-141.

—— (1952b): Angeborene Bewegungsweisen junger Katzen. *Experientia, 8*, 220-221.

—— (1953): Zur Physiologie der angeborenen auslösenden Mechanismen. I. Quantitative Untersuchungen über die Sperrbewegung junger Singvögel. *Behaviour, 5*, 32-50.

—— and Schleidt, W. M. (1950): Auslösende und steuernde Mechanismen des Saugaktes. I. Mitteilung. *Z. vergl. Physiol., 32*, 257-262.

—— —— (1951): Auslösende und steuernde Mechanismen des Saugaktes. II. Mitteilung. *Z. vergl. Physiol., 33*, 53-62.

Russell, E. S. (1934): *The Behaviour of Animals.* London.

Schenkel, W. (1947): Ausdrucks-Studien an Wölfen. *Behaviour.* 1, 81-130, 173-195.

Schiller, P. H. (1937): Purposeless manipulations. *XI. Congr. Internat. Psychol.,* Paris.

———— (1949): Analysis of detour behavior: I. Learning of roundabout pathways in fish. *J. Comp. Physiol. Psychol., 42,* 463-475.

———— (1950): Analysis of detour behavior: IV. Congruent and incongruent detour behavior in cats. *J. Exper. Psychol., 40,* 217-227.

———— (1951): Figural preferences in the drawings of a chimpanzee. *J. Comp. Physiol. Psychol., 44,* 101-111.

———— (1952): Innate constituents of complex responses in primates. *Psychol. Rev., 59,* 177-191.

Schjelderup-Ebbe, T. (1922/23): Zur Sozialpsychologie des Haushuhnes. *Z. Psychol., 132,* 289-303.

———— (1924): Zur Sozialpsychologie der Vögel. *Z. Psychol., 95,* 36-84.

Seitz, A. (1940): Die Paarbildung bei einigen Cichliden I. *Z. Tierpsychol., 4,* 40-84.

———— (1943): Die Paarbildung bei einigen Cichliden II. *Z. Tierpsychol., 5,* 74-101.

———— (1951):Vergleichende Verhaltensstudien an Buntbarschen (*Cichlidae*). *Z. Tierpsychol., 8.*

Selous, E. (1905-07): Observations tending to throw light on the question of sexual selection in birds, including a day-to-day diary on the breeding habits of the Ruff, *Machetes pugnax. Zoologist, 10,* 201-219, 285-294, 419-428; *11,* 60-65, 161-182, 367-380.

———— (1909): Observational diary on the nuptial habits of the Blackcock, *Tetrao tetrix. Zoologist, 13,* 401-413.

———— (n.d.): An observational diary of the domestic life of the Little Grebe or Dabchick. *Wild Life, 7.*

———— (1929): Schaubalz und geschlechtliche Auslese beim Kampfläufer (*Philomachus pugnax* L.). *J. Ornithol., 77,* 262.

Siewert, H. (1930): Bilder aus dem Leben eines Sperberpaares zur Brutzeit. *J. Ornithol., 78,* 245-254.

———— (1932*a*): Der Schreiadler. *J. Ornithol., 80,* 1-30.

———— (1932*b*): Beobachtungen am Horst des schwarzen Storches (*Ciconia nigra* L.). *J. Ornithol., 80,* 533-541.

———— (1933): Die Brutbiologie des Hühnerhabichts. *J. Ornithol., 81,* 1.

Skinner, B. F. (1948): "Superstitions" in pigeons. *J. Exper. Psychol., 38,* 168-172.

Stresemann, E. (1927-1934): Aves. *Kukenthal's Handb. Zool., 7,* 2. Berlin und Leipzig.

Tinbergen, N. (1934): Enkele proeven over het ei als broedobject. *Ardea, 23,* 82-89.

———— (1935): Waarnemingen en proeven over de sociologie van een zilvermeeuwenkolonie. *De levende Natuur.*

———— (1936): Zur Soziologie der Silbermöwe (*Larus a. argentatus* Pontopp.). *Beitr. Fortpfl. Vögel, 12,* 89-96.

———— (1940): Die Übersprungbewegung. *Z. Tierpsychol., 4,* 1-40.

———— (1948): Social releasers and the experimental method required for their study. *Wilson Bull., 60,* 6-52.

—— (1950): The hierarchical organization of nervous mechanisms underlying instinctive behaviour. *Symp. Soc. Exper. Biol., 4,* Cambridge: Univ. Press.

—— (1951): *The Study of Instinct.* Oxford: University Press.

—— (1952): 'Derived' activities: their causation, biological significance, origin, and emancipation during evolution. *Quart. Rev. Biol., 27,* 1-32.

—— (1953): Fighting and threat in animals. *New Biology, 14,* 9-24.

—— and Booy, H. L. (1937): Nieuwe feiten over de sociologie van de zilvermeeuwen. *De levende Natuur, 41,* 325-344.

—— and Iersel, J. J. A. van (1947): 'Displacement reactions' in the three-spined stickleback. *Behaviour, 1,* 56-63.

—— and Kuenen, D. J. (1939): Über die auslösenden und die richtunggebenden Reizsituationen der Sperrbewegung von jungen Drosseln *(Turdus m. merula* L. und *T. e. ericetorum* Turton). *Z. Tierpsychol., 3,* 37-60.

—— and Meeuse, B. J. D., Boerema, L. K., Varossieau, W. W. (1942): Die Balz des Samtfalters, *Eumenis* (= *Satyrus) semele* (L.). *Z. Tierpsychol., 5,* 182-226.

—— and Perdeck, A. C. (1950): On the stimulus situation releasing the begging response in the newly hatched Herring Gull chick *(Larus a. argentatus* Pontopp.). *Behaviour, 3,* 1-38.

Tolman, E. C. (1932): *Purposive Behaviour in Animals and Men.* New York: The Century Company.

Uexküll, J. von (1921): *Umwelt und Innenwelt der Tiere.* Berlin.

—— (1928): *Theoretische Biologie.* Berlin.

—— (1934): *Streifzüge durch die Umwelten von Tieren und Menschen.* Berlin: Springer.

Verwey, J. (1930): Die Paarungsbiologie des Fischreihers. *Zool. Jahrb. Allg. Zool. Physiol., 48,* 1-120.

Volkelt, H. (1914): *Die Vorstellungen der Tiere. Arb. Entwicklungspsychol.,* Leipzig: Engelmann.

—— (1937): Tierpsychologie als genetische Ganzheitspsychologie. *Z. Tierpsychol., 1,* 49-65.

Werner, H. (1957): *Comparative Psychology of Mental Development.* New York: International Universities Press (rev. ed.).

Whitman, C. O. (1898): Animal Behaviour. *Biol. Lectures Marine Biol. Lab.,* Woods Hole, Mass.

Winterbottom, J. M. (1929): Studies in sexual phenomena. VI. Communal display in birds. *Proc. Zool. Soc. London,* 189-195. VII. Transference of male secondary display characters to the female. *J. Genetics* (Cambridge), *21,* 367-387.

Yeates, G. K. (1934): *The Book of Rooks.* London.

Yerkes, R. M. (1916): The mental life of monkeys and apes. *Behav. Monog., 3,* iv + 145.

—— (1925): *Chimpanzee Intelligence.* Baltimore: Williams & Wilkins.

—— (1927): The mind of a gorilla. *Genet. Psychol. Monog., 2,* 1-193, 377-551.

—— and Yerkes, A. (1929): *The Great Apes.* New Haven: Yale University Press.

Ziegler, H. (1920): *Der Begriff des Instinktes einst und jetzt.* Jena.

Index

Index

Accumulation of energy, *see* Energy, endogenous
Adaptive behavior
  appetitive, 184
  in domestication, 95
Adaptiveness of instinctive behavior
  individual (ontogenetic), 133 f., 174
  phyletic, 121
Ahlquist, 245
Allen, 124, 311
Allochthonous drive, 205, 296 ff.
Alopochen, 149, 303
Alternative movements, 299
Altum, 135
Alverdes, 130, 142, 311
Anas, see Duck, mallard
Anatides, 242, 297, 303
Anatinae, 303 f.
Animals as subjects, 6 ff., 162 f., 170, 205 f.
Anser, 149
Appetitive behavior, 122, 139 ff., 152, 168, 171, 183, 202 ff., 207 f., 251, 289, 292, 305 ff.
Astatotilapia, 260 f.
Avocet, 296, 304

Baboon, 304
Baer, 29
Baerends, 292, 306, 311
Bakay, 265, 311
Bally, 292, 311
Bechterev, 164, 311
Bee, 17, 40
Beetle, 75
Behavior, innate
  vs. acquired, 126 ff.
  feeding, 209 ff.
  filial, 102 ff., 115
  mating, 109, 124
  parental, 87, 94 f., 157

Behaviorism, VII ff., XIII ff., 100 f., 131, 172
Bethe, 100, 133 f., 165, 311
Betta, 52 f., 168
Bierens de Haan, 91, 311
Bingham, 84, 278, 280, 311
Biological meaning, 13 ff., 40, 63, 170, 173, 185, 195, 254
Birch 265, 311
Bittern, 114
Blackbird, 211, 213 ff., 224 f., 231 f.
Blocking, 180, 205, 237, 295, 298, 306 ff.
Bodenheimer, 12
Botaurus, 114
Bradley, 124
Brown, 311
Brückner, 94, 95, 125, 311
Budgerigar, 112 f.
Bullfinch, 133
Butterfly, 292
Bühler, C., 105, 311
Bühler, K., 146, 154, 177, 311

Canary, 158
Captivity phenomena
  miscarrying behavior, 170
  pathological disintegration of behavior, 133
Carmichael, 97, 132, 311
Carpenter, 242, 280, 312
Casarca, 303
Chaffinch, 294
Chaulelasmus, 244
Chimpanzee, 265 ff.
Chionis, 241
Coburn, 84, 312
Co-innervation of antagonistic muscles, 185, 188 f., 200 f.
Coloeus, see Jackdaw
Columba, 97, 148

Companion
  definition, 83 ff., 116 ff.
  in different functional cycles, 59 f.,
    89, 111, 234 f.
  flight, 114
  general, 57 ff.
  illustrations, 57 ff., 87
  IRM, 110 ff., 119 f.
  love, 60 f.
  parent, offspring, sex, social, sibling,
    102 ff., 120, 233
  substitute, 57 ff., 102 ff., 115
Comparative method, 239 ff., 288 ff.,
  305
Congruent vs. incongruent behavior,
  274, 299
Constancy
  of motor form, 200, 207, 245, 248
  of stimulus, 84
Consummatory act, 144, 153, 251, 290,
  305 ff.
Coordinate system, 15, 51
Cormorant, 304
Corvidae, 137 f., 152, 304
Craig, 122, 124, 138, 143 f., 153 f., 158,
  168, 175, 251 f., 289 ff., 312
Cricket, 43 f.
Curlew 102, 111
Cyon, 16

Darwin, 37, 258
Demoll, 259
Didunculus, 148, 241
Directional
  cues, 14 ff., 55
  planes, 15 ff., 50 f.
  signs, 14 ff., 51
  steps, 14 ff., 50 f.
Displacement activity
  characteristics, 296 f.
  definition, xiii
  in humans, 298
  illustrations, 205, 257 f., 296
  and orienting reactions, 297
  phyletic evolution, 257
  and posture, 297
  types, 205, 295 ff.
Dog, 48, 50 f., 64 f., 205, 301 f.
Drees, 294, 299 f., 312
Driesch, 122, 177

Drive, 130 f., 156, 161 f., 171 f., 251 ff.,
  295 ff.
Dual quantification, 261 f., 291
Duck
  Hybrid, 244
  Mallard, 87, 96 f., 109, 115, 146,
    149 f., 157, 243 f., 260, 304
  Mandarin, 258
  Pintail, 260
  surface feeding, 303 f.

Earthworm, 37 ff.
Effector
  cue, xiii, 10, 12, 72
  image, 46 ff.
  sign, xiii, 9
Egg-rolling
  description, 187 ff.
  experiments, 192 ff.
  miscarrying, 190 f.
  observations, 187 ff.
  taxis and instinctive action in, 176 ff.
Energy, endogenous
  accumulation, 167 ff., 180, 247 ff.,
    254, 261 f., 290
  as basis of vacuum reactions, 169, 247
  generation of impulses, 179 f., 249,
    309
Environment and Umwelt, see Umwelt
Equides, 205
Estrilda, 88
Ethology
  and behaviorism, ix ff., xv ff.
  as method, 240, 305
Etroplus, 300
Evolution of behavior, see Instinctive
  behavior, evolution
Excitation
  action-specific, 169, 247 ff., 254, 295,
    299
  autochthonous vs. allochthonous, 205,
    296 f., 298 f., 302
  pressure, 167 ff., 180, 247
Exhaustibility, 169, 186, 199, 202 ff.,
  207 f., 247, 254, 262, 294 f.
Experience
  adaptive influence on instinct, 131 ff.,
    136
  role, in facilitating learning, 265 f.
Expression, see Superposition
Extinction, 10, 168 f., 202 f., 296

Fabre, 42, 68
Falcon, 144, 306
Familiar path, *see* Orientation
Familiarization, 135 f.
Farthest plane, 21 ff.
Fatigue, 135 f., 202, 294
Feeding behavior, 209 ff.
Fish
   cichlid, 294, 299
   fighting, 52 f., 168
Fowl, 43, 71, 94 f., 163
Friedmann, 124, 312
Frobenius, 67
Functional cue (sign), *see* Effector, cue,
   sign
Functional cycles, 10 ff., 32 ff., 42, 72,
   86 f., *see also* Companion
Functional tone, 47 f., 61, 64, 72
Funnel-roller, 69 f.

Gadwall, 244
Gaping reaction
   description, 209 ff.
   orientation, 221 ff.
   release, 213 ff., 293
Garganey, 259
Gasterosteus, *see* Stickleback
Gestalt, 258 ff., 290, 293
Goal and plan, *see* Purposiveness
Goal-directed behavior, 130, 135, 138 f.,
   143 f., 183 ff., 251, 309
Godwit, 102
Goethe, 193, 242, 255, 257, 289, 312
Goldfinch, 91
Goose
   Egyptian, 149, 303
   Greylag, 58, 103, 111, 160, 181 ff.,
   245, 253
   Hybrid, 147
Goura, 148, 241
Grasl, 112
Grasshopper, 43
Grohmann, 132
Groos, 99, 312
Grosbeak, 88
Guillaume, 265, 274, 294, 312
Gull, 245, 293

Hartmann, 310

Heinroth, 60, 93, 103 f., 112, 129 f.,
   147, 241 f., 256 f., 288 f., 297 f.,
   303, 312 f.
Helmholtz, 27
Hemichromis, 299
Hempelmann, 91
Hen, *see* Fowl
Hermit crab, 47
Hess, 309, 313
Hesse, 27
Heterogeneous summation, 261, 290
Hierarchy of instincts, 306 ff.
Hingston, 293, 313
Hippocampus, 183, 248
Holistic theory, 125 ff.
Home, *see* Territory
Homology
   illustrations, 240 f., 243 f., 253
   phyletic, 99, 121, 148 f., 241 f., 258,
   303 f.
Horse, 205
Housefly, 27 f., 50
Howard, 135, 167, 297, 313
Hummingbird, 181
Huth, 73
Huxley, 300, 302 f., 313

Imprinting
   in captivity, 110, 145
   dependence on specific stimuli, 104,
   107, 109 ff., 146
   in different functional cycles, 108 f.
   distinguished from learning, 102 ff.
   irreversibility, 105, 146
   nature, 102 ff., 118 f., 145 ff., 174
   susceptible period, 104, 146
Inductive
   determination, 105 f., 146
   redetermination, 107
Innate behavior patterns
   vs. acquired, 85 ff., 99, 127 f., 264 ff.
   generalization, 265
   inventory, 90 f., 242 ff., 265, 286
   regression in domestication, 94 f.,
   115, 125, 154 f.
   as taxonomic characters, 121, 148,
   174, 240 f., 288
Innate motor action
   as a basis of learning, 264 ff., 286 f.
   definition, 271
Insight, 86, 139, 205, 254, 286

Instinct
  definitions, see Instinct, theories
  and experience, see Experience
  independent of receptors, 143, 178 ff.,
    193, 207, 247
  invariability, 96 ff., 122, 131 ff., 181,
    193, 199, 207, 245 ff.
  mood, 47 ff., 64, 123 f., 161 f., 298
  nature, 129 ff., 295
  plasticity, 100, 122, 133 f., 155, 249
  subjective accompaniment, 123, 144,
    162 f., 167, 172, 184
  vs. taxis, 176 ff., 185 ff., 206 f.
  theories, 95 ff., 122 f., 131 ff., 137,
    139, 147, 156 ff., 163 ff., 176 f.,
    289
Instinctive action
  exhaustibility, see Exhaustibility
  as forerunner of learned and intelli-
    gent behavior, 131, 151 ff.
  incomplete, 134 f., 149, 173, 177 ff.,
    245, 295 ff., 305
  inertia, 262, 296
  superposition, 300 ff.
Instinctive behavior
  evolution, 99, 147 ff., 153, 174, 239 ff.
  and hunger, 300
  maturation, see Maturation
  physiology, 169, 245 ff., 295 ff., 307 ff.
  rudimentation, 151, 155, 255
  social, 125, 149, 257
Intensity, 134 ff., 167, 180 f., 200 f.,
  245, 296 f., 299 f.
Intention movements, 134, 149, 170,
  245 f., 257, 297
  in evolution, see Instinctive behav-
    ior, evolution; Phyletic compari-
    son
Interlocking
  faculty to acquire, 98, 137, 145, 155
  illustrations, 141, 144, 184 ff., 234
  of instinct and taxis, 141, 174, 181 ff.,
    206 f., 209 f., 233 ff., 250
  of instinct and training, 97 f., 102 f.,
    117, 137, 141 ff., 175
  simultaneous vs. successive, 184 f.,
    235
IRM, see Releasing mechanism, innate

Jackdaw, 36, 52 f., 53 ff., 58 ff., 99,
  106, 108 f., 112, 114, 146, 152

Katz 95, 128, 313
Key stimuli, see Sign
Kinesthesia, 14
Kirkman, 193, 313
Kitten, 306
Klüver, 275, 313
Koehler, O., 98, 144, 193, 255, 288, 314
Köhler, W., 96, 264, 269, 274 f., 276 f.,
  278, 314
Kolibri, 247
Kortlandt, 257, 295 f., 314
Kramer, 98, 147, 314
Kuenen, 292, 317
Kuhlmann, 237 f., 314
Kühn, 177, 314

Lanius, 98
Lashley, 247 f., 286, 314
Learning
  as based on instinctive motor pat-
    terns, 138, 264 ff., 286 f.
  differentiation from instinct, 98, 117,
    120 f., 158 f., 235 ff.
  interlocking, see Interlocking
  latent, 269
  vs. maturation, see Maturation
Leiner, 261
Limosa, 102
Lissmann, 168, 257, 262, 314
Local signs, 19 ff.
Localization, 83 f.
Lorenz, 59 f., 97, 98, 102, 145, 179, 181,
  232, 234, 264, 314 f.

McDougall, 123, 128, 156 ff., 161 f.,
  250, 288, 315
Makkink, 242, 258, 304, 315
Manipulation
  in the chimpanzee, 264 ff.
  determined by matured motor pat-
    terns, 286
  independent of releasers, 283 f.
  spontaneous vs. problem-solving,
    265 ff., 269
  unmotivated, 269
Manipulative patterns
  as a basis of learning, 264 ff.
  of chimpanzees, 272, 273 f., 275, 279,
    283
  spontaneous, see Spontaneous behav-
    ior

Mareca, 243

Maturation
of instincts and organs, 96 f., 131 f.,
174
vs. learning, 96 ff., 132, 233 ff., 238,
267 ff.
of motor form, 223, 234
role in learning to manipulate, 267,
270, 286
of stimulus dependence (of the releasing mechanism), 218, 233 f.
"Measuring," 279 ff.
Mechanistic interpretation of behavior,
5 ff., 125 f., 164, 289
Medusa, 32
Melopsittacus, 112 f
Merkmal, see Receptor cue
Merkorgan ("receptor organs"), 9
Merkzeichen, see Receptor sign
Methods
observation *vs.* experiment, 90 ff.,
186, 211 ff., 232 f.
total survey of behavior, 90 f., 100,
242 ff.
Meyerson, 265, 274, 294, 312
Miscarrying behavior, 111 ff., 135,
168 ff., 180, 190 f., 195, 199, 204,
208, 247 f., 253 ff., 292 ff., *see also*
Displacement activity, Substitute
companion, Vacuum activity
Mole, 55
Monkeys, 205, 242, 275
Morgan, 93, 96 f., 130, 131 ff., 315
Motion as releaser, *see* Releasers,
motor
Motivation, internal, level, 159 ff., 291,
295 f.

Nannacara, 294
Nest-building
in relation to territory, 54 ff.
rudiments, 137 f., 153 f., 245 f.,
277 f.
Night heron, 134 f., 150, 168 f., 296
Nissen, 278, 315
Noble, 124, 293, 315
Numenius, 102, 111

Operational cue (sign), *see* Effector
cue, sign

Orientation
acoustic, 196, 208
familiar path, 50 ff., 55
gravitational, 222, 234
innate path, 69 ff.
magical path, 69 f.
maturation, 221 ff., 237
mechanical, 222, 234
operational, 7, 16 f., 50 ff., 55, 69
operational *vs.* visual, 17
spatial, of instinctive actions, 297
tactile, 19 ff., 190, 192 ff., 198, 207
tropotactic, 182, 184, 246
visual, 50 ff., 69, 83 f., 222 ff.
Orientational signs, steps, *see* Directional
Orienting
mechanism and instinctive pattern,
182, 185 ff., 191, 207
movements, 140, 177 f., 182, 194,
209, 221, 250
Oriole, 218
Owl, 74

Paramecium, 31
Partridge, 107
Passeres, 147, 209, 238, 300
Patella, 17, 30 f.
Pavlov, 101, 144 f.
Pea-weevil, 68 f.
Peckham, 257, 315
Pelkwijk, 257, 260
Perceptual cue (sign), *see* Receptor
cue, sign
Perdeck, 292 f.
Perdix, 107
Phasianus, 108
Pheasant, 108, 146, 293
Phyletic comparison, 121, 149 ff., 174,
240 ff., 304 f.
Phyletic relations of instinctive to
learned and intelligent behavior,
96, 147 ff., 151 ff.
Pigeon, crowned, 148
Pigeons, 148, 240 f.
Plan in behavior, 32, 42 ff., 46, 59, 68,
70, 101
Play
in acquiring skills, 99
as appetitive activity, 292
manipulative, 269 ff., 278 ff.

Play *(cont.)*
role in problem-solving, 269 ff., 286
and work, correlated by experience, 277
Plover, 205
Poll, 242
Portielje, 114, 218, 238, 315
Prechtl, 292, 294, 300, 305, 315 f.
Problem-solving, development, 265 ff.
Purposiveness, 42 ff., 100 ff., 130 f., 135, 140 f., 153, 156 ff., 170 f., 177, 289

Rand, 293
Raven, 99 f., 152
Reaction readiness, *see* Excitation, Threshold decrease
Receptor
cue, xiii, 9, 12 f., 36 ff., 72
image, 46 ff., 72
sign, xiii, 9
Recurvirostra, 304
Reflex
animal, 32
arc, 8, 165
chain, 11, 97, 101
chain theory, 122, 131, 163 ff., 245 f.
definitions, 8, 164, 166
and instinctive action, 144 f., 166, 171 f., 175, 178, 181 f., 193, 249 ff.
person, 32, 126
postural, 182
republic, 34, 125 f.
and taxis, 178, 203
Regulation, 100, 122, 133 f., 165
Release
acoustic, 215
of egg-rolling, 194
of gaping reaction, 213 ff.
of innate reactions, model illustrating, 169, 291, 295 ff.
motor, 220
photic, 215
tactile, 214
thermal, 215
vibratory, 213 f.
visual, 194, 217 ff.
Releasers
conspicuousness, 259 f., 293
definition, 88, 121, 141, 292
differentiation, 117 f., 254 ff., 293

simplicity, 259 ff., 293
social, 83, 88, 102 ff., 116 f., 256 ff., 292
visual, 194, 217, 255
Releasing mechanism
acquired, 85 f., 111, 117
of the companion, 110 ff., 119 f.
definition, 116, 292
exhaustibility, 294
experiments, 193 ff., 255 f.
and hunger, 294 f.
innate, 85 f., 111, 141 ff., 193 ff., 233 f., 238, 254 ff., 290, 292 ff., 306 ff.
innate, definition, 116, 193, 292
innate, improbability, 85, 117
innate, loss in domestication, 194
innate, simplicity, 85, 116, 259 f.
selectivity, 117, 194, 208, 253, 294 f.
specialization, 117 f.
Releasing stimuli
relative effect, 261 f.
threshold decrease, 101, 122, 142 f., 167 ff., 171, 179 ff., 247, 253, 262, 289
Rhizostoma, 32
Rigidity, 96, 100, 121 f., 193 ff., 199, 207, 245, 289
Ring dove, 97
Ritualization
illustrations, 303 ff.
as means of expression, 296, 302
of motor releasers, 257
rigidity, 302 f.
Rock pigeon, 97
Romanes, 152
Russell, 130, 135, 250, 316

Salamander, 292
Satiation, *see* Exhaustibility
Satyrus, 292
Scallop, 37 f.
Schaff, 253
Schenkel, 264, 301, 316
Schiller, 264, 274, 284, 286, 298, 316
Schjelderup-Ebbe, 95, 316
Schleidt, 305
Sea horse, 183, 248
Sea urchin, 32 ff., 86
Search
image, 62 ff.
tone, 64

Seitz, 261 f., 290, 296, 299, 316
Selectivity
  increased, 208
  of receptors, 7 ff., 11, 49
  reduced, 168, 194
  of releasing mechanisms, 117, 254 f., 294 f.
Self-training of animals, 85 f., 138 f., 259
Selous, 302, 316
Sensation
  kinesthetic, 14
  projection, 9, 83
  visual, 21 ff.
Sensory cue (sign), *see* Receptor cue, sign
Sheldrake, 303
Sherrington, 248, 289
Shrike, 98
Sign stimuli, 11 ff., 32 f., 36 f., 42 f., 86, 193 ff., 208, 211 f., 254, 258 ff., 290, 293 f., 308
Skinner, 286, 316
Snail, 17, 30 f.
Social
  behavior, animal and human, 125 ff.
  challenge, 275 ff., 280 f., 284, 303 f.
  structure in animals, 125 ff., 149, 257
Space
  effector, functional or operational, 14 ff., 50 f., 55
  perception, 13 ff., 28 f., 84
  tactile, 19, 83
  in the *Umwelt*, 14 ff.
  visual, 19 ff., 26 ff., 50 f.
  visual *vs.* tactile, 20
Sparrow, 108, 253, 296
Specificity of sensation and response, 9
Spemann, 105 f.
Spencer, 130 ff., 152
Sphaerechinus, 32, 86
Spider, 257, 295, 299 f.
Spinal contrast, 248
Spontaneous behavior patterns
  breaking through in emotion, 274 ff.
  developing into skills, 275 ff., 281 ff.
  with implements, 269
Spragg, 278
Squirrel, 74
Starling, 68, 145
Steiner, 294

Stickleback, 54, 260 f., 297, 300, 307
Stimulus situation
  complex quality, 85, 117, 234, 259
  as determining reaction, 7, 209, 254
  effectiveness, 168, 194, 210, 233, 291, 293
  releasing and directing, 194, 209 ff., 233 ff.
Stork, 112
Superposition
  of excitations, 300
  of expressive motions, 301 ff.
  of innate reactions, 249, 300 f., 305
Survival value, xv f., 153, 170, 177, 206, 294, 296, 301, 305
Symbolic actions, 257 f., 297, 303 ff.

Tadorna, 147
Taxis
  definition, 177 f., 250
  experiments, 198 ff., 250
  and instinctive action, 140 f., 176 ff., 184, 190, 206 f., 234, 242, 250 ff.
  menotaxis, 246
  phobotaxis, 177
  phototaxis, 250
  and reflex, 178
  telotaxis, 191
  topotaxis, 177 ff., 250
  tropotaxis, 182, 184, 246
Teal, 259
Territory and home, 54 ff.
Threshold decrease, *see* Releasing stimuli
Thrush, 209, 294
Tick, 6 ff., 254, 257
Time
  contraction, 30
  perception, 12, 29 ff.
  subjective, 29
Tinbergen, 193, 234, 242, 257, 260 f., 264, 292 f., 295 ff., 316 f.
Titmouse, 91
Toad, 64, 66
Tolman, 100, 101, 130, 138, 142 f., 247, 317
Tool reactions, 91, 158 ff., 252 f.
Tool-using behavior
  in the chimpanzee, 264 ff.
  problem-solving, 265 f., 271, 274, 276 f., 281 f., 286

Tool-using behavior (cont.)
   after removal of prefrontal areas,
     268
   stereotypes, 268, 286
   unmotivated (in play), 269 ff., 278 ff.
Tragopan, 293
Training, *see* Interlocking, Self-training of animals
Turdus, 209 ff., 294

Umwelt
   definition, xiii, 5 ff.
   dependence on observer, 73 ff.
   and environment, 13 f., 31 f., 37, 40,
     50, 65 ff., 71 f.
   magic, 64 ff., 71
   simple, 31
   subjective factors, 15 ff., 19 f., 50 ff.,
     54 f., 62 ff., 67, 69 ff.

Vacuum activity
   definition, 101, 142 ff., 167, 179 f.
   discussion, 122, 127, 170, 173, 180 f.,
     247, 253
   illustration, 143, 159 ff., 181, 191,
     199 ff., 201, 247

van Iersel, 297, 300, 313
Verwey, 123, 147, 162, 242, 317
Vitalistic interpretation of behavior,
   156 ff., 164, 263, 289
von Holst, 178 ff., 246, 248 f., 290, 300,
   309, 313
von Uexküll, 84, 85, 89, 101, 111, 116,
   118, 126, 202 f., 288, 317

Waxbill, 88
Wallace, 124
Watson, 131
Weber, 19
Weiss, 309
Werner, 99, 124 f., 126, 317
Whitman, 139, 147, 154, 240, 288, 317
Widgeon, 243 f.
Wirkmal, see Effector cue
Wirkorgan ("Effector organs"), 9
Wirkzeichen, see Effector sign
Wundt, 239

Yerkes, 264, 278, 317

Zagarus, 193
Ziegler, 100, 122, 131, 163 ff., 245, 317